D1716533

Assessing Hispanic Clients Using the MMPI-2 and MMPI-A

Assessing Hispanic Clients Using the MMPI-2 and MMPI-A

James N. Butcher
Jose Cabiya
Emilia Lucio
Maria Garrido

AMERICAN PSYCHOLOGICAL ASSOCIATION

WASHINGTON, DC

Published by
American Psychological Association
750 First Street, NE
Washington, DC 20002
www.apa.org

To order
APA Order Department
P.O. Box 92984
Washington, DC 20090-2984
Tel: (800) 374-2721
Direct: (202) 336-5510
Fax: (202) 336-5502
TDD/TTY: (202) 336-6123
Online: www.apa.org/books/
E-mail: order@apa.org

In the U.K., Europe, Africa, and the Middle East, copies may be ordered from
American Psychological Association
3 Henrietta Street
Covent Garden, London
WC2E 8LU England

Typeset in Goudy by World Composition Services, Inc., Sterling, VA

Printer: Maple-Vail Book Manufacturing Group, Binghamton, NY
Cover Designer: Berg Design, Albany, NY
Technical/Production Editor: Harriet Kaplan

The opinions and statements published are the responsibility of the authors, and such opinions and statements do not necessarily represent the policies of the American Psychological Association.

Library of Congress Cataloging-in-Publication Data

Assessing hispanic clients using the MMPI-2 and MMPI-a / By James N. Butcher ... [et al.].—1st ed.
    p. cm.
    Includes bibliographical references and index.
    ISBN-13: 978-1-59147-924-6
    ISBN-10: 1-59147-924-X
    1. Personality and culture. 2. Hispanic Americans—Psychology. 3. Personality assessment. 4. Minnesota Multiphasic Personality Inventory. 5. Minnesota Multiphasic Personality Inventory for Adolescents. I. Butcher, James Neal, 1933-

    BF698.9.C8A87 2007
    155.2'808968073—dc22   2006034729

British Library Cataloguing-in-Publication Data
A CIP record is available from the British Library.

Printed in the United States of America
First Edition

CONTENTS

v

LIST OF EXHIBITS, TABLES,
AND FIGURES

EXHIBITS

TABLES

FIGURES

PREFACE

The largest ethnic minority group in the United States today is the fast-growing population of people from Latin American countries. Many of these individuals live and work under difficult and highly stressful circumstances, as is common with refugees and immigrants. Many Hispanic clients are seen in mental health and correctional facilities today, often presenting a challenge to the practitioner, particularly if the client has low English language proficiency. The goal of this volume is to orient psychological assessment practitioners to the issues, strengths, and limitations of incorporating an objective personality assessment instrument for psychological evaluations with clients who have a Hispanic background.

The Minnesota Multiphasic Personality Inventory (MMPI) instruments are the most extensively researched and widely used personality assessment instruments with Spanish-speaking clients. Much of what is known about the use of objective personality assessment instruments like the MMPI comes through the measure's broad dissemination around the globe by Spanish-speaking psychologists in other countries. The MMPI, for example, has been widely used with Spanish language populations since it was first adapted for use in Cuba by Alfonso Bernal del Riesgo in 1951.

In this volume we provide an overview of the research base and describe the most effective interpretive strategies for both the revised version of the MMPI (MMPI-2) and the version designed for use with adolescents (MMPI-A) in assessing Hispanic clients. As a background for understanding the test with this subpopulation, the international use of the MMPI-2 and MMPI-A is surveyed and applicable findings are summarized.

The main focus of this book is on the practical application of the MMPI-2 and MMPI-A with Spanish-speaking clients. Practical information concerning the MMPI-2 and MMPI-A use in the United States is provided along with numerous case examples, drawn from practice but extensively modified to protect patients' confidentiality, that illustrate the applications. Chapter highlights summarize key interpretive points made in each chapter. Useful supportive information, such as T-score tables for the Mexican MMPI-2 and MMPI-A norms and a listing of Spanish-language translations, is included for the reader's convenience.

A number of people have supported our work in developing this volume. We thank Betty Kiminiki and Holly Butcher for their editorial assistance in the early stages of the initial draft of the book. We also acknowledge the assistance of the editorial team at APA Books for their assistance during the editorial process. We especially thank Susan Reynolds for her support; her guidance and understanding have been important assets in our work.

We also acknowledge the continued support of our families in our efforts; without their understanding, a project like this would not be possible. James N. Butcher thanks his wife Carolyn Williams and children Jay, Sherry, and Holly for their support; Jose Cabiya thanks Mari and Alejandro; Emilia Lucio acknowledges Francisco, Adriana, Emilia, and Max for their support and Consuelo Duran for all the years of collaboration with the MMPI; and Maria Garrido acknowledges the encouragement and patience of her husband Rob and of her parents Jose and Iraida. Her personality assessment students in Rhode Island and Puerto Rico have also been a source of inspiration. This work is also dedicated to them.

Assessing Hispanic Clients
Using the MMPI-2 and MMPI-A

1

THE CHALLENGE OF ASSESSING CLIENTS WITH DIFFERENT CULTURAL AND LANGUAGE BACKGROUNDS

The American ideal of being a melting pot in which people from foreign lands will be welcomed and ultimately integrated into society is far from reality. Though still a land that offers relative safety, freedom, and opportunity compared with many other countries, the full integration ideal is often not realized. Many immigrants experience persistent roadblocks and resistance to fully realizing the American dream. The United States is a heterogeneous multicultural and multiethnic society, and psychologists working in applied fields—clinical, counseling, industrial, and educational specialties—often encounter this situation in their clients.

In the clinical practice of psychology, practitioners may often be faced with the complicated task of providing a psychological assessment on a client from a different cultural and language background. Is it appropriate to use psychological tests that have been developed from an American perspective to assist in clinical decisions for clients from different cultural backgrounds? Consider the following circumstances:

- A 28-year-old Mexican, non-English-speaking immigrant worker who has been living in the United States for 12 months is arrested for a drug-related crime. He is facing a sentence of up to 7 years in federal prison. The court-appointed psychologist

3

is asked to conduct a psychological evaluation to provide information for the presentencing hearing.

- A Mexican American man, age 29, who has lived in the United States for 10 years, applies for a position as a police officer at a California municipality. Employment policies require that applicants undergo a psychological evaluation to determine if they are emotionally well adjusted and reliable.
- A 32-year-old Puerto Rican woman, whose English language skills are minimal, is being evaluated by a psychologist appointed by the court in a case of likely child neglect to determine if her parental rights should be terminated.
- An American citizen of Peruvian birth (and with early education in Peru) is being evaluated in a government personnel screening program to determine if there are any psychological factors that suggest any unreliable behavior as part of his application for a security clearance.

These common evaluation situations require that the assessment psychologist make recommendations based on the most valid and reliable methods available. Yet, the techniques relied on need to be vetted for the multicultural context.

This chapter briefly reviews (a) the question of how culture, personality, and psychopathology are interrelated; (b) the various biases that might be present in instruments and test users; (c) the most important test construction challenges that affect instruments often used with ethnically and linguistically diverse individuals; and (d) cautions for users concerning test selection, application, and interpretation of test results. Overviews of the demographics of the Hispanic population in the United States and of the test use and interpretation issues that are relevant for this population are included.

THE NEED FOR RESEARCH ON CLIENTS WITH DIFFERENT CULTURAL AND LINGUISTIC BACKGROUNDS

Over the past 30 years, there has been a surge in research into the relationships among culture, personality, and psychopathology. The numerous scholarly works addressing these concepts and their interrelationships have thrust scholars and practitioners from diverse fields (e.g., sociology, anthropology, and psychology) into the tasks of defining and distinguishing concepts such as culture, ethnicity, and race (which have often been used interchangeably) and of examining whether culture has any relationship with psychopathology and determining the nature of that relationship (e.g., Atkinson, Morten, & Sue, 1998; Helms & Cook, 1999; Phinney, 1996).

The need to conduct intercultural research is spurred by two interrelated issues, one historical and the other demographic. First, it is widely recognized that the fields of psychology and psychiatry originated in Western–European culture; thus, conceptions of human behavior, behavioral health, distress, assessment, methodologies, and approaches to healing have all been based on Eurocentric worldviews. These conceptions may be appropriate to describe members of that culture but not necessarily members of non-Western, non-European-origin cultures (Comas-Diaz, 1992; Pinder-hughes, 1989). The second major issue is the demographic reality that currently characterizes major industrialized nations such as the United States and many European countries. Examination of psychology's (especially clinical and assessment psychology's) ability to describe human experience beyond that of the cultural group of its origin has become increasingly urgent as a result of the great demographic shift occurring today (discussed more fully later in the chapter). Key considerations for conducting culturally competent assessments of Hispanic clients in the mainland United States and Puerto Rico and interpreting the results are provided in the chapters to follow.

CULTURE, PERSONALITY, AND PSYCHOPATHOLOGY

The presence in health and mental health systems of growing numbers of individuals from diverse national, ethnic, and cultural origins has created a need to review and sometimes challenge traditional Western assumptions underlying human behavior, distress, assessment, and healing. Therefore, researchers have explored questions concerning the influence of culture on human behavior and psychopathology. For example, Butcher, Coelho Mosch, Tsai, and Nezami's (2006) review of existing research on the relationship between culture and human behavior and the relationship between culture and psychopathology suggests that there are cross-cultural similarities in the underlying personality structures and that some psychological correlates of different personality dimensions are present across similar cultural groups. Marin and Triandis (1985) identified *allocentrism* (or group orientation, as opposed to individual orientation) as an important characteristic of multiple Latin American nationalities. Therefore, personality assessment instruments designed with standards contrary to an allocentric orientation may characterize those for whom allocentrism is a cultural norm in a potentially negative manner as "dependent" or "unassertive."

Butcher, Coelho Mosch, et al. (2006) also reviewed the complex question of how culture may influence psychopathology. They cited previous classic studies, such as Good and Kleinman's (1985), that concluded that some psychiatric diagnoses are present across cultures but sometimes with different emphases in the expression of symptoms. Other disorders, such as anxiety and acute distress reactions, are thought to present more variation across cultures and to even be highly specific to a cultural group. For example, among Puerto Ricans, the syndrome of *ataque de nervios* (literally, "nervous attack") has been described as an acute stress reaction triggered by, for example, the death of a loved one or the discovery of a marital infidelity. The syndrome has been described as a seizurelike state of a dissociative character whereby the person falls to the floor while thrashing the limbs, clenching the fists, and engaging in other behaviors that may require others to protect the individual from him- or herself. The person with the "ataque" is usually not deliberately aggressive toward others. These attacks tend to be triggered by extreme grief or repressed anger that may have been precipitated by overt interpersonal discord. The repression of negative emotions, especially anger, is culturally sanctioned in Puerto Rican society. Therefore, only an extreme event permits its expression as described here. Furthermore, the person suffering the "ataque" tends to not recall the incident or to claim, "I don't know what came over me," which provides a degree of disassociation from the behavior (Abad & Boyce, 1979; Guarnaccia, Lewis-Fernández, & Marano, 2003).

For providers of mental health services and assessment, the complex relationship between culture and psychopathology has been taken into account in the fourth edition of the *Diagnostic and Statistical Manual of Mental Disorders* (*DSM–IV*; American Psychiatric Association, 1994). The efforts to make culture more relevant in the *DSM–IV* are manifested in (a) the consideration of specific culture, age, and gender features for many diagnoses; (b) the expansion of Axis IV to consider psychosocial and environmental problems; (c) the addition of V codes pertaining to identity, spiritual, and acculturation problems; (d) inclusion of an outline for cultural formulation; and (e) inclusion of a glossary of culture-bound syndromes (American Psychiatric Association, 1994). Nevertheless, Manson and Kleinman (1998) and Hays (2001) cautioned clinicians about limitations that persist in how culture is incorporated in the *DSM–IV*, especially in the understanding of culture-bound syndromes. For example, the various culture-bound syndromes described in *DSM–IV* appear as a glossary separate from the traditional axial formulations. Furthermore, there are no guidelines for clinicians to help them link the descriptions of these disorders with established diagnostic categories. This, in turn, tends to limit the use of these syndromes by clinicians. Additionally, the placement of the culture-bound syndromes separate from the multiaxial system and the lack of guidelines to link the syndromes to the diagnoses in Axis I or Axis II may reinforce the notion that cultures other than "majority" or "mainstream" may shape certain disorders, whereas disorders seen among nonminority individuals tend not to be seen as influenced by the majority culture (Hays, 2001).

A number of authors have cautioned that clinicians need to weigh the likelihood that recent immigrants to the United States experience adjustment problems that can affect the outcomes of psychological testing (A. M. Padilla, 1992). Butcher, Coelho Mosch, et al. (2006) cautioned clinicians to evaluate the extent of the client's level of adaptation–acculturation to the new, complex culture of the United States. For example, it is not unusual for individuals who are evaluated shortly after having arrived in the new culture to reflect higher levels of distress than those who have been in the new culture for a longer period of time (Deinard, Butcher, Thao, Moua Vang, & Hang, 1996; Velasquez, Maness, & Anderson, 2002).

Moreover, Comas-Diaz and Grenier (1998) pointed out that many immigrants (and especially immigrants of color) become ethnic minorities when they relocate to North America and are likely to experience discrimination along with being perceived as inferior by the nonminority community because of their lack of political power. These immigrants may be under pressure to adapt to the host culture while being viewed as persons of lower status. These pressures can lead to the development of potentially ineffective coping strategies.

OVERVIEW OF ISSUES IN PERSONALITY ASSESSMENT OF ETHNIC MINORITIES

When assessing ethnic minority clients, test users need to be particularly aware of the issues of test construction and appropriate test use.

Test Construction

Butcher, Coelho Mosch, et al. (2006) enumerated four key areas of concern in test construction: (a) linguistic equivalence, (b) construct equivalence, (c) psychometric equivalence, and (d) psychological equivalence.

Linguistic equivalence encompasses the aspect of vocabulary, syntactic, and idiomatic equivalence (Sechrest, Fay, & Zaida, 1972) and is most often achieved through a process of initial translation from the original to the target language followed by an independent retranslation back to the original language. It is then determined whether the translated items have retained their meaning. Any discrepant items are subject to additional translation and back-translation until consistency in meaning can be achieved between the original and target language. This process was used in the translation of the Minnesota Multiphasic Personality Inventory–2 (MMPI-2) to the various languages in which it has been published. A detailed description of this process can be found in Butcher (1996a).

Construct equivalence refers to whether the personality concepts that an instrument examines can be generalized across cultures. Rogler (1999) described in detail the consequences for cross-cultural research of the uncritical use of Western or American concepts of human behavior or experience—in particular, the risk of yielding invalid research results. The implications would be no less serious with respect to the cross-cultural use of personality assessment instruments with constructs that are irrelevant in the culture being assessed. Therefore, test users are encouraged to evaluate the instrument's construct relevance for clients representing different cultural groups. Users may ascertain this by determining whether bilingual test–retest studies with different language versions of the instrument have been conducted and whether the findings indicate that there is sufficient equivalence between the versions of the instrument to be considered alternative forms (Butcher, Nezami, & Exner, 1998). In the case of the MMPI-2, research by Velasquez, Chavira, et al. (2000) with bilingual (English and Spanish) participants has found a high degree of similarity between the English and Spanish MMPI-2 profiles of college students. The researchers have also examined the comparability of different Spanish versions of the instrument and have found high levels of similarity in the resulting profiles.

The *psychometric equivalence* of an instrument, or how the measure performs statistically across cultures, is strongly linked to the two equivalence constructs discussed above in that it is concerned with the internal structure of the instrument. In particular, the techniques of factor analysis and item responding across cultures are ways to ascertain the psychometric equivalence of instruments. In brief, factor analysis examines the similarity of latent factors to determine whether a test has a similar factor structure across cultural groups (Ben-Porath, 1990). The technique of confirmatory factor analysis in particular (Bryant & Yarnold, 1995) is useful in examining whether the items hypothesized to tap into a given dimension of an instrument (e.g., fear of social stigma within a measure of fear of HIV infection) in the source population also tap into the same dimension when applied cross-culturally. For a more detailed explanation of the basic concepts of factor analysis, the reader is referred to Bryant and Yarnold (1995).

With respect to item responding, the technique of item response theory (IRT) has recently been applied to explore psychometric equivalence between test translations. IRT, unlike classical test theory, allows for distinguishing examinee characteristics from test characteristics. Therefore, IRT explores an examinee's performance on a test item on the basis of factors called *traits*, *latent traits*, or *abilities*. Classical test theory, unlike IRT, is test oriented, which indicates a focus on the analysis of the test as a whole, such as its test–retest reliability and coefficient alpha (Henard, 2000).

Gaining psychometric equivalence may be attempted by developing local norms, especially if two cultures (the source of the instrument and the target culture) are substantially different in their patterns of responding to items (see Cusick & Fafrak, 1992; Ricks, 1971). For example, G. E. Lucio, Ampudia, Duran, Leon, and Butcher (2001) reported some differences in several MMPI-2 validity and clinical scales for Mexican males and females (although most were small and within the standard error of measurement) that are attributable to cultural differences. The authors concluded that the use of local norms in Mexico would be preferable for that indigenous population because these norms account for cultural differences.

Finally, the *psychological equivalence* of a test should be determined. This refers to whether the meaning or cultural significance of test items is similar across cultural groups (Butcher, 1996a). This is exemplified by differences in meaning for a given interpersonal or nonverbal communication such as eye contact. For instance, direct eye contact in Euro-American culture is commonly associated with self-confidence and assertiveness, but in other cultures, such as some Native American groups, it is associated with disrespect toward elders and authority figures. Therefore, the indirect eye contact that is normative and appropriate in some cultures may mistakenly be interpreted as a sign of depression, unassertiveness, or other emotional distress in a Euro-American context (Sue & Sue, 1999).

Appropriate Test Use

Psychologists seeking to use instruments in a culturally competent manner must bear in mind a range of issues and cautions when using a personality assessment instrument with culturally and linguistically diverse clients. These issues pertain to the biases (potentially present in both the test and the assessor), the need to exercise critical thinking in the overall assessment process, and the need to consider key characteristics of the test's construction that may affect its applicability across cultures.

Moreover, psychologists conducting psychological evaluations are encouraged to follow the ethical guidelines of the American Psychological Association (APA), which encourage psychologists to take into consideration appropriate cultural factors in conducting an assessment. The APA Ethics Code (APA, 2002) has stated,

> When interpreting assessment results, including automated interpretations, psychologists take into account the purpose of the assessment as well as the various test factors, test-taking abilities, and other characteristics of the person being assessed, such as situational, personal, linguistic, and cultural differences, that might affect psychologists' judgments or reduce the accuracy of their interpretations. They indicate any significant limitations of their interpretations. (p. 1072)

Beyond these general issues, practitioners would benefit from guidelines they could follow "on the ground" or at the time of using an instrument.

In the case of the culturally competent use of the MMPI-2 with Hispanics, Velasquez, Chavira, et al. (2000) recommended that test users consider not only the issues of appropriateness of the test for particular clients but also the preferred language people have for the expression of emotional issues, rapport, and appropriateness of the test format. In addition, Velasquez et al. recommended (a) that standard administration procedures be followed, (b) that computerized interpretive reports be used cautiously, (c) that scales other than just the standard validity and clinical scales be used, and (d) that the potential impact of acculturative pressures be considered. In particular, the authors cautioned test users against using unofficial translations of the test, using shortened versions, or allowing clients to take the test home. All of these can potentially affect test results to the extent of providing inaccurate or even exaggerated profiles. Concerning the use of scales beyond the traditional validity and clinical scales, Velasquez et al. encouraged users to examine results of content and supplementary scales, because they may provide important information relevant to the functioning of ethnic minorities if research supports their use. The reader is referred to Garrido and Velasquez (2006) for additional discussion and review of case studies involving content and supplementary scales and for discussion of MMPI-2 interpretation with Hispanic clients. Finally, although the exact impact of acculturation on MMPI-2 results is not clear, Velasquez et al. recommended that users of the MMPI-2 determine whether and to what extent their clients are experiencing stress as a result of their process of acculturation. This information may be more easily obtained in a qualitative manner (by interview) at this time and may help illuminate the interpretation of obtained MMPI-2 results among Hispanic immigrants (Garrido & Velasquez, 2006).

BIASES IN ASSESSMENT

The challenges of understanding the relationships among culture, behavior, and psychopathology also affect all aspects of personality assessment. These include the design and adaptation of assessment instruments that can be appropriately applied to people of diverse cultural and linguistic origins, the selection and administration of those instruments, and the interpretation of results. Much like the prevailing concepts of mental health and distress in the fields of psychology and psychiatry, the prevailing methodologies of assessment were developed in a Western–European cultural context (Dana, 1997). Therefore, many measures, especially those involving standardization, that are used to evaluate people of diverse cultural origins have been developed in populations that are (nearly) exclusively Western–European. This requires that users of these measures be alert to the possibility of Eurocentric biases that may result in inaccurate or off-target assessments of culturally diverse clients.

Hays (2001) highlighted some of the biases that can affect standardized instruments. One problem she noted is the lack of culture-specific norms, which in the case of the original MMPI resulted in some significant differences in scale scores between White Euro-American and non-White or non-English-speaking (e.g., African American, Hispanic) populations. As indicated by Hays, a remedy for this lack of culture-specific norms is the restandardization of an instrument with the inclusion of representative samples of diverse populations. The original MMPI underwent such a process of restandardization and improved the cultural relevance in the MMPI-2 by using a diverse sample standardization sample (Greene, 1991) showing no prominent differences based on ethnicity in the normative groups (Butcher, Graham, et al., 2001).

Another potential source of bias is the very fact that such tests do not originate in the target culture and therefore may not reflect the value systems or worldviews (Lindsey, 1998) of the target population. This issue evokes the distinction between etic and emic approaches to cultural understanding. In brief, this is the distinction between approaches based on universal assumptions about human experience that transcend races and cultures (*etics*) and those based on indigenous, culture-specific assumptions of experience (*emics*; Triandis, 1994). As with the first bias, the development of tests from a purely emic perspective, with highly culturally specific content, would require substantial resources and research commitment that are typically not available to many countries. Moreover, such a specifically designed instrument would not likely adapt well across different cultures.

A third source of potential bias is the lack of standardized mechanisms or procedures to allow for the adjustment of test results to account for the level of acculturation of the test taker (see Exhibit 1.1). For example, Cuellar (2000) proposed the use of an Index of Correction for Culture, derived from correlating a measure of acculturation to a criterion variable (i.e., the instrument being applied). The use of this index might provide a more accurate interpretation of test results in light of knowledge of the level of acculturation of the test taker. However, research using such a strategy has not been explored with standardized psychological measurements such as the MMPI-2. Moreover, there is still a relative lack of consensus concerning the conceptualization and measurement of acculturation. As indicated by J. W. Berry (1997) and Phinney (1996), acculturation is a complex, nonlinear process in which individuals may retain aspects of their culture of origin relatively intact while becoming more assimilated and learning the host culture. Zane and Mak (2003) reviewed multiple existing measures of acculturation and concluded that the complexity of the changes associated with acculturation virtually precludes its comprehensive assessment for the

EXHIBIT 1.1
A Case for Culturally Sensitive Assessment

Ms. Lopez, a 34-year-old mother of two preadolescent children, was referred for a parenting competency evaluation by a state child protective agency. A monolingual Spanish-speaking immigrant, Ms. Lopez was employed in the second shift of a factory and had lived in the United States for approximately 3 years before being referred. She and her children had come to join her husband, who had already settled in the United States seeking a better economic future for the family. Ms. Lopez's involvement with the child protective agency was related to her alleged inability to set appropriate behavioral limits for her children and provide them with appropriate supervision after her husband abandoned the family shortly after she had joined him in the United States. Her husband had allegedly become involved in illicit activities as a means to provide for the family, which caused serious conflicts between him and Ms. Lopez and resulted in their eventual divorce. Her son and then her daughter had started to skip school and stay away from home, to associate with what Ms. Lopez considered to be "bad company," and to spend the night in the homes of various unknown friends. The children were in foster placements at the time of the referral. Ms. Lopez was still grieving the death of her oldest child, who had been murdered in their country of origin several years earlier.

Ms. Lopez was referred to a Latina, Spanish-speaking clinician for the evaluation. The clinician's ability to communicate in Spanish initially appeared to help Ms. Lopez feel at ease. Soon, however, it was apparent that Ms. Lopez was extremely anxious about the evaluation process and about its purposes, both of which she repeatedly questioned. Ms. Lopez talked at length about the numerous struggles and heartaches she had so far endured in her life, especially in her role as a mother. She emphasized her distress about discovering her husband's illicit activities and about the poor example that it set for the two younger children, while praising the value of "earning your livelihood cleanly even if you remain poor, because God will look after you after all if you live honestly." Another major source of distress for Ms. Lopez was related to not having succeeded in managing her children's behavioral issues according to the cultural values she adhered to. She repeatedly lamented that she had only limited English language proficiency and also no reliable, trustworthy sources of support that could have helped her deal with her children in the absence of their father (i.e., extended family nearby who could "give them a good example"). As someone with very limited income, she felt she had no social power, would not be believed in her concerns about her children, and may even be penalized for using corporal punishment or the type of discipline generally accepted in her country of origin. In sum, she saw herself as completely powerless in addressing her family's situation in a society whose child-rearing values she considered alien to hers. Ms. Lopez also had serious concerns about her daughter because of her relationship with a somewhat older man whose family had allowed her to stay overnight several times. This family, also of Hispanic background, was barely known to Ms. Lopez, who frequently decried their apparent support of this relationship and their dismissal of her concerns. In her frustration, Ms. Lopez once demanded that her daughter allow herself to be examined for virginity. This precipitated an incident in which the daughter allegedly assaulted the mother, further adding to the concerns of the child protective agency.

Ms. Lopez approached the overall evaluation process with a high level of anxiety and frequently voiced concerns that "everyone" (including the evaluating clinician) was conspiring to cause her harm and to separate her from her children permanently and did not respect the cultural values she believed in, which she felt were under attack. Therefore, the administration of any instrument, including the Spanish version of the MMPI-2, required extensive explanation and reassurance. Still, during administration, Ms. Lopez would occasionally voice her objections to the content of items she found offensive and point to them as evidence that she had to be extremely careful not to respond the "wrong" way. On occasion she threatened to walk away from the testing.

(continued)

EXHIBIT 1.1   (Continued)

Ms. Lopez's MMPI-2 profile revealed an elevated level of defensiveness (*L* [Lie] = 86), a high-normal endorsement of psychopathology (*F* [Infrequency] = 61), and some degree of randomness (*VRIN* [Variable Response Inconsistency] = 70). The majority of the clinical scales appear elevated, especially Scales 1 (Hypochondriasis), 3 (Hysteria), and 8 (Schizophrenia). Content scales *FRS* (Fears), *HEA* (Health Concern), and *BIZ* (Bizarre Mentation) were also elevated. Her reading score in Spanish was commensurate with her level of education.

In light of the presenting concerns of this evaluation and of the value conflicts expressed, clinicians (including Hispanic Spanish-speaking clinicians!) who are called to evaluate clients like Ms. Lopez must approach their work with a keen sense of the linguistic and acculturation factors that may challenge the evaluation. Although some of the findings from Ms. Lopez's profile could be interpreted as indications of significant psychopathology, a more culturally informed interpretation of her suspiciousness, alienation, pervasive health concerns, and overt emotionality would consider the severe conflict between the values she wanted to uphold in raising her children and the many cultural pressures she and her children encountered in their new society. The breakup of her marriage and the ongoing trauma and grieving for her oldest child, together with her zeal to protect her younger children from their brother's fate, added themselves as individual factors to the more general issues related to her low level of acculturation—or perhaps, her rejection of several cultural values sanctioned in her host society. More specifically, this case highlights the need for the following:

1. Learning about the current saliency of the client's sociocultural values related to family relations, behavioral expectations for the children, and parental roles that are sanctioned in the country of origin.
2. Learning about the client's own experience of being raised according to the values sanctioned in the country of origin (i.e., behavioral, gender role expectations).
3. Acknowledging that the client articulates his or her experience of cultural value conflicts—namely, the client's experience of acculturation pressures to change or modify culturally sanctioned behavioral or gender expectations within the family.
4. Considering the migration circumstances, expectations of adjustment or success in the new society, and challenges to these expectations (which could originate within or outside the family).
5. Considering the client's socioeconomic experience as well as experiences of discrimination and sociopolitical power status vis-à-vis the host society.
6. Considering the lifecycle stages (i.e., transition to adolescence, initiation into sexuality), the client's values around these stages, and the acculturation pressures on these values.
7. Considering the existence of past collective and/or individual trauma, losses, and how these are dealt with (via spiritual or religious practices, social support, or other rituals).
8. Considering the availability of support resources that the client may consider trustworthy and congruent (e.g., extended family).

individual. However, they observed that acculturation research has helped identify specific psychosocial domains that have changed in individuals as a result of cultural change. Therefore, citing Betancourt and López (1993), they proposed that the assessment of acculturation focuses on "capturing specific psychological elements from a particular domain such as cultural values" (p. 54). By examining which domains have experienced change (or not) within an individual, the assessment of acculturation becomes more idiographic and relevant to the individual's experience.

As it now stands, there are no psychometric "adjustments" available that could correct for a lack of acculturation for tests like the MMPI-2. The most effective uses of acculturation assessments are (a) to determine whether a U.S.-based measure would likely provide relevant and reliable information on the client given his or her ability to understand the language of the instrument and familiarity with the behaviors being assessed and (b) to decide which language version and normative set should be used in the evaluation (see Exhibit 1.1)

A fourth source of bias mentioned by Hays (2001) is the tendency to conduct assessment in an almost exclusively quantitative manner, often at the expense of direct observation, interviewing, and other sources of information outside of standardized assessment. (Keep in mind that interviews and behavioral observations are generally unreliable and when conducted with culturally different clients can be highly vulnerable to misinformation.) Although this has affected the intellectual assessment of ethnic minority children, resulting in large numbers of these children being placed in special education classes (Suzuki & Valencia, 1997), it is also an issue in the area of adult personality assessment, especially when only limited sources of information or a noncontextual assessment may lead to inaccurate diagnoses.

Addressing Biases: Cautions Related to Test Selection and Use

In addition to the potential sources of bias discussed above, test users must be aware of other practical issues as they consider applying standardized tests to ethnically and linguistically diverse populations. As noted by Geisinger (1998), the following issues are critical:

- Test users must take into account the dominant language, socioeconomic status, ethnicity, and gender of their clients, especially if a test is being used that was developed with a different cultural group from that of the test taker.
- Test users need to be aware of the meaningfulness of the results obtained from adapted versions of a test. Being able to ascertain this may require test users to consider a number of psychometric issues, including the construction of the test, scoring, reliability, validity, impact, and fairness. Among these issues, validity is of central importance to the meaningfulness of results, because it encompasses the content, criterion, and construct dimensions of test validity.

- As applied to the use of tests with non-English-speaking populations, test users need to be aware that performance of the non-English speakers may be related to their English language skills in addition to (or even instead of) their knowledge of the test content.
- As for criterion validity, test users must be aware of the potential for differential prediction. This may occur when the relationship between the predictor (test score) and the criterion is significantly different between groups. This may indicate that a test is invalid for a given group and that a different instrument altogether may be needed for that group.
- When using a translated or otherwise adapted version of an instrument, test users should find out whether the adapted version correlates with variables that theoretically it should (thus indicating convergent validity) and whether it does not correlate with variables it should not (indicating the presence of divergent validity).
- Test users should be concerned with the impact and fairness of the instruments they apply to diverse groups. The fairness of a test is related to the issue of differential prediction discussed above. Test users should be aware of any differences between groups in the relationships among predictors and behavioral, performance, or other criteria of interest. Such differences indicate that the test may not be fair across different groups.

Addressing Biases: Toward Culturally Competent Interpretation of Test Results

Test users also need to critically examine their approach to the overall process of assessment. Handler and Meyer (1998) described psychological assessment as a complex, dynamic, integrative, and interpersonal process that is the hallmark of professional psychology. The complexity of this process is what distinguishes *assessment* (as leading to interpretation of test results and comprehensive formulation of human behavior) from *testing* (the application of instruments). The power of assessment to describe and formulate human behavior resides in the clinician's ability to critically examine the adequacy of how tests have been applied, the impact of any modifications or adaptations on the validity of the findings, whether enough information has been collected to cross-validate the findings, and whether the conclusions have been influenced by errors in judgment (e.g., confirmatory bias, use of prototypical examples, over- or underconfidence, or "hindsight" bias; Handler & Meyer, 1998). Consideration of these issues is all the more critical in the interpretation of test results of individuals representing diverse ethnic and linguistic origins.

Therefore, test users who assess ethnically and linguistically diverse populations are called on to ask themselves the following critical questions, which incorporate elements of critical thinking on the basis of the recommendations of Sandoval and Duran (1998), to guide their interpretations from the assessment of ethnically and linguistically diverse clients:

1. What barriers and/or facilitating factors are present in the assessor? This requires consideration of the assessor's level of skill in the field of assessment, willingness to refer to another practitioner if necessary, the assessor's ability to communicate with the client, and the assessor's knowledge of alternative resources (translators, interpreters, assessment of language proficiency, native-language versions of test instruments), the assessor's familiarity with the client's culture and rules for building rapport, the appropriate interpretation of nonverbal behavior, the ability to understand the client's accent, and the availability of experts with whom the assessor might want to consult.

2. What are the assessor's biases or preconceptions about the client's cultural and language origins, and how might they impact the interpretation of the results? Hays (2001) described a model of self-assessment that assessors might find helpful here.

3. Has the assessor ensured that the test to be used actually assesses the construct in question as opposed to having assessed English language proficiency? Assessors need to consider carefully their clients' proficiency in both their native and second (usually English) languages to determine the impact of language on test results. As it pertains to personality tests and the MMPI-2 in particular, a detailed discussion of this issue can be found in Garrido and Velasquez (2006).

4. Has the assessor considered the client's level of acculturation and familiarity with test-taking skills and the test materials that are used in available tests (e.g., self-reports, paper-and-pencil tests)? Assessors need to evaluate this and train their clients in the use of these materials to prevent the results from being affected by variables other than those being assessed. Likewise, assessors must consider other culture-related variables that may affect results, such as speed of response, the cognitive effort involved in dual-language processing, and the level of rapport between the client and the assessor.

5. Has the assessor collected sufficient information and assessed the right types of information (e.g., direct observations, interviews, collateral reports) to cross-validate findings, especially in light of inconsistent test performance?
6. Has the assessor presented his or her findings in clear language, noting any modifications made to the testing procedures and any limitations or reservations regarding the conclusions?

ASSESSING HISPANIC PEOPLE IN THE UNITED STATES

We next provide an overview of recent demographics of Hispanics living in the United States to give a needed perspective on the assessment context.

Demographic Overview

The most recent data from the U.S. Census Bureau (2004) indicate that people of Hispanic origin are now the largest ethnic minority group in the United States and are projected to increase substantially by the year 2025. This diversification in the ethnocultural composition of the general population is due to increases in migration, which in turn may be the result of various pressures affecting these individuals in their countries of origin. For people of Hispanic origin, as well as for others, these pressures may include the need for better economic conditions, a desire (or need) to leave situations of sociopolitical oppression, and the search for greater educational opportunities (Santiago-Rivera, Arredondo, & Gallardo-Cooper, 2002).

The Hispanic population in the United States grew from 35 million in the year 2000 to over 40 million in the year 2004, representing 14.2% of the U.S. population. The same report indicates that African Americans now represent 12.2% of the population; Asians, 4.2%; Native Americans, 0.8%; and Native Hawaiians/Pacific Islanders, 0.1%.

Among Hispanics, the largest groups continue to be those of Mexican (64%), Puerto Rican (10%), and Cuban (3.5%) origin, with other Hispanic groups accounting for the remaining 22%. The information on language use indicates that in 2000, 51% of Hispanics described themselves as able to speak English "very well," 20.7% as "well," 18.3% as "not well," and 10% as "not at all." In 2004, over 30 million Hispanics reported that they spoke Spanish at home (75% of Hispanics), and 36.5% reported that they spoke English "less than very well" (U.S. Census Bureau, 2004).

Aside from language considerations and the diversity of reasons and circumstances around migration, the most recent U.S. Census data, the Current Population Survey of March 2002 (U.S. Census Bureau, 2004), provide information concerning relevant characteristics of the Hispanic population in the United States. Specifically, Hispanics tend to be concentrated geographically in the West and South of the United States (nearly 78% of Hispanics live in those regions) and tend to live in the central cities of metropolitan areas, compared with non-Hispanic Whites (nearly 46%). Consistent with previous demographics, Hispanics are more likely than Whites to be under age 18 (34.4% of Hispanics in 2002 were under age 18 compared with 22.8% of non-Hispanic Whites). As many as two in five Hispanics are foreign born and tend to live in households that are larger than those of non-Hispanic Whites.

Educational level was also noted in the same report. As of 2002, more than two in five Hispanics age 25 and over had not completed high school. This means that among Hispanics, approximately 57% had high school diplomas compared with 88.7% of non-Hispanic Whites. Additionally, over 25% of Hispanics had less than a ninth-grade education compared with 4% of non-Hispanic Whites. In addition to the disparities in educational attainment, disparities in employment are noted. For instance, among people ages 16 and over in the labor force, 8.1% of Hispanics were unemployed, compared with 5.1% of Whites. Among the employed, Hispanics were more likely than non-Hispanic Whites to be employed in service occupations and twice as likely to be employed as machine operators and laborers. Only 14.2% of employed Hispanics were in professional or managerial occupations compared with 35% of non-Hispanic Whites. A final but no less important economic indicator concerns poverty levels. In 2002, 21.7% of Hispanics were living in poverty compared with 7.8% for non-Hispanic Whites. At the time of the report, Hispanics represented 13.3% of the total population yet represented 24.3% of the population living in poverty.

Assessment of U.S. Hispanics With the MMPI-2: Integrating Their Context

These data serve to underscore the critical role of context in the assessment of culturally and linguistically diverse populations, and in this particular case, of the Hispanic population being assessed with the MMPI-2. As indicated by Hilliard (1996) and Lonner and Ibrahim (1996), assessment psychologists are called on to understand their clients' contexts as a priority within the overall treatment and/or assessment process. More specifically, these authors recommended the use of constructivist approaches to the assessment of their clients, such as content analysis of clients' responses, qualitative examination of clients' interactions, and the use of assessment techniques that may allow clinicians to determine how their culturally diverse clients may construct reality. For example, clients' responses to projective techniques may serve to identify how their cultural background and other significant experiences may have shaped their view of reality. The authors, however, recommended using great caution given the difficulties in interpreting projective techniques across cultures.

Another example of contextual assessment is described by Nieves-Grafals (1995), who looked at how specific test items from standardized tests, such as the Wechsler Adult Intelligence Scale, have been answered by immigrants and interpreted the responses on the basis of their cultural context. Perhaps one of the most comprehensive models for contextual assessment, which considers many of the demographic variables that characterize Hispanics discussed above, is the ethnocultural assessment described by Comas-Diaz and Jacobsen (1987) and explained in detail in Comas-Diaz and Grenier (1998).

It is imperative that assessment psychologists pay close attention to their Hispanic clients' language proficiency and incorporate methods for assessing language proficiency before using any English-language instrument with these clients. This is especially important in the case of clients whose English language competencies have been acquired relatively recently or who may have oral language competencies in English but not equally developed reading, reading comprehension, or writing abilities. As described by Cummins (1984), this calls for understanding the difference between an individual's proficiency in basic interpersonal (oral) communication and proficiency in language tasks associated with reading, reading comprehension, writing, and conceptual use of language. Test users may consider using parallel English–Spanish forms of language assessment instruments such as the Woodcock–Munoz Language Survey—Revised (Woodcock, Munoz, Ruef, & Alvarado, 2005) with their Hispanic clients prior to using a given test. This is especially important when any kind of testing (e.g., cognitive, achievement, or personality) is being conducted in what Sandoval and Duran (1998) described as "high stakes" testing, in which the results of a test might determine or predict an examinee's job performance, a student's educational placement, or the outcome of a forensic evaluation. On the basis of the Bureau of Census data concerning the language proficiency levels of Hispanics in the United States, it is likely that over 70% of the population could read and understand the English language well enough to take the MMPI-2 in English either by booklet or by audiotape to provide a valid assessment.

With respect to the MMPI-2, test users are called on to apply contextual assessment principles to the interpretation of resulting profiles. For instance, Garrido and Velasquez (2006) enumerated interpretive possibilities for the validity and clinical scales of the MMPI-2 of Hispanic clients that supplement the traditional interpretation of the scales and that may prove essential to formulating culturally competent profile interpretations and therapy recommendations. The reader is referred to Garrido and Velasquez for a scale-by-scale listing of interpretive considerations that may affect Hispanic MMPI-2 profiles. (A listing of Spanish language MMPI-2 and MMPI-A adaptations is presented in Appendix A.)

However, although these cultural contextual considerations need to be made, extensive research with the MMPI-2 and MMPI-A (summarized in Appendix B) attests to both the validity of the test and its adaptability with Hispanics. (For a current listing of general MMPI-2 and MMPI-A research references, see the following Web site: http://www.umn.edu/mmpi.) Moreover, Hall, Bansal, and Lopez (1999) performed a meta-analysis of many of the available studies among non-Hispanic Whites, African Americans, and Hispanics covering 31 years of research. In their review of 31 years of comparative MMPI and MMPI-2 research, Hall et al. concluded that in the aggregate, MMPI and MMPI-2 differences among non-Hispanic Whites, Blacks, and Hispanics are quite small between non-Hispanic Whites and Hispanics (only on the L [Lie] and Mf [Masculinity–Femininity] scales). In sum, the findings by Hall and colleagues indicate that as a general approach to personality assessment, the MMPI-2 provides comparable information for both Hispanic and non-Hispanic White respondents.

In addition, although it is true that on the original MMPI some results with culturally diverse individuals and Hispanics in particular were due to the lack of diversity in the original norms, the factor structures of MMPI item dimensions can be found across diverse cultures (see Butcher & Pancheri, 1976). Studies of the factor structure of the MMPI-2 (e.g., Butcher & Han, 1996) also indicate factor similarity across cultures. Because of these findings and of the development of new norms and international adaptations of the MMPI-2, test users are urged to use and be informed about the MMPI-2 in international and multicultural contexts. For example, psychologists assessing a Spanish-speaking client in the United States who is unacculturated to American ways can use the Mexican version of the test, including the Mexican norms, and obtain highly usable results, as is discussed in chapter 2, this volume.

Test users may also be attracted to computer-generated interpretive reports, which can facilitate the overall assessment task. Readers are cautioned against the uncritical use of conclusions from these reports. It is also important to consider the existence of established cross-cultural comparisons of computer-based reports that suggest their cross-cultural utility, as described by Butcher, Berah, et al. (1998) and Shores and Carstairs (1998).

Finally, the need for useful assessment techniques in clinical and forensic settings to provide information needed for decisions far outweighs the current limitations in assessment methodology noted by Hays (2001) and Dana (2005). Although there are no perfect clinical assessment instruments (including interview and behavioral assessment) for providing useful, valid information in multicultural assessment contexts, this task often needs to proceed in order to address important treatment or administrative decisions that will be made. Even Dana (2005), one of the most eloquent proponents of the need for cross-culturally equivalent assessment tools, acknowledged that the MMPI-2 can be administered to Hispanics and had developed guidelines for its interpretation. He stated that with these guidelines "interpretation bias can be addressed by using specific steps to increase reliability of interpretation with multicultural populations including Hispanics" (p. 164). The suggestions inherent in the guidelines do include considerations of the cultural orientation of the assessor and service delivery issues as well as acculturation issues and response sets with the client that have been discussed so far in this chapter and will continue to be addressed throughout the rest of this book.

This book was not written to make a political statement or to disclose or explore problems and issues of acculturation in contemporary society, nor was it written as a theoretical treatise to persuade mental health professionals of the merits of including (or excluding) psychological testing from contemporary practice. The primary goal of this book is to provide the necessary research background and clinical guidelines for using the MMPI-2 and MMPI-A for practitioners who need to make assessments of clients from a Hispanic background.

SUMMARY

This introductory chapter has presented a number of issues that test users who work with culturally and linguistically diverse populations need to consider to accomplish equitable, culturally competent assessments. These issues are pertinent to the use of tests developed in Western–Euro-American traditions of assessment, primarily in English, and with original norms that tend not to include (or underrepresent) members of different ethnic or linguistic groups. Tests of cognitive ability, academic achievement, aptitude, and personality are all affected by these issues. Nevertheless, the focus of this chapter is personality tests, more specifically, the MMPI-2 as used with Hispanic populations in the United States. The discussion of the various biases that may affect the assessment of ethnic and linguistic minorities, the potential barriers to the culturally appropriate application and interpretation of tests, and the various methodological challenges inherent in the construction and application of culturally appropriate instruments serve to underscore the complexity that characterizes appropriate and ethical use of tests across cultures. In the case of U.S. Hispanics, now the largest ethnic minority group, this complexity is further enhanced by within-group diversity of origins, sociopolitical identifications (Comas-Diaz, 2001), migration circumstances, acculturation, and language use. Nevertheless, the latest demographic information also indicates that U.S. Hispanics remain in positions of socioeconomic and educational disadvantage, consistent with previous information.

Although socioeconomic disadvantage affects a large proportion of U.S. Hispanics compared with non-Hispanic Whites, it is critical that users of standardized measures such as the MMPI-2 focus on the impact of multiple aspects of clients' cultural experience (with the experience of poverty being one) and also search for a contextual understanding of their clients. It is clear that explanations of behavior with a complex, heterogeneous group such as Hispanics may not always be found in strictly linear formulations. Test users who seek to work in a culturally competent manner with Hispanics are called to use alternative interpretive hypotheses that incorporate knowledge of the complexity and diversity of this group.

In the chapters that follow, we consider in detail the issues of applying the MMPI-2 and MMPI-A with Hispanic clients. Chapter 2 addresses Spanish language adaptations of the MMPI and MMPI-2. Chapter 3 more specifically describes the assessment of Hispanics living in the United States. In chapter 4, we turn to the importance of evaluating response attitudes of clients to appraise the validity of the profile, looking specifically at how Hispanic clients might invalidate a protocol. Chapter 5 is devoted to a review of the MMPI-2 measures and how the interpretation of some scales might need some adjustment to provide a clearer picture of Hispanic clients who are marginally acculturated. Chapter 6 provides a practical examination of the MMPI-2 with a number of cases to illustrate the test's applicability with this population. Chapter 7 is devoted to a description of the MMPI-A and the various Hispanic versions of the test. Chapter 8 provides case illustrations of the MMPI-A with Hispanic adolescents. Finally, chapter 9 concludes this book with an overview of the use of the MMPI-2 and MMPI-A and a look at future directions the field might take.

CHAPTER HIGHLIGHTS

- Hispanics in the United States constitute the largest ethnic minority group, representing 14.2% of the total population in the year 2004. They tend to be young and to be at educational and socioeconomic disadvantage relative to non-Hispanic Whites; many are foreign born, are heterogeneous in their national origins and sociopolitical background, and tend to speak Spanish at home in large numbers.
- The relationships among culture, personality, and psychopathology are highly complex; however, research suggests that there are cross-cultural similarities in personality and that some

psychological correlates of different personality dimensions are present in diverse cultural groups.

- Biases that may affect the assessment process in general include the fact that instruments originate in and reflect the worldviews of cultural majority groups.
- Clinicians need to be aware that recent immigrants to the United States often experience adjustment problems that can affect the outcomes of psychological testing.
- Users of standardized tests must be aware of a range of issues that may affect the conclusions derived from them.
- The extensive literature on the cross-cultural applications of the MMPI-2 and MMPI-A provides substantial support for interpreting these instruments with Hispanic clients.

2

THE INTERNATIONAL ASSESSMENT CONTEXT: SPANISH LANGUAGE ADAPTATIONS OF THE MMPI, MMPI-2, AND MMPI-A

The original MMPI was widely translated and used in many countries, even though some of the items were difficult to translate and adapt culturally because of their culture-bound content—the religion items, for example. Despite this problem, there were more than 150 translations of the original MMPI.

When the MMPI was revised in the 1980s, the MMPI Restandardization Committee (Butcher, Dahlstrom, Graham, Tellegen, & Kaemmer, 1989) made efforts to develop a revised instrument that would reduce cultural content and more readily lend itself to translation and adaptation. There have been 33 test translations of the MMPI-2 since it was published in 1989 and 12 of the MMPI-A published in 1992.

The MMPI-2 restandardization project was aimed at providing a more current and more representative normative sample. All of the participants were administered the English-language MMPI-2. The large normative sample of the MMPI-2 (N = 2,600) included Black, Hispanic, Native American, and Asian participants in proportions consistent with the 1980 census. The Hispanic samples (n = 35 men, n = 38 women) are underrepresented, given the large increases in the population over the past 20 years. Further, the

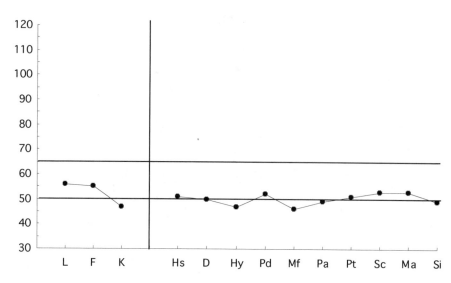

Figure 2.1. MMPI-2 validity and clinical scale profile of Hispanic normative men (N = 35) plotted on U.S. norms (N = 1,138). The scales include L (Lie), F (Infrequency), K (Defensiveness), Hs (Hypochondriasis), D (Depression), Hy (Hysteria), Pd (Psychopathic Deviation), Mf (Masculinity–Femininity), Pa (Paranoia), Pt (Psychasthenia), Sc (Schizophrenia), Ma (Hypomania), and Si (Social Introversion).

Hispanic sample was obtained in large part from one geographic area of the United States (Southern California). Analyses of MMPI-2 profile differences between White men and women and their Hispanic counterparts (using the normative sample) have revealed some differences by ethnicity, with Hispanics obtaining higher scores; however, these differences have been found to be small (López & Weisman, 2004) and of no statistical or clinical importance (Hall, Bansal, & Lopez, 1999).

The Hispanic subsample in the standardization sample (see Figures 2.1 and 2.2) falls within the standard error of measurement of the normative population. The largest differences are on the validity scales L (Lie) and F (Infrequency) for women.

In appraising the utility of the MMPI-2 and MMPI-A in the assessment of Hispanic clients in the United States, it is important to gain a broader picture of the extent of the instruments used in the international context. The original MMPI, MMPI-2, and MMPI-A have been widely adapted into other languages and cultures for several reasons.

First, the test items on the original MMPI, and to a greater extent the expanded item pool on MMPI-2 and MMPI-A, address mental health problems and personality characteristics across cultures with demonstrated validity. Many psychological problems—for example, schizophrenia—have universal manifestations and can be assessed by the same items regardless of culture (Butcher, 2004, 2005b; Butcher, Tsai, Coelho, & Nezami, 2006).

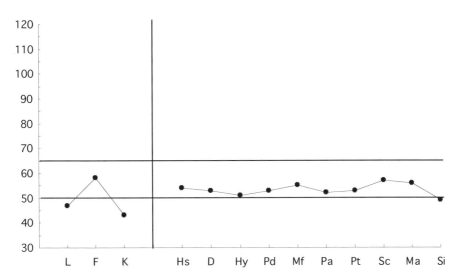

Figure 2.2. MMPI-2 validity and clinical scale profile of Hispanic normative women (*N* = 38) plotted on U.S. norms (*N* = 1,462). See Figure 2.1 for scale definitions.

Second, the MMPI-2 is an objectively scored instrument that is relatively easy to process. Protocols can be machine scored, making research on the instrument more efficient. The test can be interpreted by computer, and several international test interpretation projects have shown the generalizability of computer-derived interpretations in other countries (Butcher, Berah, et al., 1998; Shores & Carstairs, 1998).

Third, the extensive research base available on the MMPI instruments make them ideal for cross-cultural research because subjectivity and bias can be substantially less than with other psychological methods. There is a rapidly growing international research base on the MMPI-2 and MMPI-A that provides assurance that the instruments have construct validity in other cultures (Butcher, 1996a; Butcher, Cheung, & Lim, 2003; Butcher, Derksen, Sloore, & Sirigatti, 2003; Butcher & Pancheri, 1976; G. M. E. Lucio & Reyes-Lagunes, 1996).

Fourth, there is a clearly established test adaptation methodology available to guide test developers interested in adapting the instruments in their own culture (Butcher, 1996a; Butcher & Pancheri, 1976). Finally, the MMPI-2 test publisher, the University of Minnesota Press, has been supportive of international test adaptations and is willing to provide a license for this copyrighted instrument to psychologists and international publishers who can develop an equivalent version in their country and assure proper distribution.

We turn now to a more detailed historical survey of the use of the MMPI and MMPI-2 in several Spanish-speaking countries, some beginning more than 55 years ago. This will provide the reader with an understanding of the generalizability and adaptability of the objective assessment instruments in such countries.

MMPI AND MMPI-2 ASSESSMENT IN CUBA

Despite almost a half century of disagreeable relationships between Cuba and the United States and the U.S. embargo against Cuba that placed severe limitations on scholarly exchanges, Cuban psychologists have managed to persist in their efforts to develop the profession of psychology through continued use of the Minnesota personality test in clinical and health assessment (Quevedo & Butcher, 2005). The development and use of the MMPI and MMPI-2 in Cuba is an interesting history and one that is highly pertinent to this book, because many Cubans have migrated to the United States.

The original MMPI was introduced in Cuba more than 55 years ago, in 1949, when Cuban psychologist Alfonso Bernal del Riesgo consulted with one of the developers of the original MMPI, Starke Hathaway, in an effort to bring the new assessment technology to Cuban psychology. Prior to the Cuban revolution in 1959, the MMPI was used in a number of clinics in Cuba. Although the teaching and practice of psychology underwent dramatic changes after the revolution when Cuban psychology adapted models from Soviet psychology in an effort to be free of American influence, several psychologists in Cuba continued their clinical work and research on the MMPI.

Quevedo and Butcher (2005) pointed out that during the early years of the Cuban revolution, the attitude toward psychological testing was beginning to change toward the negative as a result of the antitesting influence of Soviet psychology. However, this attitude did not hamper the use of the MMPI in mental health settings during those years, because according to Valcarcel and Rios (1974), most psychological practice settings included the test in the diagnostic battery.

Published research in Cuba during this period addressed a number of topics. These include, for example, utility of the validity scales (Valcarcel & Rios, 1974), antisocial personality (Valdes, 1979), scale length (Barroso, Alvarez, & Alvisa, 1982), hyperthyroidism (Alvarez, Alvarez, & Lastra, 1982; Gonzalez, Martin, Despaigne, & Espinosa, 1983), psychosomatic problems (Arqué, Segura, & Torrubia, 1987), medical conditions such as blood disease (Triana, Delgado, Sarraff, & Felipe, 1999; Triana, Espinosa, Triana, Espinosa, & Abaascal, 1987; Triana, Espinosa, & Valdes, 1995; Triana, Espinosa, Valdes, & Gonzales, 1988; Triana, Valdes, & Felipe, 2000), cancer patients (Gomez de Borda, Gonzalez, & Llorca, 1988), depression among hemophiliacs (Loy, Alvarez, Duran, & Almagro, 1981), and psychological characteristics in leprosy (Rincon & Lastra, 1987). For a detailed discussion of this history, see the review by Quevedo and Butcher (2005).

Practicing Cuban psychologists found the Cuban MMPI to be effective in addressing mental health problems in Cuba during this period. However, in 1993, shortly after the publication of the Spanish translation of the MMPI-2, Guillermo Arias, from the University of Havana, met with James Butcher at the University of Minnesota about adapting the revised version, Garcia–Azan's MMPI-2 Hispania (Garcia-Peltoniemi & Azan Chaviano, 1993), for use in Cuba. Arias returned to Cuba enthusiastic about using a revision that had much promise because of psychometric and linguistic improvements. Over the past several years, Arias has applied the Garcia–Azan translation of the MMPI-2 to both psychiatric patients and nonpsychiatric or normative persons (Quevedo & Butcher, 2005). He collected a substantial sample of clinical and normal persons across Cuba to determine the comparability of the MMPI-2 across cultures.

Arias, Mendoza, Atlis, and Butcher (2002) reported on the effectiveness of the MMPI-2 in the Cuban populations. MMPI-2 profiles for both clinical and nonclinical samples from Cuba appear to be generally similar to those of comparable groups from the United States for both psychiatric and nonpsychiatric samples.

SOUTH OF THE BORDER: USE OF THE MMPI AND MMPI-2 IN MEXICO

The developments of the MMPI, MMPI-2, and MMPI-A in Mexico are important landmarks to review because these test adaptations are highly influential in our present-day test interpretation strategies with Hispanic clients living in the United States. Thus, we cover these developments in detail.

At the end of the 1960s, when researchers of the MMPI in the United States were beginning to question some of the items of the original MMPI and discuss the need for a revision of the instrument, the test was first published in Mexico, adapted to Spanish by Rafael Núñez in 1976. The MMPI became one of the most widely used personality inventories in Mexico, although some people questioned the extension of the test and several cultural issues apparent in some of the items. At the time, American norms were used to assess Mexican people.

In 1992, at the National Autonomous University of Mexico (UNAM), psychologists began working with the new version of the inventory: the MMPI-2 (G. M. E. Lucio & Reyes-Lagunes, 1996). Since that time, Mexican psychologists have had extensive experience with the test and have unequivocally concluded, as this section summarizes, that this new version is highly useful as a means of assessing Mexican people. The development of the Mexican adaptation followed several steps.

1. *Literal translation.* A preliminary translation was made using five bilingual psychologists as translators. One psychologist was American, one was Mexican American, and the other three were Mexican. All of the MMPI-2 items were translated without considering the previous translation of the original MMPI into Spanish.

2. *Semantic and cultural adaptation.* This version was corrected by the project researchers, who worked in collaboration with an expert bilingual translator, examining the semantic and syntactic content as well as the cultural and clinical relevant issues. Thus, a revised Spanish version was obtained that included more culturally appropriate wordings. One of the project researchers was a clinical psychologist and the other was a psychologist with measurement expertise.

3. *External validity.* The Spanish version obtained by this procedure was next examined by external clinical experts in the MMPI, who worked on its validation issues, obtaining an agreement of over 90% of the item renderings by the judges. This version also was administered to a group of students from different Latin American countries—Venezuela, Nicaragua, and Puerto Rico—to determine whether it would be appropriate with other Latin American populations.

4. *Content readjustment.* The resulting comments and elements of the analysis were considered by researchers in completing the final Spanish version of the inventory.

5. *Back-translation.* The agreed-on Spanish version was next retranslated to English by a bilingual translator who was unfamiliar with the MMPI. Then, the two English versions were compared to test the adequacy of the item renderings. Overall, the results showed a high degree of agreement.

6. *Equivalence research.* Test adapters often conduct an equivalency study of the completed version of the inventory to assure that the reading level allows participants to understand the test item wordings adequately. Once the translation of the inventory was complete, an initial study was conducted with Mexican students to assess this equivalence. The study was conducted at UNAM, the largest university in Latin America, because of its fairly heterogeneous student population; many of the students come from diverse regions of Mexico. The probabilistic representative sample of this study was obtained by the cluster method. On the basis of this technique, three of the schools in the main UNAM campus were selected: science, arts, and business administration. Students in 71 courses were tested, taking into account schedules and shifts. The original sample comprised 2,246 participants, or about 10% of the UNAM population. A total of 254 partici-

pants were eliminated because they did not meet one or several of the inclusion variables: age (17 to 36 years old), gender stated clearly, Gough's F minus K index below a score of +9, true and false percentages no more than 80 and no answer less than 30, *TRIN* (True Response Inconsistency) between 5 and 13, *VRIN* (Variable Response Inconsistency) maximum 13, *F* (Infrequency) scale maximum 11.

The final sample for the initial comparability study comprised 1,920 participants (813 men and 1,107 women). In this first study, the groups were compared with the U.S. college normative sample published by Butcher, Graham, Dahlstrom, and Bowman (1990). The results suggested that male and female Mexican students were significantly different on the clinical and validity scales, except on Scales *L* (Lie) and 8 (Schizophrenia). Thus, as found also in the United States, separate norms for men and women were needed (E. Lucio, Reyes-Lagunes, & Scott, 1994). The results indicated also that there were significant statistical differences between Mexican and American male university students in all the clinical and validity scales except in Scale 4 (Psychopathic Deviate). The greatest differences were found in Scales *L*, 2 (Depression), and 6 (Paranoia). There were significant differences between the Mexican and American female university students in all the scales, except in Scales *F* (Infrequency), 1 (Hypochondriasis), and 3 (Hysteria). The differences between Mexican and American female college students were greater than those found between Mexican and American male college students. The greatest difference between Mexican and American female college students was in Scale 5 (Masculinity–Femininity), which may be due to cultural factors. The differences obtained in this study were not as great as those found with the original MMPI in Mexico showing that normal populations had elevated pathological indexes (E. Lucio, 1976; Navarro, 1971; Núñez, 1979).

The factor analysis with the Mexican student group (Durán, Lucio, & Reyes-Lagunes, 1993) showed great similarity to American students. Several studies confirmed the internal consistency, reliability, and discriminant validity of the MMPI-2.

7. *General population study.* A probabilistic, multistage sampling procedure was used to develop the normative sample. The Mexican general population was classified using some qualitative criteria taking into account the different regions of the country in which the test could be applied and considering the kind of populations to which the instrument could be applied in Mexico. The criteria used were gender, age, and education level.

The instrument was applied to 2,077 volunteers. Fifteen percent (*n* = 330) of the initial sample were excluded using the exclusion criteria followed by the MMPI-2 restandardization project. Thus, the normative sample contained 1,744 volunteer adults (860 men and 884 women) between ages 18 and 80. The mean age was 31.4 years for men and 31.6 years for women.

The levels of education of the men and women, respectively, were as follows: junior high school, 15.1% and 9.8%; senior high school, 44.6% and 44.3%; college, 33.7% and 39.2%; and graduate school, 4.7% and 4.5%. The sample was considered representative only of the segments of the general population who possessed a high enough level of literacy to take the test, according to the data shown in the 1990 census. Participants were from different regions of the country. They answered the inventory anonymously, in groups of 10 to 100. In this study, the procedure used to standardize the MMPI-2 in the United States was followed carefully (Butcher, Dahlstrom, et al., 1989), but there were some methodological differences; for example, the North American participants were paid whereas the Mexicans were not. Special software programs (Monzon & Lucio, 1996) were developed to score the test and to obtain the uniform T scores that are used with the MMPI-2.

The means and standard deviations, with respect to the validity, clinical, content, and supplementary scales, were obtained. Also, the differences between Mexican and American norms were calculated in all the scales with t test. The results of the differences between Mexican and American norms with respect to the basic scales have been published (G. E. Lucio, Ampudia, Duran, Leon, & Butcher, 2001). With respect to basic scales, the results show that there were some differences between the Mexicans and the U.S. population. However, the majority of these differences referred to the attitudes of the Mexicans toward the inventory, because the scores of the Mexican population did not show psychopathological indexes as with the MMPI original. The differences seemed to be lower with respect to the content scales (see chap. 5, this volume). The results obtained with respect to this group of scales indicate greater differences in the CYN (Cynicism), FRS (Fears), and ASP (Antisocial Personality) scales with respect to men. In these scales, Mexican men scored higher than American men. The greater differences with respect to women were found in the same scales as in men: the ASP, FRS, and CYN scales. In these three scales, the Mexican women scored higher than the American women. The differences between American and Mexican women were also lower in this group of scales. The differences in this group of scales may be due to cultural or social determinants, with the elevation in the FRS scale related to socioeconomic conditions and the elevation with respect to the ASP scale related to the fact that different things are considered to be antisocial in each culture.

With respect to the supplementary scales, some differences were observed in the O-H (Overcontrolled Hostility), R (Repression), and GM (Gender Role Masculine) scales. In the O-H and R, Mexican men scored higher, whereas in GM American men scored higher. With respect to females, differences were found in the O-H, R, and GF (Gender Role Feminine) scales. In the O-H and the R, the Mexican women scored higher, whereas in GF the American women scored higher.

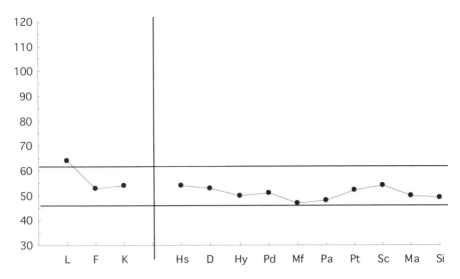

Figure 2.3. MMPI-2 validity and clinical scale profile of Mexican men (*N* = 860) plotted on U.S. norms (*N* = 1,138). See Figure 2.1 caption for scale definitions.

Norms for the MMPI-2 were developed on the Mexican normative population (see Appendix C). See the Mexican normative sample compared with American norms on the validity and clinical scales in Figure 2.3 for men and Figure 2.4 for women.

Because the test was to be applied to participants from 18 to 80 years, the Mexican research group wanted to know if there were age differences

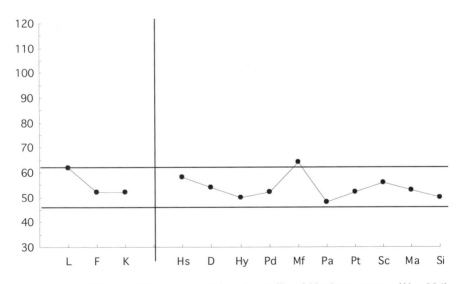

Figure 2.4. MMPI-2 validity and clinical scale profile of Mexican women (*N* = 884) plotted on U.S. norms (*N* = 1,462). See Figure 2.1 caption for scale definitions.

within the normative sample. The normative sample was divided into four groups on the basis of age. The scores of the 355 oldest participants were compared with the other three groups. The data were analyzed by analysis of variance (ANOVA) to obtain the differences in all the scales of the inventory among the four groups. The results indicated that the older group showed higher elevation on some of the scales, for example, in the L, F, and FRS scales. The older group showed lower scores in Scales 6 (Paranoia), LSE (Low Self-Esteem), and Es (Ego Strength). These results were similar to those found in other studies in the United States. From this study, it was concluded that many of these differences may be due to changes in the life span, to which the MMPI-2 is sensitive. The differences were observed only in these scales, and although they must be taken into consideration, these differences show that it is not necessary to have special norms for this age group.

Comparative Research in Mexico

A number of studies completed in Mexico provide valuable information on the utility of the test in Mexican populations. Several cultural issues should be considered when the test is administered to Mexican people. The first one is that Mexicans tend to score higher on the L scale compared with Americans, probably because members of Mexican communities are more inclined to project a good image of themselves than are people from the United States. This may be due to one or more factors: Mexican society is more traditional than North American society; Mexican people may think that if they are too self-disclosing, they may be judged in a stricter way; or Mexican people may simply have difficulty understanding the double negatives in some of the items. Whatever the reason, the clinician should make efforts to motivate clients to be honest when tests are administered to them to get valid results. When the MMPI-2 is administered to people of lower socioeconomic levels, it is probable that they will have greater difficulties in understanding some of the items and especially double negatives, so very clear instructions need to be given and assessment of their comprehension of these items conducted.

Other Studies Carried Out With the MMPI-2 in Mexico

The MMPI-2 has been available in Mexico for several years, so the test is widely used in assessing students, in clinical populations, and also in personnel selection. We highlight some of the published studies to provide the reader with a perspective on the research efforts with the test.

TABLE 2.1

Multivariate Analysis of Variance of the Substance Abuse Scales
of the MMPI-2 for Mexicans With Alcoholism ($n = 136$) and
Nonalcoholic Volunteers ($n = 136$)

Scale	Alcoholics		Volunteers		F(1, 270)
	M	SD	M	SD	
MAC-R	27.30	4.47	22.47	4.02	87.56*
APS	24.19	3.64	19.54	3.55	113.46*
AAS	6.02	2.15	1.65	1.48	371.60*

Note. Wilks's lambda = 27.87. MAC-R = MacAndrew Alcoholism—Revised scale; APS = Addiction Potential Scale; AAS = Addiction Acknowledgment Scale.
*p = .00

Studies With Clinical Groups

Substance abusers. Leon and Lucio (1999) carried out a study to assess the validity and reliability of the substance abuse scales: MAC-R (Mac-Andrew Alcoholism—Revised), AAS (Addiction Acknowledgment Scale), and APS (Addiction Potential Scale). This study was conducted with the aim of determining the internal consistency and effectiveness of the test to obtain an exact diagnosis of Mexican patients with alcoholism. This study focused on the usefulness of the MMPI-2 to assess personality traits in Mexican alcoholic patients because an adequate validity and internal consistency was obtained with a group of 136 alcoholic patients compared with a group of 136 volunteers. Higher scores were obtained in the group of patients than in the group of volunteers, so it was concluded that the test could discriminate between the two groups. The results of the multivariate analyses of variance, using all the scales of the MMPI-2, also indicated the existence of differences between the normal sample participants and the alcoholic patients' sample, especially in the addiction scales: MAC-R, APS, and AAS (see Table 2.1). Thus, these scales discriminate one group from the other. The greatest differences in the basic scales were observed in the F, K (Defensiveness), D (Depression), Pd (Psychopathic Deviate), Pa (Paranoia), Pt (Psychasthenia), Sc (Schizophrenia), Ma (Hypomania), and Si (Social Introversion) scales. The most meaningful differences within the supplementary scales were observed in the A (Anxiety), Es (Ego Strength), MAC-R, Re (Social Responsibility), Mt (College Maladjustment), PK (Keane Posttraumatic Stress Disorder), PS (Schlenger Posttraumatic Stress Disorder), Fb, APS, and AAS scales.

A statistical analysis based on signal detection theory (Berry, 1996; Egan, 1975; Macmillan & Creelman, 1991; Swets, 1988) was carried out to obtain the most suitable cutoff score for the MAC-R, APS, and AAS scales, using the receiver operating characteristic curves. To obtain the sensitivity and the specificity, it was necessary to consider the data provided by the two samples studied. The results indicated that to determine the best sensitivity and specificity for the diagnosis of persons with alcoholic problems with a 50% prevalence, the most suitable cutoff scores for the addiction scales were 24 for the MAC-R, 22 for the APS, and 4 for the AAS. For the supplementary scales, a good model fit was also obtained on the basis of four predictors that provide the classification, $\chi^2(4, N = 272) = 243.19, p < .001$, with 88.24% accuracy; the scales included in the equation were GM, GF, Fb, and AAS. Finally, by using addiction scales, a good model fit was obtained on the basis of two predictors that provide the classification, $\chi^2(2, N = 272) = 227.53, p < .001$, with 88.60% accuracy of classification; the scales included in the equation were MAC-R and AAS.

From this study, the researchers concluded that the MMPI-2 scales provide an accurate differential diagnosis of people with alcoholism. In this study the validity of the substance abuse scales of the MMPI-2 was established for the Mexican population with respect to the differences in personality traits in a group of alcoholic patients and a group of volunteers who did not use alcohol excessively. This was the first step in validating that the scales can be useful in the treatment of identified alcoholic patients, because there is no other instrument in Mexico that estimates alcohol abuse in relation to other personality factors.

Another step in the use of the MMPI-2 with patients with alcoholism was to determine the discriminative sensitivity of the Koss–Butcher and Lachar–Wrobel critical item sets as alcoholism indicators. The answers on the MMPI-2 Spanish version of 122 alcoholics and 122 nonalcoholics were compared (G. M. E. Lucio, Córdova, & Hernández, 2002a, 2002b). The participants from the alcoholic sample were all under treatment for substance abuse. Statistically significant differences were found in all the 17 groups between both samples with the Student t test ($p = .001$). The highest t values obtained were found in Depressed Suicidal Ideation (16.5), Situational Stress Due to Alcoholism (28.4), Mental Confusion (16.02), Antisocial Attitude (16.21), Family Conflict (12.06), Depression and Worry (15.17), and Substance Abuse (19.85). High scores within the alcoholic sample were in the Depressed Suicidal Ideation ($M = 8.75$, $SD = 4.33$), Acute Anxiety State ($M = 7.34$, $SD = 3.97$), Somatic Symptoms ($M = 6.34$, $SD = 3.80$), and Depression and Concern ($M = 6.00$, $SD = 3.31$) groups, whereas in the nonalcoholic sample the highest scores were found in the Anxiety ($M = 2.04$, $SD = 1.81$), Depressed Suicidal Ideation ($M = 1.70$, $SD = 1.87$), Antisocial Attitude ($M = 1.40$, $SD = 1.23$), and Somatic Symptoms ($M = 1.81$, $SD = 11.87$) groups. Findings support the existence of significant differences in the answers given to the Koss–Butcher and Lachar–Wrobel 17 groups of critical items by alcoholics and nonalcoholics, with sets 2, 4,

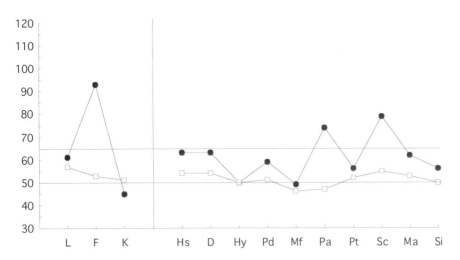

Figure 2.5. MMPI-2 validity and clinical scale profiles of men from a Mexican psychiatric hospital (*N* = 135; black dotted line) compared with men from a university population (*N* = 813; open box line). See Figure 2.1 caption for scale definitions.

5, 7, 8, 14, and 16 being the ones exhibiting the highest *t* values. Therefore, critical items can be used effectively as alcoholism indicators that facilitate diagnosis and intervention strategy integration. Furthermore, their use as interview guidelines to approach specific issues in MMPI-2 invalid profiles is suggested.

Psychiatric patients. To assess the effectiveness of the MMPI-2 in detecting mental health problems in Mexico, the scale adapters conducted a study comparing the responses of psychiatric patients with a sample of nonpatients (G. M. E. Lucio, Palacios, Duran, & Butcher, 1999). An inpatient psychiatric sample diagnosed as having psychotic or severe personality disorders according to the third edition of the *Diagnostic and Statistical Manual of Mental Disorders* (*DSM–III*) was obtained from three psychiatric hospitals in Mexico. The sample consisted of 233 patients (135 men and 98 women): 41% had schizophrenia, 15% had organic psychosis, 8% had toxic psychosis, 10% had major depression, 8% had dysthymic disorder, 4% had chronic psychosis, 6% had antisocial personality disorders, and 8% had other diagnoses. The patients ranged in age from 17 to 67 years, with a mean age of 32.79 years. The control comparison sample was composed of normal individuals (university students) who volunteered to take the MMPI-2 as part of the test adaptation study (G. M. E. Lucio & Reyes-Lagunes, 1996).

The performance of psychiatric patients on the MMPI-2 clinical scales (see Figures 2.5 and 2.6) shows that psychiatric patients in Mexico respond in a manner similar to inpatient samples in the United States. For a discussion of MMPI-2 assessment of inpatients, see Nichols and Crowhurst (2006; see also Butcher, Tsai, et al., 2006).

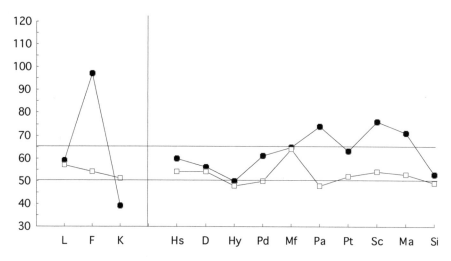

Figure 2.6. MMPI-2 validity and clinical scale profiles of women from a Mexican psychiatric hospital (*N* = 98; black dotted line) compared with women from a university population (*N* = 1,107; open box line). See Figure 2.1 caption for scale definitions.

Medical patients. A study was carried out to assess the personality traits of a group of 44 patients suffering from a medical condition, dermatitis. These patients, 33 men and 11 women, attended one of the principal dermatological centers in Mexico City. All of the patients were diagnosed by dermatologists. The personality traits of the patients were compared with the Mexican students' norms. All of the participants were volunteers and were asked to answer the inventory while they were waiting to see the specialists. Only those patients who had finished elementary school were considered for the study. The main hypothesis was that scales *Hs* (1, Hypochondriasis) and *HEA* would be elevated. Several differences were observed between both groups. With respect to female participants, the higher differences in the group of the basic scales were observed in scales *Hs* (t = 3.43, p = .01) and *Es* (t = 5.41, p = .01), in which patients scored higher than students. There was also an important difference in scale *F* (t = 5.45, p = .01), in which patients scored lower than students. With respect to the content scales, the higher differences were in *ANG* (t = 4.19, p = .01); *DEP* (t = 4.74, p = .01); and *TRT* (t = 4.73 p ≤ .01). In the group of supplementary scales the greatest differences were observed in scales *Es* (t = −6.13, p ≤ .01; *Do* (Dominance) (t = −6.01, p ≤ .01), in which patients scored lower; and also in *DEP* (t = −4.08, p ≤ .01).

With respect to the group of male participants, the most important differences were as follows: In the group of basic scales, there were significant differences only in scale *F* (t = 4.33, p ≤ .01) and *K* (t = 3.45, p ≤ .01). In scale *F*, patients scored higher than students, whereas in scale *K*, patients scored lower than students. With respect to content scales, the higher differences were in scales *HEA* ($t = 3.73$, $p \leq .01$) and *DEP* ($t = 3.89$, $p \leq .01$), in which patients scored higher than students.

Differences in the group of women were similar to those observed in the group of men. From the results obtained, the main hypothesis was partially proven, because in the group of women there were high scores in the scales *Hs* (1) and *HEA*, but in the group of men there were not high scores in *Hs* (1). Results show also that there were significant differences in the group of women compared with men; for example, women had negative attitudes to treatment and, surprisingly, had high scores in *SOD* (Social Discomfort; i.e., indicating that they avoided relationships with others), which may be due to the fact that their self-image was negatively affected by the illness. Scores for *Es* were low in both groups, which indicates, along with the fact that posttraumatic stress scores were high, that they did not have enough resources to cope with stress. The elevation in the scales of the MMPI-2 that suggests emotional problems such as anxiety must be taken into account by physicians who treat the illness. The results of this study led to a proposal to introduce supportive group sessions with these patients.

A second study with a larger group of dermatitis patients, 64 females and 26 males, was conducted to examine the relationship between personality traits and recent life events. The higher scores in this second study were similar to the higher scores in the first study, and statistically significant correlations between personality traits and life events were also found. This study tried to find out how emotional problems detected with the MMPI-2 were related to the environment in which these patients lived.

Some of the life events related to dermatitis were divorce, death of a partner, conflicts, economical losses, working difficulties, economic difficulties, and assaults. These two studies show the usefulness of the MMPI-2 with Mexican groups in medical settings.

Personality disorders. A study of patients with borderline personality disorder was carried out (Ordaz & Villegas, 2000) to obtain the discriminant validity of the test between borderline patients previously diagnosed by a psychiatrist according to *DSM–IV* on Axis II; the other group were controls with the same characteristics as the borderline patients but without any psychiatric diagnosis. Results confirmed the hypothesis that borderline patients would show higher scores in many of the scales of the inventory than the comparison group. The scales in which there were higher differences between both groups were as follows: In clinical scales, the more noticeable differences were in scales 2 (*D*; $t = 5.31$), 4 (*Pd*; $t = 4.98$), and 8 (*Sc*; $t = 4.31$); in the content scales, the higher differences were in scales

DEP (*t* = 5.36) and *LSE* (*t* = 4.58); and in the supplementary scales group, the highest differences were in the posttraumatic stress scales (*t* = 5.06 and *t* = 4.97 for patients and controls, respectively).

Studies With the MMPI-2 in Treatment Settings

Díaz, Jurado, Lucio, and Cuevas (2003) carried out a study assessing whether the MMPI-2 could discriminate those patients who remain in psychotherapy treatment for a longer period of time from those who give up psychological treatment at an early stage. To accomplish this, they applied the MMPI-2 to all college students who attended a university mental health service during a 7-month period. The study also assessed personality traits related to attending treatment so the students could receive enough sessions to assure a permanent therapeutic effect.

A descriptive comparison study with two independent groups was carried out using a quota sampling method. All of the students who asked for a psychological treatment referral during 7 months were considered for the study. The final sample comprised 163 participants (106 female and 57 male). Initially, the MMPI-2 was administered to all the students who attended a second psychotherapy session. A total of 258 students attended this second session, but later 67 participants did not show up, and 28 protocols were not valid. Because this was a clinical sample, the validity criteria were as follows: Scale *F* up to 23, *Fp* up to 16, *VRIN* up to 13, *TRIN* between 5 and 13, and *CNS* (Cannot Say) up to 30. The participants were split into two groups: One group attended 4 or fewer sessions, and the other group continued the treatment and attended from 5 to 20 sessions.

Data were analyzed through ANOVA to take into account sex and number of sessions. Results show that statistically significant differences were obtained on the following scales. With respect to the clinical scales, differences were found in scales 2 (*D*), (*F* = 2.321, *p* ≤ .02) and *Hi* (*F* = 3.00, *p* ≤ .003) in which the group that attended more sessions had a higher score. With respect to the content scales, differences between both groups were obtained on scales *HEA* (*F* = 2.06, *p* ≤ .04) and *ANG* (Anger; *F* = 2.39, *p* ≤ .01). Moreover, in the supplementary scale, *Es*, students who attended more sessions had a lower score (*F* = 1.97, *p* ≤ .05). With respect to gender, the significant differences were obtained in *L* (*t* = 2.10, *p* = .03), *Hs* (1; *t* = 4.3, *p* ≤ .001); *Hi* (3; *F* = 2.5, *p* ≤ .01), *HEA* (*t* = 2.90, *p* ≤ .004), and *O-H* (*t* = 2.54, *p* ≤ .01), in which female students obtained a higher score. There was also a significant difference with respect to scale 5 (Masculinity–Femininity), in which male students obtained a higher score.

With respect to the interaction between gender and number of sessions attended, there were significant differences in three scales: *Hs* (*F* = 7.5, *p* ≤

.001), Hy ($F = 5.7$ $p \leq .001$) and HEA ($F = 3.93$, $p < .01$). It was concluded that there are scales in the MMPI-2 that can predict the adherence to psychological treatment. It seems that when people feel more depressed and manifest more symptoms, they attend more psychological treatment sessions. They also attend more sessions when they feel that they do not have enough resources to cope with their problems. It also seems that those who express a higher need for emotional support stay for a longer period in psychotherapy.

In this study some of the students also received pharmacological therapy. Thus, it would be desirable to carry out more research with the MMPI-2 to get more precise results on the effects of medication on continuation in treatment.

Criminal Offenders

A study was carried out in a forensic setting by Villatoro and Ramírez (1998) to find out the personality traits of a group of 200 offenders in one of the largest preventive reclusion prisons in Mexico City. The participants were divided into four groups based on the four more frequent crimes committed in Mexico according to the crime committed: robbery or assault, possession or dealing with prohibited substances, homicide, and rape. From this sample of 200, 40 were excluded because of validity problems with the MMPI-2. The group finally considered included 160 inmates: 38 for rape, 43 for robbery, 38 for homicide, and 41 for dealing and possession of prohibited substances. The test was administered in the facility in small groups of no more than 5 inmates. Results show that there were significant differences between the four groups only in the FRS and MacAndrew scales. On the FRS scale, the homicide and possession or dealing with substances groups had a significant clinical score (T = 67), whereas the other two groups had a lower score (T = 60). This elevation may be due to the fact that they knew that they were going to receive a more severe punishment. On the MacAndrew scale, the group for robbery had the highest score (T = 60), whereas the other three groups had scores of less than 55. This might be due to the fact that robbery is frequently associated with addiction in Mexico.

It is noticeable that most of the scores of all the four groups were lower than might be expected, probably because the participants may not have been truthful—the test was administered in the facility and by psychologists who, although they did not work in the prison, could influence the inmates' punishment. This can be concluded because the four groups had an L score of T = 70 or higher.

Another important finding was that with the exception of the robbery group (T = 62), the other three groups had a significant elevation in O-H (Overcontrolled Hostility), which is a scale that has been shown to be related to a subtype of violence. Although this is an exploratory study and there can be other external variables that may explain the results, the usefulness of the MMPI-2 with this population was shown.

As the research in Mexico clearly shows, the MMPI-2 is an effective adaptation and provides comparable information on Mexicans taking the test in Spanish. The importance of this equivalence is highlighted later in the book when the norms of this version of the test are illustrated on cases in the United States.

USE OF THE MMPI-2 IN PUERTO RICO

The MMPI has been used clinically in Puerto Rico since the 1950s by early doctoral-level clinical psychologists trained in the continental United States. It continued to be used mainly clinically in the diagnostic process and personnel selection until the 1990s, when the MMPI-2's Hispanic version and the MMPI-A's Hispanic version were published. Since then, the MMPI-2 and MMPI-A have been regularly used to evaluate Puerto Ricans in both clinical and nonclinical settings. For instance, the MMPI-2 is frequently used to evaluate clients referred for psychological treatment, psychiatric hospitalization, neuropsychological evaluations, forensic evaluations, and personnel selection. The MMPI-2 and MMPI-A are more likely to be administered to Puerto Ricans in Spanish because this is the dominant language on the island, although there are some Puerto Ricans who can be evaluated in English, depending on their proficiency in the language. Indeed, Puerto Ricans were included in the norms for the Spanish version of the MMPI-A. In 1996, Cabiya published the first summary of research in Puerto Rico in the book, *International Applications of the MMPI-2* (Butcher, 1996a). The chapter focused on the adaptation of the Spanish translation to Puerto Rican Spanish, and specific rephrasing in eight items was recommended.

Research consistently indicates that the MMPI-2 has differentiated well between normal and clinical samples, for instance, between normal samples and samples of depressed and psychotic patients (Cabiya & Davila, 1999b), of prison inmates (C. Pena, Cabiya, & Echevarria, 1995), and of battered women (Cabiya, Colberg, Pérez, & Pedrosa, 2001). The MMPI-A also has been shown to differentiate well between normal adolescents, depressed adolescent patients, and juvenile delinquents (Cabiya, Reuben, et al., 2001). Thus, these results do suggest that these tests are likely to be valid tools in the assessment of psychopathology in Puerto Ricans. These patterns of results are consistent with those reported by Cabiya (1996), E. Lucio et al. (1994), Whitworth and McBlaine (1993), and Whitworth and Unterbrink (1994) with other Latino samples in the continental United States.

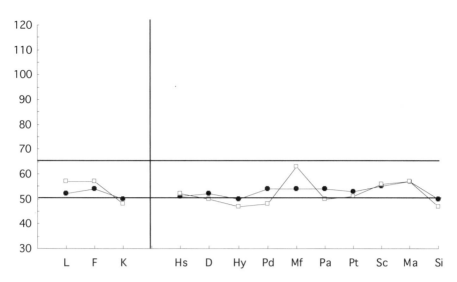

Figure 2.7. Group mean MMPI-2 validity and clinical scale profile of Mexican American college students (*N* = 173, black dotted line; Whitworth & McBlaine, 1993) and Puerto Rican women (*N* = 117, open box line; Cabiya, 1996). See Figure 2.1 caption for scale definitions.

However, there still is a need to conduct studies on Puerto Ricans who reside in the mainland United States to determine the extent to which the research in Puerto Rico is applicable to them. For example, Puerto Ricans in the United States are a numerical minority, whereas those on the island represent the majority. There are also many Puerto Ricans who now maintain permanent residency on the mainland, whereas others move to and from Puerto Rico on a frequent basis. There is a need for further study to see if this "cultural shift" and the status of majority–minority affect their MMPI-2 performance. Furthermore, there is a need to study the role of acculturation on the MMPI-2 performance of Puerto Ricans on both the mainland and the island. To date, all studies on the role of acculturation have been conducted with Chicanos. Clearly, Puerto Ricans face acculturative stress on both the mainland and island. For example, there is a need for further studies to see whether the acculturative stress affects the performance of Puerto Ricans who are more acculturated toward a traditional culture than those who are more acculturated toward mainstream European values on the MMPI-2.

Figures 2.7 and 2.8 present the MMPI-2 profile for samples of Puerto Rican college students compared with Mexican American college students reported by Whitworth and McBlaine (1993). The MMPI-2 clinical profiles of the Puerto Rican students are highly similar to those of Mexican American college students studied by Whitworth and McBlaine. Moreover, these mean profiles are within the range of MMPI-2 scores of Anglo college students

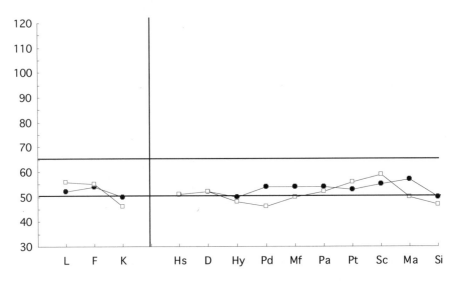

Figure 2.8. Group mean MMPI-2 profile of Mexican American college students (*N* = 40, black dotted line; Whitworth & McBlaine, 1993) and Puerto Rican men (*N* = 94, open box line; Cabiya, 1996). See Figure 2.1 caption for scale definitions.

that have been reported in the assessment literature (Butcher, Graham, Dahlstrom, & Bowman, 1990).

USE OF THE MMPI-2 IN CHILE

One of the most extensive assessment projects in psychology has been conducted with the MMPI and MMPI-2 in Chile. Research adapting the original MMPI in Chile began in 1976 at the Catholic University of Chile; in 1989, when MMPI-2 became available, the Chilean psychologists adapted this newer version for their research programs. Psychologists in the Student Affairs Department were interested in developing an effective program for evaluating students entering the university with the aim of providing counseling services to those in need of mental health services (Rissetti, Himmel, & Gonzalez-Moreno, 1996). Over a period of more than 20 years, the psychology staff collected MMPI data on over 40,000 students.

Translation and Adaptation of the Original MMPI

The translation and adaptation of the original MMPI in Chile was conducted from 1976 to 1978. During this time, an interdisciplinary committee developed the translation from English, producing a Spanish version by consensus. This form of the test was back-translated by a bilingual psychologist, and the committee compared the Spanish version with the English original, making adjustments to the Spanish version as necessary. The final translation was also checked by James Butcher and Rosa Garcia, from the University of Minnesota. The Chilean form of the MMPI was administered to university students, and item analyses were performed to evaluate comparability of the endorsement frequencies for Chilean compared with American students (Rissetti & Maltes, 1985a). Once the translation was complete, a number of studies were conducted to standardize and validate the instrument for general Chilean populations (Rissetti et al., 1979a, 1979b, 1979c; Rissetti, Montiel, Maltes, Hermosilla, & Fleischili, 1978), for the university student population (Rissetti & Maltes, 1985a, 1985b), and for the general adult population (Rissetti, Himmel, Maltes, Gonzalez, & Olmos, 1989a, 1989b).

During the research program, the MMPI was administered to students entering the university during their freshman year. This testing provided a database for the mental health professionals of the Student Health Department. For example, students who later were seen in counseling or were interested in career counseling had access to this entry information. As information on the psychometric characteristics of the inventory accumulated, several prospective studies on high-risk groups among university students were conducted to provide information on the mental health status of students at the university.

Before the MMPI came to be used in clinical evaluations in Chile, a large normative sample of 3,325 students from the university (ages 16 to 25 years) was randomly selected. Linear T scores were computed according to the standard method proposed by Butcher and Pancheri (1976). Rissetti et al. (1996) found that subsequent administrations of the MMPI showed the high stability of the local norms. Moreover, a factor-analytic study of a subset of the student population showed that the factor structure was congruent with the factor analyses of MMPI data sets reported by Butcher and Pancheri (1976; see Rissetti & Maltes, 1985a, 1985b). In addition, the test showed discriminant validity in differentiating normal from abnormal individuals (Himmel, Maltes, & Rissetti, 1979; Rissetti & Maltes, 1985a).

General Populations Norms

In 1988, Rissetti et al. (1989a) conducted a normative study (N = 608) of a general population from a random sample of Chileans to evaluate the utility of the MMPI with the general populations. As part of their study, the researchers compared the discriminant validity of the MMPI in differentiating clinical patients (N = 284). Linear T scores were derived for the reference population (Rissetti et al., 1989a).

Translation and Adaptation of the MMPI-2 in Chile

After the MMPI-2 was published in 1989, the adaptation project for this revised version of the test was initiated in 1991. Several modifications were made in the original translation to produce a Chilean version that would be equivalent to the English original. Two versions of an instrument are considered psychometrically equivalent when they have the same psychometric properties at the item as well as scale levels. The investigators assured that the item endorsement percentages and the factor structures were equivalent. A multidisciplinary translation committee was formed of two psychologists, two physicians, and a person with a master of arts in education and psychometrics to develop the MMPI-2 adaptation (Rissetti et al., 1996).

The following steps were taken in their adaptation work:

1. Each member of the committee individually translated the 567 items from the English original into the Spanish version.
2. Each member's translated versions were compared by the committee and evaluated for acceptability.
3. This final combined version was given to two bilingual individuals who then back-translated into English.
4. A bilingual test–retest study was conducted to determine if the item translations resulted in a comparable version of the instrument. The test–retest correlations of the scale raw scores for both administrations have a high mean correlation of about .80, confirming the comparability of the translation.
5. A new standardization study was conducted. The investigators made an effort to obtain a representative sample from the four most representative regions in the country. Participants were recruited from several institutions and communities. The MMPI-2 was group administered under controlled conditions. The final normative sample included 1,111 participants (522 men and 589 women). Age ranges for male and female participants, respectively, were 52.1% and 45.0% under 24 years of age, 27.2% and 22.1% between the ages of 25 and 34, 11.5% and 13.4% between the ages of 35 and 44, and 9.2% and 19.6% over the age of 45. The mean age of the men was 27.9 years (SD =10.8) and of women, 31.9 years (SD = 14.6). The education levels of the male and female participants, respectively, were 24.0% and 15.5% with elementary education, 44.0% and 37.9% with high school education, 9.0% and 16.5% with vocational education, and 22.6% and 29.9% with higher education. This sample composition was considered to be representative of the general Chilean population.

6. A large clinical sample was obtained to provide a validation sample. The MMPI was administered to 518 people who were undergoing mental health treatment. This group was selected to meet the demographic parameters as was the normative sample. Their clinical problems and mental health diagnoses were defined by the presence of some type of psychopathology at the time of taking the test, previously assessed through clinical judgment or other evaluation procedure that led to a psychiatric diagnosis and to the formulation of a treatment strategy. All of the participants were undergoing public or private outpatient or inpatient psychiatric or psychotherapeutic treatment at the time they took the test. For further information about the generalizability and validity of the Chilean MMPI-2, see Rissetti et al. (1996).

The Chilean standardization study provided substantial evidence concerning the congruence of the MMPI-2 in Chile. The profiles of the Chilean and U.S. normative samples were highly similar; and the high internal consistency of the scales, sometimes higher than those found in the original version, support the psychometric soundness of the Chilean version (Rissetti et al., 1996).

THE MMPI-2 IN ARGENTINA

The MMPI has been used extensively in Argentina since the 1960s. The original MMPI was translated into Spanish in Argentina in 1964 by the Psychological Assessment Service of the University of Buenos Aires Vocational Guidance Department (Casullo, 1964) and by Montoya (1977; see also Barbenza, Montoya, & Borel, 1978). This version of the MMPI was not widely used in clinical settings but was used extensively in personnel screening and for clinical research. Casullo, Samartino Garcia, Brenella, Marquez, and Dupertuis (1996) began developing the Argentine MMPI-2 in 1991 by obtaining the Spanish version developed for Chile by Risetti et al. (1989b).

When the revised version became available, Casullo et al. (1996) conducted a number of projects to adapt the Spanish language MMPI-2 for populations in Argentina. In adapting the Chilean version of the test, they took into account the need for linguistic and conceptual equivalence in modifying the translated items. As the project developed, they conducted training courses on the use, administration, scoring, and interpretation of the test to facilitate work with professionals on the MMPI-2 in Argentina. The researchers conducted several studies of the Argentine version of the MMPI-2 (Casullo et al., 1996).

Procedures for the Adaptation of the Argentine Version of the MMPI-2

The Argentine adaptation of the MMPI-2 was derived from the Chilean Spanish translation of the test and from a translation and back-translation developed by two bilingual psychologists. Casullo et al. (1996) took into consideration the linguistic and conceptual equivalence of the items for people in Argentina. In addition, they considered the accuracy and cultural sensitivity of the items; that is, they changed some words to adapt them to local verbal expressions in Argentina. The accuracy of the final adaptation was evaluated by two back-translation studies into English. When there were item discrepancies, the item content was modified to apply to Argentineans. In addition, the researchers took further steps to facilitate MMPI-2 research in Argentina. For example, they developed an MMPI-2 test manual (Brenella, Dink, & Maristany, 1992) to train people participating in research and Argentinian students who do not read or speak English. The manual provided current information on MMPI-2 history, development, structure, administration, and scoring procedures. Casullo et al. also incorporated the MMPI-2 into the academic curriculum in a course on psychological assessment taught at the Faculty of Psychology of the University of Buenos Aires, and they developed several training workshops for professional psychologists and physicians working in the psychiatric and general hospitals participating in the project and for professionals working on the Forensic Medical Board.

Research on the MMPI-2 in Argentina

Casullo et al. (1996) conducted research on a number of groups. Initially, data were collected on a sample composed of 600 Argentine normal individuals from Belgrano and Buenos Aires; from two universities in the metropolitan Buenos Aires area; and from the National University of La Plata, located in the capital city of Buenos Aires state. The normative data on the general population included participants from the middle socioeconomic level, all of them living in the two large urban areas of Buenos Aires and La Plata. Research on the validity and clinical scales was also conducted to provide information on normal individuals. Although Argentine men and women, in comparison with U.S. normative data, showed some higher mean scores on several scales, these differences were small, and most fell within the standard error of measurement (Casullo et al., 1996).

Several studies have also been conducted on other populations, such as applicants to a military college, psychiatric patients, forensic psychiatric patients, prison inmates, and college students. Although there may be some cultural differences, Casullo et al. (1996) concluded that in general, the MMPI-2 shows a clear sensitivity to psychological problems in Argentina. They reported that when mean scores from the general population sample and the psychiatric outpatient sample are compared, the MMPI-2 discriminates well between them as with studies reported in other countries. Casullo et al. (1996) concluded that the present Argentine studies of the MMPI-2 suggest a valuable role for future research and clinical personality assessment. The most readily available Spanish version of the MMPI-2 for use in Argentina is the Castilian version (see subsequent discussion and the publisher information in Appendix A).

USE OF THE MMPI AND MMPI-2 IN PERU

Rather than translate the MMPI or MMPI-2 into Spanish for their own country, some psychologists have chosen simply to use successful Spanish versions that have been developed for other countries. Psychologists in Peru, for example, have successfully followed this strategy. The MMPI and MMPI-2 have a long history of research and clinical use in Peru. The original version of the MMPI was the subject of a number of research investigations involving both the Nunez translation and the Garcia translation (MMPI Hispania). For example, Zanolo (1993) surveyed the findings of 20 Peruvian studies on the MMPI that focused on such factors as evaluating the comparability of test scores in various clinical groups, studying the effectiveness of the test in evaluating personality characteristics as measured by various clinical scale elevations, examining the relationship of the MMPI with other personality measures, and appraising the utility of shortened versions of the test in an effort to make the test easier to administer to clients in Peru.

Research in Peru has established that the Garcia–Azan version of the Spanish language MMPI-2 with the American norms is appropriate for use in clinical assessments in Peru (Scott & Pampa, 2000). These investigators conducted a comparative study of the MMPI-2 on two samples of men and women with a diverse range of occupational, educational, and socioeconomic backgrounds. They found that the Peruvian participants scored similarly on the MMPI-2 clinical and content scales as the American normative sample. The mean score of their samples of men and women from the general population are shown in Figure 2.9 for men and Figure 2.10 for women plotted on American norms. As noted by Scott and Pampa, the scores of Peruvians fall very close to the means for the American general population, with the exception of scale F for women. This difference is similar to findings for Mexico.

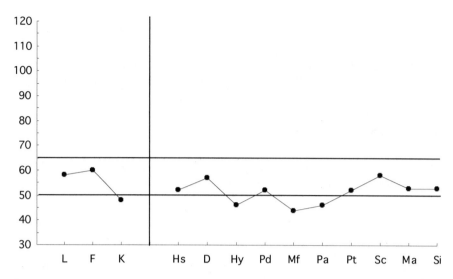

Figure 2.9. MMPI-2 validity and clinical scales scores of Peruvian men (*N* = 56) plotted on U.S. norms (*N* = 1,138; Scott & Pampa, 2000). See Figure 2.1 caption for scale definitions.

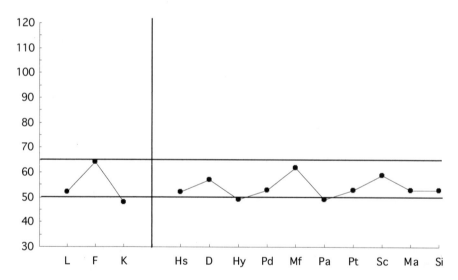

Figure 2.10. MMPI-2 validity and clinical scales scores of Peruvian women (*N* = 67) plotted on U.S. norms (*N* = 1,462; Scott & Pampa, 2000). See Figure 2.1 caption for scale definitions.

USE OF THE CASTILIAN MMPI AND MMPI-2 IN SPAIN

The original MMPI was used in Spain since it was first translated in 1975 (Avila-Espada & Jimenez-Gomez, 1996). The broadest use of the MMPI was in the areas of personnel selection and academic counseling; however, a number of clinical practitioners also included it in their assessment batteries. There were several problems that hampered broader acceptance of the MMPI among psychologists. First, the original Castilian MMPI translation was somewhat problematic in Spain (particularly in preemployment screening), because it contained several items whose meanings were ambiguous, strange, or culturally or socially outdated. Some of the items raised legal concerns because they were thought to possibly violate the Spanish constitution, which protects the freedom of the individual with regard to his or her social, political, and religious ideas. That is, the original MMPI contained a number of items that inquired about religious beliefs (these items were dropped in the revision of the MMPI in 1989). The second reason that the test did not gain wide acceptance in Spain involved the fact that the initial translation of the instrument contained a number of items that were inaccurately translated. The third reason was that the norms used were not sufficiently broad to represent the general population (Avila-Espada & Jimenez-Gomez, 1996). There were more appropriate Spanish norms available, published by Seisdedos (1977) and Seisdedos and Roig Fuste (1986), but these were not included in the MMPI that was officially available (Avila-Espada & Jimenez-Gomez, 1996). These problems with the original Spanish MMPI prompted adaptation of the MMPI-2 when it was published in 1989. In 1992, a research team made up of professors and investigators from 11 Spanish universities and coordinated by A. Avila-Espada was formed at the University of Salamanca.

Castilian MMPI-2

The research team followed the available translation guidelines for test adaptation developed by the University of Minnesota Press. They initially directly translated the items as follows. Six professional psychologists with translation experience (three of whom were fully bilingual) translated the items independently. The translators were instructed to carefully consider the original sense of the item and to assure that the sentences were understandable for participants from middle and low cultural levels and from different geographical locations in Spain. Then the team met and developed a consensus version. Following the effort to arrive at a consensus item pool, the agreed-on version was administered to two groups of postgraduate clinical psychology students and to a number of people from the general population to determine if the items were understandable. These results allowed the research team to refine the test version further (Avila-Espada & Jimenez-Gomez, 1996).

The research team conducted a normative study of the Castilian version of the MMPI-2 by obtaining a normal population comprising a number of samples from diverse population subgroups on the basis of 1989 census. They obtained samples from all the geographical areas of Spain of men and women across three age ranges: 19 to 29 years, 30 to 44 years, and 45 to 65 years. Moreover, sociodemographic representativeness was also an important consideration.

Structural Characteristics of the Castilian Version With the Normal Population

The normative population for the Castilian version of the MMPI-2 showed endorsement patterns similar to those of the normative population in the United States (Avila-Espada & Jimenez-Gomez, 1996). The mean scores, though slightly higher among the Spanish population, were generally consistent with the American norms. Moreover, for the most part, item endorsement patterns between U.S. and Spanish samples were similar. The correlations of endorsement percentages were .850 for females and .871 for males, further confirming the equivalence between the English language MMPI-2 and the Castilian version. Furthermore, the factor structure of the Castilian version was comparable to the factor analysis of the American normative sample.

Overall, the psychometric studies of the Spanish normative sample provided clear support for the transcultural consistency of the MMPI-2 and in particular for the equivalence of the Castilian and U.S. versions in general populations.

SUMMARY

To gain a full appreciation of the utility of the MMPI and MMPI-2 in the assessment of Hispanic clients in the United States, it is important to gain a broader picture of the instrument's use in the international context, particularly in Spanish-speaking countries. This chapter has provided a historical survey of the use of the MMPI and MMPI-2 in several Spanish-speaking countries to illustrate their generalizability. The original MMPI was widely translated and used in many countries even though some of the items were difficult to translate and to adapt culturally. It has been estimated that there are more than 150 translations of the original MMPI around the world. The 1989 MMPI revision included item changes that made the instrument more adaptable to other languages and countries. There are 33 test translations available of the MMPI-2, and there are 12 of the MMPI-A. In the MMPI-2 revision, efforts were made to provide a more representative normative sample of African American, Hispanic, Native American, and Asian participants to match the makeup of the U.S. population. In spite of disagreeable relationships between Cuba and the United States, Cuban psychologists have maintained an interest in using the American test—the MMPI—for assessment of clinical problems.

The extensive adaptation and validation research on the Spanish language version of the MMPI-2 for Mexico has been reviewed in this chapter. The norms for the Mexican version of the test are generally similar to the American norms. The MMPI-2 has become widely used in personality assessment in Mexico since it was published in the 1990s. Research on the test in other Spanish-speaking countries also has been reviewed.

CHAPTER HIGHLIGHTS

- The original MMPI was widely used in Cuba between the 1950s and 1990s. The MMPI-2 Hispania was incorporated in research and clinical applications in Cuba in the 1990s.
- The MMPI and MMPI-2 have been used in Mexico since their publication in 1967 and in the 1990s, respectively. Extensive adaptation and validation research has been performed on the Mexican version of the MMPI-2.
- The MMPI has been used in Puerto Rico since the 1950s, with adaptations of the MMPI-2 Hispania and MMPI-A Hispania versions conducted in the 1990s. Both versions of the test have been widely used in clinical assessment and research in Puerto Rico.
- One of the most extensive translation and adaptation projects has been conducted with the MMPI and MMPI-2 in Chile. Research adapting the original MMPI in Chile began in 1976. The MMPI-2 was translated and normed in Chile after the MMPI-2 was published in 1989.
- The MMPI has been used extensively in Argentina since it was published in 1964. Its early use focused on personnel screening and clinical research. When the revised version was published in Chile, psychologists in Argentina began to use it as well.
- Psychologists in Peru adapted the MMPI and, more recently, the MMPI-2 for research and clinical use in Peru. The original MMPI, both the Núñez translation and the Garcia translation, were the subject of a number of studies in Peru. Researchers

have concluded that the Garcia–Azan translation of the MMPI-2 used with the American norms works well in characterizing mental health problems in Peru.

- The original MMPI began to be used in Spain in 1975 primarily for personnel selection and academic counseling. The MMPI-2 was carefully translated into Castilian Spanish, and new norms were collected from a diverse sampling of the population based on the 1989 census.

3

USING THE MMPI-2 TO ASSESS HISPANIC CLIENTS LIVING IN THE UNITED STATES

The assessment of clients from differing cultural backgrounds can present the clinician with a number of challenges. This chapter addresses the use of the MMPI and MMPI-2 with Hispanic clients living in the United States. For example, it can assist in the determination of whether a Mexican immigrant charged with a capital crime is guilty by reason of insanity.

Our goal in this chapter is to provide an overview of considerations that are important for clinicians who are assessing Spanish-speaking clients with the MMPI-2. First, a historical perspective on past research and on applications of the use of various forms of the MMPI with Hispanics in the United States is provided, followed by pertinent background information needed for assessing Spanish-speaking clients in applied settings.

OVERVIEW OF RESEARCH

The use of the MMPI instruments in assessing clients of Hispanic origin who are living in the United States has a long history and involves several versions of the MMPI, both English and Spanish.

55

Using the English Language Version of the MMPI-2 With Hispanic Clients

The English language version of the MMPI-2 is widely used with Hispanics living in the United States, as was the original MMPI. The use of the English language version of the test is based on the assumption that the client reads and understands English. This form of the test is typically used for clients who are bilingual or who have lived, worked, or attended school in the United States for a period of time. The use of the English language version of the MMPI-2 is clearly an appropriate form for Hispanics who can read and understand the items and are familiar with American culture; census data suggest, as noted in chapter 1, that a high proportion of Hispanics living in the United States do in fact read and understand English sufficiently and are well enough versed in American culture to be administered the test in English. Moreover, Hispanics were included in the normative population when the MMPI-2 norms were collected on the English language version (Butcher, Dahlstrom, Graham, Tellegen, & Kaemmer, 1989), and as noted earlier, the mean scores of the Hispanic normative sample on the clinical scales did not differ substantially from the Caucasian sample.

The Núñez Translation of the MMPI Into Spanish

Although the earlier Cuban version of the original MMPI (Bernal & Fernandez, 1949) had been used experimentally in the United States, the Spanish MMPI version most widely used in this country during the 1960s and 1970s was the translation developed by Rafael Núñez. The Núñez version of the Spanish language MMPI was published in 1967 (see Núñez, 1967, 1979, 1987) for use in Mexico and was also used in the United States as a means of assessing Hispanic clients who could not read or understand the English language version.

In the 1960s, Núñez, a psychology professor at the University of the Americas in Mexico City, studied briefly with Starke Hathaway in Minneapolis. On his return to Mexico, he initiated a translation of the items by having bilingual college students from the university translate the item pool; the items were divided up so that each student who participated only translated a subset. Back-translation or bilingual test–retest studies were not conducted before the test came into wider use; thus the inventory contained a number of items that were inadequately translated. Also, the Núñez translation of the original MMPI was completed prior to the development of the present-day stringent guidelines for item translation and consequently was not translated or adapted to Mexico with the thoroughness applied to today's instruments.

The MMPI Hispania and MMPI-2 Hispania

The MMPI Hispania was developed by Garcia, Hoffman, and Butcher (1983) to provide a more accurate translation of the items. This version was published by National Computer Systems, the MMPI distributor, in 1984. This translation was carefully accomplished using initial translations by mental health professionals from Cuba, Mexico, and Ecuador. A back-translation of the completed translation assured that the items attained equivalence (Butcher & Garcia, 1978). In addition to the booklet version, the test publisher also published a tape-recorded version of the items. Psychologists using the MMPI Hispania scored the results on the American norms for the MMPI and followed traditional test interpretation strategies. The availability of this translation of the MMPI enabled psychologists to test clients who had a marginal English language reading level and came to be widely used in clinical and forensic settings.

When the MMPI-2 replaced the original MMPI in the United States, the MMPI-2 Hispania was developed by Rosa Garcia and Alex Azan in 1993 (Garcia-Peltoniemi & Azan Chaviano, 1993) to provide a means of assessing clients from Hispanic backgrounds who live in the United States but do not speak English well enough to complete the test in English. The translated version of the MMPI-2 was developed from Garcia et al.'s MMPI Hispania. Azan (1989) translated the additional items from MMPI-2 that were not included (and translated into the original MMPI) and conducted an adaptation and comparability study of the test on Hispanics in the United States (Azan, 1989). The Garcia–Azan version of the MMPI-2 has come to be used extensively in the United States and Puerto Rico and is also used in Argentina and distributed there by the test publisher Paidos in Buenos Aires. As with the original MMPI Hispania, the American norms for the MMPI-2 are used with this form of the MMPI-2 in part on the basis of the comparability found by Azan (1989).

Given the fact that there are several possible Spanish translations available, the question arises whether a single translation into Spanish might not suffice for all Spanish-speaking countries as the English version does in English-speaking countries like Canada, England, Ireland, and Australia. However, psychologists in the various Spanish-speaking countries have noted that some item renderings do not convey the same meaning in all Spanish-speaking countries and need to be modified. For example, Cabiya (1994) found that 22 items in the Chilean MMPI-2 translation would need to be altered for the instrument to be applicable in Puerto Rico. He found, however, that only 8 items of the Garcia–Azan translation had to be modified locally. Overall, the Garcia–Azan version of the MMPI-2 was considered to be the most appropriate form for use in Puerto Rico (Cabiya, 1994).

TABLE 3.1

Bilingual Test–Retest Correlations (Spanish–English) for MMPI-2 Validity and Clinical Scales of the MMPI-2 Hispania and 6-Month Retest of 30 Participants Selected Randomly From the Normative Sample of 200 (Cruz-Niemiec, 2004)

Scale	1-week test–retest study	6-month test–retest study
L	.68	.56
F	.66	.84
K	.76	.75
Hs	.60	.40
D	.76	.73
Hy	.68	.51
Pd	.62	.63
Mf	.77	.61
Pa	.76	.32
Pt	.77	.68
Sc	.76	.68
Ma	.77	.56
Si	.63	.88

Note. The scales include L (Lie), F (Infrequency), K (Defensiveness), Hs (Hypochondriasis), D (Depression), Hy (Hysteria), Pd (Psychopathic Deviation), Mf (Masculinity–Femininity), Pa (Paranoia), Pt (Psychasthenia), Sc (Schizophrenia), Ma (Hypomania), and Si (Social Introversion). From Velasquez, Callahan, et al. (1998) and Cruz-Niemiec (2004).

Research studies involving a bilingual test–retest design have shown that the MMPI-2 scores are comparable. Bilingual test–retest evaluations of the MMPI-2 Hispania by Velasquez, Callahan, Reimann, and Carbonell (1998) and Cruz-Niemiec (2004) provided verification that the Spanish version is equivalent to the English form. They tested 57 Hispanics (42 women and 15 men) with the Garcia–Azan MMPI-2. (See Table 3.1 for test–retest correlations between the two forms.) They also compared Spanish-speaking Hispanics on the MMPI-2 Hispania and Mexican version in a counterbalanced design and found no differences between the two Spanish translations. Research on the Spanish language MMPI-2 has shown that this version of the MMPI-2 is an effective and equivalent translation of the inventory. Scott and Pampa (2000) concluded that the Garcia–Azan version of the MMPI-2 was a significant improvement over the earlier Nunez translation for assessing clients in Peru.

Validity Research on the MMPI-2 Hispania

The validity of the Garcia–Azan version of the MMPI-2 (studies involving the Spanish language administration and U.S. norms) has been established in a number of research studies in a variety of clinical problem areas. These areas include psychiatric inpatients (Callahan, 1997; Colon,

1993), trauma experience (Alamo, Cabiya, & Pedrosa, 1995), abusive and neglectful parents (Garrido, Parsons, Velasquez, Reimann, & Salazar, 1997), sex offenders (Frank, Velasquez, Reimann, & Salazar, 1997), DUI offenders (Flores, Chavira, Velasquez, Perez, & Engel, 1996), outpatients and inpatients with depression (Cabiya & Davila, 1999b), and improvement in therapy (C. Pena, Cabiya, & Echevarria, 1995).

A number of studies have been conducted on substance abusers with the Spanish language version of the MMPI-2 in the United States mainland as well as in Puerto Rico. Hispanic men with alcohol or drug abuse problems have been found to have similar MMPI-2–based personality features to those of Euro-Americans (Flores et al., 1996; Lapham, Skipper, & Simpson, 1997; Steinman, 1993; Velasquez et al., 1997). Finally, the Megargee Felon Classification System developed for the MMPI-2 worked equally well for Hispanic and African American inmates as it did for Whites (Garrido, Gionta, Diehl, & Boscia, 1998). In this study, inmates were given the option of taking the MMPI-2 in English or Spanish either in booklet form or audiotape.

Cabiya and his colleagues (Cabiya, 1994) have conducted a number of external validation studies on the MMPI-2 Hispania. In one study, Cabiya (1994) evaluated the effectiveness of the MMPI-2 in detecting mental health problems in a psychiatric sample compared with a nonpsychiatric student sample. In this study, the investigators tested 30 male and 33 female patients and compared their responses with those of a nonpatient sample of 198 male and 146 female students. The MMPI-2 clinical measures significantly differentiated these populations, as did the results of G. M. E. Lucio, Palacios, Duran, and Butcher (1999) in Mexico and Rissetti et al. (1996) in Chile. In another study, C. Pena et al. (1995) conducted an evaluation of a representative sample of inmates in prison in Puerto Rico. These results are comparable to studies of Hispanic correctional samples on the United States mainland (Garrido, Diehl, Gionta, Boscia, & Bailey, 1999).

Imported Spanish Language Versions of the MMPI-2

As described in chapter 2, the MMPI-2 has been widely adapted in Spanish-speaking countries. It might be appropriate, for example, for some recent immigrants to the United States from a Latin country to be administered a different Spanish language version developed in another country (e.g., Mexico or Chile).

The most common imported Spanish version in use in the United States for assessing Hispanic clients is the Mexican version of the MMPI-2 by G. M. E. Lucio and Reyes-Lagunes (1996; see chap. 2, this volume). Consequently, the Mexican norms (T-score conversion tables) for MMPI-2 are provided in Appendix C, and the T scores for MMPI-A are provided in Appendix D to allow psychologists to plot profiles on these norms.

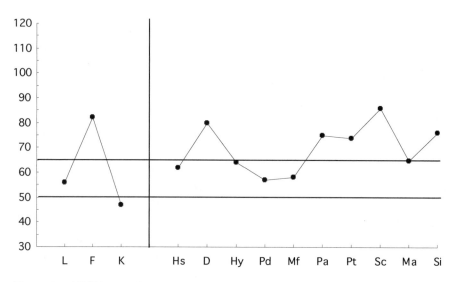

Figure 3.1. MMPI-2 validity and clinical profile for Juan G., an immigrant worker from Mexico living in the United States (plotted on U.S. norms). The scales include *L* (Lie), *F* (Infrequency), *K* (Defensiveness), *Hs* (Hypochondriasis), *D* (Depression), *Hy* (Hysteria), *Pd* (Psychopathic Deviation), *Mf* (Masculinity–Femininity), *Pa* (Paranoia), *Pt* (Psychasthenia), *Sc* (Schizophrenia), *Ma* (Hypomania), and *Si* (Social Introversion).

The figures accompanying the following case illustrate the profile similarity when the test is scored on both U.S. and Mexican norms.

> Juan G., a 38-year-old immigrant worker from Mexico, was admitted into an inpatient psychiatric facility in the United States. He had been in the United States for approximately 9 months when his psychiatric symptoms became severe enough to require hospital admission. At the time of admission he was disorganized and delusional; he threatened to kill his cousin and a coworker with whom he was living. During the admission interview, Juan appeared quite disturbed and disoriented. He reported visual hallucinations. After he had been in the hospital for 2 weeks, he was administered the tape-recorded version of MMPI-2 Hispania (see Figure 3.1 for the profile plotted on American norms). His profile was also plotted on Mexican norms (see Figure 3.2).

Criticisms of Psychological Test Use With Hispanics

As discussed in chapter 1, two criticisms of the use of psychological tests, including the MMPI-2, with Hispanic clients have been published and need to be viewed in an appropriate perspective (Dana, 1988; Hays, 2001). Both reviews, although making some valid points about the need to attend to cultural factors in assessment, essentially go to the extreme and counter a reasoned use of psychological assessment procedures in cultural

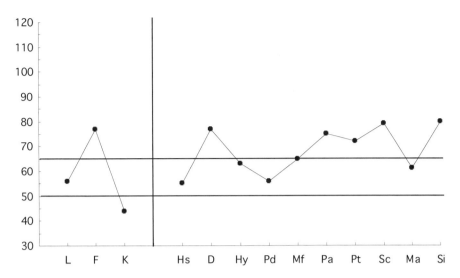

Figure 3.2. MMPI-2 validity and clinical profile for Juan G., an immigrant worker from Mexico living in the United States (plotted on Mexican norms). See Figure 3.1 caption for scale definitions.

contexts. If one were to take their advice unqualifiedly, all international personality assessment research would be curtailed!

As described in chapter 1, these criticisms have failed to take into consideration a number of demonstrated facts: (a) MMPI items clearly address universal problems—a broad range of mental health symptoms, beliefs, and attitudes—that are relevant and appropriate for people in different cultures; (b) the MMPI scales group these symptoms in meaningfully descriptive ways (or scales) that have broad generality and validity; and (c) the factor structures of these item dimensions can be found across diverse cultures (see Butcher & Pancheri, 1976). The item domain represented in the MMPI-2 item pool provides a sufficient mental health review or screening in a mental health assessment in different cultures.

The extreme "culturist" viewpoints fail to recognize and acknowledge cultural dispersion and linguistic and behavioral commonality among people from diverse cultures. These critics tend to use the idea of cultural uniqueness the same way anthropologists do—to counter universalist viewpoints in cross-cultural comparisons.

Summary of MMPI and MMPI-2 Research With Hispanics in the United States

Velasquez, Ayala, and Mendoza (1998) reviewed the existing research literature on using the MMPI and MMPI-2 with Hispanics and reported the results of 173 studies on Hispanics across several different settings, including studies on adolescents (18), in college settings (36), in community settings (7), in correctional settings (21), on personnel in work settings (5), on psychiatric patients (33), in rehabilitation settings (15), and on people with substance abuse (22). Velasquez et al. noted that many of the studies, although strong, were never published and are often difficult to gain access to. A summary of many of these studies can be found in Velasquez et al.'s resource manual (Velasquez et al., 1998). These authors provided a favorable view toward using tests like the MMPI in assessing Hispanic clients when factors such as acculturation and reading comprehension are taken into consideration. (For a listing of relevant references, see Appendix B.)

A well-designed and comprehensive review of extensive research on several ethnic groups to examine the potential effects of ethnic minority status on personality profiles was published by Hall, Bansal, and Lopez (1999). These investigators conducted a meta-analysis of the research bearing on ethnic groups and the MMPI and MMPI-2. They performed analyses on several comparative MMPI and MMPI-2 studies of the following samples: 1,428 male African Americans and 2,837 male European Americans (25 studies); 1,053 female African Americans and 1,470 European Americans (12 studies); and 500 male Hispanic Americans and 1,345 male European Americans (13 studies). They found that ethnic membership has a minimal influence on measured personality.

In a study of Hispanic and Euro-American parents referred for parenting competency evaluations by a state child protective agency, Garrido et al. (1997) used both the English and the Spanish versions of the MMPI-2. Even with sociodemographic differences between the Hispanic and Euro-American parents (i.e., Hispanics had lower levels of educational attainment, lower rates of employment, and larger families), the MMPI-2 revealed relatively few significant differences. One of these, higher L (Lie) scale scores in the Hispanic sample, is consistent with the findings of previous studies in a variety of settings. In this study, significant differences were also observed in basic scales Hs (Hypochondriasis), D (Depression), and Sc (Schizophrenia), all higher for Hispanics. Likewise, content scales FRS (Fears), HEA (Health Concerns), and BIZ (Bizarre Mentation) were higher for Hispanics. The existence of these differences, taken together with the significance of family and the parental role among Hispanics (e.g., Coohey, 2001; Ortega, 2001), indicates that the MMPI-2 provides useful information about Hispanic parents' functioning while at the same time being sensitive to the unique sociocultural characteristics of these parents.

The MMPI-2 has also been used to describe the characteristics of Hispanic and Euro-American prison inmates and to predict their prison adjustment. In a study of state prison inmates awaiting their custody classification, Garrido et al. (1998) found that consistent with previous research, the Hispanic inmates obtained higher *L*, *Hs*, *Pt* (Psychasthenia), *Sc*, *HEA*, and *BIZ* scale scores compared with the European American inmates. When the Megargee Offender Classification system was applied to this sample, there was no statistically significant relationship found between ethnicity and offender type, consistent with previous findings with the MMPI (Carey, Garske, & Ginsberg, 1986). Limitations in the size of this sample, however, require that this finding be interpreted cautiously and suggest further investigation with a larger sample. The MMPI-2 was also able to discriminate between inmates with few or no disciplinary sanctions and those with frequent sanctions. The analysis revealed that scales *Ma* (Hypomania), *ASP* (Antisocial Practices), *FAM* (Family Problems), and *TPA* (Type A) were, as a group, the strongest predictors. For Hispanic inmates, content scale *FAM* emerged as the strongest single predictor of number of disciplinary actions, although it was not a significant predictor for the Euro-American inmates. This suggests that for the Hispanic inmates the quality and characteristics of their family relationships may have a strong influence on their overall adjustment to the prison experience. This also suggests the MMPI-2's ability to capture a culturally meaningful aspect of these inmates' functioning, with implications for their institutional adjustment. Finally, this study examined the ability of the MMPI-2 to predict the type of disciplinary infractions (none, assaultive infractions, and nonassaultive infractions). Both age and MMPI-2 scales that confirm antisocial and impulsive dimensions provided the strongest differentiation between types of infractions committed.

On the basis of these overview comparisons of the extensive research on the comparability and use of the test with Hispanic populations, we conclude that a cautious use of the MMPI-2 can provide valuable hypotheses about personality functioning and symptomatic behavior.

ADMINISTRATION AND SCORING GUIDELINES

We next turn to important factors for practitioners to consider when using the MMPI-2 with Hispanic clients.

Culturally Sensitive Assessment

As discussed in chapter 1, an important consideration to review in the use of any psychological assessment procedure with Hispanic clients is the appropriateness of the testing situation and procedures used (American Psychological Association, 2002). Clinicians who conduct MMPI-2 evaluations of Hispanics in any setting should be guided by consideration of both individual psychological characteristics and the family, sociocultural, and sociodemographic contexts. Clinicians should address the following questions: What are the economic, familial, health, and community supports available to this client? What could be the impact on this client's evaluation of the presence (or absence) of these resources? What are the client's cultural assumptions around the presenting issue (i.e., competency as parent; the existence of emotional distress; managing loss, change, or other life transitions), and how might these assumptions contrast with those of the host society?

To this end, clinicians should ask themselves the following questions:

1. Have I built adequate rapport with the client by providing an adequate explanation of the purposes of this evaluation? Have I explained clearly the limits and obligations of my role as an evaluator?
2. Does my interview include questions about family-of-origin experience, values, education, and socioeconomic experience?
3. Does my interview include questions about migration circumstances, possible sociopolitical conflicts that may have affected the family, and possible migration-related violence and/or trauma?
4. Does my interview explore this client's strengths or potential sources of support even in the face of socioeconomic or other disadvantage?
5. Does my interview give the client an opportunity to describe ways in which he or she might be helped in a culturally congruent manner?
6. How appropriate are the specific testing instruments I am considering for this evaluation in terms of language, translations, and norms? How is this going to influence the way in which I have to interpret the results? What alternative explanations should I consider, especially when standardized test results appear outside the "normal" range?

Test Administration Considerations

Before the MMPI-2 is administered, to maximize cooperation the practitioner needs to ensure that the client is comfortable in the test situation. Practitioners need to take the time to tell the client how the test results are to be used and who will have access to them. It is important to assure the client that the results will be kept in confidence and that he or she would need to sign an appropriate release form before results are made available to any other party.

The clinician should have a clear picture of the client's background and experience with testing as well as an understanding of his or her cultural history. For example, Velasquez et al. (1997) pointed out that the majority of Mexican American clients are good candidates for assessment with the MMPI-2 because they are accustomed to responding to surveys or questionnaires related to health or opinions. However, many Mexican immigrant clients may have not been exposed to this type of evaluative process in Mexico.

Many clients who have recently entered the United States from Mexico only speak Spanish and may only possess a low level of education or have limited experiences in dealing with the mental health system in either this country or Mexico. Therefore, they are less likely to understand the purpose or meaning of this style of testing in a mental health or health care setting. These individuals may also be less likely to openly self-disclose their emotional problems or issues because of a fear that they may be accentuating feelings of marginality, alienation, or hopelessness. Malgady, Rogler, and Constantino (1987) pointed out that there is a need "for a preliminary assessment of the client's language dominance and preference as well as a situation-specific assessment of the client's degree of identification with the Anglo-American versus Hispanic cultures" (p. 233).

Another factor that needs to be considered, as discussed in chapter 1, is the possibility that new immigrants to the United States might have a different response set than people who have been living here for some time; for example, they may have a strong need for approval that gets reflected in a questionable profile (for a discussion of assessing protocol validity, see chap. 4, this volume). They may, for example, respond to items in a more socially desirable way because their own culture emphasizes a sense of privacy or personal restraint and the belief that strangers, including the counselor or social worker, should not have access to their feelings related to marginality, social awkwardness, or mental illness. Thus, many clients may view the assessment task as intrusive and may minimize their problems.

Administration Language

It is important for the practitioner to determine the most appropriate language for assessing Hispanic clients with the MMPI-2. Hispanic clients living in the United States may be monolingual Spanish speaking, monolingual English speaking, or bilingual (Butcher & Garcia, 1978; Velasquez et al., 1997). If they are bilingual, they may be Spanish or English dominant, or their level of proficiency in English or Spanish may vary depending on many factors, including time spent in this country or exposure to English in Mexico. The best way to determine which language to use is simply to ask the clients about their level of language proficiency, their preference of language when disclosing feelings or attitudes, or the language most commonly used to relate or resolve emotional problems (Velasquez et al., 1997).

Malgady et al. (1987) pointed out that

> when . . . bilingualism [in clients] . . . is acknowledged, the following questions arise: In which language, English or Spanish, do bilinguals express greater psychopathology? And, of course, which language conveys the true nature and extent of pathology? (p. 231)

Velasquez et al. (1997) noted that bilingual clients may show the phenomenon of *language switching*, in which the client shifts from English to Spanish and back to English depending on the depth or intensity of the issues or feelings being discussed. It may well be the case that observed differences in the type of psychopathology that is manifest by the client may be the result of language usage.

Which version of the MMPI-2 should be used with a particular client? Several factors need to be considered by the psychologist choosing the proper form of the MMPI-2 to use with a Spanish-speaking client in the United States. There are several possible forms of the MMPI-2 to choose from in assessing Hispanic clients. Both the English and Spanish versions are available in booklet and audiotaped formats. The English language MMPI-2 can be used for clients who read and comprehend English at greater than a sixth-grade level. This form of the instrument is equivalent to the Spanish language version and appropriate to use with Hispanics who understand English.

The MMPI-2 Hispania is recommended for clients in the United States who cannot speak English and for clients in Puerto Rico. Research on the Hispanic version of the MMPI-2 in the United States and Puerto Rico shows that the MMPI-2 Hispania is an appropriately translated instrument for use with literate individuals being assessed in clinical contexts in the United States—that is, when the evaluation is being conducted for assessment purposes in this country (Cabiya, 1994).

Other alternatives for Spanish-speaking clients are the Mexican version of the MMPI-2 (booklet form; *El Manual Moderno*) and a different translated version (e.g., the translation for Chile or Spain) for nationals from those countries being assessed in the United States. Immigrants who have been in the United States a short time (e.g., less than a year or so) and who may prefer being assessed in the Spanish of their home country could be evaluated with an appropriate language adaptation of their native country, for example, the Mexican version of the MMPI-2 (see G. M. E. Lucio & Reyes-Lagunes,

1996). This version uses idioms to which recent immigrants from Mexico are more accustomed.

In sum, the practitioner must decide which particular version of the MMPI-2 to use in the assessment on the basis of the considerations described above. In any case, the United States norms (the standard MMPI-2 norms) should be used for all cases except when the Mexican version or the version for Spain or Chile are used, which have their own established norms. It is important for the practitioner to administer the full MMPI-2 whatever form is used.

NORMS FOR HISPANIC CLIENTS EVALUATED IN THE UNITED STATES

Which norms should be used when assessing Spanish-speaking clients living in the United States? It was the view of Hathaway (1970), a coauthor of the original MMPI, that the development of different sets of norms for different populations should be avoided. Rather, just like we have standard units of measure for length or weight, Hathaway felt that we should measure psychopathology in a comparable manner—with a single reference standard rather than multiple value sets. However, other factors need to be considered to assure that a client's problems are weighed appropriately—for example, level of comprehension, degree of acculturation to the normative population, and the extent to which the particular normative base is generally representative of the client's cultural experiences.

Several questions need to be considered in determining which norms should be used to evaluate a particular client. Is it appropriate to use the American English language norms for the MMPI-2 that were developed in the United States, the Spanish language norms developed in the United States, or norms based on a different language version (e.g., Mexican version) that have been developed in the client's home country? The question as to whether to use the American norms for evaluating clients who have emigrated from other countries is an important one because there are several possible administration formats and appropriate norms available. Several possibilities need to be considered.

The American English Language Norms

In the event that the practitioner has determined that the client reads and understands English well enough to be administered the MMPI-2 in English, then the standard MMPI-2 English language norms can be used because the normative sample included a subset of Hispanic individuals. This normative group might be considered the most appropriate comparison sample for evaluations of Spanish-speaking people living in the United States as long as they can read English at the sixth-grade level and have lived in the United States long enough to become familiar with U.S. culture. For example, Whitworth (1988) concluded,

> On the contrary, these results suggest that if Mexican-Americans are fluent enough to be tested in English, given the choice of English or Spanish, then the differences in performance on the MMPI between the two ethnic groups should be relatively small and should have little effect on the clinical interpretation of the MMPI. (p. 896)

The American norms appear to work effectively in assessing Hispanic clients (Cabiya, 1994). Strong support for the use of the American norms to assess Hispanic clients living in the United States has been provided by a number of studies. Construct validation was provided in several MMPI-2 studies in which Hispanics were administered the English language version of the MMPI-2 and scored on U.S. norms. One study reported that the Hispanic and White clients with posttraumatic stress disorder produced comparable results (Mason, 1997). In another study, Haskell (1996) found essentially the same pattern for Hispanic and Anglo clients with only a small difference on the L scale. Rowell (1992), using the English version of the MMPI-2 and the U.S. norms, found that there were no ethnic differences (Hispanic, African American, or European American) but that the instrument did discriminate well between problem drinkers and nonproblem drinkers.

It should also be noted that research on a parallel instrument (the Spanish language MMPI-A for the United States) has provided additional assurance of the relevance and appropriateness of the Spanish language versions in the United States. In the adolescent normative study, separate norms were developed for the MMPI-A for Hispanic adolescents living in the United States (Butcher, Cabiya, et al., 1998). As will be discussed in chapter 7, this research showed that specially constructed adolescent norms with young people from Florida, San Juan, California, and Mexico produced norms that were similar to the U.S. norms for the MMPI-A. T scores generated from the two data sets are highly comparable and do not result in different interpretations.

At present there are no norms available on a Spanish-speaking American population for a number of reasons. First, an appropriate normative population is somewhat difficult to define in that it is an ever-changing and highly diverse group comprising Hispanics from different cultural groups (e.g., Puerto Rico, Mexico, Peru, etc.) and not a single homogeneous population. Second, the research access to many people in this group for developing a normative study is often difficult. For example, during the time that the

MMPI-2 revision committee was collecting norms for the revision, the goal of obtaining a large representative sample of Hispanics was frustrated by factors including, among others, difficulty in locating participants and the unwillingness of targeted participants to volunteer for the project for fear of disrupting their immigration status. No matter how hard one tries, it is unlikely that a test standardization effort would result in an adequately representative and time-resistant sample; this is not a homogeneous population. Although there has been some preliminary research to develop norms for the MMPI-2 Hispania in the United States mainland and Puerto Rico (Butcher, 2004; Cabiya, Cruz, & Bayón, 2002), an effective set of norms is not available at this time. However, the generalizability of the English language norms and the availability of Mexican norms provide clear options for the clinician in having a relevant reference group for evaluating client profiles. The most appropriate reference population can be used, or the practitioner might plot a profile on both American and Mexican norms, as shown in Figures 3.1 and 3.2, respectively. The absence of a specific norm set for this transitory population is not a deterrent to application of the MMPI-2 with this population when important mental health decisions are required by the circumstances.

Norms From Other Countries

Research has supported the use of the Spanish language MMPI-2 that is most appropriate to the client, but psychologists should also consider using norms developed in Mexico on Hispanics who have been in the United States for fewer than 5 years and who do not communicate well in English (G. E. Lucio, Ampudia, Duran, Leon, & Butcher, 2001; G. M. E. Lucio et al., 1999). For a client who has recently migrated to the United States and does not speak English or comprehend the American culture, the practitioner might decide that it would be more appropriate to administer the MMPI-2 developed in the client's home country, for example, Mexico. The psychologist might then use the Lucio–Reyes version of the MMPI-2 for Mexico and score the answer sheet on Mexican norms to obtain a more appropriate assessment (see http://www.manualmoderno.com). Although T scores generated by the Mexican norms are similar to the American norms, one might make a case that given the client's recent arrival, it might be better to use the Mexican norms. It is likely that the interpretations would be similar.

Whether the American norms or the Mexican norms are used, it is important to keep in mind that additional factors need to be considered in evaluating Hispanic clients. In the next chapter we turn to a discussion of important interpretive considerations for Hispanic clients.

The Inadequacies of Altered Forms of the MMPI-2

In efforts to get a briefer measure, a number of studies of MMPI short forms were conducted in Latin American countries during the 1970s and 1980s—for example, in Costa Rica (Adis-Castro & Arayo-Quesada, 1971; Arayo-Quesada, 1967), in Peru (Mendizabal, 1993), and in Cuba (Barroso, Alvarez, & Avisa, 1982). These investigators were interested in obtaining MMPI scale scores with a reduced number of items under the belief that patients would not want to complete a full, standard administration. This research was conducted with the idea that reducing the items administered would provide an adequate assessment and would be an appropriate modification. Both of these assumptions have proved incorrect. First, MMPI short forms have not fared well in comparability studies and have not been recommended for use in making clinical decisions. The short forms of the test have not been shown to measure the scale constructs in a valid manner and fail to assess important dimensions (Butcher & Hostetler, 1990). Second, the test publisher and copyright holder has not typically approved of such test modifications.

Problems of Unvalidated MMPI-2 Scales

The development of new scales for the MMPI-2, possibly reflecting refined approaches to symptom description, can result in improved discrimination of clinical problems. However, it is important for the developer to verify empirically the new measures for proposed applications. There has been a tradition among MMPI researchers to develop new assessment measures for personality characteristics, and there were hundreds of scales published for the original MMPI covering a broad range of characteristics, most of which were not widely used (for a discussion of the plethora of MMPI scales, see Dahlstrom, Welsh, & Dahlstrom, 1975). New scales need to be thoroughly researched and compared with existing measures before they can be relied on for making decisions about people (for a discussion on developing new scales, see Butcher, Graham, Kamphuis, & Rouse, 2006).

Several new MMPI-2 scales are available in the United States that have not yet been researched and validated sufficiently with Hispanic or Latin American populations. The Psychopathology Five (abbreviated as PSY-5) Scales (Harkness, McNulty, Ben-Porath, & Graham, 1999) and the Restructured Clinical Scales (Tellegen et al., 2003) are not included for interpretation in this book because they are too novel to have an established interpretive base at this time with Hispanic populations.

Moreover, the Restructured Clinical Scales have not been without controversy. There are a number of unanswered questions about their psychometric properties that require clarification with further research. For example, the extent to which the scales have captured the basic core of the original clinical scales as postulated in the initial publication (Tellegen et al., 2003) has been questioned (Butcher, Hamilton, Rouse, & Cumella, 2006; Nichols, 2006). In addition, their potential insensitivity to psychological problems (e.g., two studies have reported that these measures tend not to be elevated in clinical cases in which the traditional clinical scales are elevated [Rogers, Sewell, Harrison, & Jordan, 2006; Wallace & Liljequist, 2005]) has raised the possibility that the Restructured Clinical Scales may actually provide contradictory hypotheses to the clinical scales that result in conflicting interpretations of the test. Finally, there is some evidence to suggest that they are simply redundant measures of existing MMPI-2 scales such as the MMPI-2 content scales (Butcher, Hamilton, et al., 2006; Nichols, 2006), confirming the need for caution in interpreting these scales until data are available on Hispanic populations.

The application of new measures needs to be supported by research. The Restructured Clinical Scales (Tellegen et al., 2003) have not been sufficiently researched (Rogers et al., 2006), particularly with multicultural populations (i.e., there have been no published studies with Hispanics) to use clinically at this time.

SUMMARY

A primary goal of this chapter has been to provide an overview of important considerations for clinicians who are assessing Spanish-speaking clients with the MMPI-2. Several versions of the MMPI, both English and Spanish, have been available for this population since the test was initially translated in the 1950s. The English language version of the MMPI-2 is often used with Hispanics living in the United States, as was the original MMPI, on the assumption that the client reads and understands English. The American norms are typically used with this version.

A single translation into Spanish does not suffice for all Spanish-speaking countries as the English language version does in English-speaking countries such as Canada, England, Ireland, and Australia. Psychologists in the various Spanish-speaking countries have noted that some item renderings do not convey the same meaning in all Spanish-speaking countries.

Bilingual test–retest studies have shown that the scale scores on MMPI-2 are comparable whether the test was administered in English or Spanish. The most frequently "imported" Spanish language version of the

MMPI-2 in use in the United States for assessing Hispanic clients is the Mexican version. Research has shown this form of the test to be comparable to the American (English language) version. If the client reads and understands English well enough to be administered the MMPI-2 in English, then the standard MMPI-2 English language norms can be used because the normative sample included a subset of Hispanic individuals.

CHAPTER HIGHLIGHTS

- Many of the early applications of the original MMPI with Hispanics in the United States in the 1960s and 1970s involved the Nunez translation. Some of the earlier criticism of the use of the MMPI with Hispanic clients as not being equivalent to the U.S. version resulted from its inadequacies.
- The MMPI Hispania was developed by Garcia, Hoffman, and Butcher (1983) to provide a more accurate translation of the items. This version, using the American norms, was published by the MMPI publisher and distributor in 1984.
- The Hispanic MMPI-2 was initially developed from the MMPI Hispania (for the original MMPI) by Azan (1989) and published by Garcia-Peltoniemi and Azan Chaviano (1993). The Garcia–Azan version of the MMPI-2, using the American norms, has come to be used extensively in the United States and Puerto Rico.
- The validity of the Garcia–Azan version of the MMPI-2 (studies involving the Spanish language administration and the U.S. norms) has been established in a number of research studies.
- U.S. norms should be used for all cases except when the Mexican version or the versions for Spain or Chile are used; these versions have their own established norms. Cabiya (1994) has shown that the U.S. norms appear to work effectively in assessing Hispanic clients.

4

ASSESSING THE CREDIBILITY OF A HISPANIC CLIENT'S TEST RESPONSES

Regardless of the form used to administer the MMPI-2 to Hispanic clients or the norms used to plot the profiles, the interpretation strategy for the profiles remains the same as it does for MMPI-2 interpretation of clients in general. It is important to assess protocol validity before interpretive statements are made about the clinical or content scale profiles. The assessment psychologist needs to determine whether the profile is valid and interpretable and that the client has approached the task with frankness before making clinical inferences. The practitioner can gain a ready understanding of the genuineness of the client's test-taking approach by careful consideration of the validity scales. It is especially important in the assessment of clients from diverse cultural backgrounds to try and obtain a clear perspective on the clients' understanding of the items and adaptation to the cultural environment in which they are being evaluated. The MMPI-2 validity scales can provide clues as to the client's general comfort level with the assessment—information that can provide the practitioner with a perspective on the client's willingness to be assessed.

The practitioner can have considerable confidence in the utility of the MMPI-2 validity scales in the task of determining the credibility of the profile being assessed. The MMPI-2 validity scales have been found to provide valuable information about the client's cooperation with the testing in a number of cross-cultural contexts. Thus, clients who have not provided adequate data (e.g., defensive or exaggerated responding) can be identified. There is an extensive literature on the use of the MMPI-2 validity scales in assessing invalidating test conditions (for a comprehensive review, see Bagby, Marshall, Bury, Bacchiochi, & Miller, 2006; for a listing of malingering and defensiveness references, see Pope, Butcher, & Seelen, 2006).

Several studies in other languages and cultures have provided verification on the usefulness of the MMPI-2 validity scales in detecting invalid profiles cross-culturally. In China, Cheung, Song, and Butcher (1991) found that the F (Infrequency) scale of the original MMPI needed to be modified because of culture-specific content (religious items). These items were later dropped in the MMPI revision, making the F scale more culturally appropriate for other cultures. In Korea, Hahn (2003) conducted a study appraising the utility of the validity scales of the Korean MMPI-2 in differentiating malingered and defensive profiles. She administered the MMPI-2 twice to a sample of 169 Korean college students (82 men, 87 women). The participants initially completed the MMPI-2 with standard instructions to answer the items as they applied to themselves. Then, she administered the test in a second condition in which the participants were assigned to one of three experimental conditions to answer the items to (a) fake bad, (b) deny psychological problems, or (c) claim extreme virtue. Hahn found that F, Fb (Back F), and the F raw score minus the K (Defensiveness) raw score index of the Korean MMPI-2 were successful in differentiating fake-bad participants from honest participants and from psychiatric patients. Those participants who were asked to deny problems or claim extreme virtues were also detected by the L (Lie), K, and S (Superlative) scales.

None of the numerous Spanish language MMPI-2 and MMPI-A translations demonstrate such extreme item frequency differences on the F scale as the original MMPI did with the Chinese sample. Research on the use of the MMPI-2 with Spanish-speaking populations from Mexico (G. M. E. Lucio & Reyes-Lagunes, 1996), Chile (Rissetti, Himmel, & Gonzalez-Moreno, 1996), Spain (Avila-Espada & Jimenez-Gomez, 1996), and Argentina (Casullo, Samartino Garcia, Brenella, Marquez, & Dupertuis, 1996) have used the Spanish adaptations of the F scale without modifications in item membership.

Other MMPI-2 validity scales have been effective in other countries as well. In Australia, Shores and Carstairs (1998) found that the computer interpretation system for the MMPI-2, the Minnesota Report, detected malingering. Sirigatti and Giannini (2000) in Italy and Crespo and Gomez (2003) in Spain found that the S scale operated in a similar manner in their countries as in the United States in detecting defensiveness.

Research on the MMPI-A has also confirmed the cross-cultural generalizability of the validity indicators. G. E. Lucio, Duran, Graham, and Ben-

Porath (2002) conducted a study in Mexico on the MMPI-A F scales and demonstrated that the F scales performed as intended without modifications (G. E. Lucio et al., 2002). The MMPI-A F scales function in China as they do in the United States, according to research by Cheung and Ho (1997), who compared Chinese adolescents on American norms and reported that Chinese adolescents scored very close to the American normative sample on the F scale. They made no recommendations for modifying the F scale on the Chinese MMPI-A.

GENERAL CONSIDERATIONS

Cultural Nuances With Hispanics

Some research has shown that the F scale and the L scale may be slightly higher in normal samples of Hispanics living in the United States as a result of their not being acculturated to this country (Whitworth & McBlaine, 1993). In addition, infrequent responding (as measured by the F scale) can be influenced by stress the client might be undergoing—a commonplace occurrence among immigrants. These findings need to be taken into consideration when interpreting profiles by allowing more elevation (e.g., 5 T-score points or half of a standard deviation) on these scales before considering them invalid.

Earlier reviews by Greene (1987) and Hall, Bansal, and Lopez (1999) have pointed out that although in general MMPI differences between Hispanics and Anglos were minimal, there was a trend toward higher L scale and lower scale 5 (Masculinity–Femininity) scores among Hispanics. It is interesting that the L scale has been shown to reflect cultural influence in at least one other country, the Netherlands. Scale L was found to be slightly higher (about 2 raw score points) among Dutch normative group respondents compared with U.S. normative group respondents; however, this has not apparently diminished the effectiveness of the scale in profile interpretation in the Netherlands (see Derksen, de Mey, Sloore, & Hellenbosch, 1993).

Some validity scale elevations have been found for minority groups. Greene, Robin, Albaugh, Caldwell, and Goldman (2003) examined the empirical correlates of MMPI-2 scales that showed a difference between Native Americans and Whites and found significant correlations between scale elevations and several symptoms. Therefore, the MMPI-2 differences identified previously appear to correspond to actual symptoms among the Native American participants rather than just test bias or self-presentation differences.

Assessing Protocol Validity in Hispanic Profiles

The most pertinent scales for determining if the Hispanic client is able to read and understand English sufficiently to provide a valid test picture are the Cannot Say (CNS) scores, the response consistency scales (variable [VRIN] and true [TRIN]), and the Infrequency scales (F, Fb, and Fp). It is also useful to examine the true and false percentages to assure that the client has not simply checked all true or all false.

In the sections that follow, we provide more specific information about the use of each of the validity scales in assessing protocol validity. Several case examples are provided to illustrate their use.

INCONSISTENT RESPONDING

The following scales help determine if the client has understood the test content and has endorsed the items in a sufficiently cooperative manner to produce a valid, interpretable profile.

Cannot Say (CNS) Score

This scale assesses the total number of unanswered items on the answer sheet. The score can serve as an index of cooperativeness and may suggest items that the person had difficulty reading or comprehending. The examiner should check the client's answer sheet to see if any items have been omitted and make sure that the person was able to understand the content. This step is particularly important with Hispanic clients who may have marginal reading comprehension in the language of administration of the test.

The CNS score can reflect unwillingness on the part of a client to endorse the items. If the client has omitted items, the practitioner can inquire as to whether the person left them blank because he or she did not understand the content or was avoiding responding to the particular content.

Variable Response Inconsistency (VRIN)

This scale measures the tendency to endorse items in an inconsistent or random manner. An elevated score on this validity scale can suggest that the client did not understand the item; the possibility that the client did not fully comprehend the item content should be followed up in interview. Meanwhile, the test administration should assure that the instructions are clear to rule out the possibility of response sets resulting from unclear instructions.

If the client has produced a high score on this scale (T ≥ 100), it is likely that he or she has not responded to the content of the items either as a means of not complying with the testing or else because he or she did not read or understand the items well enough. In either case, the resulting profiles probably do not provide useful personality or symptom information. Some research has suggested that the *TRIN* scales on MMPI-A can be influenced somewhat by demographic factors (Schinka, Elkins, & Archer, 1998).

True/False Response Inconsistency (TRIN)

This scale measures the tendency to endorse items in an inconsistent true or false manner scale. High scores (T ≥ 100) on this scale suggest an all-true or all-false endorsement pattern. Some Hispanics produce high *TRIN* scores as a result of cultural factors; they tend to answer false to a large number of items to deny problems.

CASE: THE NEED TO LOOK GOOD IN THE ASSESSMENT

Carlos V., a 23-year-old convicted felon, was awaiting a parole hearing after serving 6 years of his 12-year sentence for drug and weapons charges for which he had been found guilty. As part of the parole evaluation, he was administered a psychological test battery that included the MMPI-2.

Carlos had come to the United States from Mexico with his mother and had lived in the country for 11 years. He attended junior high school and 2 years of high school before dropping out in the 12th grade. Although his English language skills were considered to be sufficient for taking the MMPI-2, he opted to be administered the test in Spanish, his native language.

The MMPI-2 validity profile in Figure 4.1 (the Garcia–Azan version scored on American norms) shows a clear pattern of extreme false responding throughout the protocol. The extremely high score on *TRIN* indicates that the client responded in a predominantly "false" manner to the items regardless of content, even endorsing highly similar items in opposite directions. This extreme approach to problem denial is also shown to have had an impact on other validity scales. The *L* scale (a scale in which all of the items are scored in the false direction) is significantly elevated; the *K* scale, reflecting test defensiveness, is also extremely elevated—in part because of the high number of false responses scored on the scale. Moreover, the client's defensiveness is also reflected in the large number of item omissions. He had 15 CNS items, indicating an unwillingness to respond to a significant number of items. All of these indicators suggest that the client's MMPI-2

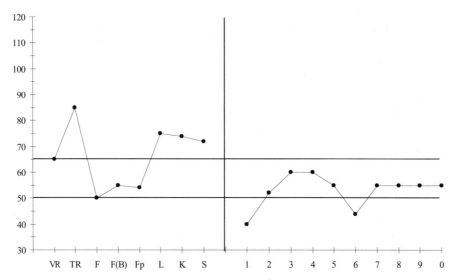

Figure 4.1. MMPI-2 validity and clinical scale profile for Carlos V. showing a pattern of test defensiveness and inconsistent responding. The scales include *VR* (Variable Responding), *TR* (True Responding), *F* (Infrequency), *Fb* (Infrequency Back), *Fp* (Infrequency Psychopathology), *L* (Lie), *K* (Defensiveness), and *S* (Superlative Self-Presentation). The numbered scales include 1 (*Hs*, Hypochondriasis), 2 (*D*, Depression), 3 (*Hy*, Hysteria), 4 (*Pd*, Psychopathic Deviate), 5 (*Mf*, Masculinity–Femininity), 6 (*Pa*, Paranoia), 7 (*Pt*, Psychasthenia), 8 (*Sc*, Schizophrenia), 9 (*Ma*, Hypomania), and 0 (*Si*, Social Introversion).

profile is likely to underreport problems in an effort to appear problem free. The MMPI-2 clinical and content scales should not be interpreted in this case because they are not likely to provide a useful picture of the client's present personality functioning and symptomatic behavior.

ASSESSING EXTREME RESPONDING

Extreme item responding is found to be reflected in elevations of the following validity measures:

Infrequency Scale (F)

This scale measures the tendency to exaggerate psychological problems or endorse an extreme number of problems in the first part of the booklet; it also detects random responding. If the F scale is elevated in the high ranges (T > 90), it is likely that the client has not been careful in responding to the content of the items as a noncompliance strategy or it suggests that he or she did not read or understand the items well enough to provide a valid result. High scores on this scale could also suggest that the individual is endorsing a great number of symptoms to call attention to problems. Regardless of the source of symptom exaggeration, the profiles are going to be of limited utility in high ranges of scale elevation.

Keep in mind when evaluating the F scale for recent immigrants that as a group, they tend to endorse more extreme items compared with more acculturated populations. F scores in the 100-T or more range, however, clearly indicate that the person has endorsed too many extreme items to produce an interpretable record. The infrequency measures on MMPI-A can be influenced somewhat by demographic factors (see Schinka et al., 1998).

Infrequency Back Scale (Fb)

This scale measures the tendency to exaggerate psychological problems. As with the F scale, if the Fb scale is elevated in the high ranges (>90 T), it is likely that the client has exaggerated his or her symptom presentation by endorsing an extreme number of problems toward the end of the booklet. This index detects random responding to items at the back of the booklet. As with the F scale, if the Fb scale is elevated in the high ranges (>100 T), it is likely that he or she has extremely exaggerated symptom presentation to the point of producing an invalid record. As with the F scale noted above, when evaluating the Fb scale for recent emigrants, recognize that they tend to endorse more extreme items than more acculturated populations do. Fb scores in the 100-T or more range, however, clearly indicate that the person has endorsed too many extreme items to produce an interpretable record.

Infrequency Psychopathology Scale (Fp)

This scale measures the tendency to endorse extreme items compared with a general psychiatric sample. If the Fp scale is elevated in the high ranges (>90 T), it is likely that the client has exaggerated his or her symptom picture by endorsing an extreme number of mental health problems that even inpatient psychiatric patients do not claim.

Percent True

This scale measures the extent to which the individual has endorsed true responses. This index detects "yea-saying" response attitudes—for example, records with high numbers of "true" (greater than 30%) suggest that the person has responded "true" to items without considering carefully their content.

Percent False

This scale measures the extent to which the individual has endorsed false responses in an incredible manner. This index detects a "nay-saying" response attitude—for example, records with high numbers of "false" (greater than 30%) are likely to produce an invalid record because the individual has responded "false" to a large number of items that most people would endorse as true.

CASE OF ELANA G.: QUESTION OF ATTENTION SEEKING, EXAGGERATED RESPONDING, OR NEED FOR PSYCHIATRIC ATTENTION?

The following case illustrates extreme item endorsement in the context of an inpatient psychiatric evaluation.

Elana G., a 29-year-old unemployed migrant worker from Mexico who presently lives with her sister in the United States, was being seen at a mental health center following a suicide attempt. She has been in the United States for 4 years. Elana is now living apart from her husband, who was returned to Mexico because of his illegal immigrant status, and she is caring for two children, ages 3 and 4. Although she could communicate socially in English, the initial interview was conducted in Spanish because she felt more comfortable discussing her problem situation in Spanish. The MMPI-2 Hispania was administered and scored on American norms (see the profile in Figure 4.2). Because of her low level of acculturation to the United States, the MMPI-2 was also scored on Mexican norms (see Figure 4.3).

Elana was referred to the mental health center by her sister, who has been concerned over Elana's mood in recent months. She has reportedly made two suicide attempts in the past 2 months. Elana has been depressed since she came to the United States; however (according to her sister), her mood has deteriorated following her husband's arrest and deportation to Mexico and her losing her job as a maid in a hotel that closed. At present, Elana lives with her sister and her children. She has no income except for financial assistance from welfare to support her children.

MMPI-2 Interpretation of Elana's Profile

The MMPI-2 profile shown in Figure 4.2 is one that requires careful consideration to assure that the client's scores are in an acceptable range

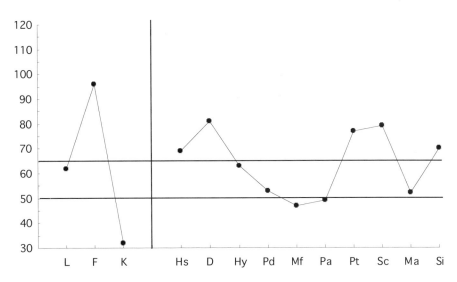

Figure 4.2. MMPI validity and clinical scale profile (U.S. norms) for Elana G. showing a pattern of exaggerated symptom endorsement. See Figure 4.1 caption for scale definitions.

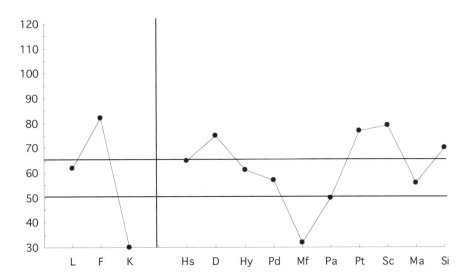

Figure 4.3. MMPI-2 validity and clinical scale profile (Mexican norms) for Elana G. suggesting some symptom exaggeration. See Figure 4.1 caption for scale definitions.

before clinical interpretation can be undertaken. The high degree of extreme responding, as reflected in the elevations on the F scale, suggests that the client has endorsed a number of items in the pathological direction. Does this represent a problem of misinterpretation of the items? Or, is this an attempt to malinger? Or, could this reflect an expressed need for attention for her genuine psychological problems? Are the clinical scales interpretable? To answer these questions, we have presented the profile as scored on both American norms (see Figure 4.2) and on Mexican norms (see Figure 4.3).

On the American norms, Elana's profile suggests that she has responded to a number of extreme symptoms, as reflected in the high elevations on F and Fb, although her Fp scale (T = 75) does not suggest invalidity. With the F scale elevated, one might question whether the client understood the items sufficiently to produce a valid protocol. An examination of the VRIN scale (T = 79), however, suggests that her elevated score does not result from random or careless responding. She endorsed the items in a fairly consistent manner, which shows that her infrequent responding was toward select items and not just meaningless exaggeration. In all likelihood, her endorsement of the high degree of extreme symptoms results in part from psychopathology, because her clinical profile showed selective endorsement of symptoms and not just problem expression "across the board." Her low scores on the L and K scales suggest that she does not appear to have operating defenses at this time. Overall, her validity and clinical scale profile is relatively common among individuals being evaluated in outpatient mental health settings.

Elana's MMPI-2 clinical profile suggests that she has severe psychological problems at this time. She reports being very depressed and anxious and feeling hopeless about the future. She shows some symptoms of personality disorganization and unusual thinking that can lead to self-destructive behavior. She is apparently bothered by feelings of low self-esteem and feelings of inadequacy. She tends to be a shy and introverted person who lacks self-confidence and feels alienated from other people. Individuals with this profile may be seen by others as passive, distant, and perhaps apathetic. She is a moody person who tends to have more than her share of problems and who tends to be easily hurt in relationships. Insecurity and low self-confidence characterize her typical mode of interacting with others.

Information From the Use of Mexican Norms

When Elana's scores are plotted on the Mexican norms (see Appendix C), we see that she obtains virtually the same clinical scale pattern as she obtained on the American norms. The clinical interpretation of the MMPI-2 profile suggests severe and chronic mental health symptoms (depression, severe anxiety, disruptive thinking, and extreme social isolation) regardless of the reference group used.

ASSESSING DEFENSIVE RESPONDING

It is equally important to determine if the client has cooperated with the assessment by answering the items in a frank and open manner. As noted earlier, some Hispanics are overly compliant in the testing and respond in a socially desirable way just to please the examiner. For example, some elevation on the L scale is not uncommon. Careful examination of the "self-presentation" scales L, K, and S will provide information as to whether the client was responding in an overly positive way to impress the examiner with his or her categorically strong qualities at the expense of being honest about his or her problems.

Lie Scale (L)

This scale measures the tendency to claim excessive virtue or attempt to present an overall favorable image. High scores (T > 65) indicate that the person has presented in an overly positive manner. Keep in mind that Hispanics, as a group, have been found in some studies to have slightly higher L scores than non-Hispanic Whites. In evaluating the elevations on L, allow a slightly higher cutoff before invalidity is concluded.

Defensiveness Scale (K)

This scale measures the tendency to see oneself in an unrealistically positive way. A score of 65 to 69 suggests a tendency to present oneself in an overly positive manner. Scale scores above 70 are likely to reflect test defensiveness resulting in an uninterpretable profile.

Superlative Self-Presentation (S)

Similar to the K scale, this scale measures the tendency to present oneself in an extremely positive or superlative way.

CASE: POLICE APPLICANT PRESENTING A FAVORABLE IMAGE

Eduardo F., age 25, was evaluated in the context of a personnel assessment program by a police department in California where he applied for a

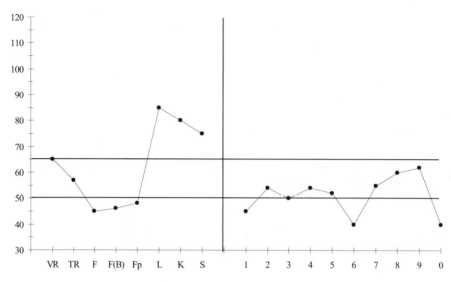

Figure 4.4. MMPI-2 validity and clinical scale profile for Eduardo F. showing a defensive test response pattern. See Figure 4.1 caption for scale definitions.

police officer position. Eduardo had been in the United States since he was 12 years old and had graduated from high school and a 2-year community college in California. He was administered the English language MMPI-2, and his test protocol was processed through the American norms (see profile in Figure 4.4).

MMPI-2 Interpretation

Eduardo's extreme scores on the *L, K,* and *S* scales indicate that he has not responded to the items in an open, cooperative manner. Instead, he has presented an overly favorable view of his personality and life functioning. His MMPI-2 profile is invalid as a result of defensive responding and provides no useful information for the decision to be made.

Defensive profiles occur with some frequency among samples of job applicants taking personality tests. People in this context may attempt to present themselves as well adjusted and free of any weaknesses or personality flaws; they deny even minor problems that most people would acknowledge, thereby invalidating the test as a result of underreporting. Eduardo's test invalidity is probably not a function of his being originally from a different culture but results from the job application context (see Butcher, Ones, & Cullen, 2006). Consequently, his test defensiveness has made the MMPI-2 results (and any other personality test he might have been administered) unusable in the employment process.

Psychologists using personality testing like the MMPI-2 in employment screening should be aware of the problem of test defensiveness in this context and make efforts to obtain more usable information. For example, a well-established practice in personnel assessment with the MMPI-2 involves an administration procedure that produces more valid (less defensive) results— a retest procedure in the event that the applicant has invalidated the test because of defensiveness (for a discussion, see Butcher, Ones, & Cullen, 2006). This procedure involves readministering the MMPI-2 to an applicant who has invalidated the test with instructions to be less defensive the second time. In the majority of retests, applicants produce a valid test protocol, and in about 15% of retest cases the test results show demonstrable psychopathology (Cigrang & Staal, 2001; Fink & Butcher, 1972; Gucker & McNulty, 2004). In the case of Eduardo's testing, this retest procedure was not used; therefore, it is not known whether he would have produced a more valid result on retest.

SUMMARY

The MMPI-2 validity scales have been found to provide valuable information about the client's cooperation with the testing in a number of cross-cultural contexts. Careful interpretation of these measures can aid the clinician in making a determination about the credibility of the profile being interpreted. Some research has shown that the F scale and the L scale may be slightly higher in nonclinical samples of Hispanics living in the United States as a result of the lack of acculturation or cultural differences. This finding needs to be taken into consideration when interpreting profiles by allowing more elevation (e.g., 5 T-score points) on these scales before considering them invalid.

If the validity scales are within the interpretable range, then it is likely that the client was able to understand and respond to the items in an appropriate manner. Valid profiles can provide the interpreter with assurance that the clinical scale correlates will apply for the Hispanic clients as with the general population of Americans.

CHAPTER HIGHLIGHTS

- In evaluating profiles of Hispanic clients, it is important to consider protocol validity before interpretive statements are made about the clinical or content scale profiles.
- Of particular importance in assessing the interpretability of profiles for Hispanic clients is the need to consider whether

they can read and understand the items sufficiently to respond appropriately to the content, and to evaluate the extent of the client's acculturation to the U.S. culture.

- There is an extensive literature available on the use of the MMPI-2 validity scales in assessing invalidating test conditions and a growing literature on the utility of the MMPI-2 validity scales in detecting invalid profiles cross-culturally.
- Even though minimal MMPI differences have been found between Hispanics and non-Hispanic Whites in research, some studies have suggested that two validity scales, L and F, require more careful consideration with Hispanics because of possible cultural influences.

5

PERSONALITY AND CLINICAL
ASSESSMENT OF HISPANIC CLIENTS

The application of standardized assessment procedures with minority clients requires careful attention to possible differences in interpretation resulting from cultural factors. Even with a psychological test like the MMPI-2, which has been widely used with Spanish-speaking clients around the world, there might be nuances that result in improved interpretation if incorporated into conclusions.

This chapter reviews the main clinical and content measures on the MMPI-2, with a special emphasis on factors that can influence their interpretation with Hispanic clients. Later in the chapter, we provide an interpretive strategy that can aid the clinician in applying MMPI-2 scales in assessing Hispanic clients.

SPECIAL CONSIDERATIONS IN CLINICAL INTERPRETATION WITH HISPANIC CLIENTS

Garrido and Velasquez (2006) and Greene (2000) pointed out that ongoing research with the MMPI-2 indicates that Hispanic test takers appear to obtain profiles that are similar to those of non-Hispanic White test takers. This finding applies to research with the English language version of the instrument and with normative (nonclinical) groups (see Velasquez, Maness,

& Anderson, 2002). More recently, MMPI-2 research with Hispanics has focused on exploring the comparability of the English and Spanish language versions of the MMPI-2. Research with bilingual college students has resulted in nearly identical profiles in the English and Spanish language versions (Velasquez, Chavira, et al., 2000).

Garrido and Velasquez (2006) summarized a number of cultural issues that could influence the responses of Hispanic clients on the MMPI-2—for example, their adherence to socially and culturally sanctioned ways of interacting within the cultural group and with the broader society. They provided guidelines for interpreting profiles to prevent test users from reaching inaccurate conclusions or conclusions that may reflect stereotypical or even overpathologized views of Hispanic clients (see Exhibit 5.1).

Confidence in the interpretation of the MMPI-2 with Hispanics follows from the universal nature of the clinical scale constructs, which have been demonstrated in research. As described in chapter 2, the clinical scales have been shown to measure psychopathology across diverse cultures (Butcher & Pancheri, 1976; Butcher, Tsai, Coelho, & Nezami, 2006; Manos, 1985; Savacir & Erol, 1990).

BASIC CLINICAL SCALES OF THE MMPI-2

A brief summary of the constructs measured by the MMPI-2 clinical scales are presented below (for a more detailed review of these scales and their research base, see Butcher, 2005a, 2006; Graham, 2006).

Scale 1: Hypochondriasis (Hs)

People who score high on the Hs scale present numerous vague physical problems. They tend to endorse items that suggest that they are generally unhappy, self-centered, and hostile toward others. They are usually viewed by others as demanding, whiny, and complaining—focusing great attention on their physical symptoms, which are usually numerous and, at times, seem exaggerated, extensive, and unconnected. The high-scoring person tends to demand attention for his or her symptoms. The problems shown by high-scoring clients tend to be chronic; the symptoms are typically resistant to psychological treatment efforts.

Scale 2: Depression (D)

People who have their peak score on the D scale (T > 65) report having a depressed mood, low self-esteem, and strong feelings of inadequacy. High-scoring individuals are typically described as being moody, pessimistic,

EXHIBIT 5.1
Some Interpretive Cautions Provided by Garrido and Velasquez (2006)

1. The manner in which Hispanics approach structured inquiries, such as surveys or questionnaires, may influence the validity of these data collection methods, including the MMPI-2 profiles. For example, some Hispanics have been found to respond with extreme response sets (i.e., yea-saying or nay-saying). This tendency has been identified especially among Hispanics with lower levels of socioeconomic status.

2. Many Hispanics hold beliefs in spirituality that could influence their responses to some personality items. For example, some may hold devotions to the saints of the Catholic faith, and some Hispanic nationalities (especially of Caribbean origin) practice spiritism, Santeria, or other variations of African-origin religions. Some people of Hispanic religious background may adhere to a more traditional value orientation of the power of saints to influence outcomes, for example in their impact on physical or mental illness. These beliefs might influence the way some MMPI-2 items are endorsed and may result in scale elevations on measures that are associated with unusual experiences or psychotic symptoms, such as the *Sc* (Schizophrenia) or *BIZ* (Bizarre Mentation) scales.

3. Many Hispanics place considerable importance on the quality of interpersonal relationships as opposed to individualism, a quality often referred to as *personalismo*, which has been described as a characteristic of a collectivistic worldview. *Personalismo* describes values such as those of dignity and interpersonal respect, at the heart of which is the high level of regard for inner qualities and self-worth as opposed to material achievement, and interdependence as opposed to individualism and competitiveness. This tendency is related to the need for some Hispanics to present a dignified self and to not reveal personal problems publicly, especially to someone outside the family network; disclosure of personal problems would bring shame (*verguenza*) on the individual and his or her family.

4. There is often the expectation that Hispanics are socially competent and comfortable around their families and social network but may be alienated from the mainstream culture and even from their cultural group of origin. Therefore, for Hispanics, the interpretation of scores on the *Si* (Social Introversion) scale should take into account the existence of difficulties beyond internally experienced social anxiety or discomfort.

5. Because of cultural factors, Hispanics may find it more acceptable to endorse items related to somatic and health concerns rather than items directly related to symptoms of emotional distress. Therefore, this tendency may result in somewhat higher scores on scales such as *Hs* (Hypochondriasis) and *HEA* (Health Concerns).

6. Many Hispanics hold a strong alliance and loyalty toward their families, both nuclear and collective, referred to as *familismo*. *Familismo* derives from a collectivistic worldview that values the sharing of responsibilities, emotional and financial support when needed, and participation in decision making. Interdependence as opposed to independence tends to be fostered. Direct, personal contact with members is valued over other forms of communication such as telephone calls. Hispanics who do not have this level of access to their family may experience emotional or other adjustment difficulties.

7. The clear demarcation of male and female roles within the family has long characterized traditional Hispanic families. The concepts of *machismo* and *marianismo* are most important to understanding gender role views of Hispanics. These views are likely to have important implications for the interpretation of the *Mf* (Masculinity–Femininity) scale (typically different from Whites) on the MMPI-2. *Machismo* refers

(continued)

EXHIBIT 5.1 *(Continued)*

to a Latino man's responsibility, loyalty, and integrity toward his family, his community, and friends rather than what has often been described as "an emphasis on virility and chauvinism in other definitions of machismo. *Marianismo* refers to the expectation that women adopt a nurturing, pious, virtuous, and humble role in the family. Garrido and Velasquez noted that recent studies on Scale 5 of the MMPI-2 have found that women show more variability on this scale than Latino men, who tend to obtain scores below 50 T. In fact, some research has suggested that Latina women show comparatively less adherence to traditional gender role expectations, possibly as a result of increased independence from their families and of pursuing professional advancement.

8. The expression of aggression and emotional distress found in Hispanics may reflect clear cultural rules. Specifically, it is not unusual for many Hispanics to report somatic symptoms underlying which may be sources of emotional distress such as depression, anxiety, and interpersonal or family conflict.

distressed, high-strung, lethargic, and guilt-prone. They tend to be very emotionally withdrawn and overcontrolled. They have characteristic introversive personality features, such as being shy and despondent. Elevated scores reflect great discomfort and a need for change or symptomatic relief. These clients tend to be responsive to treatment.

Scale 3: Hysteria (Hy)

Patients in mental health or medical settings who score high on the *Hy* scale, from a psychodynamic perspective, often display neurotic defenses such as denial and repression to deal with stress. They tend to be dependent, naive, outgoing, infantile, and narcissistic. Their symptom picture is typically mixed. They frequently show a lack of insight concerning possible underlying causes of symptoms and their own motives and feelings; they are often described as psychologically immature, childish, and infantile.

High scorers often feel overwhelmed and have symptoms that may appear and disappear suddenly; they typically do not seem to be experiencing acute emotional turmoil. They view themselves as having medical problems and want medical treatment. They often receive diagnoses of conversion disorder, somatoform disorder, or pain disorder.

People with high *Hy* scores often have interpersonal conflicts and show little insight into problems. High levels of stress are often accompanied by the development of physical symptoms. (This scale usually has the peak score among female medical patients who have no diagnosable illness.) They may report headaches, stomach discomfort, chest pains, weakness, or tachycardia. High-scoring patients often respond to suggestion but often resist insight-oriented treatment. They may show little interest in examining psychological processes. Very high scorers (T scores > 80) tend to react to stress and avoid responsibility by developing physical symptoms.

Scale 4: Psychopathic Deviate (Pd)

The Pd scale assesses antisocial behavior, such as rebelliousness, disrupted family relations, and impulsive acting out. People who score high on this scale tend to exhibit problems in school or work and often have legal difficulties, and become involved in alcohol or drug abuse. They tend to show personality traits associated with personality disorder, such as antisocial behavior. High scorers tend to be outgoing, sociable, and likable but also deceptive, manipulative, hedonistic, and exhibitionistic. They typically show poor judgment and are unreliable, immature, hostile, and aggressive toward others. Life problems are common among people who have Pd as a high point profile (elevated above T = 65)—they may show marital or family relations problems and have run-ins with the law. High Pd scorers often show long-standing character problems that are highly resistant to treatment. It is not uncommon for high Pd scorers to terminate psychological treatment prematurely if they do become engaged in therapy.

Scale 5: Masculinity–Femininity (Mf)

This scale is not a measure of psychopathology but of gender role attitudes. Of the scales on the standard clinical profile, this scale is most susceptible to cultural variation—gender roles often differ cross-culturally. Males with high Mf scores tend to have traditionally feminine interests and deny having more traditional male interests; they also tend to report conflicts regarding sexual identity and low heterosexual drive, whereas low-scoring males admit to having more sterotypically masculine interests and deny having feminine ones. The direction of scoring is reversed for females: High-scoring females endorse more traditionally male interests and deny more sterotypically feminine roles, whereas low-scoring females describe themselves as having sterotypically feminine interests and deny having more masculine ones.

As noted, scores on the Mf scale have been found to be more variable in Hispanic samples and to differ somewhat from those of non-Hispanic groups. Samples of Latino men have often been found to have somewhat higher mean scores (G. E. Lucio, Ampudia, Duran, Leon, & Butcher, 2001), but scores are lower in other groups such as Puerto Ricans (Cabiya, Cruz, & Bayón, 2002). Interpretation concerning gender roles should be made only with extreme caution (this same caution holds with interpreting Hispanic clients in the United States).

Scale 6: Paranoia (Pa)

People with high scores on the Pa scale are characteristically suspicious, mistrustful, and externalize blame. They are typically wary, aloof, and distant in relationships and are often described by others as shrewd, guarded, and overly sensitive in personal relationships. High scorers tend to project blame to others, externalize their anger, and harbor grudges against others. They are often viewed as hostile and argumentative. Extremely high scores on Pa (T > 75) suggest serious cognitive problems such as delusions and personality disorganization.

Individuals who have Pa as their peak scale score are not likely to benefit from psychotherapy because they do not typically accept responsibility for their own actions and are not amenable to changing their behavior in response to outside influence.

Scale 7: Psychasthenia (Pt)

The Pt scale measures anxiety and general maladjustment. High scorers endorse items that suggest they are feeling tense, anxious, ruminative, pre-occupied, obsessional, phobic, and rigid. These individuals often have obsessive–compulsive rumination. People who score high on the Pt scale are frequently self-condemning and guilt prone; they feel inferior and inadequate. Clients with Spike 7 elevations overintellectualize, overrationalize, and resist psychological interpretation in treatment.

Scale 8: Schizophrenia (Sc)

The Sc scale measures behavior, symptoms, and attitudes that are often associated with severe mental health problems. People who have high scores (T ≥ 65) have an unconventional, schizoid lifestyle. They are typically withdrawn, shy, and moody. They often report feeling inadequate, tense, and confused. They may have unusual or strange thoughts, poor judgment, and erratic moods. High Sc scorers usually experience difficult interpersonal relationships. They are often viewed by others as unusual or bizarre in their thinking and relationships.

People who obtain very high scores (T scores of 80 or above) may have poor reality contact, bizarre sensory experiences, delusions, and hallucinations. High Sc scorers may have difficulty relating in therapy; they generally lack self-awareness and have poor problem-solving skills. The Sc scale is the highest score on the profile for Mexican psychiatric patients (G. M. E. Lucio, Palacios, Duran, & Butcher, 1999) and Puerto Ricans (Cabiya & Davila, 1999a, 1999b).

Scale 9: Hypomania (Ma)

The Ma scale was devised as a measure of personality factors and affective symptoms related to hypomania, a subclinical syndrome of bipolar disorder. High scorers (T = 65–74) are viewed by others as sociable, outgoing, impulsive, overly energetic, and optimistic. They tend to be high risk takers and have overly lax moral views. They are often seen by others as flighty, impulsive, and grandiose and overly optimistic in their approach to life. They are also seen as irritable and impatient. Many individuals with elevations on Ma drink excessively and develop problems with substance abuse. They often fail to follow through on plans; they exaggerate their self-worth and are manipulative. Very high scorers (T ≥ 75) may show affective disorder, bizarre behavior, erratic moods, impulsive behavior, and delusions.

Scale 0: Social Introversion/Extroversion (Si)

People who score high on the Si scale are viewed by others as introverted, shy, withdrawn, socially reserved, submissive, overcontrolled, lethargic, conventional, tense, inflexible, and guilt-prone. Those who score low tend to be extraverted, outgoing, gregarious, expressive, aggressive, talkative, impulsive, uninhibited, spontaneous, manipulative, opportunistic, and insincere in social relations. The personality construct underlying the Si scale (introversion/extroversion) operates in Mexican populations as it does in the United States, showing comparable T-score elevations.

USE OF MMPI-2 CODE TYPES

In many instances, more than one clinical scale is elevated in the interpretable range, at or over a T score of 65. Early in MMPI history, clinicians observed that many patients who manifested similar clinical problems produced similar MMPI profile patterns with multiple scale elevations. For example, the profiles of patients with depression often had elevations on both Scale 2 (D) and 7 (Pt). The interpretation of profile scale configurations came to be as important in MMPI interpretation as the use of single scale elevation. The profile scale pattern, or *code type*, is simply the highest configuration of scale scores in the clinical profile; for example, a two-point code type is the two most elevated scores, such as the 4/9–9/4 code describing a profile with scale 4 (Pd) and 9 (Ma) being the highest points on the profile. Several three-point and four-point code types have also been researched. These are code types in which three scales are elevated above the T score of 65; for example, the 2/7/8 profile code type describes elevations

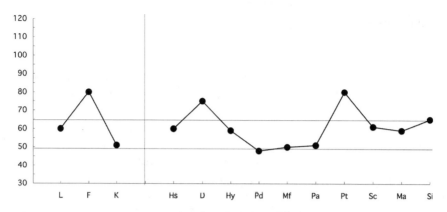

Figure 5.1. MMPI-2 validity and clinical profile illustrating high-profile definition. The scales include *L* (Lie), *F* (Infrequency), *K* (Defensiveness), *Hs* (Hypochondriasis), *D* (Depression), *Hy* (Hysteria), *Pd* (Psychopathic Deviation), *Mf* (Masculinity–Femininity), *Pa* (Paranoia), *Pt* (Psychasthenia), *Sc* (Schizophrenia), *Ma* (Hypomania), and *Si* (Social Introversion).

of Scale 4 (*D*), 7 (*Pt*), and 8 (*Sc*). (See Figure 5.1 for a very well-defined profile and Figure 5.2 for a profile that is not well defined.)

Well-researched descriptors for many of the MMPI code types (group-ings based on the two, three, and sometimes four most elevated scales) are available for the most frequently appearing profile types (see Archer, Griffin, & Aiduk, 1995; Gilberstadt & Duker, 1965; Graham, Ben-Porath, & McNulty, 1999; Gynther, Altman, & Sletten, 1973; Marks, Seeman, & Haller, 1974). For further discussion of code type interpretation, see Butcher (2005a) and Graham (2006).

In interpreting MMPI-2 code types, it is also important to analyze how distinctive the profile code is from the rest of the profile. That is, the

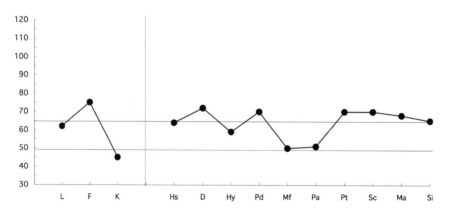

Figure 5.2. MMPI-2 validity and clinical profile illustrating a "not well-defined" scale configuration. See Figure 5.1 caption for scale definitions.

interpreter should take into consideration how clearly elevated the code type of the elevated score is above the next highest scale in the profile. This concept is referred to as *profile definition*, or the extent to which an MMPI scale score or code type is elevated above the next highest scale. Several levels of profile definition are considered in clinical interpretation. The profile code or single point score that is 10 or more points higher than the next score in the profile is referred to as "very well defined," the code or score that is more than 5 points but less than 10 points higher than the next scale is considered to be "well defined," and profiles that are 4 points or less than the next highest score in the profile are referred to as "not well defined" (see discussion in Butcher, 2005a).

MMPI-2 scales and profiles that are well defined or very well defined are considered to be more reliable over time than profiles that are not well defined. In addition, one can be more confident the personality correlates that have been established for that code are likely to apply with profiles that are very well defined or well defined. Profiles that are not well defined need to be interpreted somewhat more cautiously because the profile pattern might change if the client is retested (Butcher, 2005a; Graham, 2006).

ITEM CONTENT AND THE SHARING OF PERSONAL INFORMATION

Once the credibility of a client's responses can be assured and the MMPI-2 profiles are considered valid, then one can assume that the client's item responses are veridical representations of their symptoms and behavior. The MMPI-2 content scales are summary variables that provide a normative framework for a client's endorsement of similar items or problem areas. For example, a high point score on the *D* content scale (e.g., a T score of 80) indicates that the client has endorsed a substantial number of symptoms and behaviors that are associated with depressed mood and suicidal ideation. It is important, in the clinical evaluation, to attend to this shared information and address those feelings and possible suicidal behavior in the clinical context.

The similarity of performance of Mexican normal population compared with the American normative sample for the MMPI-2 content scales is shown in Figures 5.3 and 5.4. Moreover, the item and scale statistics of these measures cross-culturally provide confidence that they are measuring similar constructs across the Spanish language and Mexican culture (G. M. E. Lucio & Reyes-Lagunes, 1996). Overall, the similarity of performance of these groups suggests that one can have considerable confidence that the content scales are addressing similar problems in Hispanic samples. In the interpretation of an MMPI-2 content scale profile with a Hispanic client

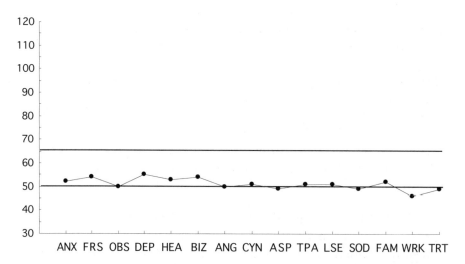

Figure 5.3. MMPI-2 content scale profile of Mexican normal men (*N* = 813) plotted on U.S. norms (G. M. E. Lucio, Palacios, et al., 1999). The scales include *ANX* (Anxiety), *FRS* (Fears), *OBS* (Obsessiveness), *DEP* (Depression), *HEA* (Health Concerns), *BIZ* (Bizarre Mentation), *ANG* (Anger), *CYN* (Cynicism), *ASP* (Antisocial Practices), *TPA* (Type A), *LSE* (Low Self-Esteem), *SOD* (Social Discomfort), *FAM* (Family Concerns), *WRK* (Work Interference), and *TRT* (Negative Treatment Indicators).

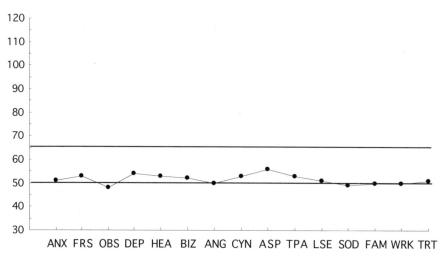

Figure 5.4. MMPI-2 content scale profile of Mexican normal women (*N* = 1,107) plotted on U.S. norms (G. M. E. Lucio, Palacios, et al., 1999). See Figure 5.3 caption for scale definitions.

(whether one has determined it more appropriate to use Mexican norms or American norms), one can feel confident that one is obtaining an indication of the client's acknowledged problem description as reflected in the elevated scores of the content scales.

The constructs being assessed by the MMPI-2 content scales are as follows:

Anxiety (ANX, 23 items). Individuals who score above a T of 65 on the *ANX* scale are acknowledging a high number of general symptoms of anxiety, including tension, somatic problems (e.g., heart pounding and shortness of breath), problems with sleeping, being overwhelmed by worry, and having poor concentration. They report being concerned over losing their mind. Moreover, they find life a strain and have difficulty making decisions. They acknowledge being aware of these symptoms and problems and are willing to discuss them with others. Psychological treatment could be directed toward anxiety reduction.

Fears (FRS, 23 items). A high point score on the *FRS* scale (T score > 65) indicates that an individual has many specific fears and feels overwhelmed by their presence. These fears can include the sight of blood; high places; money; animals such as snakes, mice, or spiders; leaving home; fire, storms, and natural disasters; water; the dark; being indoors; and dirt. People with a high point score on this scale are likely to feel vulnerable to periods of intense anxiety.

Obsessiveness (OBS, 16 items). People who score in the clinical range (T score > 65) on the *OBS* content scale are reporting great difficulty making decisions. They are likely to ruminate excessively about issues and problems (even minor problems or events), causing others to become impatient with them. They have great difficulty making changes and become distressed over even minor changes in their lives. They tend to have some compulsive behavior, such as compulsive counting or saving unimportant things. They tend to be excessive worriers who may become overwhelmed by their own thoughts.

Depression (DEP, 33 items). People who score high on the *DEP* scale (T score > 65) have significant depressive thoughts. They acknowledge feeling depressed, uncertain about their future, and lacking interests in life. They are likely to report considerable unhappiness, tend to cry easily, and feel hopeless about the future. High *DEP* scorers also may report thoughts of suicide or wishes that they were dead. They tend to believe that they are condemned or have committed unpardonable sins and to view other people as not being supportive of them. Clients who have their highest point on the *DEP* scale tend to be open to therapeutic intervention and feel the need for support.

Health Concerns (HEA, 36 items). People who have an elevated high point score on the *HEA* scale (T score > 65) acknowledge many physical symptoms across several body systems, such as neurological problems (e.g., convulsions, dizzy and fainting spells, paralysis), gastrointestinal symptoms (e.g., constipation, nausea and vomiting, stomach trouble), sensory problems (e.g., poor hearing or eyesight), cardiovascular symptoms (e.g., heart or chest pains), skin problems, pain (e.g., headaches, neck pains), and respiratory troubles (e.g., coughs, hay fever, asthma). High-scoring HEA clients tend to worry excessively about their health and to feel they are in poorer health than most people or than they actually are.

Bizarre Mentation (BIZ, 23 items). This scale assesses unusual thinking. High *BIZ* scorers (T score > 65) acknowledge having psychotic thought processes and may have auditory, visual, or olfactory hallucinations. They may recognize that their thoughts are strange and peculiar. These high scorers also acknowledge paranoid ideation (e.g., the belief that they are being plotted against or that someone is trying to poison them). These individuals may feel that they have a special mission or special powers.

Anger (ANG, 16 items). This scale assesses anger control problems. High scores on the *ANG* scale (T score > 65) suggest temper-related problems and loss of control in the expression of aggression. High scorers acknowledge being irritable, grouchy, impatient, hotheaded, annoyed, and stubborn. They indicate that they often feel like swearing or smashing things. They may also report having been physically abusive toward other people.

Cynicism (CYN, 23 items). This scale addresses a general personality characteristic that centers on dislike and mistrust of other people. Misanthropic beliefs are central themes acknowledged by high *CYN* scorers. They tend to view other people in a negative light—they suspect hidden, negative motives behind the acts of others; for example, they believe that most people are honest simply for fear of being caught. They believe that others are not to be trusted because people use each other and are only friendly for selfish reasons. They tend to harbor negative attitudes about people close to them.

Antisocial Practices (ASP, 22 items). This scale addresses personality problems associated with acting-out behavior, impulsive lifestyle, and engaging in behavior that is against the law. High scorers on the *ASP* scale (T score > 65) also tend to have misanthropic attitudes similar to high scorers on the *CYN* scale, but high scorers on the *ASP* scale report antisocial behavior—being in trouble with the law, stealing, or shoplifting. They report sometimes enjoying the activities of criminals and believe that it is all right to get around the law.

Type A (TPA, 19 items). This scale assesses characteristics known as the Type A personality. High scorers on the *TPA* scale (T score ≥ 65) are viewed as hard-driving, fast-moving, work-oriented individuals who frequently become impatient, irritable, and annoyed. High-scoring clients do not like to wait or to be interrupted at a task. They complain that there is never enough time in the day for them to complete their tasks. They are usually direct, blunt, and overbearing in interpersonal relationships.

Low Self-Esteem (LSE, 24 items). People who score high on the *LSE* scale (T > 65) are characterized by having low opinions of themselves. They feel as though other people do not like them. They acknowledge many negative attitudes about themselves, including beliefs that they are unattractive, awkward, clumsy, useless, and a burden to others. They appear to lack self-confidence and find it hard to accept compliments from others. They may at times be overwhelmed by all the faults they see in themselves.

Social Discomfort (SOD, *24 items*). This scale was developed to provide a measure of social discomfort and interpersonal ineffectiveness. People obtaining high *SOD* scores (T > 65) are very uneasy around others,. They prefer to be by themselves. In social situations, they are likely to sit alone rather than join the group. They see themselves as shy and dislike parties and other group events.

Family Problems (FAM, *25 items*). This scale was developed to provide an assessment of a client's family relationships and his or her attitudes toward members of the family. People who have high *FAM* scores (T > 65) report having considerable family discord. They describe their families as loveless, quarrelsome, and unpleasant. They may acknowledge that they hate members of their families and may view their childhoods as abusive and their marriages as unhappy and lacking in affection.

Work Interference (WRK, *33 items*). This scale was developed to assess a client's attitudes toward work and his or her confidence with respect to capability to work. A high score on the *WRK* scale is indicative of behavior or attitudes that are likely to contribute to poor work performance. Some of the problems addressed in the scale relate to low self-confidence, concentration difficulties, obsessiveness, tension, and personal questioning of career choice. A number of items focus on relationships with and possible negative attitudes toward coworkers.

Negative Treatment Indicators (TRT, *26 items*). This scale was devised to assess personality features and attitudes toward treatment. A high score on the *TRT* scale indicates a negative attitude toward doctors and mental health treatment. High scorers do not believe that anyone can understand or help them. People who score high (T > 65) tend to have issues or problems that they are not comfortable discussing with anyone. They may be resistant toward changing anything in their lives. In addition, high scorers may not feel that change is possible. They prefer to give up rather than face a crisis or difficulty in their lives.

SUPPLEMENTARY SCALES

The MMPI-2 supplementary scales, such as the substance abuse indicators, have also been researched with Spanish-speaking populations (León & Lucio, 1999) and can be of value in exploring potential problems with Hispanic clients (see chap. 2, this volume). The supplementary scales include the following:

MacAndrew—Revised (MAC-R). High scorers are prone to developing problems of addiction, such as alcohol or drug abuse, pathological gambling, and so on.

Addiction Potential Scale (APS). This 39-item scale was developed for the MMPI-2 using an empirical scale construction strategy developed by Weed, Butcher, McKenna, and Ben-Porath (1992). This scale assesses the potential for individuals to develop problems of addiction such as drug or alcohol abuse.

Addiction Acknowledgment Scale (AAS). This 13-item scale was developed by rational–statistical scale methods to assess the extent to which the individual acknowledges alcohol or drug abuse problems (Weed et al., 1992). High scores (T > 60) suggest a high endorsement of alcohol or drug use problems.

Keane Post-Traumatic (PK). This scale (Keane, Malloy, & Fairbank, 1984) was developed using an empirical scale construction strategy. In developing the scale, the authors used a group of 100 male veterans who had been diagnosed as having posttraumatic stress disorder (PTSD) in contrast with 100 male veterans with other psychiatric problems. They found that 49 items significantly discriminated the PTSD group from the general psychiatric sample. This scale was found to have an 82% hit rate in the classification of veterans with PTSD. As expected, the *PK* scale shows a strong relationship to other anxiety scales, such as the Welsh A scale and *Pt* scale, and it is negatively correlated with the *Es* scale.

Hostility (Ho). This scale was developed by Cook and Medley (1954) with the original MMPI and retooled for MMPI-2 by Han, Weed, Calhoun, and Butcher (1995) to identify an individual's ability to work harmoniously with others. The scale was found to be an effective measure of hostility (Han et al., 1995). Individuals who score high on this scale (T ≥ 65) tend to be aggressive and openly confrontative, even when not provoked. Research on this scale has shown it to be effective in assessing health-related behavior, such as the Type A behavior pattern in which anger often plays a significant role.

Marital Distress Scale (MDS). The MDS is a newly developed scale for the MMPI-2 (Hjemboe, Almagor, & Butcher, 1992). The scale was conceived and empirically constructed to detect marital distress. A sample of 150 couples in marital counseling was used as the primary development group. The correlation of each MMPI-2 item to the Spanier Dyadic Adjustment Scale (DAS; Spanier, 1976) was computed, and the items with the highest correlations among both males and females were retained. These were then compared with the same correlations among 392 couples from the MMPI-2 restandardization normative sample, and those items that showed strong correlations in this sample were retained as well. Other items that were significant, on the basis of their assessment of general maladjustment—

for example, anxiety and depression content—were deleted. The items retained were then correlated with Dyadic Adjustment Scale scales and content scales to permit direct comparability with other standardized MMPI scale scores. In tests of the *MDS* hit rate for both counselees and the normative sample, participants reported poor adjustment at a T score of 60. In both the normative and counselee samples, levels of dyadic adjustment clearly declined with an elevation on the *MDS*. Results are reported only for clients who indicated that they were married or separated.

DEVELOPING AN MMPI-2 PSYCHOLOGICAL EVALUATION STRATEGY FOR HISPANIC CLIENTS

Developing psychological test reports for Hispanic clients that are based on or derived, in part, from their responses to the MMPI-2 should follow a systematic interpretive strategy (see discussions by Butcher & Williams, 2000; Graham, 2006). This process should take into consideration not only the great congruencies between Hispanic and Anglo MMPI-2 performance but also some differences that have been noted. As in any diagnostic evaluation, caution in reporting test results is encouraged.

In developing the report, it is important to confirm that the evaluation as a whole and the test administration in particular have provided an interpretable test result—that is, that the testing situation was controlled and monitored and that the instructions for taking the test were understood. The examiner needs to ensure that the client has read and comprehended the language in which the test is being administered, whether English or Spanish. In addition, it is also important to provide information about any extraneous factors that might have affected the client's performance on the testing. For example, did the Hispanic client conduct himself or herself in the interview in ways that may have produced questionable results? Was he or she sufficiently familiar and comfortable with the assessment procedures to provide credible test results? Once the testing situation has been vetted, then the psychologist can have confidence in proceeding.

The client's performance on the test needs to be consistent with those of the people who took the test in the standardization sample on which the test norms were developed to produce interpretive results. That is, for tests to be credible, the test conditions need to be "standard." Ensure that the client did not omit a significant number of items and that no invalidating response sets were present. Carefully weigh the client's performance on the validity scales to guarantee a meaningful and interpretable result. Are any validity scales elevated in the extreme? Allowing for the fact that some Hispanic clients might score higher on the *L* (Lie) or *F* (Infrequency) scales than non-Hispanic clients, consider whether the elevation on the scale was sufficient to produce invalidity or cautionary statements. Could the client be using the testing as a means of making a point, such as "I am in despair and need help," or "I am a very virtuous person who needs to be treated with great respect," or "I need to present a positive, acceptable self to the professional; I can't bring shame onto me or my family"? The psychological evaluation needs to be based on the conclusion that the client's response attitudes were appropriate and credible.

In the clinical interpretation, it is important to gain an understanding of the client's major symptom elements (e.g., anxiety, depression, or cognitive deterioration) to obtain a picture of his or her present emotional state. Determine which of the clinical scales or code types will be focused on in the report. The practitioner does not provide interpretations for all eight of the clinical scales but only those most salient or most important in describing the client's problems. In selecting which of possible elevated clinical scales to interpret, several steps are taken. First, it is important to consider scale elevation and the configuration of the elevated scales in the profile that are in the clinical range (T > 65). Then, if more than one scale is elevated in this range, they are given most prominent attention. What is the configuration of scores in the profile? Are there interpretable code types? Next, it is important to weigh the reliability of these measures for the evaluation by examining the scale definition. Was the profile sufficiently defined (e.g., having 5 points separating the next scale) to be considered stable and reliable over time?

Provide a clear description of the client's expressed symptoms at the present time as reflected in prominent MMPI-2 scales. For example, is the person depressed (elevations on D or DEP > 65 T), delusional (elevations on Sc > 75 T or BIZ > 65 T), or anxious (elevation on Pt or ANX > 65 T)?

Describe the client's personality functioning that could be influencing the profile elevations. For example, is the client extroverted or introverted (on the basis of elevations of the Si scale), does the person have an impulsive lifestyle (are Pd and/or Ma elevated), or is the person obsessive–compulsive in approach to tasks or situations (elevations on Pt or OBS)?

What are the major symptomatic themes that are represented in the client's MMPI-2 responses? What content themes (as summarized by the content scales and content component scales) can be viewed as representing major concerns of the client? Do these symptom expressions coincide with the information being obtained in other testing or interview? Are there particular "critical items" that need to be addressed? For example, how has the client responded to the suicide items?

Include an estimate of the extent of psychological maladjustment on the basis of the MMPI-2. Are there personality or psychological problems reflected in the profiles? Would this person be considered to have a psychological adjustment disorder? How severe would the psychological problems be on the basis of MMPI-2 elevations? Do the hypotheses derived from the MMPI-2 results fit into the personality pattern and diagnostic information being obtained in other assessment results such as interview or past history?

SUMMARY

This chapter has provided an interpretive framework for understanding and developing psychological evaluations of Hispanic clients. We summarized the established personality and symptomatic correlates for the clinical scales of the MMPI-2, and some clinical or content scales that have been reported to be influenced by cultural differences for Hispanic clients were noted and interpretative changes suggested. Guidelines for interpreting profiles were presented as an aid to practitioners in developing accurate conclusions about Hispanic clients' test scores. In some cases, some scale elevations that may reflect stereotypical or even overpathologized views of Latino clients were noted. We presented an MMPI-2 interpretive strategy and described the pertinent questions to address in developing MMPI-2 interpretations for Hispanics.

CHAPTER HIGHLIGHTS

- An interpretive framework was provided for understanding and developing a psychological evaluation of Hispanic clients.
- The established personality and symptomatic correlates for the clinical scales of the MMPI-2 were summarized. Scales that have been shown to have possible cultural differences for Hispanic clients were noted.
- Guidelines for interpreting profiles were presented to keep practitioners from reaching inaccurate conclusions or conclusions that may reflect stereotypical or even overpathologized views of Hispanic clients.
- An MMPI-2 interpretive strategy was presented and the pertinent questions to address in developing MMPI-2 interpretations for Hispanics were described.

6

CLINICAL INTERPRETATION OF THE MMPI-2 WITH HISPANIC CLIENTS: CASE STUDIES

In this chapter we provide several case studies to illustrate the process of MMPI-2 interpretation with Hispanic clients. The cases were selected from different settings to highlight the utility of the test in contemporary practice. In each case we provide relevant background and referral information, the scored profiles with the pertinent test information, and a computer-based interpretive report to illustrate objective interpretation.

CASE 1: A CHILD MURDERER IN PUERTO RICO

Daniella A. was raised by her grandmother after the early death of her father; however, her mother was very significant in her life. Her mother had been critical of her while providing little support. She had always been resentful of her mother for not raising her like the rest of her brothers and sisters.

Daniella had an average performance in school but dropped out to live with an older man when she was 13 years old. She left this man and went to live with another man, an alcoholic, when she was 17 years old. At that time she abused alcohol and marijuana. She then studied and passed

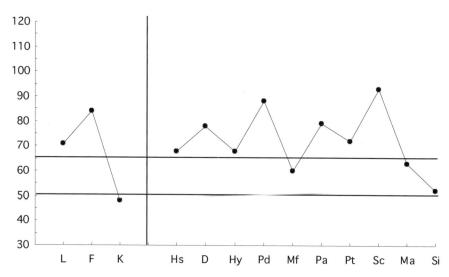

Figure 6.1. MMPI-2 validity and clinical scale profile for Daniella A., a Puerto Rican child murderer. The scales include *L* (Lie), *F* (Infrequency), *K* (Defensiveness), *Hs* (Hypochondriasis), *D* (Depression), *Hy* (Hysteria), *Pd* (Psychopathic Deviation), *Mf* (Masculinity–Femininity), *Pa* (Paranoia), *Pt* (Psychasthenia), *Sc* (Schizophrenia), *Ma* (Hypomania), and *Si* (Social Introversion).

her high school qualifying exams and completed a 1-year training course as an office clerk. At that time, she married and eventually had two children with a man who frequently abused her physically.

By this time, she had stopped drinking and abusing drugs and had become devoted to a Christian sect. During this time she also developed a delusional belief that the only way that she could relieve her children from the "tortures of this life" was by killing them. She murdered her children in an apparent psychotic episode in which she also attempted to take her own life.

She was immediately arrested and charged with homicide. At trial, she was found to be not guilty by reason of insanity and was sent to a state psychiatric hospital. After 10 years in the hospital, she was referred to Jose Cabiya for a psychological evaluation because she did not appear to the staff to be psychotic. Her clinical diagnosis had been paranoid schizophrenia, although she was asymptomatic. As part of the evaluation to determine her mental state, she was administered the MMPI-2 Hispania. Her MMPI-2 basic profile (plotted on the U.S. English language norms) is shown in Figure 6.1, and her content scale profile is given in Figure 6.2. The Minnesota Report computer-based interpretation of Daniella's MMPI-2 profiles is presented in Exhibit 6.1.

The MMPI-2 results suggest an elevated profile that is consistent with general maladjustment (see the discussion in the Minnesota Report Forensic

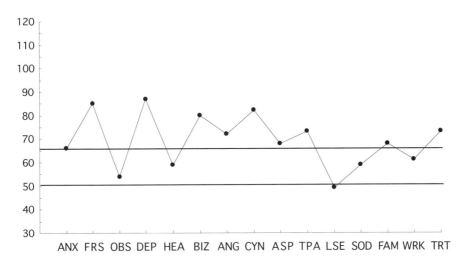

Figure 6.2. MMPI-2 content scale profile for Daniella A., a Puerto Rican child murderer. The scales include *ANX* (Anxiety), *FRS* (Fears), *OBS* (Obsessiveness), *DEP* (Depression), *HEA* (Health Concerns), *BIZ* (Bizarre Mentation), *ANG* (Anger), *CYN* (Cynicism), *ASP* (Antisocial Practices), *TPA* (Type A), *LSE* (Low Self-Esteem), *SOD* (Social Discomfort), *FAM* (Family Concerns), *WRK* (Work Interference), and *TRT* (Negative Treatment Indicators).

Considerations narrative in Exhibit 6.1). This client's MMPI-2 clinical profile is often found among women who commit the crime of murder (Berger, 1995). Her 8-4 code type suggests that she has many features of personality disorder, does not seem to fit into her environment, and is resentful of authority, which is consistent with her social history. Her history of erratic impulsive and marginal adjustment is also consistent with this code type, as are the drug history and radical religious beliefs. Finally, the murders of her children are consistent with this tendency toward impulsive and criminal acts. This code type is also consistent with poor capacity for empathy, mistrust, and poor social skills.

However, elevations in Scales 2 (*D*, Depression) and 7 (*Pt*, Psychasthenia) suggested the possibility that the client did have potential to respond to psychotherapy because of her depressed mood and experience of anxiety. This possibility was reinforced by the fact that the *ANX* (Anxiety) and *FRS* (Fears) scales were the highest content scales and that the *TRT* (Negative Treatment Indicators) scale, although high, was not very elevated. In fact, the high *FRS* and *LSE* (Low Self-Esteem) scales did suggest the possibility that she was not more open to relate to others because of her insecurities and poor self-esteem, also predicted by the 8-4 code type. Thus psychotherapy was directed to improving her self-esteem and sense of security through analysis of her relationship with her mother and cognitive restructuring.

EXHIBIT 6.1

Validity Considerations

This MMPI-2 profile should be interpreted with caution. There is some possibility that the clinical report is an exaggerated picture of the client's present situation and problems. She is presenting an unusual number of psychological symptoms. The assessment psychologist needs to consider her extreme tendency to endorse a broad range of nonspecific symptoms in the evaluation; symptom malingering is a strong possibility.

This client's responses to items that appear near the end of the MMPI-2 were somewhat more exaggerated than her responses to items that appear in the beginning of the test. There is a strong possibility that she responded to the last section of items carelessly, randomly, or deceitfully, thereby invalidating that portion of the test. Although the standard clinical and validity scales can be scored from items in the first two thirds of the test, caution should be used in interpreting the MMPI-2 content and supplementary scales, which depend on items found throughout the entire item pool.

Symptomatic Pattern

The client's MMPI-2 clinical profile suggests that she has many psychological problems at this time. She appears to be angry and alienated and tends to act out impulsively and unpredictably in antisocial ways. She may engage in dangerous or extremely pleasure-oriented behavior just for the thrill of it, and she has probably had many sexual problems. She is likely to be viewed as immature and irresponsible, and she may have a long history of deviant behavior, including poor achievement, poor work history, and problems with authority.

The client's response content suggests that she feels intensely fearful about a large number of objects and activities. This hypersensitivity and fearfulness appear to be generalized at this point and may be debilitating to her in social and work situations. She has endorsed a number of items suggesting that she is experiencing low morale and a depressed mood. She reports a preoccupation with feeling guilty and unworthy. She feels that she deserves to be punished for wrongs she has committed. She feels regretful and unhappy about life, and she seems plagued by anxiety and worry about the future. She feels hopeless at times and feels that she is a condemned person. She has endorsed a number of unusual, bizarre ideas that suggest some difficulties with her thinking.

Profile Frequency

This elevated MMPI-2 two-point profile configuration (4-8/8-4) is very rare in samples of normals, occurring in less than 1% of the MMPI-2 normative sample of women.

This elevated MMPI-2 two-point profile configuration (4-8/8-4) is found in 2% of the women in the Pearson-NCS–outpatient sample. Similarly, Graham, Ben-Porath, and McNulty (1999) reported that 1.8% of the outpatient women in a community-based outpatient study had a well-defined 4-8/8-4 profile code. However, 5.7% of the women in this sample produced 4-8/8-4 profiles though not necessarily in the elevated range or well defined.

This elevated MMPI-2 two-point profile configuration (4-8/8-4) is also found in 5.3% of the women in the Graham and Butcher (1988) sample and in 2.8% of the women in the Pearson-NCS inpatient sample. Among women veteran inpatients, this profile code was found as the high-point pair in 4.7% of the cases, although these were not necessarily well-defined profiles. Only 1.2% of the female veterans had well-defined codes at or above a T score of 65. The 4-8/8-4 configuration was found to be of similar frequency in the sample studied by Arbisi, Ben-Porath, and McNulty (2003), who reported that this high-point configuration occurred with 4.7% frequency but with less than 1% having well-defined code types.

(continued)

EXHIBIT 6.1   *(Continued)*

Profile Stability

The relative scale elevation of the highest scales in the client's clinical profile reflects high profile definition. If she is retested at a later date, the peak scores on this test are likely to retain their relative salience in her retest profile pattern. Her high-point score on *Sc* (Schizophrenia) is likely to remain stable over time. Short-term test–retest studies have shown a correlation of .80 for this high-point score.

Interpersonal Relations

The client appears to have poor social skills, and although she is insecure in relationships, she may manipulate others through aggression and intimidation. She is overly sensitive and frequently misunderstands the motives of others.

She appears to act impulsively and may become embroiled in relationship problems. She may hedonistically use other people for her own satisfaction without concern for them. Her lack of trust may prevent her from developing warm, close relationships. She is probably behaving in unpredictable and erratic ways that may produce a great deal of marital strain.

Her acting-out behavior is likely to put great strain on her marriage or relationships. She seems to have great difficulty relating to the opposite sex. She may use other people for her own gratification with little concern for their needs. Rocky interpersonal relationships are the norm among individuals with this profile. Marital breakup is relatively common.

Mental Health Considerations

Many individuals with this profile receive a diagnosis of severe personality disorder. The possibility of a schizophrenic disorder should also be considered.

Individuals with this MMPI-2 clinical profile appear to have long-term personality problems that impede psychological treatment. Psychotropic medication is frequently the treatment of choice. Some individuals with these extreme problems require treatment in a controlled setting. Outpatient therapy may be difficult with this client because of her social alienation and poor ego controls. Insight-oriented psychotherapy tends to be unproductive with individuals of this type because they are likely to act out in unpredictable ways and frequently do not trust the therapist sufficiently to establish a treatment relationship. The client is so emotionally and socially alienated from other people that it would be difficult for a therapist to gain her confidence.

She may respond better to behavioral management therapy than to verbal psychotherapy. Progress is likely to be limited regardless of the treatment approach because of her tendency to act out against others. Medication abuse is a possibility because many individuals with this profile develop drug or alcohol problems.

Forensic Considerations

The client's response content is consistent with the antisocial features in her history. These factors should be taken into consideration in arriving at a clinical diagnosis.

The client endorsed item content that seems to indicate low potential for change. She may feel that her problems are not addressable through therapy and that she is not likely to benefit much from psychological treatment at this time. Her apparently negative treatment attitudes may need to be explored early in therapy if treatment is to be successful. Examination of item content reveals a considerable number of problems with her home life. She feels extremely unhappy and alienated from her family. She reports that her home life is unpleasant and that she does not expect it to improve. Any psychological intervention will need to focus on her negative family feelings if progress is to be made. Her very high score on the Marital Distress Scale suggests that her marital situation is problematic at this time. She has reported a number of problems with her marriage that are possibly important to understanding her current psychological symptoms.

The client did respond to therapy and was discharged after a year, and she has lived most of the time since then in supervised foster homes.

CASE 2: INCARCERATED MAN BEING EVALUATED BY A CHILD PROTECTIVE AGENCY REGARDING PARENTAL RIGHTS

Raul T. was a 30-year-old, Spanish-language-dominant man of Puerto Rican background who was evaluated while he was serving an 18-month prison term for a drug-related offense. Raul spent portions of his childhood and youth between New York City and Puerto Rico. In addition to the criminal charges for which he was serving a sentence, Raul was evaluated on referral by the local child protective agency (CPA) to determine his suitability to parent his young son once he was released. Among the concerns of the CPA were Raul's history of domestic violence and of violating no-contact orders.

Raul was interviewed extensively as part of his evaluation. He described his family of origin as nurturing and invested in his and his brother's education. He stated that the extended family network, especially his grandparents, supported education and regular school attendance. He denied the existence of family violence or substance abuse. Raul described himself as "quite close" to his father.

Raul was 16 years old when his father was diagnosed with a terminal illness for which he required specialized care outside Puerto Rico. Because the family had made extended summer visits to relatives in New York during Raul's childhood, and because the father had been referred to a facility specializing in his condition in that city, Raul's parents traveled to New York hoping that the father would be treated successfully and survive. Raul and his brother remained in Puerto Rico under the supervision of the grandparents.

Once Raul learned of his father's serious health condition, he acknowledged, "I changed completely, started to run with the wrong people, to mess with and sell drugs and guns." Within 6 months, Raul's father passed away in New York. By the time of his father's death, Raul already had a criminal record in Puerto Rico and had been sentenced to incarceration as a juvenile. He added, "I was a good student until the 10th grade, but at that point, everything turned bad." He obtained some carpentry skills while incarcerated but did not complete a GED. In fact, Raul was being transported to take his GED exam when he escaped from custody and traveled to New York with a girlfriend who had family there.

Over the next several years, Raul was involved in a number of relationships and frequently changed jobs. He acknowledged that in between jobs he would sell drugs to secure an income. He was certain of having fathered two children but believed there might have been others. Raul described himself as "a generally good worker in whatever job I got, the only problem is that I have always had trouble taking orders from others at work and also got bored very easily, so I would just quit." He acknowledged that

> my problem is that I get angry very quickly and don't give the other person a chance, I just go ahead and throw the first punch; even if someone looks at me the wrong way I don't know how to ignore them, I go after them.

Raul expressed interest in changing this aspect of his behavior and hoped to begin attending an anger management group during his current incarceration. He was adamant that he would never strike his children and that he greatly enjoyed their visits, "even if it has to be with the supervision of the social workers." During the interview, Raul repeatedly expressed anxiety about the future of his situation and especially about whether he would ultimately have any parental rights. Although he affirmed that he still loved the mother of his children, he expressed a great deal of ambivalence about the future of the relationship and appeared to feel overwhelmed about the number of issues that would have to be addressed for the relationship to survive. Finally, Raul also expressed considerable distress about being confined, because he had never "dealt well with being locked up or in one place for too long, so I try almost anything to get my mind off the fact that I am stuck here."

Because of his reported level of education and the fact that Raul reported that he could speak "some English, just to get by but really can't read or write it, I am better in Spanish," the evaluation included an assessment of Raul's current level of native language proficiency for vocabulary, verbal reasoning, and basic reading and spelling tasks. This assessment revealed that even in his native language, Raul functioned below his reported level of educational attainment (10th grade) on many of the language tasks listed above. Nevertheless, his reading level was sufficient for him to complete the MMPI-2 Spanish version. An estimate of his cognitive ability was obtained nonverbally, revealing average-level cognitive ability. An inventory of experiences as a parent was also administered in Spanish, as was a semistructured interview of parenting skills. Despite the length of the evaluation session, Raul was compliant and cooperative. He also asked questions when he needed clarification on the meaning of test items. On the basis of his general approach to the evaluation, the obtained results are considered to represent Raul's current level of functioning.

All 567 items of the MMPI-2 Spanish version were administered. The Minnesota Report computer-based interpretation of his MMPI-2 profile is presented in Exhibit 6.2. An analysis of Raul's validity profile indicates that he approached the inventory in a generally open, nondefensive manner

EXHIBIT 6.2
Minnesota Report: General Corrections Interpretive Report (Raul T.)

Profile Validity

This MMPI-2 profile should be interpreted with caution. There is some possibility that the clinical report is an exaggerated picture of the client's present situation and problems. He presented an unusual number of psychological symptoms. This extreme response set could result from poor reading ability, confusion, disorientation, stress, or a need to call attention to his problems.

His test-taking attitude should be evaluated for the possibility that he produced an invalid profile. He may have been uncooperative with the testing or may have attempted to present a false picture of mental illness. Determining the source of his response style, whether conscious distortion or personality deterioration, is important because he reported extreme problems. He was somewhat inconsistent in his responses to the test items. He may not have attended carefully to item content.

Symptomatic Patterns

This report was developed using the *Pa* (Paranoia) and *Pt* (Psychasthenia) scales as the prototype. The client's MMPI-2 clinical profile suggests that he is experiencing many psychological problems at this time. He appears to ruminate a great deal and may manifest obsessive or compulsive behavior. He holds beliefs that others are not likely to accept and tends to obsess about them to the point of alienating others. He appears to be quite intense, anxious, and distressed. Individuals with this profile may be overreacting to environmental situations with intense anxiety, suspicion, and concern. He feels insecure and inadequate when dealing with his problems. He may feel angry with himself and others, and he may feel guilty about his fantasies or beliefs. Often rather rigid, he may have problems controlling and directly expressing his anger.

In addition, the following description is suggested by the content of the client's item responses. He reports a preoccupation with feeling guilty and unworthy. He is full of regret and unhappy about life, and he is plagued by anxiety and worry about the future. He feels hopeless at times and feels that he is a condemned person.

According to his response content, there is a strong possibility that he has seriously contemplated suicide. The client's recent thinking is likely to be characterized by obsessiveness and indecision. He endorsed a number of items reflecting a high degree of anger. He appears to have a high potential for explosive behavior at times. He feels somewhat self-alienated and expresses some personal misgivings or a vague sense of remorse about past acts. He feels that life is unrewarding and dull, and he finds it hard to settle down. He reports some antisocial beliefs and attitudes, admits to rule violations, and acknowledges antisocial behavior in the past. He views the world as a threatening place, sees himself as having been unjustly blamed for others' problems, and feels that he is getting a raw deal from life. He is rather high-strung and believes that he feels things more or more intensely than others do. He feels lonely and misunderstood at times.

He endorsed a number of extreme and bizarre thoughts, suggesting the presence of delusions or hallucinations. He apparently believes that he has special mystical powers or a special mission in life that others do not understand or accept. The possibility that he could act out in an aggressive manner on his delusional ideas should be further evaluated. He endorsed statements that indicate some inability to control his anger. He may physically or verbally attack others when he is angry. His high endorsement of general anxiety content is likely to be important to understanding his clinical picture.

(continued)

EXHIBIT 6.2 *(Continued)*

Profile Frequency

It is usually valuable in MMPI-2 clinical profile interpretation to consider the relative frequency of a given profile pattern in various settings. The client's MMPI-2 high-point clinical scale score (*Pt*) is found in only 4.9% of the MMPI-2 normative sample of men. Only 3.1% of the sample have *Pt* as the peak score at or above a T score of 65, and only 1.6% have well-defined *Pt* spikes. The client's elevated MMPI-2 pattern (6-7/7-6) is rare, occurring in less than 1% of the MMPI-2 normative sample of men.

His MMPI-2 high-point clinical scale score (*Pt*) is found in 5.8% of military men (Butcher, Jeffrey, et al., 1990). Moreover, 3.6% of these men have *Pt* scale peaks at or over a T score of 65, and only 1.9% actually have well-defined *Pt* spikes in that range.

The relative frequency of this profile in various correctional settings is informative. Megargee (1993) reported that this MMPI-2 high-point clinical scale score (*Pt*) occurred in 4.3% of men in a state prison and less than 1% of men in a federal prison. Only 3.3% of the state prison sample and less than 1% of the federal prisoners had the *Pt* scale spike at or above a T score of 65.

Butcher (1997) reported a study of high-point and code type frequencies for men undergoing psychological evaluations in prison. The high-point MMPI-2 score on *Pt* that the client received occurred with only 5.4% frequency in that sample, the second lowest frequency of any scale peak. Additionally, only 1.9% of these were well-defined profiles at or above a T score of 65. This high-point MMPI-2 code (6-7/7-6) can best be understood in the context of Butcher's (1997) heterogeneous sample of men in prison. This profile configuration occurred with moderate frequency (5%), and 1.1% were well-defined scores at or above a T of 65.

Cabiya (1997) conducted an evaluation of incarcerated Puerto Rican men (almost 75% of whom were substance abusers) using the Spanish translation of the MMPI-2. In this study, this high-point MMPI-2 code (6-7/7-6) occurred with some frequency (3.7%), but less than 1% were well-defined scores at or above a T of 65.

Profile Stability

The relative elevation of the client's highest clinical scale scores suggests some lack of clarity in profile definition. Although his most elevated clinical scales are likely to be present in his profile pattern if he is retested at a later date, there could be some shifting of the most prominent scale elevations in the profile code. The difference between the profile type used to develop the present report and the next highest scale in the profile code was 4 points. So, for example, if the client is tested at a later date, his profile might involve more behavioral elements related to elevations on *Pd*. If he is retested, responses related to acting-out, aggressive, and irresponsible behaviors might become more prominent.

Interpersonal Relations

Individuals with this profile tend to be experiencing some interpersonal distress. The client seems somewhat shy and may have excessively high moral standards by which he judges others. His inflexibility in interpersonal situations may put a great strain on close relationships because he seems to test other people to reassure himself. He appears to be touchy or hostile interpersonally, and he may brood over what he imagines others have done to him. His mistrusting and jealous behavior may put strain on his marriage. Individuals with this profile are often petulant and testy in relationships. He is likely to quarrel a great deal and continually bring up old issues in his arguments. His aloofness and detachment may make his marital relationship difficult at times. He tends to be argumentative and may not be able to "forgive and forget" after a quarrel.

(continued)

EXHIBIT 6.2   *(Continued)*

He is an introverted person who has trouble meeting and interacting with other people. He is shy and emotionally distant. He tends to be uneasy, rigid, and overcontrolled in social situations. His shyness is probably symptomatic of a broader pattern of social withdrawal. Personality characteristics related to social introversion tend to be stable over time. His generally reclusive behavior, introverted lifestyle, and tendency toward interpersonal avoidance may be prominent in any future test results. His very high score on the Marital Distress Scale suggests that his marital situation is problematic at this time. He reported a number of problems with his marriage that are possibly important to understanding his current psychological symptoms.

The content of this client's MMPI-2 responses suggests the following additional information concerning his interpersonal relationships. He feels intensely angry, hostile, and resentful toward others, and he would like to get back at them. He is competitive and uncooperative and tends to be very critical of others. His relationships are likely to be viewed by others as problematic. He may be visibly uneasy around other people. He probably sits by himself in a group and dislikes participating in group activities.

Mental Health Considerations

The client's excessive anxiety and obsessive behavior should be taken into consideration in the final diagnosis. In addition, the possibility of a paranoid disorder or paranoid personality should be evaluated. His response content is consistent with the antisocial features in his history. These factors should be taken into consideration when arriving at a clinical diagnosis. His unusual thinking and bizarre ideas should be taken into consideration in any diagnostic formulation.

He has a number of personality characteristics that are associated with a substance use or abuse disorder. The client's scores on the addiction proneness indicators, along with the personality characteristics reflected in the profile, suggest that he resembles some individuals who develop addictive disorders. A substance abuse evaluation should explore this possibility through a careful review of his personality traits and typical behavior. In his responses to the MMPI-2, he acknowledged some problems with excessive use or abuse of addictive substances.

Inmates with this MMPI-2 clinical profile usually have severe psychological problems as well as some physical health concerns. This individual is feeling extremely vulnerable to outside threat at this time. Psychiatric treatment should focus on his tension and self-doubts. It may be appropriate to use medication to relieve his intense anxiety. The possibility that he has suspicious or paranoid ideas should be kept in mind when considering psychological rehabilitation options. He may have trouble forming a treatment relationship.

He is rigid and intellectualizes a great deal; therapeutic progress is likely to be slow. Individuals with this MMPI-2 clinical profile tend to have unrealistic expectations and perfectionistic beliefs that may require some challenging if their personal vulnerability is to be diminished. An approach such as rational-emotive therapy might enable him to acquire more self-acceptance. The client endorsed item content that seems to indicate low potential for change. He may feel that his problems are not addressable through therapy and that he is not likely to benefit much from psychological treatment at this time. His apparently negative treatment attitudes should be explored early in therapy if treatment is to be successful. His acknowledged problems with alcohol or drug use should be addressed in therapy.

(continued)

EXHIBIT 6.2 *(Continued)*

General Correctional Considerations

The symptoms or problems reported by the client should be carefully evaluated and may have an important bearing on his current situation. His present symptoms and outlook are likely to be important considerations in his case. Individuals who score high on the *Pt* scale, as he has, tend to feel overwhelmed by anxiety. They feel tense and agitated to the point that their discomfort, worry, and apprehension spill over into their daily activities and relationships. They are high-strung and "jumpy" people who have trouble concentrating. They often feel insecure, unable to deal effectively with their lives, and plagued by self-doubt. In fact, they are often seen by others as ruminative, indecisive, obsessive, and compulsive. They tend to be rigid in their thinking. They would probably have trouble following through on plans and taking effective, direct action to resolve problems. They also tend to intellectualize and rationalize problems, and they may be resistant to interpretations of their behavior. They tend to need and seek reassurance in anything they undertake.

In addition to the problems indicated by the client's MMPI-2 clinical scale scores, he endorsed some items on the content scales that could reflect difficulties for him. His numerous family problems should be taken into consideration in the evaluation. His proneness to experience anxiety, depression, obsessive thinking, and unusual thoughts might make it difficult for him to think clearly or function effectively. His low self-esteem probably characterizes a somewhat ineffective manner of approaching new tasks. His basic insecurity and lack of self-confidence might make it difficult for him to implement change-oriented plans. His anger-control problems are likely to interfere with his functioning in interpersonal relationships at this time. His antisocial attitudes and behavior are likely to make him vulnerable to further legal problems. He is likely to have substance abuse or use problems that could be a possible source of future problems.

(*L* [Lie] = 52; see Figure 6.3), although he tended to respond rather randomly (*VRIN* [Variable Response Inconsistency] = 80). Indeed, Raul commented on the length of the inventory, which may suggest that he was somewhat tired when he was nearly 75% finished. It is possible that being fatigued may have caused some carelessness, especially when responding to items phrased in double negatives (which were pointed out to him at the beginning of the inventory). Therefore, some of the elevation noted in the *F* (Infrequency = 89) scale may be accounted for by the randomness index. His score on *Fb* (Back F = 71), however, is lower than on *F*, indicating a more frequent endorsement of items reflective of unusual or disordered thinking than items reflective of panic or anxiety-related symptoms. Raul's score on *K* (Defensiveness = 43) is rather low, suggestive of the existence of fragile defenses.

Raul's clinical scales profile reveals multiple elevations (code type= 7648; see Figure 6.4). Because of the infrequent responding noted above, it is necessary to interpret this profile cautiously. Nevertheless, several elevations appear to capture accurately key aspects of Raul's functioning. Specifically, elevations on Scales 6 (*Pa*, Paranoia) and 7 (*Pt*, Psychasthenia) appear to be consistent with Raul's tendencies to be highly anxious, self-doubting, and self-critical in a somewhat covert manner. These characteristics are not

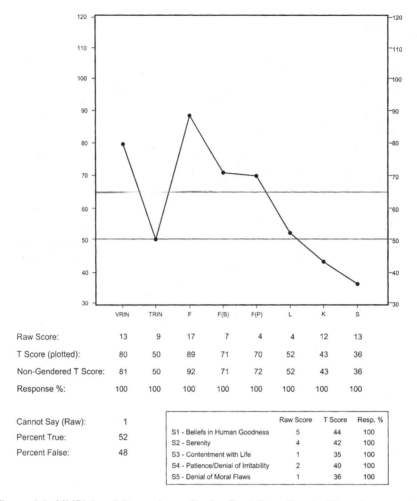

	VRIN	TRIN	F	F(B)	F(P)	L	K	S
Raw Score:	13	9	17	7	4	4	12	13
T Score (plotted):	80	50	89	71	70	52	43	36
Non-Gendered T Score:	81	50	92	71	72	52	43	36
Response %:	100	100	100	100	100	100	100	100

			Raw Score	T Score	Resp. %
Cannot Say (Raw):	1	S1 - Beliefs in Human Goodness	5	44	100
Percent True:	52	S2 - Serenity	4	42	100
Percent False:	48	S3 - Contentment with Life	1	35	100
		S4 - Patience/Denial of Irritability	2	40	100
		S5 - Denial of Moral Flaws	1	36	100

Figure 6.3. MMPI-2 validity scale profile for Raul T., a Puerto Rican incarcerated male being tested in a parental rights evaluation. The scales include *VRIN* (Variable Responding Inconsistency), *TRIN* (True Responding), *F* (Infrequency), *F(B)* (Infrequency Back), *F(P)* (Infrequency Psychopathology), *L* (Lie), *K* (Defensiveness), and *S* (Superlative Self-Presentation).

inconsistent with a general lack of trust and alienation from others, reflected in Scale 6, or with the experience of dysphoria and pessimism reflected in Scale 2 (*D*, Depression). His acknowledged impulsivity, anger, interpersonal difficulties, and involvement in illicit activities appear reflected by elevations in other clinical scales such as 4 (*Pd*, Psychopathic Deviate), 8 (*Sc*, Schizophrenia), 9 (*Ma*, Hypomania), and 0 (*Si*, Social Introversion).

Examination of the content scales profile also reveals multiple elevations, with the highest being on the *ANX* scale (see Figure 6.5). This appears consistent with the multiple worries he described in the interview as well as

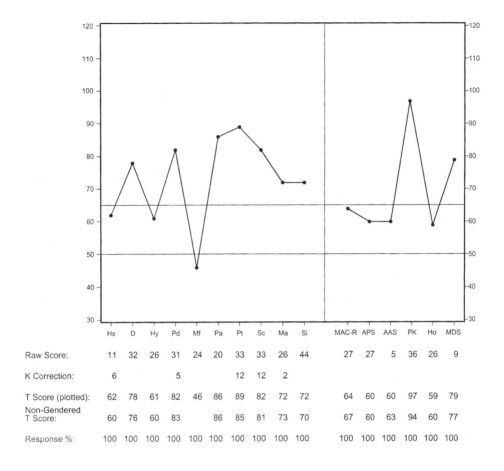

	Hs	D	Hy	Pd	Mf	Pa	Pt	Sc	Ma	Si		MAC-R	APS	AAS	PK	Ho	MDS
Raw Score:	11	32	26	31	24	20	33	33	26	44		27	27	5	36	26	9
K Correction:	6			5			12	12	2								
T Score (plotted):	62	78	61	82	46	86	89	82	72	72		64	60	60	97	59	79
Non-Gendered T Score:	60	76	60	83		86	85	81	73	70		67	60	63	94	60	77
Response %:	100	100	100	100	100	100	100	100	100	100		100	100	100	100	100	100

Welsh Code: 7648"290'+13-/5: F'''+-L/K:

Profile Elevation: 76.5

Figure 6.4. MMPI-2 clinical and supplementary scales profile for Raul T., a Puerto Rican incarcerated male being tested in a parental rights evaluation. The scales include *Hs* (Hypochondriasis), *D* (Depression), *Hy* (Hysteria), *Pd* (Psychopathic Deviation), *Mf* (Masculinity–Femininity), *Pa* (Paranoia), *Pt* (Psychasthenia), *Sc* (Schizophrenia), *Ma* (Hypomania), *Si* (Social Introversion), *MAC-R* (MacAndrew Alcoholism—Revised), *APS* (Addiction Potential), *AAS* (Addiction Acknowledgment), *PK* (Posttraumatic Stress Disorder), *Ho* (Hostility), and *MDS* (Marital Distress).

with the elevation in Scale 7 (*Pt*), described above. Among other significant elevations are those on the *DEP* (Depression), *ANG* (Anger), and *ASP* (Antisocial Practices) scales. Elevations on these scales are consistent with Raul's own description of his behavioral functioning (unresolved grief over the loss of his father, difficulties controlling anger, choosing to engage in illicit activities) and also with several of the elevations described in the clinical scales profile. The elevation on the *WRK* (Work Interference)

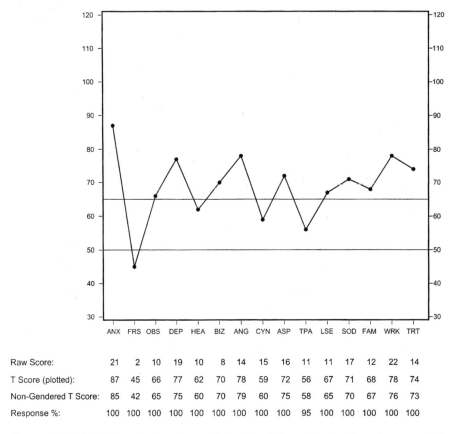

	ANX	FRS	OBS	DEP	HEA	BIZ	ANG	CYN	ASP	TPA	LSE	SOD	FAM	WRK	TRT
Raw Score:	21	2	10	19	10	8	14	15	16	11	11	17	12	22	14
T Score (plotted):	87	45	66	77	62	70	78	59	72	56	67	71	68	78	74
Non-Gendered T Score:	85	42	65	75	60	70	79	60	75	58	65	70	67	76	73
Response %:	100	100	100	100	100	100	100	100	100	95	100	100	100	100	100

Figure 6.5. MMPI-2 content scale profile for Raul T., a Puerto Rican incarcerated male being tested in a parental rights evaluation. See Figure 6.2 for scale definitions.

scale is also consistent with Raul's poor adjustment to various employment settings, especially because he acknowledged having difficulties accepting orders and feedback from coworkers and supervisors. Other elevations, such as on the *FAM* (Family Problems), *SOD* (Social Discomfort), and *LSE* (Low Self-Esteem) scales, appear to be highly consistent with his history and his generally poor interpersonal adjustment. Consistent with the elevation on Scale 7 (*Pt*), Raul's content profile reveals an elevation on the *OBS* (Obsessiveness) scale. This reflects what appears to be a covert struggle among feelings, ideas, and coping behaviors that Raul was engaged in. Of particular concern, however, is the elevation seen on the *TRT* scale, which indicates that despite his strong need for therapeutic intervention, Raul may have difficulties engaging in a productive therapy relationship because of his difficulties with interpersonal trust.

Finally, Raul's supplementary scales reveal that although at the time he took this test he did not endorse difficulties related to substance abuse, he acknowledged a high level of relationship distress, as indicated by the elevation on the MDS (Marital Distress = 77) scale.

CASE 3: JOB APPLICANT IN AN EMPLOYMENT SCREENING PROGRAM FOR A STATE HIGHWAY PATROL

Roberto C., age 28, applied for a position as a police officer for the state highway patrol in a midwestern state. Roberto was interviewed by the police department assessment psychologist a week following the group administration of the MMPI-2. He was administered the English language booklet version of the MMPI-2. The test was scored and interpreted on the U.S. norms and initially interpreted by the Minnesota Report, Personnel Setting (see the validity profile in Figure 6.6, clinical profile in Figure 6.7, and the content scale profile in Figure 6.8). The computer-derived Minnesota Report narrative report is shown in Exhibit 6.3.

Roberto was the second son of a Mexican immigrant family who came to the United States when he was 9 years old. His father migrated to the Midwest and found employment in an auto assembly plant. His family joined him after 6 years when he established residency status. Roberto's mother worked as a housekeeper for a motel chain. His parents were legally separated at the time this study was done following his mother's involvement with another man. Roberto's older brother became an active gang member and was in federal prison for drug-related offenses.

When Roberto began school in the United States, his low English language skills resulted in his placement in a grade lower (second grade) than his age level and school experience in Mexico warranted. Roberto received a suspension for 6 months when he was a junior in high school for fighting with other students at school.

Following high school, he attended a 2-year junior college program while working as a clerk in a large retail store. He received his associate of arts degree at age 24. Roberto began working full time as a security guard at a retail store after he completed his college program. However, this position was terminated after a disagreement with his supervisor after 3 months. Roberto was late for the job interview, complaining that he had been given the wrong time by the administrative assistant who set up appointments. (She later confirmed that he had been given the correct time.) He appeared to be somewhat frustrated and was initially hesitant in responding to questions that the psychologist asked about problematic behavior that he experienced in the past. For example, he showed visible irritation over questions into his past work relationships and the reasons for his dismissal from the security guard position 2 years ago. He was also

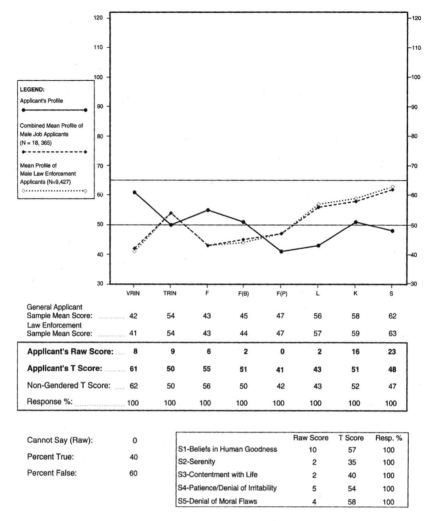

	VRIN	TRIN	F	F(B)	F(P)	L	K	S
General Applicant Sample Mean Score:	42	54	43	45	47	56	58	62
Law Enforcement Sample Mean Score:	41	54	43	44	47	57	59	63
Applicant's Raw Score:	8	9	6	2	0	2	16	23
Applicant's T Score:	61	50	55	51	41	43	51	48
Non-Gendered T Score:	62	50	56	50	42	43	52	47
Response %:	100	100	100	100	100	100	100	100

Cannot Say (Raw):	0
Percent True:	40
Percent False:	60

	Raw Score	T Score	Resp. %
S1-Beliefs in Human Goodness	10	57	100
S2-Serenity	2	35	100
S3-Contentment with Life	2	40	100
S4-Patience/Denial of Irritability	5	54	100
S5-Denial of Moral Flaws	4	58	100

Figure 6.6. MMPI-2 validity scale profile for Roberto C., a Mexican American police applicant in a preemployment setting. See Figure 6.3 for scale definitions.

blunt in his response to questions regarding the problems he experienced in high school when he was suspended for 6 months.

The assessment psychologist, on the basis of the psychological testing and background information from the background check, recommended against offering the applicant a permanent position on the police force. Both his personality testing and his personal history suggested that he had serious interpersonal problems that would likely affect his work performance as a police officer.

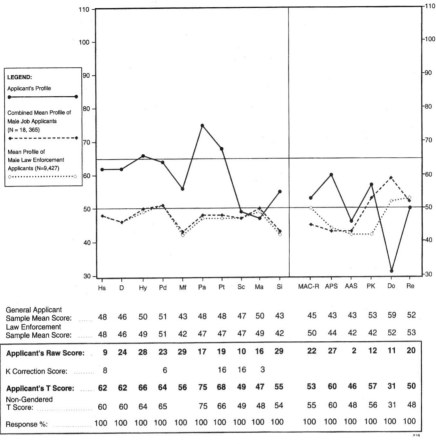

	Hs	D	Hy	Pd	Mf	Pa	Pt	Sc	Ma	Si	MAC-R	APS	AAS	PK	Do	Re
General Applicant Sample Mean Score:	48	46	50	51	43	48	48	47	50	43	45	43	43	53	59	52
Law Enforcement Sample Mean Score:	48	46	49	51	42	47	47	47	49	42	50	44	42	42	52	53
Applicant's Raw Score:	9	24	28	23	29	17	19	10	16	29	22	27	2	12	11	20
K Correction Score:	8			6			16	16	3							
Applicant's T Score:	62	62	66	64	56	75	68	49	47	55	53	60	46	57	31	50
Non-Gendered T Score:	60	60	64	65		75	66	49	48	54	55	60	48	56	31	48
Response %:	100	100	100	100	100	100	100	100	100	100	100	100	100	100	100	100

Welsh Code: 6'73+412-50/89: FK/L:

Profile Elevation: 61.6

Figure 6.7. MMPI-2 clinical and supplementary scales profile for Roberto C., a Mexican American police applicant in a preemployment setting. See Figure 6.4 for scale definitions.

CASE 4: PSYCHIATRIC PATIENT IN MEXICO

This case is presented to illustrate the use of the MMPI-2 with a mental health client in Mexico and to provide an illustration of how the Mexican norms and the U.S. norms of the MMPI-2 profiles compare. The client was a woman who had several depressive episodes and was evaluated with the MMPI-2 in a private treatment context. She was being seen by a psychiatrist in Mexico City. The MMPI-2 profiles that are presented are scored and graphed against both the Mexican and U.S. norms.

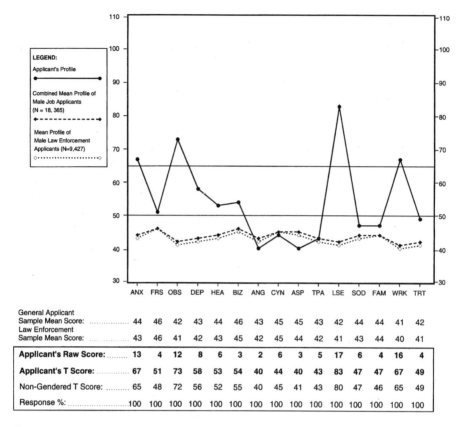

	ANX	FRS	OBS	DEP	HEA	BIZ	ANG	CYN	ASP	TPA	LSE	SOD	FAM	WRK	TRT
General Applicant Sample Mean Score:	44	46	42	43	44	46	43	45	45	43	42	44	44	41	42
Law Enforcement Sample Mean Score:	43	46	41	42	43	45	42	45	44	42	41	43	44	40	41
Applicant's Raw Score:	13	4	12	8	6	3	2	6	3	5	17	6	4	16	4
Applicant's T Score:	67	51	73	58	53	54	40	44	40	43	83	47	47	67	49
Non-Gendered T Score:	65	48	72	56	52	55	40	45	41	43	80	47	46	65	49
Response %:	100	100	100	100	100	100	100	100	100	100	100	100	100	100	100

Figure 6.8. MMPI-2 content scale profile for Roberto C., a Mexican American police applicant in a preemployment setting. See Figure 6.2 for scale definitions.

Ana A., a 35-year-old architect, experienced a depressive episode several months before testing during which she attempted suicide. She consumed alcohol with Rivotril because she was feeling very depressed and did not want to live any longer. As a result of this attempt, she was committed to a psychiatric hospital for 2 weeks.

Ana was married and had one child. She had been doing well at her work, but her job setting became conflict ridden because she felt that many people there were jealous of her. She had a conflict with her supervisor and, as result, had been fired 2 months before. When her problems at work intensified, she began abusing alcohol more. After being fired, she attempted to commit suicide. This was the third depressive episode Ana had experienced; the first one was when she was 16 years old and was in high school.

Her childhood was problematic. During her infancy, her family situation was difficult because her father was violent. She often felt rejected at school because of the darker color of her skin and also because her family

This applicant's approach to the MMPI-2 was open and cooperative. This suggests that he appears to be able to follow instructions and to respond appropriately to the task. This may be viewed as a positive indication of his involvement with the evaluation.

Personal Adjustment

This applicant is sensitive to criticism and overreacts to minor problems with anger or hostility. He may be suspicious, and he may feel that he has to constantly protect himself against perceived threats from others. Individuals with this profile are frequently argumentative and tend to blame others for their problems. In addition, the following description is suggested by the content of this applicant's responses. At times, he may seem naive in relationships. His denial of negative impulses and his espousal of high moral standards probably influence his attitudes toward others. He endorsed a number of attitudes that reflect low self-esteem and long-standing beliefs about being inadequate. His current thinking is likely to be characterized by obsessiveness and indecision. He has endorsed items indicating that he is experiencing some symptoms or that he believes that he is impaired in his capacity to work at this time.

Interpersonal Relations

Intractable and aloof in social relationships, the client appears to not fully trust other people and is critical of them. He tends to be hostile and to harbor grudges for long periods of time.

Profile Frequency

Profile interpretation can be greatly facilitated by examining the relative frequency of clinical scale patterns in various settings. An elevated score on the *Pa* scale occurred in 9.6% of the MMPI-2 normative sample of men (*N* = 1,138). Only 3.16% of the normative sample of men obtained clinical scale spikes on *Pa* above a T score of 65. This elevated MMPI-2 pattern (6-7/7-6) is very rare, occurring in less than 1% of the MMPI-2 normative sample of men. This profile pattern and scale elevation were obtained by about 1% of the men in the law enforcement database (Pearson Assessments–National Computer Systems, 1994).

Contemporary Personnel Base Rate Information

Additional up-to-date profile frequency information is available to serve as a basis for interpreting law enforcement applicants' profiles. The relative frequency of this profile in various personnel settings is useful information for clinical interpretation because highly elevated *Pa* patterns can suggest possible negative interpersonal factors in police officers. The relative frequency of this MMPI-2 high-point *Pa* score is 8.0% in job applicants in the large NCS Assessments (Butcher et al., 2000) applicant sample (*N* = 18,365 males) regardless of elevation. This high-point clinical scale score (*Pa*) occurs in 4.7% of the men with this high-point scale spike at or above a T score of 65 and as a well-defined peak. In a specific law enforcement personnel sample (*N* = 9,427 men), male applicants produced a *Pa* high-point score with a frequency of 8%. As in other studies of elevated profile types, 4.1% of male applicants had well-defined high-point *Pa* spikes at or above a T score of 65. This elevated MMPI-2 pattern (6-7/7-6) is found in 1.7% of the men in the NCS Assessments (Butcher et al., 2000) combined personnel sample (*N* = 18,365 men) regardless of elevation; only 0.3% had this as a well-defined score at or above a T of 65. Less than 1.5% of men applying for law enforcement positions (*N* = 9,427 males) had this code as a high point, regardless of elevation. However, only 0.2% of the cases showed this pattern as a well-defined and elevated 6-7/7-6 code type.

(continued)

EXHIBIT 6.3   *(Continued)*

Profile Stability

The relative elevation of the highest scales in the client's clinical profile reflects high profile definition. If he is retested at a later date, his peak scores are likely to retain their relative salience. His high-point score on *Pa* is likely to show moderate test–retest stability. Short-term test–retest studies have shown a correlation of .67 for this high-point score. Spiro, Butcher, Levenson, Aldwin, and Bosse (1993) reported a moderate test–retest stability of .55 in a large study of normals over a 5-year test–retest period. Individuals with this profile tend not to change much over time. They are inflexible. When they feel threatened, their suspicious behavior and mistrust are likely to increase.

Possible Employment Problems

Law enforcement applicants with this MMPI-2 profile may have some personality problems that interfere with work and social relationships. They may find it somewhat difficult to approach tasks with an open mind. Individuals with this pattern tend to have problems with their anger and with maintaining their self-control. They often feel threatened and blame others for their problems. Overly critical and hostile relationships are likely, particularly if they feel threatened. They may withdraw from other employees because they are unable to trust other people.

---

had a lower status than that of her classmates. She fell in love when she was 16, and when her boyfriend went to work in Canada, she cried all day and dropped out of school for a time. She also gained 20 pounds because she ate compulsively. That was the first time she was treated by a psychiatrist. She had another depressive episode when she was 20 and went to a psychiatrist again, who placed her on antidepressant medications.

When Ana was 23, she met her future husband, and she became pregnant before they married. She reported that the first 2 years of their marriage were pleasant and quiet. However, later she obtained a time-consuming job and earned more than her husband, who did not like this fact.

Ana was administered the MMPI-2 because her psychiatrist wanted to have more data to guide her therapy. Figure 6.9 shows her performance plotted against both the Mexican and U.S. norms. Her profile should be interpreted with caution because she left 10 items unanswered and also produced an elevated *F* scale, suggesting some symptom exaggeration. The profiles suggest that she may have distorted her image or exaggerated the severity of psychopathology in an attempt to gain attention for her problems. Her MMPI-2 profile, whether plotted on Mexican or U.S. norms, is consistent with those of people who have severe psychopathology as shown in an elevated *F* scale, a common elevation among psychiatric inpatients.

A review of Ana's MMPI-2 profile indicates that she obtained clinically significant elevations (scores > 65 T) on the following scales: *Pd, Pa, Sc, Ma,* and *D.* This client is admitting personal and emotional problems, is

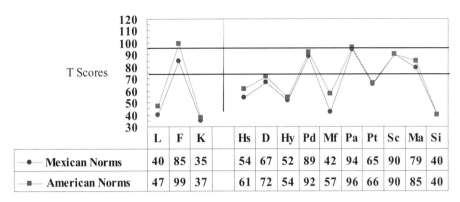

	L	F	K		Hs	D	Hy	Pd	Mf	Pa	Pt	Sc	Ma	Si
— •— Mexican Norms	40	85	35		54	67	52	89	42	94	65	90	79	40
— ■— American Norms	47	99	37		61	72	54	92	57	96	66	90	85	40

Figure 6.9. MMPI-2 validity and clinical scales profile for Ana A., a Mexican psychiatric patient. See Figure 6.1 for scale definitions.

requesting help with her problems, and is unsure of her own resources for dealing with them.

In addition, she is likely to have a relatively poor self-concept, as shown by the elevations on Scales 2 (*D*, Depression) and 8 (*Sc*, Schizophrenia) in Figure 6.9. She appears to be strongly dissatisfied with herself, lacks the skills necessary to change her situation, and is highly self-critical. Ana shows a lack of insight into her motivation and behavior and shows ineffectiveness in dealing with the problems of daily life. She is experiencing a moderate level of emotional distress that is characterized by brooding, anger, resentment, agitation, and perhaps anhedonia (as reflected in the *Sc* scale). She has difficulty controlling or expressing her emotions, as shown by her high *Pa* score, and she is also experiencing a great deal of anger (see the *Pd* scale and the *ANG* content scale). In response to stress, she is likely either to withdraw completely or to act out her angry impulses. She feels insecure, isolated, rejected, and unwanted. She is threatened by a world that she views as hostile and dangerous. Although until recently she was professionally successful, at present she finds it difficult to get things done and has little hope of being successful even if something could motivate her. She always works under a great deal of stress and tension (see Figures 6.10 and 6.11).

Ana exhibits poor judgment and often is unpredictable and impulsive as reflected in her high scores on *Pd* and *Sc*. She is suspicious of the motives of others and is sure that she is being talked about. She believes that she would have been more successful if someone "had not had it in for her." She believes that people say insulting and vulgar things about her and may be plotting against her. She thinks and dreams about things that she knows are best kept to herself. She is worried that there is something wrong with her mind and she reports a number of personality disorder symptoms that

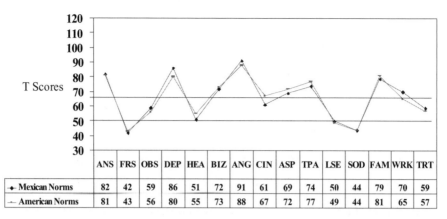

	ANS	FRS	OBS	DEP	HEA	BIZ	ANG	CIN	ASP	TPA	LSE	SOD	FAM	WRK	TRT
Mexican Norms	82	42	59	86	51	72	91	61	69	74	50	44	79	70	59
American Norms	81	43	56	80	55	73	88	67	72	77	49	44	81	65	57

Figure 6.10. MMPI-2 content scale profile for Ana A., a Mexican psychiatric patient. See Figure 6.2 for scale definitions.

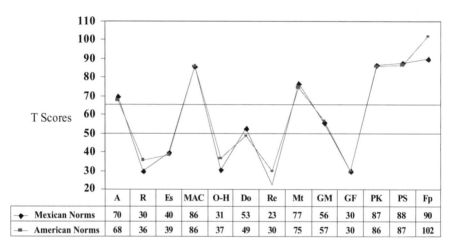

	A	R	Es	MAC	O-H	Do	Re	Mt	GM	GF	PK	PS	Fp
Mexican Norms	70	30	40	86	31	53	23	77	56	30	87	88	90
American Norms	68	36	39	86	37	49	30	75	57	30	86	87	102

Figure 6.11. MMPI-2 supplementary scale profile for Ana A., a Mexican psychiatric patient. The scales include *A* (Anxiety), *R* (Repression), *Es* (Ego Strength), *Mac* (MacAndrew Alcoholism—Revised), *O-H* (Overcontrolled Hostility), *Do* (Dominance), *Re* (Social Responsibility), *Mt* (College Maladjustment), *GM* (Gender Role Masculine), *GF* (Gender Role Feminine), *PK* (Posttraumatic Stress Disorder), *PS* (Psychoticism), *Fp* (Infrequency–Psychopathology).

may reflect long-term, characterological problems (see the elevation on the *Pd* scale in Figure 6.9).

Ana's interpersonal relations are marked by conflict, distress, defensiveness, and a lack of empathy. She has difficulty with close, emotional relationships. She sees the world as dangerous and other people as rejecting and unreliable. Her tendency to feel rejected by others often leads to hostility and conflict, which only exacerbates her feelings of being alienated. She sees her family as extremely uncaring and critical and her home life as very unpleasant (see her elevation on FAM in Figure 6.10). She believes that no one understands her and her way of doing things.

She is likely to have suicidal ideation, which should be evaluated carefully. She is isolated, feels hopeless, and is prone to act out impulsively toward herself or others, increasing the potential for suicide. She is likely to abuse substances, which also increases the probability of her acting out (see the elevation on MAC [MacAndrew Alcoholism—Revised] in Figure 6.11). Her previous suicide attempts were related to substance abuse. Her problems sometimes involve inappropriate sexual behavior.

She remains at risk for suicide because she is very depressed, anxious, and wants to evade her responsibilities and problems. Her prognosis is generally poor and psychopharmacologic interventions are unlikely to be effective because of the long-term characterological nature of her problems. Her difficulties in forming emotional relationships and her reluctance to self-disclose make the establishment of a therapeutic alliance problematic at best. Any form of insight-oriented therapy is contraindicated at this time. Short-term, behavioral interventions that are presented in a direct and explicit manner might be effective.

An examination of the profiles plotted on both the Mexican and U.S. norms provide the practitioner with a great deal of confidence that the MMPI-2 is working well at describing the client's problem situation regardless of which set of norms is used to typify her problems.

7

ASSESSING HISPANIC ADOLESCENTS WITH THE MMPI-A

Normal developmental processes during adolescence can be challenging at times even for well-adjusted adolescents. These developmental years are often burdened with high risk for emergence of psychological problems. The stress of adolescence is even more difficult for those who are required to adjust to new environmental demands of a different language and culture, as many Hispanic adolescents living and attending schools in the United States face.

Adolescents who are undergoing severe stress or experiencing mental health problems can pose difficult issues for practitioners. The clinician must be able to determine whether symptoms shown by adolescent clients indicate underlying personality or mental health problems or are a function of normal stressful developmental circumstances. To obtain a clear picture of the symptomatic pattern being assessed, it is usually important for the clinician to evaluate the adolescent from a normative perspective by comparing their attitudes and symptoms with those reported by a broad, representative sample of nontroubled adolescents. Psychological assessments need to determine if troubled adolescents are experiencing problems that are different from those of other adolescents.

The use of an objective personality assessment instrument, like the MMPI–Adolescent (MMPI-A) that can assess adolescent problems and behavior across cultural boundaries, provides a unique perspective on personality adjustment and can make an important difference in multicultural assessment. This chapter addresses the application of the MMPI-A with Hispanic adolescents. We provide an overview of the Spanish version of the MMPI-A developed for the United States as well as the Spanish version of the test developed and standardized in Mexico. Chapter 8 is devoted to providing a number of cases to illustrate the use of the MMPI-A with adolescents.

DEVELOPMENT OF THE MMPI-A

The original MMPI was used with adolescents in a broad range of settings, beginning with the initial work of Dora Capwell with adolescent girls in 1945 (Capwell, 1945). Applications included assessment in mental health settings (Archer & Gordon, 1988), medical problem populations (Colligan & Osborne, 1977), alcohol and drug treatment programs (Brook, Kaplun, & Whitehead, 1974; Burke & Eichberg, 1972; Fitzgibbons, Berry, & Shearn, 1973), and correctional or juvenile delinquency programs (Genshaft, 1980; Green & Kelley, 1988; Gregory, 1974; Hathaway & Monachesi, 1951, 1952, 1957, 1961, 1963; Lindgren, Harper, Richman, & Stehbens, 1986; Lueger & Hoover, 1984; Smith, Monastersky, & Deisher, 1987).

Although the original MMPI became the most widely used personality inventory for assessing adolescents in mental health and correctional settings in the 1960s and 1970s, there were some clear limitations with its use. One of the main limiting factors was that the item pool of the original MMPI (Hathaway & McKinley, 1940) was constructed to assess adults; adolescent problems and behaviors were not addressed. Moreover, the interpretation of adolescent MMPI scores was always somewhat difficult because of the lack of an appropriate reference or normative group with which to compare clients' profiles—that is, the lack of specific adolescent age-appropriate norms (Archer, 1992; Butcher & Williams, 1992).

During the 1980s, an extensive program of research was directed toward developing an MMPI-based instrument for adolescents to remedy these measurement problems. This work resulted in publication of the MMPI-A in 1992 (Butcher et al., 1992). The revision project to develop the MMPI-A included several major elements: eliminating items from the original test that were obsolete or otherwise inappropriate for adolescents and expanding the pool to include new items containing content specifically relevant to the problems of adolescents. Moreover, prior research on the original MMPI with adolescents had not produced a sufficient number of specific adolescent psychopathology measures to address the problems that young people experience. Therefore, a major goal of the MMPI-A project was to develop a number of scales specific to adolescent problems (Butcher & Williams, 2000). Perhaps the most serious limitation of using the original MMPI with adolescents was the lack of specific appropriate norms that were representative of adolescents in the United States (Archer, 1992; Butcher & Williams, 1992). Thus a more extensive, broad-based reference sample was needed.

The original MMPI validity and clinical scales were retained for the revised versions of the test, the MMPI-2 and MMPI-A, to assure continuity with the MMPI-2 and the original instrument: L (Lie), K (Defensiveness), F (Infrequency), 1 (Hs, Hypochondriasis), 2 (D, Depression), 3 (Hy, Hysteria), 4 (Pd, Psychopathic Deviate), 5 (Mf, Masculinity–Femininity), 6 (Pa, Paranoia), 7 (Pt, Psychasthenia), 8 (Sc, Schizophrenia), 9 (Ma, Hypomania), and 0 (Si, Social Introversion). In addition, several scales developed for the MMPI-2 were adapted for the MMPI-A: $TRIN$ (True Response Inconsistency) and $VRIN$ (Variable Response Inconsistency). With respect to the F scale, the items incorporated in MMPI-A were somewhat different from the original version of the test. Items were selected for the infrequency measures that were endorsed by no more than 20% of the MMPI-A normative sample. Another feature in the assessment of infrequency with MMPI-A was that the F scale was divided into two subscales, $F1$ and $F2$, covering the first and second halves of the test booklet, to assess the relative infrequent responding to both the beginning and the end of the booklet. (Fuller discussion of the MMPI-A can be found in Archer, 2005, and Butcher and Williams, 2000; see also Exhibit 7.1 for a description of the MMPI-A validity and clinical scales.)

In addition to the traditional scales, a new set of content-based measures was developed for MMPI-A, the content scales, to address specifically adolescent problem areas, incorporating problem areas that had been absent from the original adult-oriented MMPI (Williams, Butcher, Ben-Porath, & Graham, 1992). See Exhibit 7.2 for a description of the MMPI-A content scales. These scales were derived according to a rational–empirical scale construction strategy to provide several measures of problems that are specific to adolescents.

The development of a specific normative sample for the MMPI-A was an important step in establishing the adolescent version of the test as an assessment standard. The collection of data on a substantial and nationally based sample of adolescents provided an appropriate reference population for the test. This was considered to be crucial because of important ways in which adolescents differed from adults in their response to personality test items (Butcher & Williams, 1992; Colligan & Offord, 1992). The normative group sample included 1,620 adolescents ages 14 to 18 years old, approximately 76% White, 12% Black, 3% Asian American, 3% Native American, and 2% Hispanic (Butcher et al., 1992). The normative study of the MMPI-A was developed on the English language version of the test;

EXHIBIT 7.1
MMPI-A Validity Indicators and Clinical Scales Validity Indicators

VRIN (Variable Response Inconsistency). As with the MMPI-2, the *VRIN* scale on MMPI-A was developed to identify response inconsistency. *VRIN* consists of specially selected pairs of items. The members of each *VRIN* item pair have either similar or opposite content; each pair is scored for the occurrence of an inconsistency in the responses to the two items. The raw score on the *VRIN* scale is the total number of item pairs answered inconsistently. A high *VRIN* score suggests that the adolescent may have answered the items in the inventory in an indiscriminate manner and raises the possibility that the protocol is invalid and that the profile is essentially uninterpretable. *VRIN* scores greater than 90 suggest random responding.

TRIN (True Response Inconsistency). The *TRIN* scale is comprised of pairs that are opposite in content. Inconsistency is scored as follows: If a participant responds inconsistently by answering True to both items of certain pairs, one point is added to the *TRIN* score; if the participant responds inconsistently by answering False to certain item pairs, one point is subtracted. A very high *TRIN* raw score indicates a tendency for the person to indiscriminately give an "acquiescent" or "nonacquiescent" response set.

Some tendency for Hispanic adolescents to respond in an inconsistent manner on *TRIN* has been noted. The interpreter should be alert to the possibility that the Hispanic adolescent's *TRIN* score might be somewhat more elevated than other adolescents and take this into consideration in the interpretation.

F, F1, and F2 (Infrequency). The *F* scale of the MMPI-A was developed to detect whether clients are presenting in an exaggerated manner, that is, possibly presenting themselves in a bad light or "faking bad." Several factors may contribute to high *F* scores, including symptom exaggeration, the presence of severe maladjustment, or carelessly or inconsistently responding. The MMPI-A *F* scale is divided into a 33-item *F1* scale and a 33-item *F2* scale. The *F1* and *F2* scales can be used to detect whether the client has exaggerated symptom endorsement in the front or end of the booklet. A comparison of T scores on the *F1* and *F2* scales makes it possible to identify an adolescent who, for example, may not have paid careful attention at the end of the booklet and may have changed her or his test-taking approach in the later stages of the test session.

L (Lie). The MMPI-A *L* scale consists of 14 items (1 item was deleted from the original *L* scale because the content was developmentally inappropriate for adolescents). The *L* scale was developed to detect naïve attempts by adolescents to place themselves in a favorable light, particularly regarding personal ethics or social behavior. Adolescents with high *L* scores were thought to be answering the MMPI-A items in ways that appeared to deny relatively minor flaws or weaknesses, to be fairly naïve, and to claim excessive virtue.

Some Hispanic studies have found higher *L* responding when compared with studies on non-Hispanics. In interpreting adolescent profiles, be aware of this possibility of obtaining a somewhat higher *L* score and allow a higher score (e.g., a T of 70) before considering invalidity.

K (Defensiveness). The *K* scale of the MMPI-A addresses test defensiveness. The scale is identical to the MMPI-2 *K* scale. Similar to the *L* scale, the *K* identifies individuals who respond defensively and without candor. The *K* scale can be used as a basic validity indicator in the MMPI-A suggesting the possibility of a defensive test-taking attitude.

Scale 1 (Hs, Hypochondriasis). Scale 1 of the MMPI-A contains 32 items (1 item was dropped from the original Scale 1 because of objectionable content). The *Hs* scale is a homogeneous scale containing items that reflect a preoccupation with health and illness and a variety of physical complaints, some vague and some highly specific. It is important to rule out the possibility of actual disorders in interpreting

(continued)

EXHIBIT 7.1 *(Continued)*

elevations on this MMPI-A measure. For example, moderate elevations (T scores = 60–64) can occur in adolescents with chronic illnesses. The higher the Scale 1 elevation, however, the more likely the problems are psychological in origin.

Scale 2 (D, Depression). The MMPI-A *D* scale consists of 57 items (compared with 60 on MMPI-2). Some items were eliminated because they contained objectionable content. This scale contains items that deal with general dissatisfaction with one's life, feelings of discouragement, hopelessness, and low morale. High scorers acknowledge feeling despondent and apathetic and being overly sensitive. They tend to endorse having physical problems and complaints, including psychomotor retardation. High-scoring adolescents report feeling guilty, ashamed, self-critical, and introspective. Social withdrawal and limited friendships are characteristic of high scorers.

Scale 3 (Hy, Hysteria). The MMPI-A *Hy* scale consists of items devised to identify individuals who respond to stress with hysterical reactions that include sensory or motor disorders without an organic basis. High-scoring adolescents tend to express anxiety or stress through somatization and vague physical symptoms.

Scale 4 (Pd, Psychopathic Deviate). This MMPI-A *Pd* scale was developed on the basis of responses of young women and men with patterns of lying, stealing, sexual promiscuity, and alcohol abuse. On the original MMPI, adolescents produced higher mean raw scores on this scale compared with adults. Scale 4 was the most frequent high point in code types in clinical adolescent groups. The items on the scale address familial discord, authority problems, social imperturbability, social alienation, and self-alienation. Elevations on the scale are associated with numerous behavior problems. High-scoring adolescents are more likely to be involved with the use of alcohol or other drugs. In addition, elevations on Scale 4 are related to lying, cheating, stealing, temper outbursts, and aggression.

Scale 5 (Mf, Masculinity–Femininity). The MMPI-A *Mf* scale addresses gender role attitudes and behavior. The *Mf* scale is not a measure of psychopathology but an interest scale. It is largely a measure of the masculinity or femininity of interests, with elevations in boys or men indicating interests that are more feminine than those of the average man. Similarly, elevations in girls and women were thought to indicate masculine interests.

Among boys, extreme elevations on *Mf* (i.e., T > 80) suggest endorsement of an unusual pattern of stereotypically feminine interests. Among girls, high elevations suggest unusual stereotypically masculine or "macho" interests. Hispanic boys, in some samples, have been found to have higher *Mf* scores than Anglo boys. One should be cautious in interpreting elevations on this scale as suggesting psychopathological characteristics.

Scale 6 (Pa, Paranoia). The MMPI-A *Pa* scale consists of 40 items that were initially selected to identify clients manifesting paranoid symptomatology. The items include content related to ideas of reference, suspiciousness, and feelings of persecution, rigidity, and moral self-righteousness. Moderate elevations among normal adolescents have been associated with oversensitivity to the remarks and inferred attitudes of others. High-point *Pa* elevations (T > 65) are associated with school dropout and personality features of distrust, suspiciousness, and, in extreme elevations, delusions of persecution or paranoia. High elevations on the scale appear to be associated with aggressive acting-out and argumentative behavior.

Scale 7 (Pt, Psychasthenia). The *Pt* scale is generally viewed as a measure of anxiety and general maladjustment. The content of this scale covers a wide variety of symptomatology, including physical complaints, unhappiness, problems in concentration, obsessive thoughts, anxiety, and feelings of inferiority. High-scoring adolescents show limited self-confidence and often make suicidal threats. Scale elevations are also associated with depression, low morale, and increasing discord with parents.

(continued)

EXHIBIT 7.1 *(Continued)*

Scale 8 (Sc, Schizophrenia). The items on the *Sc* scale were selected to identify clients with diagnoses of various forms of schizophrenia. The content areas include such characteristics as bizarre thought processes, peculiar perceptions, social isolation, disturbances in mood and behavior, and difficulties in concentration, impulse control, and defective inhibition. High-scoring adolescents have been described as mistrustful, vulnerable to stress, withdrawn, and interpersonally isolated. In addition, they often present with problems that more often included impaired reality testing. This scale has been associated with a number of problem behaviors and negative life outcomes. Boys with higher *Sc* scores reportedly had numerous severe problems such as somatic complaints, behavior problems, internalizing, schizoid behavior, psychotic symptoms, low self-esteem, and a possible history of sexual abuse. Clinical records for girls have noted a history of sexual abuse and an increase in disagreements with their parents.

Scale 9 (Ma, Hypomania). The *Ma* scale assesses personality characteristics such as impulsivity, overactivity, and extroverted personality characteristics. High elevations can suggest grandiosity, irritability, flight of ideas, egocentricity, elevated mood, and cognitive and behavioral overactivity. Research has suggested that this scale in adolescents was related to enthusiasm and energy. However, an abnormally high activity level could lead to antisocial acts or irrational manic behavior. Adolescents with elevations on *Ma* become restless and stir up excitement for enjoyment. Scale elevations for girls have been associated with problems both in school and at home, for example, academic underachievement.

Scale 0 (Si, Social Introversion). The MMPI-A *Si* scale contains items dealing with social relationship problems. Elevated scores are associated with social withdrawal and low self-esteem. High scorers are likely to be described as withdrawn, timid, shy, physically weak, uncoordinated, fearful, and depressed. High elevations reflect inhibitory characteristics. Adolescents with high *Si* scores are unlikely to participate in school activities. Low scores on *Si* are often informative as well. Scores below a T of 40 suggest extroversive personality characteristics, including high energy, outgoing personality features, and sociable.

---

however, the final MMPI-A sample was underrepresentative of Hispanic adolescents in the general population (Archer, 1992).

The psychometric characteristics of MMPI-A scales are comparable to those reported for MMPI-2 scales. For example, test–retest coefficients, alpha coefficients, and internal consistency coefficients were of magnitudes comparable to those of the MMPI-2 measures (Butcher et al., 1992). In addition, test–retest stability for basic scale scores in a subgroup of the normative sample ranged from .49 for the *F1* scale to .84 for Scale 0 after a 1-week retest interval (Butcher et al., 1992). Research on the external validity of the MMPI-A indicated that the test predicts the personality and behavior of adolescents with accuracy (see Archer, 2005; Ben-Porath & Davis, 1996; Butcher & Williams, 2000). Research from a number of settings, for example, has provided external validation of the MMPI-A scales (Archer, Bollnskey, Morton, & Farris, 2003; Arita & Baer, 1998; Cashel, Ovaert, & Holliman, 2000; Cumella, Wall, & Kerr-Almeida, 1999; Forbey & Ben-Porath, 2003; Gallucci, 1997; Glaser, Calhoun, & Petrocelli, 2002; Kopper,

EXHIBIT 7.2
Description of the MMPI-A Content Scales

A-anx (Adolescent–Anxiety). Adolescents who score high on *A-anx* acknowledge symptoms of anxiety, including tension, frequent worrying, and sleeping difficulties (e.g., nightmares, disturbed sleep, and difficulty falling asleep). They report feeling confused and having problems with concentration. They show an inability to stay on task and have difficulties completing requirements. High scorers tend to have concerns over losing their minds and feel as though something dreadful is about to happen to them. This scale appears to be measuring general maladjustment as well as assessing symptoms such as depression and somatic complaints.

A-obs (Adolescent–Obsessiveness). High scorers on *A-obs* report unreasonable worrying, often about trivial matters. They report having ruminative thoughts about "bad words" or unimportant items. At times they are unable to sleep because of their ruminations. They also report difficulty making decisions and dread having to make changes in their lives. They acknowledge that others tend to lose patience with them. They often regret things they have said or done.

A-dep (Adolescent–Depression). Adolescents scoring high on the *A-dep* scale acknowledge many symptoms of depression. They report frequent crying spells and problems with fatigue. They feel they are not as happy as other people are, and they are dissatisfied with their lives. They report numerous self-deprecatory thoughts, such as that they have not lived the right kind of life. They feel useless much of the time. They may feel as though they are condemned and their sins are unpardonable. They feel that life is not worthwhile or interesting. Much of the time they wish they were dead. They tend to have suicidal thinking and feel lonely a lot, even when they are with other people. Their future seems too uncertain for them to make serious plans. They have a sense of hopelessness.

A-hea (Adolescent–Health Concerns). Those who score high on *A-hea* acknowledge having numerous physical problems that interfere with their enjoyment of life. These physical complaints tend to interfere with their school, and they report numerous absences. Their physical symptoms typically occur across several body systems, such as gastrointestinal problems (e.g., constipation, nausea and vomiting, stomach trouble), neurological problems (e.g., numbness, convulsions, fainting and dizzy spells, paralysis), sensory problems (e.g., hearing difficulty, poor eyesight), cardiovascular symptoms (e.g., heart or chest pain), skin problems, pain (e.g., headaches, neck pain), and respiratory problems. High-scoring adolescents report worrying about their health a great deal.

A-aln (Adolescent–Alienation). Adolescents who score high on *A-aln* are acknowledging great emotional distance from others. They feel as though they are getting a raw deal from life and that no one cares about or understands them. They feel that no one likes them, and they do not get along with others. They often feel as though others are out to get them and are unkind to them. They complain that they do not have as much fun as other adolescents and report that they would prefer living all alone in a cabin in the woods. They have difficulty self-disclosing and report feeling awkward when they have to talk in a group. They also feel that other people often block their attempts at success.

A-biz (Adolescent–Bizarre Mentation). Adolescents who score high on *A-biz* scale admit to having strange thoughts and experiences, which might include auditory, visual, and olfactory hallucinations. They describe their experiences as strange and unusual, and they may report that there is something wrong with their minds. Paranoid thoughts may also be reported. They may report that other people are trying to steal their thoughts and ideas; some high scorers believe that other people control their minds. They may believe that evil spirits or ghosts possess or influence them. Adolescents with higher scores on this scale tend to have problems in school and to receive low marks.

(continued)

EXHIBIT 7.2   *(Continued)*

A-ang (Adolescent–Anger). Adolescents who score high on this scale report having anger-control problems. They frequently feel like swearing, smashing things, or starting a fight with someone. They sometimes get into trouble for impulsive behavior, such as breaking or destroying things. They tend to have problems with irritability and impatience with others. Temper tantrums are common with adolescents who score high on *A-ang.* They tend to be very hotheaded and often feel that they have to yell. They tend to get into fights, particularly if they have been drinking.

A-cyn (Adolescent–Cynicism). Cynical and misanthropic attitudes are assessed by the *A-cyn* scale. High scorers believe that others are out to get them and will use unfair means to gain an advantage over them. They typically look for hidden motives whenever someone does something nice for them. They tend to believe that it is safer to trust nobody because people only make friends in order to use them. High-scoring adolescents are on guard when people seem friendlier than they expect. They usually feel misunderstood by others, and they think other people are very jealous of them.

A-con (Adolescent–Conduct Problems). The *A-con* scale assesses behavior problems such as stealing, shoplifting, lying, breaking or destroying things, being disrespectful, swearing, and being oppositional toward others. Adolescents with this scale elevated often belong to a peer group that is in trouble. High-scoring adolescents also try to make other people afraid of them. They often admit to doing bad things in the past that they cannot tell anybody about.

A-lse (Adolescent–Low Self-Esteem). Adolescents who score high on the *A-lse* scale acknowledge having negative opinions of themselves and their abilities. They often feel unattractive and useless. They lack self-confidence and feel that they are unable to do anything well. They are likely to be passive and yield to others in disputes. They allow other people to take charge when problems have to be solved. They report that they feel that they are incapable of planning their own future.

A-las (Adolescent–Low Aspirations). Adolescents who score high on the *A-las* scale tend to view themselves as not being successful. They do not like to study or read about things. They do not like challenge and prefer work that allows them to be careless. High scorers on this scale do not expect to be successful. They report difficulty starting new things and tend to give up quickly when a task gets difficult. They tend to let other people solve problems for them.

A-sod (Adolescent–Social Discomfort). Adolescents who score high on the *A-sod* do not enjoy being around other people. They tend to be shy and prefer being alone. They tend not to like parties or social events such as crowds or dances. They usually will not speak to others unless spoken to first. Other people find it hard to get to know them. They have difficulty making friends and do not like to meet new people.

A-fam (Adolescent–Family Problems). The *A-fam* scale addresses family problems. Adolescents who score high on this scale report having difficulties with their parents and other family members. Family discord, jealousy, fault finding, anger, beatings, serious disagreements, lack of love and understanding, and limited communication are problems reflected in the item content of this scale. Adolescents who score high on this measure do not believe they can count on their families in times of trouble. They report feeling that they long for the day when they can leave home. They believe that their parents frequently punish them without cause and treat them like children. They usually report that their parents dislike their friends.

A-sch (Adolescent–School Problems). This scale addresses school problems. Adolescents who score high on *A-sch* tend to obtain poor grades and may have problems with school suspension, truancy, negative attitudes toward teachers, and dislike of school. High-scoring adolescents typically do not participate in school activities or

(continued)

EXHIBIT 7.2   *(Continued)*

---

sports. They believe that school is a waste of time. In addition, they usually report having been told that they are lazy. They may report being bored with school.

A-trt (Adolescent–Negative Treatment Indicators). Adolescents who score high on the *A-trt* acknowledge having negative attitudes toward doctors and mental health professionals. They usually do not believe that other people are capable of understanding them or their problems. They are usually not willing to take charge of their own lives and face their problems. They report having several faults and bad habits that they feel are insurmountable. They do not feel that they can plan their own future or do much to improve their situation. They typically do not assume responsibility for negative things in their lives. Moreover, they also acknowledge that they are not willing to discuss their problems with others.

Osman, Soman, & Hoffman, 1998; Lilienfeld, 1994; McGrath, Pogge, & Stokes, 2002; Micucci, 2002; Moore, Thompson-Pope, & Whited, 1996; Morton, Farris, & Brenowitz, 2002; Rinaldo & Baer, 2003; Stein, McClinton, & Graham, 1998; Toyer & Weed, 1998; Weed, Butcher, & Williams, 1994; Williams & Butcher, 1989a, 1989b).

The MMPI-A validity and reliability have been tested several times in different countries, including Mexico, China, Argentina, Chile, the Netherlands, and Italy, among others (Calderon, 2002; Cheung & Ho, 1997; Contini de Gonzalez, Figueroa, Cohen Imach, & Coronel de Pace, 2001; Derksen, Ven Dijk, & Cornelissen, 2003; Farias, Duran, & Gomez-Maqueo, 2003; Gómez, Johnson, Davis, & Velasquez, 2000; Negy, Leal-Puente, Trainor, & Carlson, 1997; L. M. Pena, Megargee, & Brody, 1996; Scott, Butcher, Young, & Gomez, 2002; Scott, Knoth, Beltran-Quiones, & Gomez, 2003; Sirigatti, 2000; Vinet & Alarcon, 2003).

ASSESSING SPANISH-SPEAKING CLIENTS

As noted previously, Spanish-speaking adolescents living and going to school in the United States are at an even higher risk for adjustment problems than most adolescents because of the added pressures of acculturating to a new living situation and functioning in a new language. In evaluating unacculturated teens who do not read or understand English, the psychologist wants to use an appropriate language version of the test to provide an assessment of psychopathology. It also may be valuable to use a comparable reference population or norms that are relevant to adolescents being evaluated in mental health settings that will provide an appropriate standard for Hispanic adolescents. Two options for assessing Hispanic adolescents in their own language are described in the remainder of this chapter: the MMPI-A Hispania (Butcher, Cabiya, et al., 1998) and the Mexican version of MMPI-A (E. Lucio, Ampudia, & Durán, 1998). Whichever Spanish language form of the MMPI-A is used, the resulting T scores and profile configurations are likely to be highly comparable to the English language MMPI-A.

THE MMPI-A HISPANIA NORMATIVE STUDY

In this section, we summarize efforts at providing a Spanish language MMPI-A for the United States. We first describe the development of the MMPI-A Hispania for the United States; then we discuss the development and utility of the Mexican version of the MMPI-A for practitioners who might wish to use one of these versions for assessing Hispanic clients.

Translation of the MMPI-A Items

The MMPI-A translation project was designed to develop a Spanish language version of the test that could be used by psychologists in the United States to evaluate the psychological adjustment problems of Hispanic adolescents. The MMPI-A items were translated with an eye toward being comparable to items of the Spanish language MMPI-2 for the United States and to include appropriate Spanish language translations of the MMPI-A items that do not appear on the MMPI-2. The item wordings were developed to assure that they were at a sixth-grade level as with the MMPI-2. The translation procedures for the Hispanic MMPI-A (described more fully in Butcher, Cabiya, et al., 1998) were as follows.

Phase 1. The item pool for the Hispanic MMPI-A for the United States was initially obtained by using items from two proven Spanish language test translations. Because the goal was to maintain congruence between the MMPI-2 and MMPI-A where possible, the initial item translations were obtained from the Spanish translation of the MMPI-2 by Garcia-Peltoniemi and Azan Chaviano (1993). Many of the items on MMPI-A also appear on MMPI-2. The translated versions of the remaining items (not on the MMPI-2) were initially borrowed from the Spanish language MMPI-A developed by E. Lucio et al. (1998) for the Mexican version of the test.

Phase 2. The Spanish items were next reviewed by three bilingual psychologists (one resident of Puerto Rico, one Cuban from Miami, and one Mexican American from Los Angeles). The translators were asked to consider the accuracy and appropriateness of each item translation and to determine if the content was equivalent to the item in English. Questionable item renderings were noted and discrepancies clarified. The item was then rewritten and reworked until the meaning was clear to each bilingual translator.

Phase 3. The third stage of the translation process consisted of performing a back-translation of the items into English. This back-translation was performed by linguists from the University of Minnesota Language Center. Any problematic items from the back-translation phase were retranslated and again back-translated until their meaning was considered clear and equivalent to the English language version.

Phase 4. Evaluation of item meanings was also followed up at each testing site when the normative data set was being collected to determine if participants in the study had difficulty with any items. Five items were designated for further review with this procedure. These items were modified slightly for the final version of the booklet.

The Hispanic MMPI-A Normative Sample

The selection of a normative sample that can serve as a reference population for a psychological assessment instrument requires careful consideration. Although an ideal sample is usually considered to be one that is representative of the general population, there are special reference groups that can be used effectively for specific applications. In the case of the MMPI-A, a generally representative normative sample was used to develop the English language norms (Butcher et al., 1992); however, Latinos/Latinas were underrepresented in the normative group, in part because the test was administered in English only.

The general purpose in developing the MMPI-A Hispania study was somewhat more restricted than the English language normative study: to provide a reference norm for a specific subset of the population, often referred to as a *local norm* (for informative discussions of local norms, see Anderson, 2001; Bartram, 2001). In many ways, local norms can be more difficult to define and capture than a general, representative sample because the process involves projecting the possible demographics of a particular subpopulation who would be administered the test. The goal in this Hispanic normative study was to obtain a specialized sample of adolescents who would be representative of (a) a population of Spanish-speaking adolescents who may be in the process of being acculturated to U.S. culture or (b) people who primarily communicate in Spanish within U.S. territory (e.g., those who live in Puerto Rico) and are not testable by the English language version of the MMPI-A. The primary ethnic groups of Hispanic adolescents who might be evaluated in the United States were represented in the data collection.

The plan was to obtain samples of adolescents living in the mainland United States (California and Florida) and samples of adolescents from regional sites that have been a source of Spanish-speaking adolescents who might be administered the test in the United States. These choices were made with the goal of including representation of the two major immigrant groups of Mexican and Cuban origin in the United States. In addition, two resident populations, outside the United States mainland, were included because they are significant sources of Spanish-speaking clients who might be administered the test. For example, the MMPI-2 and MMPI-A are widely used in Puerto Rico because Puerto Ricans are U.S. citizens who frequently travel to the mainland to live or work, and adolescents from Mexico are the most frequent immigrating population in the United States.

Data Collection Sites

The normative data for the Spanish language MMPI-A were collected in four sites in which a prominent percentage of Hispanic adolescents are found: Florida, California, Puerto Rico, and Mexico.

Miami, Florida. In the Miami sample, five schools that were considered to have a high concentration of Cuban Americans served as the data collection sites. The students volunteered for the project and were paid $10 for their participation. A total of 134 students (58 boys and 76 girls) participated in the study. Eight days after the initial test administration, a subset of the population was retested; the retest data were collected on 17 students from one of the schools.

Los Angeles, California. Student volunteers from Los Angeles schools were recruited to participate in the data collection. Parental consent was obtained, and ethnicity and Spanish language proficiency were verified for students. The MMPI-A Hispania was administered by a clinical psychologist with the assistance of a graduate student and a teacher from the high school. The students volunteered for the project and were paid $10 for their participation. All instructions were given in Spanish. A total of 213 adolescents (100 boys and 113 girls) participated in the study.

San Juan, Puerto Rico. The Puerto Rican sample included 186 adolescents (101 boys and 85 girls) who were recruited from five schools in Puerto Rico that were considered to be representative of the student population. The schools were from both the metropolitan San Juan area and from a semirural area outside San Juan. The proportions of participants closely resembled the distribution of the general population in these areas. The participants ranged in age from 14 to 18 years. Student volunteers were paid $10 for their participation. Parents of those who accepted signed a release authorizing participation.

Mexico City, Mexico. A sample of 304 students (146 boys and 158 girls) were recruited from two public schools in Mexico City. These schools were considered to be similar in terms of parents' educational level and other demographic characteristics to those of Mexican adolescents living

TABLE 7.1
Total Sample (Before Exclusions) and Final Sample

Location	Boys	Girls	Total
	Before exclusions		
Florida	58	76	134
California	100	113	213
Puerto Rico	101	85	186
Mexico	146	158	304
Total	405	432	837
	Final sample		
Florida	48	70	118
California	93	112	205
Puerto Rico	91	80	171
Mexico	141	151	292
Total	373	413	786

in the United States. Only 8% of the parents of these adolescents had an educational level higher than high school. One week later, a retest study was completed with a sample of 53 boys and 44 girls. As part of the same study, other groups from the same schools were administered the Spanish MMPI-A version for Mexico, which contains some differently worded items. See Table 7.1 for the samples that were included in the study.

Adolescents sometimes produce unusable test responses for several reasons: They do not understand the instructions, they simply randomly endorse items, or they do not comprehend the meaning of the items. Therefore, standard criteria of exclusion were used to ensure that the final samples included only valid protocols. The following criteria were used to eliminate invalid protocols from the analysis: CNS (Cannot Say) > 35; F > 43 raw score; $TRIN$ < 5 raw or > 14 raw; $VRIN$ > 13 raw. In all, 51 protocols were eliminated from the analysis on the basis of invalidity. The final sample consisted of 786 participants (373 boys and 413 girls; see Table 7.1).

Test–Retest

In addition to collecting a normative sample, the investigators also conducted a test–retest study of the MMPI-A to assess reliability of the measures. Students (51 boys and 77 girls) from the Puerto Rico, Miami, and Mexico data collection sites participated in a test–retest study. These students were retested 1 week after the initial test administration with the Hispanic form of the MMPI-A. The test–retest correlations for the MMPI-A validity and clinical scales were found to be comparable to those of the MMPI-A normative study.

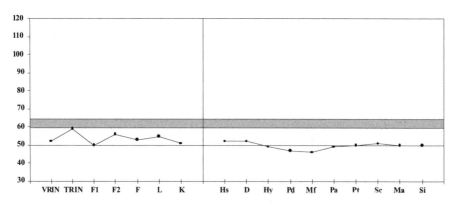

Figure 7.1. MMPI-A validity and clinical scale profile of Hispanic boys (*N* = 373) plotted on U.S. MMPI-A norms (*N* = 805). The scales include *VRIN* (Variable Responding Inconsistency), *TRIN* (True Responding), *F* (Infrequency), *L* (Lie), *K* (Defensiveness), *Hs* (Hypochondriasis), *D* (Depression), *Hy* (Hysteria), *Pd* (Psychopathic Deviation), *Mf* (Masculinity–Femininity), *Pa* (Paranoia), *Pt* (Psychasthenia), *Sc* (Schizophrenia), *Ma* (Hypomania), and *Si* (Social Introversion).

Comparison of the Hispanic Adolescent Sample With the U.S. Normative and Mexican Samples

The investigators concluded from the study that the MMPI-A scores for Hispanic samples of boys and girls fell within one standard deviation of the mean of the standard MMPI-A norms. Most of the scale scores were within the standard error of measurement, a T score of around 50. Among the validity and clinical scales, only two MMPI-A scales showed much difference between the two groups: the *Mf* (Masculinity–Femininity) scale for girls and the *TRIN* scale (see Figures 7.1 and 7.2 for scale profiles for Hispanic boys and Figures 7.3 and 7.4 for girls). These findings suggest that the adolescents in the Hispanic sample tended to respond inconsistently to a few more item pairs (in the True direction) compared with the standard normative sample; however, this pattern was not extreme, and most scale scores were highly comparable.

The Hispanic MMPI-A scores are essentially "normal variations" around the mean of the standard MMPI-A norms (Butcher, Cabiya, et al., 1998). The standard English language MMPI-A norms are likely to be highly appropriate for assessing Hispanic adolescents even if the test is administered in Spanish. The project authors concluded that special Hispanic norms are probably not necessary to provide an appropriate clinical assessment of these adolescents because Hispanic adolescents respond to MMPI-A items in much the same way as adolescents taking the English language version and compared on the standard MMPI-A norms (see Negy et al., 1997). We return

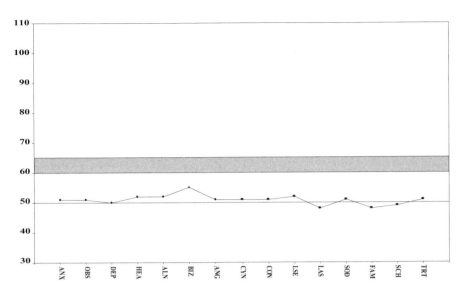

Figure 7.2. MMPI-A content scale profile of Hispanic boys (*N* = 373) plotted on U.S. MMPI-A norms (*N* = 805). The scales include *ANX* (Anxiety), *OBS* (Obsessiveness), *DEP* (Depression), *HEA* (Health Concerns), *ALN* (Alienation), *BIZ* (Bizarre Mentation), *ANG* (Anger), *CYN* (Cynicism), *CON* (Conduct Problems), *LSE* (Low Self-Esteem), *LAS* (Low Aspiration), *SOD* (Social Discomfort), *FAM* (Family Concerns), *SCH* (School Problems), and *TRT* (Negative Treatment Indicators).

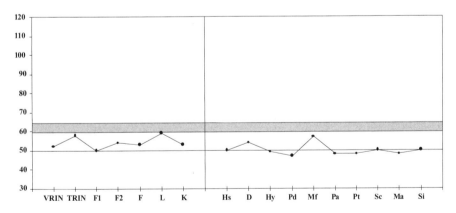

Figure 7.3. MMPI-A validity and clinical scale profile of Hispanic girls (*N* = 413) plotted on U.S. MMPI-A norms (*N* = 815). See Figure 7.1 for scale definitions.

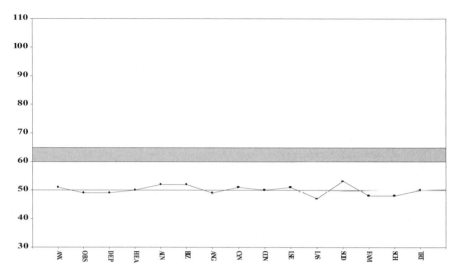

Figure 7.4. MMPI-A content scale profile of Hispanic girls (*N* = 413) plotted on U.S. MMPI-A norms (*N* = 815). See Figure 7.2 for scale definitions.

to the question of appropriate normative comparisons after we introduce the Mexican version of the MMPI-A.

The MMPI-A Hispania has been included in several research studies. Scott et al. (2002) conducted a study comparing Spanish-speaking adolescents in five countries: Columbia, Mexico, Peru, Spain, and the United States. They found a high degree of similarity across the five countries on the basic content and supplementary scales, with most scales falling within a half of a standard deviation from the U.S. normative sample (see Figures 7.5 and 7.6). Scott et al. (2003) found that a general sample of adolescents in Columbia had scores on the MMPI-A Hispania similar to those of adolescents in the United States. In addition, Scott et al. reported that adolescent earthquake victims in Columbia showed slight elevations on three scales (*D* [Depression], *Pt* [Psychasthenia], and *Sc* [Schizophrenia]) that are commonly associated with the experience of posttraumatic stress.

THE MEXICAN VERSION OF THE MMPI-A

Psychologists in Mexico considered it important to develop adequate instruments to evaluate adolescents, an extensive population in Mexico according to the 2000 Instituto Nacional de Estadistica Geografía e Informática (INEGI) survey data (INEGI, 2000). In the 2000 INEGI census, there were about 1.5 million adolescents in the Federal District of Mexico alone.

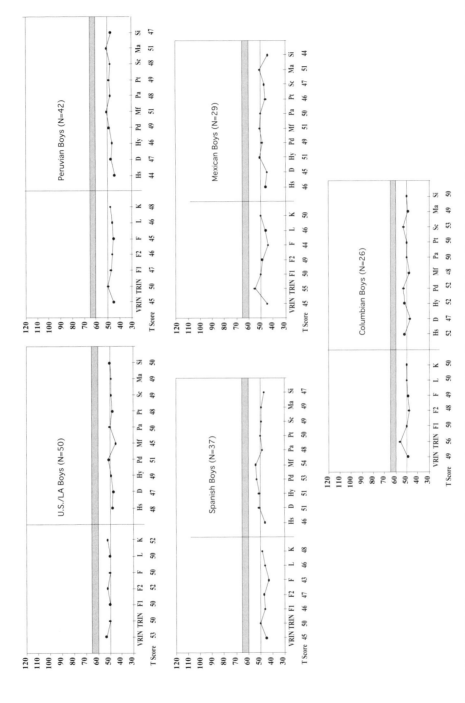

Figure 7.5. MMPI-A basic scale profiles of boys from five countries. See Figure 7.1 caption for scale definitions. From "The Hispanic MMPI-A Across Five Countries," by R. L. Scott, J. N. Butcher, T. L. Young, and N. Gomez, 2002, *Journal of Clinical Psychology*, *71*, p. 413. Copyright 2002 by Wiley & Sons. Adapted with permission.

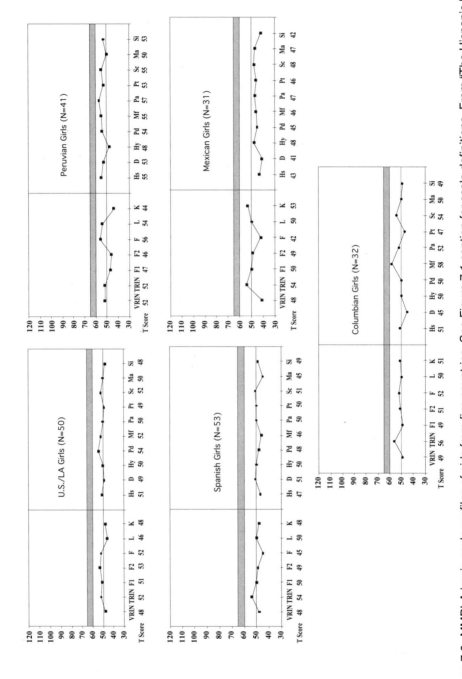

Figure 7.6. MMPI-A basic scale profiles of girls from five countries. See Figure 7.1 caption for scale definitions. From "The Hispanic MMPI-A Across Five Countries," by R. L. Scott, J. N. Butcher, T. L. Young, and N. Gomez, 2002, *Journal of Clinical Psychology, 58,* p. 414. Copyright 2002 by Wiley & Sons. Adapted with permission.

The original MMPI had been used in Mexico to evaluate adolescents since the 1970s. Izaguirre-Hernandez, Sanchez-Quintanar, and Avila-Mendez (1970) found differences in the profiles of Mexican adolescents attending the National Preparatory School of the National Autonomous University of Mexico (UNAM) and those of adolescents in the United States. Therefore, they considered it necessary to obtain norms for the scores of these Mexican adolescents and applied the inventory collectively to a group of 911 participants (679 boys and 239 girls) whose ages ranged from 15 to 22 years. The scales showing the greatest elevations with respect to the North America norms were Scales F, 8, 4, and L. The highest scores obtained by the girls were on Scales F, 8, 2, 7, and 4. The scale authors concluded that a profile of Mexican adolescents using the U.S. norms would probably have a great tendency to present high scores on Scales 2 and 8. However, because specific Mexican adolescent norms were never published, the norms of the original MMPI continued to be used to evaluate Mexican adolescents, resulting in overpathologizing.

In other studies (Madariaga & Guttin, 1980; Sesteaga, 1980), elevated scores on Scales 8 and 2 were also found. Ghiju (1982) reported that, for girls, the lower the socioeconomic level the higher the scores obtained on Scale 8. This could possibly be due to their reading comprehension. In general, the profiles of Mexican adolescents obtained with the original MMPI showed psychopathologic alterations even when normal groups were evaluated. This finding became a problem when using the instrument, although the MMPI was widely used in clinical practice because there was no other instrument that could be used as a substitute.

Because the MMPI-A had proved to be of value in assessing adolescents in the United States, it was decided that the instrument may prove to be valid and reliable in the evaluation of adolescents in Mexico as well. Many of the problems presented in the original MMPI with adolescents were eliminated in the revised version. An instrument such as the MMPI-A can be useful because it evaluates broader areas of functioning, providing the possibility of a more thorough knowledge of both normal and specific clinical groups of young people.

Translation Procedures

The translation procedures for the adaptation of the MMPI-A followed a rigorous methodology, in which the semantic, syntactic, and cultural contents of the items composing the instrument were highlighted (E. Lucio et al., 1998). This work consisted of a careful transliteration process, which included the following steps:

1. The original protocol in English was translated by Emilia Lucio and a professional translator to obtain the first version of the

inventory. This translator was a bilingual, bicultural linguist, because in adapting an instrument of this sort, it is not considered enough for the person to know both languages thoroughly; the person must also have lived at least 5 years in the country where the instrument was constructed if it is not in his or her native language.

2. This version was discussed with other clinical psychologists and several students from different Latin American countries (Mexico, Bolivia, Cuba, and Nicaragua) to modify some items, thus obtaining a second version.

3. This version was given to 10 clinical judges, who agreed on 98% of the items but commented on some that did not seem clear.

4. The person responsible for the project, some professors, and students who had participated in the study as well as the professional translator discussed the comments to obtain a third version.

5. Psychologists and linguists from the University of Minnesota analyzed this version and considered it to be an excellent and precise translation. The linguistics department suggested some slight changes in using this Spanish version for the United States.

6. Some of these suggestions were accepted for the Mexican Spanish version, whereas others were rejected on the grounds that they altered the semantic content of the items. Afterward, the final version was obtained. The Mexican Spanish version developed at UNAM by Emilia Lucio can also be used in other Latin American countries.

7. Finally, a back-translation from Spanish to English was obtained. An agreement of 90% was reached for the items (E. Lucio et al., 1998).

The Mexican Spanish version was the basis for the Spanish version recently published in the United States.

The Normative Sample of Mexican Adolescents

Mexican adolescents were selected from different geographical areas of the federal district and from different types of schools. The federal district was chosen because the population in Mexico City is heterogeneous enough to be considered representative of the Mexican population. Besides, economic resources did not allow traveling throughout the country. The test was administered to a total of 4,181 adolescents from public and private schools. Emilia Lucio, Amada Ampudia, and Consuelo Durán participated in the process of the test adaptation. Several undergraduate and graduate students from UNAM collaborated in the collection of the data.

The data collection was begun at UNAM's schools of science and humanities and the preparatory schools. The first step was to obtain authorization from the preparatory schools department. The selection of the schools and classes where the inventory would be applied was done randomly according to four geographical areas into which the federal district was divided. Once the schools were identified, authorization was obtained from the principals of the schools. Permission was granted either by the principal or the head of academic services of each school. Data collection was complicated because of school terms and class schedules and because another extensive instrument besides the MMPI was also applied. Once the sample was obtained from these schools, permission to apply the test in other schools within the urban area was solicited from the director of middle education in the secretariat of education. Schools were selected from the geographical areas considered above according to the data of the 1990 National Census (INEGI, 1990). Permission was also requested from private schools in the different geographical areas of the federal district but was only granted by some of these schools. From the schools mentioned above, various classes were selected according to the age data registered in the census. Thus, a total of 4,600 adolescents were chosen. After permission was obtained and timetables were set for the application of the inventory, students were tested in groups of 30 to 150, with one psychologist monitoring every 25 adolescents. Sometimes the teachers of the corresponding class also participated. In addition to the MMPI-A, the students answered a questionnaire (based on the questionnaire designed for adolescents in the United States by Williams et al., 1992) designed especially for Mexico asking about biographical and life events data. A small group of adolescents (151 boys and 190 girls) participated in a test–retest study 1 week later.

The schools selected differed in their requirements for administering the instrument to the students. All of the students participated voluntarily without payment. Each of the schools received group profile reports of the students and a list of the individual results obtained from each student.

Efforts were made to include several socioeconomic levels and different types of educational levels in the sample because the difficulty in answering the test increases when reading comprehension is poor. Table 7.2 shows the distribution of the Mexican normative sample by age and gender.

The Mexican normative sample is larger than the North American one. It includes 4,050 adolescents (1,904 boys and 2,146) girls. The majority of these students came from public schools, although a considerable number were from private ones. Their ages ranged from 14 to 18 years. In almost all the age ranges, except in the 18-year-old group, there were more girls than

TABLE 7.2
Age and Gender of the Mexican Adolescent Normative Sample

Age (years)	Boys			Girls			Total sample	
	n	%	Census %	*n*	%	Census %	*N*	%
14	412	21.6	18.5	511	23.8	18.4	923	22.8
15	502	26.4	19.4	649	30.3	19.4	1,151	28.4
16	400	21.0	19.7	464	21.6	19.8	864	21.3
17	372	19.5	20.9	380	17.7	21.0	752	18.6
18	218	11.5	21.5	142	6.6	21.4	360	8.9
Total	1,904			2,146			4,050	

Note. For boys, *M* = 15.7, *SD* = 1.3; for girls, *M* = 15.5, *SD* – 1.2.

boys, which may be due partly to the gender distribution of the adolescent population and also to the fact that girls collaborate much more when voluntary cooperation is required. The ages were adjusted according to the 1990 census (INEGI, 1990) except at the 18-year-old level, in which there were more boys than girls, probably because girls were at a higher grade or had left school for some reason (e.g., getting married). The average scores for Mexican adolescents (validity and clinical scales) are shown in Figure 7.7 (for boys) and Figure 7.8 (for girls) compared with American norms. Note that the Mexican norms result in highly comparable profiles to the American normative sample.

The same criteria used by Butcher et al. (1992) to exclude invalid protocols in the United States were used to ensure that only complete and valid protocols would be included in the normative sample. Only adolescents who answered both the MMPI-A and the biographical and life events questionnaire, whose ages ranged from 14 to 18 years of age, who left fewer than 35 items unanswered, whose scores on the *F* scale were less than 26

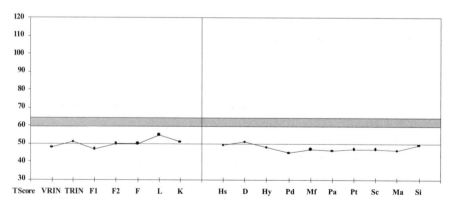

Figure 7.7. MMPI-A validity and clinical scales of Mexican boys (*N* = 1,904) plotted on U.S. MMPI-A norms (*N* = 805). See Figure 7.1 for scale definitions.

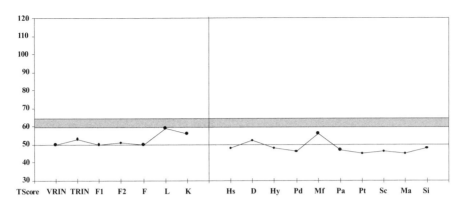

Figure 7.8. MMPI-A validity and clinical scales of Mexican girls (*N* = 2,161) plotted on U.S. MMPI-A norms (*N* = 805). See Figure 7.1 for scale definitions.

in boys and less than 23 in girls, and whose *VRIN* was up to 12 and *TRIN* was between 5 to 13 were included in the study. With these criteria, approximately 10% of the participants who answered both instruments were eliminated.

The Mexican Clinical Sample

In addition to the MMPI-A normative sample, a large clinical sample was obtained. The basic research instruments used for the normative sample were also used for the clinical one: the MMPI and the biographical and life events questionnaire. The data from the clinical history of the patients were registered in a standardized way, and in the majority of the cases the most important data obtained from a semistructured interview were written down.

In most of the cases, graduate clinical psychology students and under-graduate students in their last semesters, who had been previously trained, evaluated the patients in the clinical sample. The collaboration of several mental health institutions was solicited to gather the data of the patients in the clinical sample. Patients from several units in a psychiatric hospital, from various mental health institutions, and from the tutelary council were included in the sample. Cooperation was solicited from both the authorities in these institutions and the patients in the sample. The instruments were administered individually in most of the cases, and, when possible, the results were delivered to the institution so that they could be used in the treatment of the adolescents.

A total of 243 patients were evaluated, 25 of whom were excluded because their protocols turned out to be invalid. The criteria for exclusion were slightly different from those used for the normative sample: The ages in this group also ranged from 14 to 18 years and up to 35 items were left

TABLE 7.3
Age and Gender of the Mexican Clinical Sample

Age (years)	Boys		Girls		Total sample	
	n	%	N	%	N	%
14	42	29.8	32	41.6	74	33
15	34	24.1	26	33.8	60	27
16	27	19.1	4	5.2	31	17
17	33	23.4	10	13.0	43	19
18	5	3.5	5	6.5	10	4
Total	141		77		218	100

Note. For boys, M = 15.47, SD = 1.24; for girls, M = 15.09, SD = 1.26.

TABLE 7.4
Diagnostics for the Mexican Adolescent Clinical Sample

Diagnosis	Boys (n = 141)		Girls (n = 77)	
	n	%	n	%
Conduct disorders	28	19.9	8	10.4
Mood disorders	13	9.2	43	55.8
Family problems	3	2.1	7	9.1
Problems related to sexual abuse of child	—	—	5	6.4
Antisocial behavior	14	9.9	2	2.6
Learning disorders	5	3.5	1	1.3
Alcohol induced disorders	7	5.0	—	—
Polysubstance-related disorder	41	29.0	1	1.3
Anxiety disorders	5	3.6	—	—
Psychosis	7	5.0	4	5.2
Somatoform disorders: conversion disorder	—	—	2	2.6
Personality disorders	2	1.4	—	—
Exogen obesity	1	.7	1	1.3
Without diagnosis	15	10.6	3	3.9
Total	141	100	77	100

Note. Dashes in cells indicate data are not available.

unanswered, but VRIN scores went to 18 and TRIN scores ranged between 15 and 13 and F scale scores were up to 39 in boys and 33 in girls. The clinical sample consisted of 218 adolescents as observed in Table 7.3 (141 boys and 77 girls). As shown in Table 7.4, the majority of the participants suffered from mood disorders.

THE MEXICAN NORMS FOR THE MMPI-A

Central tendency measures, such as means and standard deviations, were obtained for the normative Mexican sample by scale. Later, T tests were used to compare the mean and standard deviation of the Mexican normative sample with those of the North American sample to observe if there were significant differences. Once the differences among the samples were established, the specific norms for the population were calculated by calculating uniform T scores. The norms are described in the test manual (E. Lucio et al., 1998). (See T-score tables presented in Appendix C.) In addition, the profiles of the participants in both studies were obtained and were graphically plotted to observe how the T scores were distributed on the scales of the inventory. The results indicate that the averages of the Mexican population are similar to those of the North American population, although there is a notable difference in some of the scales. Given that the samples are quite large, even small differences on scale elevation are statistically significant though not clinically meaningful.

The differences are greater with respect to girls because statistically significant differences (p = .001) are observed in all the scales except *VRIN*, *F1*, and *F*. Mexican girls have higher scores in *TRIN, F2, F, L, K*, and *D*, whereas North American girls have higher scores in *Hs, Hy, Pd, Mf, Pa, Pt, Sc*, and *Ma*.

When the profiles of the basic scales are examined both in boys and girls, one observes that there is a clear tendency toward normality. That is, some of the scores fall at or below a T-score elevation of 50 compared with the U.S. norms.

With respect to the comparison of the raw scores of the content scales in the Mexican normative sample with those of the North American sample, there are some differences. In the group of boys, the basic scales showed small but significant differences (p = .001) in scales *A-anx* (Anxiety), *A-biz* (Bizarre Mentation), *A-cyn* (Cynicism), *A-las* (Low Aspirations), *A-sod* (Social Discomfort), *A-fam* (Family Problems), and *A-sch* (School Problems). Mexican boys obtained higher scores in *A-biz, A-cyn*, and *A-sod*, whereas North American boys had higher scores in *A-anx, A-las, A-fam*, and *A-sch*. For girls, significant statistical differences were observed in the majority of the basic scales except in *A-aln* (Alienation), *A-biz, A-ang* (Anger), and *A-cyn*. Mexican girls had higher scores in scale *A-sod*, whereas girls in the United States had higher scores in scales *A-anx, A-obs* (Obsession), *A-dep* (Depression), *A-hea* (Health Problems), *A-con* (Conduct Problems), *A-lse* (Low Self-Esteem), *A-las, A-fam, A-sch*, and *A-trt* (Treatment).

When the natural scores obtained by the normative sample of the Mexican boys were compared with those of the boys in the United States, significant statistical differences (p = .001) were found in most of the basic scales. Nevertheless, most of the differences were small compared with the scores of the boys in the United States, less than half a standard deviation. Only in the *L* scale, in which Mexican boys scored higher, was the standard deviation greater than half, indicating that the attitude of Mexican boys toward psychological evaluation differs from that of the American boys. This L scale elevation could be due to the fact that most people are interested in giving a good impression of themselves.

With respect to girls, the differences were somewhat greater because there were significant statistical differences in most of the scales. However, the majority of the differences observed were small, less than half a standard deviation. Only in the L scale, in which the Mexican girls scored higher, was there a difference greater than 1 standard deviation with respect to the North American girls. The elevation in L scale shown by Mexican girls indicates that their attitude when answering the inventory is different from that of the girls in the United States and that probably, as in the case of boys, they have a greater interest in giving a good impression of themselves. The elevation in this scale has been observed in some studies performed with Mexican adolescents using the original MMPI and in adolescent populations in other countries (Cheung & Ho, 1997; Izaguirre-Hernandez et al., 1970). The reliability of this scale is not very high, indicating that it is necessary to make major modifications to the items to obtain norms for this scale.

Differences greater than half a standard deviation were observed in Scales 5 (Mf) and 4 (Pd) with respect to girls, with Mexican girls scoring lower. The difference in Scale 5 (Mf) shows that Mexican girls feel distant from the traditional feminine roles assigned to women by society in the United States. The elevation in Scale 5 in girls has been observed in other groups of Hispanic girls (Butcher, Cabiya, et al., 1998). The differences found between the two groups in the basic scales of the MMPI regarding personality characteristics seem due more to cultural differences than to psychopathology.

In terms of the reliability of the instrument, the data obtained are congruent with those reported in previous studies (Butcher et al., 1992; Stein et al., 1998). The relatively low internal consistency of the scales referring to alcohol and substance abuse agrees with research carried out by Weed et al. (1994), who indicated that this could be due to the fact that these scales include several factors.

When comparing these results with those obtained by Mexican adolescents for the original MMPI, it is clear that the scores of Mexican adolescents, boys as well as girls, tend toward normality; none of the scores reached an elevation of 65, considered the cutoff to indicate psychopathology; moreover, no scores reached an elevation of T = 60, which may be acknowledged as a high normal score. Only Scales L and 5 (Mf), both not clinical scales, reached T = 59 in girls. It can be concluded from these results that the MMPI-A version of the inventory does not reflect psychopathology in adolescents, as was the case with the original MMPI. The elevation of the L scale in girls has been observed in previous studies (Izaguirre-Hernandez et al., 1970; Sesteaga, 1980). With respect to the content scales, there are only minor differences between Mexican and North American adolescents with both girls and boys and of no interpretative significance. The scores of the Mexican adolescents are, in general, lower than those of North American adolescents. There are some minor differences, less than half a standard deviation, with respect to North American norms. Scale A-*fam* shows the greatest difference both in boys and girls, indicating that North American adolescents more readily admit having disagreements with their parents and other members of their family more than Mexican adolescents do. This explains the elevation in Scale 4. The results obtained in this study support those obtained by other authors who have worked with other groups of non-U.S. adolescents with regard to the greater efficiency of the MMPI-A over the MMPI when evaluating adolescents (Cheung & Ho, 1997; Negy et al., 1997).

Although the differences found between North American and Mexican adolescents are minimal with the MMPI-A, we consider it important to use the norms established for the Mexican population because this would allow us to assess adolescents' psychopathology and emotional problems more adequately. From the data obtained in the adaptation of the test, we can conclude that it is obvious that the profiles of the Mexican adolescents obtained with the MMPI-A fall into the normal expected ranges as opposed to those obtained with the original MMPI. This finding shows the MMPI-A to be a better instrument to assess the personality of the Mexican adolescents than the original MMPI.

Reliability and Validity of the MMPI-A in Mexico

A group of adolescents from the Mexican sample, 151 boys and 190 girls, answered the test on two occasions (the second time a week later) to obtain the reliability of the instrument using a test–retest. The stability obtained in most of the clinical and basic scales was high, in most cases greater than .70 in boys and girls (G. M. E. Lucio, Ampudia, & Durán, 1997). The reliability of most of the scales of the MMPI-A for the Mexican population using alpha coefficient was high. The reliability of the scales in the Mexican population was .74, fitting with the typical values between .65 and .82. Some of the scales that exhibited less internal reliability were those related to proneness to alcohol abuse (.45) and addictions (.46). With respect to the test–retest reliability, the typical values were between .65 and .80. Only the MacAndrew Alcoholism—Revised (MAC-R) scale showed a value less than .60.

A faking-bad study has been carried out with the MMPI-A (G. E. Lucio, Ampudio, Duran, Leon, & Butcher, 2002) to examine the extent to which the validity scales of the MMPI identified adolescents who were faking bad in a group of Mexican adolescents. This study also evaluated the validity scales' capacity to differentiate between nonclinical adolescents instructed to fake-bad and both clinical and nonclinical adolescents who received standard instructions. Participants were 59 male and 87 female high school Mexican students and 59 male and 87 female adolescents from clinical settings. The results of this study indicate that Scales $F1$, $F2$, F, and the raw score of F minus the raw score of K could discriminate adequately between the three different conditions. High positive and negative predictive power and overall hit rates using different base rates were obtained in this study. Higher scores were needed to discriminate in the group of girls than in the group of boys.

Other Studies Carried Out in Mexico

The study with the original clinical sample with Mexican adolescents showed that the higher scores with respect to the group of girls were found on the F scale and also on Scales 4, 8, A-dep, A-fam, and MAC-R (G. M. E. Lucio et al., 1998). All of these scales had a mean score greater than 60 T. With respect to boys, the higher scales were Scales 4, $F1$, F, A-dep, and MAC-R. All of these scores are around a T score of 60.

Various other studies have used the MMPI-A with different adolescent samples. For example, G. M. E. Lucio, Loza, and Durán (2000) studied the personalities of a group of adolescents with suicidal tendencies by using the MMPI-A with two different groups: a clinical sample consisting of adolescents who had attempted suicide and had received treatment in two public hospitals and a comparative sample of adolescents without a suicidal attempt from a public school (both groups included 38 female adolescents). The MMPI-A and a life events questionnaire were applied to both samples. The two groups were paired on the following variables: age between 14 and 18 years, female, and from medium-low or low socioeconomic background.

The test was applied individually to the clinical sample in two public hospitals in Mexico City, with each session lasting approximately 3 to 4 hours. The test was administered collectively to the control group in two sessions with half of the participants in each one. The socioeconomic background was determined using a sociodemographic questionnaire considering the type of school attended and the patients' socioeconomic characteristics. The fact that the students from the school had never attempted suicide was duly corroborated.

Significant differences were found between both groups of adolescents. With respect to the MMPI-A, the clinical group had higher scores in the following basic scales: F, 2 (D, Depression), 3 (Hy, Hysteria), 4 (Pd, Psychopathic Deviation), 6 (Pa, Paranoia), and 8 (Sc, Schizophrenia). Some differences were also found in the content and supplementary scales.

Results indicate that the adolescents in the suicidal group focused their attention on the acknowledgment of their problems in contrast to the adolescents in the normal group. The scales that showed the greatest differences were Scales 4 and 6, followed by 8. These scales show more psychopathology than the others and indicate that the suicidal adolescents behave more aggressively and impulsively than the nonsuicidal adolescents. The adolescents in the suicidal group had greater difficulty in adjusting themselves to social norms and seemed unsure, worried, and suspicious of others, all of which corresponds to the *Pa* scale. Finally, the elevation in the *Sc* scale shows that the adolescents in the clinical sample had greater behavioral difficulties in interpersonal relations. The elevation in the *Hy* scale indicates greater difficulty in facing conflictive or stressful situations because of a lack of maturity. The differences found indicate that greater psychopathology existed in girls with suicidal tendencies. These results are similar to those found by other authors (Nordström, Schalling, & Alsberg, 1995) who reported that adolescents with suicidal tendencies show greater psychopathology indexes. Probably, the profiles obtained do not show higher elevations because the girls in the clinical sample tried to conceal the importance of their symptoms in order to be released from the hospital since some of them rejected treatment.

Significant differences were also found in the content and supplementary scales; the most important were in *A-dep* ($t = 4.40$), *A-hea* ($t = 3.34$), *A-ang* ($t = 3.51$), *A-fam* ($t = 4.08$), and *A-anx* ($t = 3.46$). The results obtained in these scales confirm that adolescents with suicidal tendencies presented greater psychopathology than those who did not. This is clearly shown by the elevation in the *A-dep* and *A-anx* scales. The results of this study confirm those obtained by Kopper et al. (1998), who found that the basic scales *A-dep*, *A-sch*, and *A-fam* of the MMPI-A show an increased risk of suicidal attempt. The high scores in the profiles of the girls with a suicidal attempt and the code type they obtained indicate a tendency to direct their depression and anger toward self-destruction. The suicidal adolescents also reported more stressful life events compared with the normal group.

Figueroa (2001) used the MMPI-A in a study concerning the psychosocial and personality factors related to the academic performance of female adolescents. The object of this study was to find the personality and contextual features that influenced low and high academic performance. The study was performed in a non-coeducational school directed by a religious order. The relation between the personality profiles obtained with the MMPI-A, some sociodemographic data, life events, and family expectations to high and low academic performance was also analyzed. A semistructured interview was used to learn the reason for the school choice and to find out some of the characteristics of the family structure and the interpersonal relations within the family.

This was an ex post facto and field study in which 41 female students out of a total of 126 girls were selected to participate because of their high ($n = 26$) or low ($n = 15$) achievement. The students were chosen from the last 2 years of high school. The hypothesis was that the personalities of girls with high or low academic results would show up on the basic, content, and supplementary scales of the MMPI-A. Although the two samples were small, significant statistical differences were found in four scales in which the low-performance girls had high scores: Hs ($t = 2.8$, $p = .03$), A-hea ($t = 2.04$, $p = .04$), A-sch ($t = 3.16$, $p = .01$), and the MacAndrew scale ($t = 2.5, p = .02$). This corroborated the main hypothesis of the study and seems to indicate that the students with low results show more anxiety, worry more about school and health problems, and present a greater tendency to have problems with addictions. Although the samples were small and therefore the study must be considered preliminary, the differences found between the groups seem to highlight the importance of the use of the MMPI-A in educational environments, because both a quantitative comparison of groups and a qualitative analysis of the individual profiles of the girls were done. When the study results were discussed with the students, girls in the low-performance group reported more stressful family, school, and social events than the high-performance group. Some of the data obtained in the profiles were corroborated and complemented those obtained in the interview.

A study by Hernandez, Lucio, and Manzo (2002) with a small group of high-performance Mexican adolescents compared the MMPI-A profiles of the Mexican adolescent normative sample (E. Lucio et al., 1998) and a study sample of 16 adolescents (7 males and 9 females) to look for any statistically significant differences. Furthermore, IQ scores of the sample were obtained using the Wechsler Intelligence Scale for Children and Raven Progressive Color Matrices scales. The sampling criterion was high school students between the ages of 16 and 18 years whose average grades equaled or were above the 95th percentile of their class in the last completed academic year as established by the American National Research Council for the Gifted and Talented, the Spanish Society for the Study of Giftedness, and others (Benito & Moro, 1997). The sample was obtained from the second and third grade of a preparatory school in Morelia, Mexico, and comprised the top 5% of their class, which matches the percentages typically used in other studies of giftedness screening. The sample exhibited superior and above-average scores in both intelligence tests. For the MMPI-A results, the female profile exhibited more statistical differences using the z test ($p = .05$) than the male profile compared with their corresponding normative sample profiles, even though all of the T sores were well within normal range. For the girls, these differences are found in all scale groups, the highest being F2 and F in the validity scales; Pt, Sc, and Si in the basic scales; A-dep, A-aln, A-biz, A-cyn, A-lse, A-sod, and A-trt in the content scales; and ACK (Alcohol Problem Acknowledgment) and A (Anxiety) in the supplementary scales; in all of these, the high-performance girls displayed lower scores compared with the normative sample. For the boys, statistical differences were only found in the validity (*F2*) and content (*A-lse*) scales. Findings support that these adolescents were well adjusted, extroverted, and self-confident; had high self-esteem; and were competitive and heterogeneous in their academic, artistic, and sports preferences and interests as reported in other studies. Moreover, all of the students from the sample showed willingness to participate in enrichment or acceleration programs if they were available, and their MMPI-A profiles could be used as predictors for high academic performance.

Another study was carried out with part of the Mexican normative group (Monzon, 2001) to identify personality features implicated in academic performance and to determine the possibility of predicting the academic performance of adolescents using the scales of the MMPI-A as predictive variables. This follow-up study, carried out with 1,617 students from UNAM high schools (760 boys and 857 girls), compared the results obtained on the test by a high-performance group with those obtained by a low-performance group. The original group included 1,947 students from different areas in Mexico City and from different schools, educational levels, and ages; some were eliminated because of invalid protocols and because their academic records were not available.

The students' academic performance was classified according to the average of the grades obtained during the time they had been high school students and taking into consideration whether they had completed their studies within the period of time permitted. Gender, age, and year first registered in high school were used as variables. The instruments used were the basic, content, and supplementary scales of the MMPI-A. Differences in the means of the different scales between the high- and low-performance groups were obtained with *t* tests, and logistic linear regression was applied to the categorical dependent variables to predict the academic performance by means of the MMPI-A scales. Different variables, such as average number of years enrolled in the school system, were used to classify the students. In all the variables, girls scored higher than boys, which indicates that gender does make a difference in scholastic performance.

In the group of girls, 29 of the 39 scales of the MMPI-A showed differences between the high- and low-performance groups. In the validity scales, the greatest difference was found in the *F1* scale, $t = 12.90$, $p = .001$, in which the low-performance group obtained a higher score. In the basic scales, the greatest difference was found in Scale 4 ($t = 11.21$, $p = .001$), in which once more the low-performance group obtained a higher score. In the content scales, the greatest difference was in the *A-Sch* scale ($t = 23.81$, $p = .001$). In the supplementary scales, the greatest differences were in Scales ACK ($t = 18$, $p = .001$), and PRO (which assesses proneness toward alcohol and substance abuse; $t = 18.31$, $p = .001$). In all these scales, the low-performance group obtained higher T scores, interpreted as clinically significant.

In the group of boys, 22 of the 39 scales show statistical differences. In the validity scales, the greatest difference was found in the F scale ($t = 9.17$, $p = .001$), in which the low-performance group obtained a higher T score. In the clinical scales, the greatest difference was observed in Scale 8 (Sc; $t = 5.223$, $p = .001$), in which the low-performance group also obtained a higher score. In the content scales, the greatest difference was in A-Sch ($t = 29.02$, $p = .001$), and in the supplementary scales, in PRO ($t = 13.53$, $p = .001$). In all these scales, the low-performance boys obtained higher scores.

The MMPI-A scales that best classified a high percentage of the boys into high- and low-academic performance students were L, F2, Hs, A-sod, A-biz, A-sch, and IMM (Immaturity). For girls, the scales that proved to better predict high and low performance were L, A-lse, ACK, and MAC-R.

The results of this study indicate that personality features partly explain the differences in adolescents' academic performance and that gender makes a difference in their performance. These results also indicate that although the MMPI-A cannot fully predict academic results, it is a useful instrument in educational settings not only for diagnosing psychological alterations but also for helping to prevent other kinds of problems in this stage of development, such as low academic performance and possible school desertion, by aiding in early detection.

In this section we have tried to illustrate how the MMPI-A was adapted for adolescents in Mexico and how the inventory has been useful in research and clinical practice. Because Mexican norms (which in many of the scales are similar to the North American ones) have been established, a more accurate vision of the characteristics of individuals and groups is possible.

SUMMARY

The MMPI-A can provide a unique perspective on personality adjustment of adolescents and an objective perspective on multicultural assessment. This chapter has addressed the importance of having a clinically relevant and appropriate version of the MMPI for assessing adolescents. The development of the MMPI-A was described, and the revised clinical and validity scales were presented along with the content-based measures that address a broader range of adolescent-specific problems. The need for a Spanish language MMPI-A for assessing adolescents who are not able to read the English language items was highlighted, and two Spanish translations were described. The first translation was the MMPI-A Hispania, developed for adolescents living in the United States who cannot take the English language form of the MMPI-A. Research has demonstrated that the MMPI-A Hispania can be used effectively in other countries for assessing adolescent problems and behavior. The Mexican version of the MMPI-A also was described and the performance of Mexican adolescents was compared with that of the American normative sample. Comparisons of the normative data from these three forms of the MMPI-A show that adolescents are likely to produce similar MMPI-A scale performance (i.e., to obtain relatively similar T score elevations for the scales), regardless of which version of the test they take.

CHAPTER HIGHLIGHTS

- The MMPI was revised for adolescents in 1992 by eliminating obsolete or inappropriate items, adding new adolescent-specific items, developing a specific normative reference sample, and developing a number of new adolescent problem scales.
- Practitioners in the United States are frequently asked to assess Hispanic adolescent clients who live in the United States and do not read or understand English, many of them native Spanish speakers; thus the MMPI-A was translated into the Spanish language to evaluate the psychological adjustment problems of these adolescents.
- Appropriate norms were collected on samples of Spanish-speaking adolescents living in the U.S. mainland, Puerto Rico, and Mexico (the country of origin for the majority of Hispanic adolescent immigrants).
- The MMPI-A has also been adapted and normed in Mexico with a large sample of Mexican adolescents. This version of the MMPI-A has been widely researched and has been shown to be an effective instrument for understanding Mexican adolescents' personality and symptoms.
- The MMPI-A Hispania and the Mexican version of the MMPI-A provide norms that are highly comparable with the U.S. MMPI-A norms, with similar mean scores and standard deviations across the three normative distributions.
- Practitioners could choose the most appropriate version of these forms of the MMPI-A (with the appropriate reference population) to assess Hispanic adolescents in the United States on the basis of the adolescent client's language skills and level of acculturation.

8

CLINICAL INTERPRETATION OF THE MMPI-A WITH HISPANIC CLIENTS: CASE STUDIES

Now that we have summarized the MMPI-A scales and explored Spanish language translations and adaptations, we can look more specifically at how the instrument works in describing Hispanic clients. The six case studies included in this chapter illustrate the MMPI-A in several settings or applications and with a diverse range of adolescents. These case examples include Hispanic adolescents from the United States, Mexico, and Peru. In most cases, in addition to the behavioral history, problems, MMPI-A profiles, and interpretation points, we provide a computer-based interpretive report on the client. This interpretation allows the reader to see how objective test interpretation works in depicting mental health problems in adolescents from diverse backgrounds.

CASE 1: A DELINQUENT ADOLESCENT

Juan C., age 15, was seen for a psychological evaluation in a juvenile correctional facility where he was being held pending a court hearing. He had been arrested, along with two friends, over the previous weekend for possession of marijuana and having an open bottle in their vehicle after a driving incident involving a high-speed chase. This was Juan's second arrest for a drug offence in the past 3 months. Following the evaluation and an initial hearing with an arbitrator assigned to his case, Juan was released in his mother's custody to await a later trial date. In the meantime, the court-appointed psychologist recommended that Juan enter into a drug–alcohol treatment program for his substance abuse problems.

Juan, originally from Mexico, had lived in the United States for the past 6 years with his mother and two siblings. His father did not live with the family most of the year but worked in another state. Juan had been attending middle school and had completed the eighth grade before encountering academic difficulties in his ninth-grade classes. He had missed a great deal of school and was suspended for 3 months for fighting. When he returned to school, he was placed in a special school program for adolescents with behavior problems.

In the psychological evaluation, it was determined that Juan was able to read and understand English well enough to be interviewed and administered

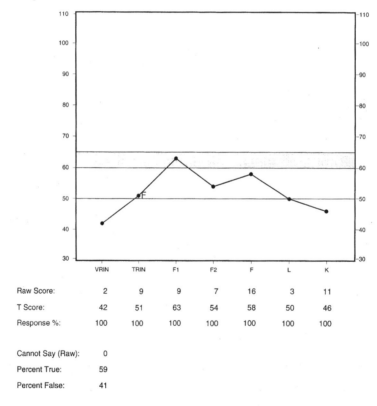

	VRIN	TRIN	F1	F2	F	L	K
Raw Score:	2	9	9	7	16	3	11
T Score:	42	51	63	54	58	50	46
Response %:	100	100	100	100	100	100	100

Cannot Say (Raw): 0

Percent True: 59

Percent False: 41

Figure 8.1. MMPI-A validity scale profile for Juan C. The scales include *VRIN* (Variable Responding Inconsistency), *TRIN* (True Responding), *F* (Infrequency), *L* (Lie), *K* (Defensiveness).

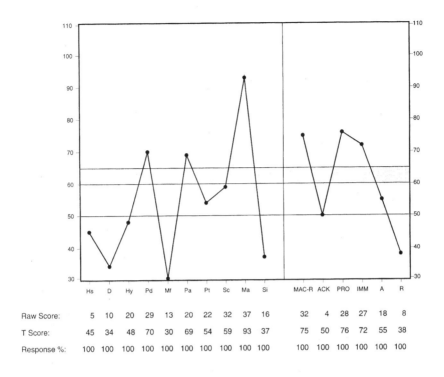

	Hs	D	Hy	Pd	Mf	Pa	Pt	Sc	Ma	Si		MAC-R	ACK	PRO	IMM	A	R
Raw Score:	5	10	20	29	13	20	22	32	37	16		32	4	28	27	18	8
T Score:	45	34	48	70	30	69	54	59	93	37		75	50	76	72	55	38
Response %:	100	100	100	100	100	100	100	100	100	100		100	100	100	100	100	100

Welsh Code: 9*"4'6+-87/31:025# FL/K:

Mean Profile Elevation: 59.0

Figure 8.2. MMPI-A clinical and supplementary scale profile for Juan C. The scales include *Hs* (Hypochondriasis), *D* (Depression), *Hy* (Hysteria), *Pd* (Psychopathic Deviation), *Mf* (Masculinity–Femininity), *Pa* (Paranoia), *Pt* (Psychasthenia), *Sc* (Schizophrenia), *Ma* (Hypomania), *Si* (Social Introversion), *MAC-R* (MacAndrew Alcoholism—Revised), *ACK* (Alcohol/Drug Problem Acknowledgment), *PRO* (Proneness Toward Alcohol and Substance Abuse), *IMM* (Immaturity), *A* (Anxiety), and *R* (Repression).

English language tests. His MMPI-A test profiles are shown in Figures 8.1, 8.2, and 8.3. The Minnesota Report narrative is presented in Exhibit 8.1.

Juan failed to follow up on the substance abuse referral and failed to show up for his court date. His mother reported to the court-appointed arbitrator that Juan had not been living at home for the past month and that she did not know his whereabouts. The Minnesota Report addresses several issues pertaining to Juan's adjustment disorder, particularly the conduct problems, substance abuse involvement, and relationship difficulties.

Comment: The MMPI-A clinical profile shown in Figure 8.2 provides a useful summary of Juan's developing personality problems. His high-point MMPI-A scores on *Ma* (Hypomania), *Pd* (Psychopathic Deviate), and *Pa* (Paranoia) reflect the possibility of extreme acting-out, aggressive behavior, as noted in the Minnesota Report in Exhibit 8.1. Moreover, his scores on

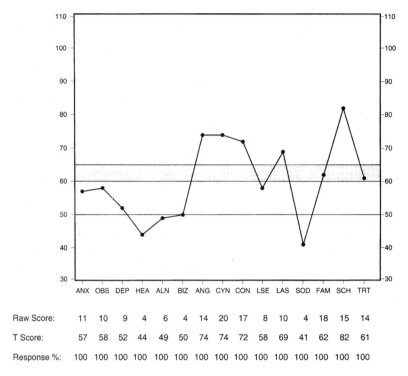

	ANX	OBS	DEP	HEA	ALN	BIZ	ANG	CYN	CON	LSE	LAS	SOD	FAM	SCH	TRT
Raw Score:	11	10	9	4	6	4	14	20	17	8	10	4	18	15	14
T Score:	57	58	52	44	49	50	74	74	72	58	69	41	62	82	61
Response %:	100	100	100	100	100	100	100	100	100	100	100	100	100	100	100

Figure 8.3. MMPI-A content scale profile for Juan C. The scales include *A-anx* (Anxiety), *A-obs* (Obsessiveness), *A-dep* (Depression), *A-hea* (Health Concerns), *A-aln* (Alienation), *A-biz* (Bizarre Mentation), *A-ang* (Anger), *A-cyn* (Cynicism), *A-con* (Conduct Problems), *A-lse* (Low Self-Esteem), *A-las* (Low Aspiration), *A-sod* (Social Discomfort), *A-fam* (Family Concerns), *A-sch* (School Problems), and *A-trt* (Negative Treatment Indicators).

the substance abuse scales MAC-R (MacAndrew Alcoholism—Revised) and PRO (Proneness Toward Alcohol and Substance Abuse) indicate a developing substance abuse problem, although his low score on the ACK (Alcohol/Drug Problem Acknowledgment) scale indicates that he was not openly admitting to problems at the time the test was administered. This scale discrepancy is found among substance-abusing individuals who deny that they have a drug or alcohol problem. The computer-based interpretation addresses the problems Juan was experiencing in the area of aggressive behavior and substance abuse problems. The report also notes the possibility that his behavior may have an affective disorder basis that should be followed up. His severe adjustment difficulties and impulse control problems would be likely to continue, and his low frustration tolerance and need for constant stimulation would likely cause him to continue to behave recklessly or irresponsibly. Juan's failure to follow up on the substance abuse referral reflects the likelihood that he was not ready to alter his pattern of behavior.

EXHIBIT 8.1
Minnesota Report (Juan C.)

Validity Considerations

This adolescent responded to the items in a cooperative manner, producing a valid MMPI-A. His profiles are likely to be a good indication of his current personality functioning.

Symptomatic Behavior

His MMPI-A clinical scales profile suggests severe adjustment difficulties including impulse-control problems. His low frustration tolerance and need for constant stimulation cause him to behave recklessly or irresponsibly. He is a risk-taker who probably abuses alcohol or other drugs. His numerous behavior problems include authority conflicts, school maladjustment, and family difficulties. Serious antisocial behavior problems are evident given his elevated *A-con* (Conduct Problems) score. These problems may have come to the attention of the courts or other officials.

Self-indulgent, hedonistic, immature, and defiant if his desires are frustrated, he appears to have an exaggerated sense of self-importance and may have quite grandiose plans. He charms and persuades others easily, but he may actually feel quite insecure and inadequate. He excessively denies problems or tends to blame others for them. He may be overactive, agitated, irritable, and moody. He is prone to angry outbursts when he becomes frustrated.

His two highest MMPI-A clinical scales, *Pd* and *Ma*, are the most frequent two-point scale elevations among adolescent boys in both mental health and alcohol/drug treatment settings. Over 20% of boys in treatment programs have these two scales prominent in their clinical profile. It should be noted that this high-point pair is the second most frequent scale pair in the normative boys' sample as well (representing almost 6% of the sample). However, *Pd* and *Ma* scale elevations are usually lower in the normative sample than in adolescent treatment samples.

His MMPI-A content scales profile reveals important areas to consider in his evaluation. He reports many behavioral problems, including stealing, shoplifting, lying, breaking or destroying property, being disrespectful, swearing, or being oppositional. He may belong to a peer group that is frequently in trouble and encourages deviant behavior. Poor academic performance and behavioral problems in school are also possible, as are behavior problems at home. Assaultive or aggressive acting-out behavior may be present given his report of considerable problems in controlling his anger. He may appear overly interested in violence and aggression.

This young person reports numerous difficulties in school. He probably has poor academic performance and does not participate in school activities. He may have a history of truancy or suspensions from school. He probably has very negative attitudes about school, possibly reporting that the only positive aspect of school is being with his friends. He has limited expectations of success in school and is not very interested or invested in succeeding.

Interpersonal Relations

He is frankly exploitive in relationships, using his charm and powers of persuasion to con others. He avoids deep emotional attachments. His social behavior might be punctuated with periods of moodiness and open expression of negative feelings.

Some problems with his relationships are evident from his extreme endorsement of items on *A-cyn* (Cynicism). He has numerous misanthropic attitudes. The world is a very hostile place to him, and he believes that others are out to get him. He looks for hidden motives whenever someone does anything nice for him. He believes that

(continued)

EXHIBIT 8.1   *(Continued)*

it is safer to trust no one because people make friends in order to use them. Because he believes that people inwardly dislike helping each other, he reports being on guard when people seem friendlier than he expects. He feels misunderstood by others and thinks they are very jealous of him.

In addition to his extreme endorsements on the MMPI-A content scales, he reports other significant interpersonal issues. Anger control problems are significant in his clinical picture. He reports considerable irritability, annoyance, and impatience with others. Temper tantrums and aggressive behavior may characterize his interactions. He indicates several family problems and may be experiencing increasing discord with his parents and other family members.

Behavioral Stability

The relative elevation of his highest clinical scales (*Pd* and *Ma*) suggests that his profile is not as well defined as many other profiles. That is, his highest scales are very close to his next scale score elevations. There could be some shifting of the most prominent scale elevations in the profile code if he is retested at a later date. This pattern of behavior problems and impulsivity may be resistant to change.

Diagnostic Considerations

Adolescents with this clinical profile may be diagnosed as having one of the disruptive behavior disorders, although the possibility of a cyclothymic disorder should also be evaluated. His highly elevated *A-con* scale may indicate the presence of an oppositional-defiant disorder or a conduct disorder. Given his elevation on the *A-sch* scale, his diagnostic evaluation could include assessment of possible academic skills deficits and behavior problems. Academic underachievement, a general lack of interest in any school activities, and low expectations of success are likely to play a role in his problems.

He obtained extremely high scores on *MAC-R* and *PRO*, indicating a high potential for developing alcohol or other drug problems. He probably engages in risk-taking behaviors and tends toward exhibitionism. He probably belongs to a peer group that uses alcohol or other drugs. His involvement in an alcohol- or drug-abusing lifestyle should be further evaluated. Problems at home or school are likely given his problems with alcohol or other drugs.

However, he has not acknowledged through his item responses substantial problematic use of alcohol or other drugs. He is not willing to admit to problems with alcohol or other drugs, or he may be unaware of the extent to which his use interferes with his ability to meet his responsibilities.

Treatment Considerations

Adolescents with this MMPI-A clinical scales profile tend to be poor candidates for traditional psychotherapy. Although they may initially appear agreeable and cooperative and may seem to "enjoy" treatment, they soon become bored or distracted by other activities and terminate before there is significant behavior change. Therefore, a behavioral management approach may be best, unless other problems are revealed.

This individual's very high potential for developing alcohol or drug problems requires attention in therapy if important life changes are to be made. However, his relatively low awareness of or reluctance to acknowledge problems in this area might impede treatment efforts.

Conditions in his environment that may be contributing to his aggressive and assaultive behaviors could be explored. Adolescents with anger control problems may benefit

(continued)

EXHIBIT 8.1 *(Continued)*

from modeling approaches and rewards for appropriate behaviors. Stress-inoculation training or other cognitive–behavioral interventions could be used to teach self-control. Observations of his behavior around his peers may provide opportunities to intervene and prevent aggressive actions toward others.

He endorsed some items that indicate possible difficulties in establishing a therapeutic relationship. He may be reluctant to self-disclose, he may be distrustful of helping professionals and others, and he may believe that his problems cannot be solved. He may be unwilling to assume responsibility for behavior change or to plan for his future. His cynical attitudes and beliefs about others and their hidden motivations may create difficulties in therapy. His therapist should be aware of his general mistrust of others.

CASE 2: A SUICIDAL MEXICAN ADOLESCENT

The next case is presented as a means of illustrating the appropriate use of the MMPI-A in Mexico. The female client, who attempted to commit suicide, was evaluated with the MMPI-A and was in treatment in a psychiatric service in Mexico City. For illustrating the comparability of the different versions of the test, the MMPI-A profile data are graphed against both the Mexican and U.S. norms.

Gabriela G. was a 15-year-old-adolescent Mexican female who attempted to commit suicide because her mother caught her having sex with her boyfriend. It is important to note that premarital sex in Mexican culture is considered inappropriate and "sinful" for unmarried teenagers because sexual activity is expected to occur only within a marital relationship. As a result, Gabriela immediately reacted by ending all contact with her boyfriend and being angry, upset, and disappointed at her mother. She became highly despondent and ingested a large quantity of sleeping pills and antidepressants. She was immediately hospitalized and stabilized over the course of a few days. She was then referred for psychiatric treatment, which continued over several months. Gabriela had protested loudly about having to be in treatment. She stated that the treatment had not been effective. Yet, at the same time, she continued to have behavioral and academic problems at school. It is important to note she was an only child and that her mother was separated from her father.

Gabriela was administered the MMPI-A in Spanish as part of treatment. Figures 8.4 and 8.5 present her performance plotted against both the Mexican and U.S. norms. Her profile is considered to be valid and interpretable. A review of the MMPI-A profile indicates that she obtained clinically significant elevations (>65 T) on the following scales: *Pd, Pa,* and *Sc* (Schizophrenia).

T Scores

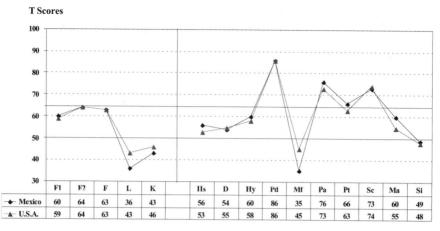

	F1	F2	F	L	K		Hs	D	Hy	Pd	Mf	Pa	Pt	Sc	Ma	Si
Mexico	60	64	63	36	43		56	54	60	86	35	76	66	73	60	49
U.S.A.	59	64	63	43	46		53	55	58	86	45	73	63	74	55	48

Figure 8.4. MMPI-A validity and clinical scale profile for Gabriela G. plotted on Mexican and U.S. norms. The scales include *F* (Infrequency), *L* (Lie), *K* (Defensiveness), *Hs* (Hypochondriasis), *D* (Depression), *Hy* (Hysteria), *Pd* (Psychopathic Deviation), *Mf* (Masculinity–Femininity), *Pa* (Paranoia), *Pt* (Psychasthenia), *Sc* (Schizophrenia), *Ma* (Hypomania), and *Si* (Social Introversion).

Clinically, it appears that Gabriela felt resentful, irritable, and angry, especially toward those whom she was closest to emotionally. An elevation on the *A-aln* (Alienation) scale indicates a tendency to withdraw from others, not share her feelings, feel misunderstood, and have poor communication skills. Her profile indicates a resentful and angry approach toward others, especially feeling marginalized. In addition, the results also suggest a tendency to be oppositional, deceptive, defiant, and perhaps manipulative and controlling.

Gabriela G. noted that she was caught cheating at school and had to be held back 1 academic year. She also stated that she had experimented with drugs and had been rejected by many friends as a result of using drugs. She said she had broken up with her boyfriend and appeared highly disillusioned over relationships. Also, she found it more and more difficult to talk about her "issues" or problems. Elevations on the *A-trt* (Negative Treatment Indicator) and the *A-cyn* (Cynicism) scales indicate that she may have been angry and resentful, defensive and guarded, cynical about treatment, argumentative and sarcastic, and generally defiant (see Figure 8.5).

A review of the supplementary scales indicates an elevation on the *PRO* scale, which assesses proneness toward alcohol and substance abuse. Although she did not admit to active substance abuse or even experimentation, the scale may have tapped into the potential for abusing substances, legal or illegal, including those that she had ingested. An elevation on

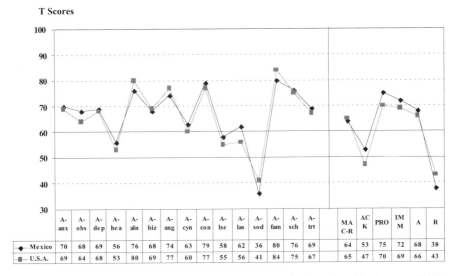

T Scores

	A-anx	A-obs	A-dep	A-hea	A-aln	A-biz	A-ang	A-cyn	A-con	A-lse	A-las	A-sod	A-fam	A-sch	A-trt	MAC-R	ACK	PRO	IMM	A	R
Mexico	70	68	69	56	76	68	74	63	79	58	62	36	80	76	69	64	53	75	72	68	38
U.S.A.	69	64	68	53	80	69	77	60	77	55	56	41	84	75	67	65	47	70	69	66	43

Figure 8.5. MMPI-A content scale profile for Gabriela G. plotted on Mexican and U.S. norms. The scales include *A-anx* (Anxiety), *A-obs* (Obsessiveness), *A-dep* (Depression), *A-hea* (Health Concerns), *A-aln* (Alienation), *A-biz* (Bizarre Mentation), *A-ang* (Anger), *A-cyn* (Cynicism), *A-con* (Conduct Problems), *A-lse* (Low Self-Esteem), *A-las* (Low Aspiration), *A-sod* (Social Discomfort), *A-fam* (Family Concerns), *A-sch* (School Problems), *A-trt* (Negative Treatment Indicators), *MAC-R* (MacAndrew Alcoholism—Revised), *ACK* (Alcohol/Drug Problem Acknowledgment), *PRO* (Proneness Toward Alcohol and Substance Abuse), *IMM* (Immaturity), *A* (Anxiety), and *R* (Repression).

the A (Anxiety) scale reaffirmed overall maladjustment, including self-undermining.

In general, it can be concluded from Gabriela's test performance and behaviors that she was immature, lacking in ego strength and self-esteem, and self-centered. It also appears that she felt like a victim, was rigid, and was unable to be flexible or open to psychological feedback. Therapeutic feedback was provided to help her with her oppositional, angry, defensive, and rigid attitudes and behaviors. This feedback, although difficult for her to accept, did appear to affect her in the long run to the point of slowly promoting some positive change.

Comment: The MMPI-A profile of Gabriela produced essentially the same T scores on the three normative data sets: Lucio's Mexican adolescent norms, the English language norms, and the MMPI-A Hispania norms, as shown in Table 8.1. All three norm sets indicate a valid and interpretable profile that reflects Gabriela's MMPI-A clinical profile (see Figure 8.4) showing her prominent high-point scale elevations on *Pd*, *Pa*, and *Sc* that predict her recent acting-out behavior history and her anger control problems.

TABLE 8.1
T Scores for Gabriela G., a Mexican Adolescent Girl, for the MMPI-A
English Language Norms, the MMPI-A Hispania Norms, and
the Lucio Mexican Norms

Scale	U.S. norms	Hispanic U.S. norms	Mexican norms
F1	59	60	60
F2	64	60	64
F	63	61	63
L	43	38	36
K	46	44	43
Hs	53	53	56
D	55	56	54
Hy	58	58	60
Pd	86	84	86
Mf	45	37	35
Pa	73	74	76
Pt	63	65	66
Sc	74	72	73
Ma	55	54	60
Si	48	47	49

Note. The scales include F (Infrequency), L (Lie), K (Defensiveness), Hs (Hypochondriasis), D (Depression), Hy (Hysteria), Pd (Psychopathic Deviation), Mf (Masculinity–Femininity), Pa (Paranoia), Pt (Psychasthenia), Sc (Schizophrenia), Ma (Hypomania), and Si (Social Introversion).

CASE 3: CHILD PROTECTION

Susana D., a 16-year-old bilingual Latina adolescent, was referred for evaluation by the state child protective agency (CPA). Susana grew up in Colombia, where she was raised by and lived with her paternal relatives following the divorce of her parents when she was an infant. Her mother migrated to the United States, where she eventually remarried, had more children, and subsequently divorced. When Susana turned 11, her paternal grandmother, who had been her main caretaker, passed away. With no other relatives willing to take on the responsibility of caring for Susana, arrangements were made for her to join her mother in the eastern United States. At the time of the evaluation, Susana had lived and attended school in the United States for at least 5 years.

Susana's family became involved with the state CPA following her disclosure to a school counselor that her mother was physically abusing her and making her take on numerous household and child-care responsibilities. Following substantiation of this report by the CPA, Susana was referred to out-of-home placement to protect her safety. It was also discovered that the mother was neglecting her own outpatient mental health treatment. In addition to these problems, Susana reported that her mother would treat her like a stranger, maybe because of our separation . . . but she expects me to be perfect, does not appreciate what I do that she tells me to do, does not care about how school is going for me, and believes that my friends are bad without even having met them.

Susana also described her mother as "isolative."

Despite these problems, Susana reported that she had a good relationship with other relatives on the maternal side of the family and that "because of their support, I am OK, I still want to go to school and succeed in the future, maybe even become a doctor or a counselor." She acknowledged feeling depressed episodically, especially "when there's an argument between me and my mother . . . I just go in my room, cry, and don't feel like eating." Susana denied substance abuse or suicidal tendencies. Because of difficulties with her out-of-home placement unrelated to her adjustment, she was evaluated at a time when she had returned to live with her mother. Because of the safety issues mentioned above, the family was being closely monitored by a caseworker.

Throughout the evaluation, which included measures of cognitive functioning, cognitive–academic language proficiency, a sentence completion task, drawings, and the MMPI-A, Susana was cooperative, compliant, and put forth a good effort. Therefore, the findings are considered to represent accurately her level of functioning. The evaluation was conducted bilingually, because Susana preferred to relate her background history in Spanish but preferred to respond to test instruments in English.

Because Susana expressed a preference for English for the testing instruments even though she had been in the United States no more than 5 years at the time of this evaluation and she preferred to use Spanish for conversation, it was important to assess her proficiency in both languages before determining the language in which the MMPI-A would be administered. When Susana started school in the United States, she was placed in an English as a second language group and was subsequently transitioned to an all-English regular education group without apparent academic difficulties.

The parallel evaluation of language proficiency in English and Spanish revealed that overall, Susana's level of proficiency was still higher in Spanish than in English for reading, spelling, verbal reasoning, and vocabulary tasks. Nevertheless, her score on a task of reading proficiency in English was well above the level required for the MMPI-A. Additionally, informal assessment of Susana's comprehension of MMPI-A items was conducted by having her read and respond to several items, which verified her comprehension of their content. In light of her lower level of English proficiency relative to Spanish, an estimate of her cognitive ability was obtained using a nonverbal measure. On this measure, Susana obtained a score in the average range.

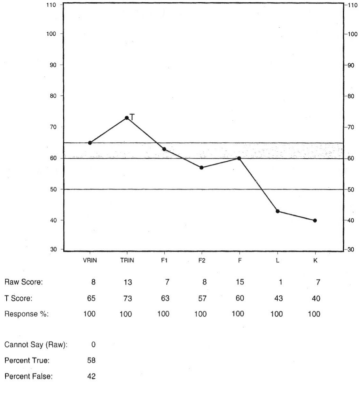

	VRIN	TRIN	F1	F2	F	L	K
Raw Score:	8	13	7	8	15	1	7
T Score:	65	73	63	57	60	43	40
Response %:	100	100	100	100	100	100	100

Cannot Say (Raw):	0
Percent True:	58
Percent False:	42

Figure 8.6. MMPI-A validity scale profile for Susana D. See Figure 8.1 for scale definitions. T = true.

Susana responded to all 478 items of the MMPI-A English version. She approached the inventory in an open, nondefensive manner, as reflected by her score of 43 on the *L* (Lie) scale. This nondefensiveness is further reflected by her *K* (Defensiveness) scale score of 40, which may indicate the existence of rather weak defenses and emotional vulnerability. Other characteristics of her approach to the inventory include the tendency to acquiesce (*TRIN* [True Response Inconsistency] raw score = 13) along with some degree of randomness (*VRIN* [Variable Response Inconsistency] = 65). It is possible that in spite of her adequate reading level in English, Susana may have become confused by the content or structure of some of the items, leading her to respond inconsistently in some instances. Her *F* (Infrequency) scale scores are in the high-normal range, indicating that she acknowledged some degree of emotional distress (see Figure 8.6).

Susana's clinical scales profile (see Figure 8.7) reveals elevations on Scales 2 (*D*, Depression), 4 (*Pd*), 7 (*Pt*), and 8 (*Sc*). These elevations indicate multiple emotional difficulties especially related to depression, preoccupations about her safety and her future, family conflict, and alienation. These

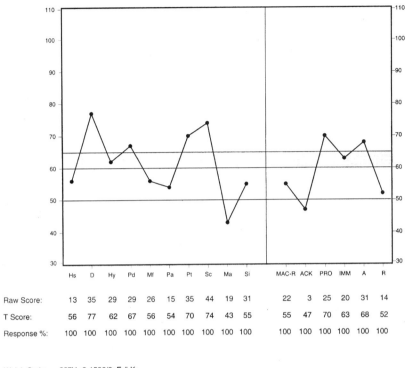

	Hs	D	Hy	Pd	Mf	Pa	Pt	Sc	Ma	Si		MAC-R	ACK	PRO	IMM	A	R
Raw Score:	13	35	29	29	26	15	35	44	19	31		22	3	25	20	31	14
T Score:	56	77	62	67	56	54	70	74	43	55		55	47	70	63	68	52
Response %:	100	100	100	100	100	100	100	100	100	100		100	100	100	100	100	100

Welsh Code: 287'4+3-1506/9: F-/LK:

Mean Profile Elevation: 62.9

Figure 8.7. MMPI-A clinical and supplementary scale profile for Susana D. See Figure 8.2 for scale definitions.

elevations appear to be consistent with Susana's experience of feeling help-less and defeated in the face of her mother's unrealistic expectations. Susana was likely to be confused and disappointed in her relationship with her mother, because she had hoped to gradually build a positive relationship after their long separation but instead the relationship, as she described it, was "like between strangers." She may have also experienced considerable confusion given her roles as child in the family but also as caretaker for the household and younger siblings and as an adolescent in a different culture. Finally, her mother's own emotional difficulties and inconsistent compliance with treatment were likely to add to Susana's overall distress and to be reflected by tendencies to be preoccupied and to experience anxiety, worry, and even confusion about her identity. The elevations in the clinical scales, in sum, seem to capture these issues accurately.

Additionally, content examination of Scale 2 (D) reveals elevations in all of the components, ranging from subjective feelings of depression to so-matic experiences of depressive affect and ruminative thoughts. Experiences

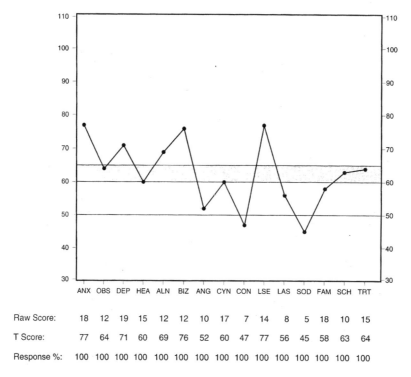

	ANX	OBS	DEP	HEA	ALN	BIZ	ANG	CYN	CON	LSE	LAS	SOD	FAM	SCH	TRT
Raw Score:	18	12	19	15	12	12	10	17	7	14	8	5	18	10	15
T Score:	77	64	71	60	69	76	52	60	47	77	56	45	58	63	64
Response %:	100	100	100	100	100	100	100	100	100	100	100	100	100	100	100

Figure 8.8. MMPI-A content scale profile for Susana D. See Figure 8.3 for scale definitions.

of self and social alienation as well as of low ego mastery are reflected in subscales of Scales 4 (*Pd*) and 8 (*Sc*).

As for the content scales profile (see Figure 8.8), there are also several elevations that are largely consistent with the elevations observed in the clinical profile. The more significant elevations are on scales A-*anx* (Anxiety), A-*dep* (Depression), A-*aln* (Alienation), A-*biz* (Bizarre Mentation), and A-*lse* (Low Self-Esteem). Susana was likely to experience pervasive anxiety around multiple issues, consistent with the elevation on clinical Scale 7 (*Pt*, Psychasthenia). In addition to the elevations in the areas of depression and alienation, the content scales reveal that Susana experienced low self-esteem (A-*lse* = 77), which is generally consistent with the multiple negative experiences in her background. Other content scales, although not at the level of clinical concern (T = 65), do approach that level and may have become significant in Susana's functioning. These include her score on A-*obs* (Obsessiveness), A-*sch* (School Problems), and A-*trt* (Negative Treatment Indicators). Although it is clear that Susana had multiple worries and tended to be preoccupied, her difficulties may also have had some impact on her overall school adjustment. She may also have had difficulty engaging in a therapeutic relationship, because she may have been afraid of further jeopardizing the status of her family, of becoming more aware of her emotional difficulties, and possibly of trusting others outside her family for fear of being punished or separated from family support. Of particular concern, however, is the elevation observed on scale *PRO*, which may point to vulnerability in her personality functioning that may have placed her at risk for substance abuse.

Comment: Susana's MMPI-2 profile shows a severe emotional disorder in which she was overwhelmed by anxiety, tension, and depression. Moreover, she felt helpless, alone, inadequate, and insecure at the time of administration. The symptoms that she reported on the MMPI-A, summarized extensively in the Minnesota Report (see Exhibit 8.2), suggest a need for psychological treatment and for development of a more supportive home environment.

CASE 4: JUVENILE COURT EVALUATION

Carlos F. was a 15-year-old Hispanic adolescent of Dominican background who was referred for evaluation following his arraignment in juvenile court on a wayward/disobedient petition. In addition to refusing to attend school, Carlos was both verbally and physically abusive toward his mother. Carlos lived in the Dominican Republic until he completed the 2nd grade of elementary school. The family had settled permanently in the United States by the time Carlos entered the 4th grade. As a 10th-grade student at the time of this evaluation, Carlos was failing all of his subjects.

In an extensive interview, his mother reported that Carlos's behavioral problems affected all members of the household, that "he is just not able to accept 'no' for an answer to whatever he wants," and that he "has set fires." At the time of this evaluation, Carlos had not had any psychiatric treatment. The mother also provided some developmental information about Carlos, describing him as a rather shy child from early on and that he developed some "unusual" habits around age 3, including refusing to eat if anyone sat in front of him and becoming extremely afraid in nearly any social situation. Additionally, Carlos developed an aversion to being touched, and at the time of this evaluation was still preoccupied with becoming dirty or contaminated, washed his hands "constantly," and took "very long" showers. According to Carlos's mother, he consistently refused to engage in any therapy. Carlos's biological father was not involved with the family, and his mother had not remarried or entered a new relationship.

When he was interviewed individually, Carlos presented as a superficially pleasant and polite adolescent. It was readily evident that he approached the evaluation process cautiously, because he tended to respond

EXHIBIT 8.2
Minnesota Report (Susana D.)

Validity Considerations

This young person had a tendency to inconsistently respond True without adequate attention to item meaning. Although her *TRIN* score is not elevated enough to invalidate her MMPI-A, caution is suggested in interpreting and using the resulting profiles.

Symptomatic Behavior

A pattern of psychological maladjustment characterizes individuals with this MMPI-A clinical scales profile. This individual is overwhelmed by anxiety, tension, and depression. She feels helpless, alone, inadequate, and insecure. She believes that life is hopeless and that nothing is working out right. She attempts to control her worries through intellectualization and unproductive self-analysis, but she has difficulty concentrating and making decisions. She is functioning at a low level of efficiency. She tends to overreact to even minor stress and may show rapid behavioral deterioration. She also tends to blame herself for her problems. Her lifestyle is chaotic and disorganized. She may be preoccupied with obscure religious ideas.

Her high-point *D* score is the second most frequent peak score in clinical samples (over 18%). This *D* score is also frequent among normative girls (over 14%). The *D* score is elevated above a T of 65 for about 20% of girls in clinical samples but for only 10% of girls in the normative sample. Extreme responding is apparent on her MMPI-A content scales profile. She endorsed at least 90% of the items on *A-anx* in the deviant direction, indicating that the following is quite important in understanding her problem situation. She reports many symptoms of anxiety, tension, and worry. She may have frequent nightmares, fitful sleep, and difficulties falling asleep. Life is very much a strain for her, and she may feel that her problems are insurmountable. A feeling of dread is pervasive, as are difficulties with concentration and staying on task.

In addition to the extreme endorsements found in her MMPI-A content scales profile, she also describes other important problem areas. She reports several strange thoughts and experiences, which may include hallucinations, persecutory ideas, or feelings of being controlled by others. She may worry that something is wrong with her mind.

Symptoms of depression are quite prominent in her responses to the MMPI-A. She reports sadness, fatigue, crying spells, and self-deprecatory thoughts. Her life may seem uninteresting and not worthwhile. Feelings of loneliness, pessimism, and uselessness are prominent. She has endorsed a number of very negative opinions about herself. She reports feeling unattractive, lacking self-confidence, feeling useless, having little ability and several faults, and not being able to do anything well. She may be easily dominated by others.

Interpersonal Relations

Problematic personal relationships are also characteristic of adolescents with this clinical profile. This individual seems to lack basic social skills and is withdrawn. Although she tends to be dependent and clingy at times, she may relate to others ambivalently, never fully trusting or loving anyone. Many individuals with this clinical profile never establish lasting, intimate relationships. This client's personal relationships are likely to be unrewarding and impoverished. She seems to feel inadequate and insecure in her relationships with others.

Some interpersonal issues are suggested by her MMPI-A content scales profile. This young person reports feeling distant from others. Other people seem unsympathetic toward her. She feels unliked and believes that no one understands her. She

(continued)

EXHIBIT 8.2   (Continued)

reports some misanthropic attitudes, indicating distrust of others and their motivations. She may be on guard when people seem friendlier than she thinks they should be.

Behavioral Stability

The relative scale elevation of her highest clinical scales (*D, Pt, Sc*) suggests clear profile definition. Her most elevated clinical scales are likely to be present in her profile pattern if she is retested at a later date. She may be developing a rather chronic behavioral pattern. Adolescents with this clinical profile live a disorganized and pervasively unhappy existence. They may have episodes of more intense and disturbed behavior resulting from an elevated stress level.

Diagnostic Considerations

Adolescents with this MMPI-A clinical scales profile may be diagnosed as having anxiety or dysthymic disorders. Characteristics of developing schizoid tendencies are also possible. This young person reports several bizarre thoughts and behaviors. If these experiences cannot be explained by alcohol or other drug intoxication, organic problems, a misunderstanding of the items, or an intentional exaggeration of psychopathology, a psychotic process should be considered. Her extreme endorsement of multiple anxiety-based symptoms should be considered in her diagnostic work-up.

Adolescents with very high scores on the *PRO* scale typically report being involved with a peer group that uses alcohol or other drugs. This adolescent's involvement in an alcohol- or drug-using lifestyle should be further evaluated. Problems at home or in school are likely, considering her involvement with alcohol or other drugs. However, she has not acknowledged through her item responses substantial problematic use of alcohol or other drugs. She may not be willing to admit to problems with alcohol or other drugs or she may be unaware of the extent to which her use interferes with her ability to meet her responsibilities.

Treatment Considerations

Many individuals with this clinical profile seek and require psychological treatment for their problems. Because many of their problems tend to be chronic, an intensive therapeutic effort may be required to bring about any significant change. Because clients with this clinical profile typically have many psychological and situational concerns, it is often difficult to maintain a focus in treatment.

This client probably needs a great deal of emotional support at this time. Her insecurity and feelings of inadequacy make it difficult for her to get mobilized toward therapeutic action. Her expectation for positive change in therapy may be low. A positive attitude is important for her if treatment is to be successful.

Adolescents with this clinical profile tend to be overideational and given to unproductive rumination and self-doubt. They tend not to do well in unstructured, insight-oriented therapy and may actually deteriorate in functioning if they are asked to be introspective. This individual may respond more to supportive treatment of a directive, goal-oriented type.

Her very high potential for developing alcohol or drug problems requires attention in therapy if important life changes are to be made. However, her relatively low awareness of or reluctance to acknowledge problems in this area may impede treatment efforts.

Adolescents with this clinical profile may present a clear suicide risk. This adolescent client should be evaluated for the presence of suicidal thoughts and any possible suicidal behaviors. If she is at risk, appropriate precautions should be taken.

(continued)

EXHIBIT 8.2   *(Continued)*

She endorsed some items that indicate possible difficulties in establishing a thera-peutic relationship. She may be reluctant to self-disclose, may be distrustful of helping professionals and others, and may believe that her problems cannot be solved. She may be unwilling to assume responsibility for behavior change or to plan for her future.

This adolescent's emotional distance and discomfort in interpersonal situations must be considered in developing a treatment plan. She may have difficulty self-disclosing, especially in groups. She may not appreciate receiving feedback from others about her behavior or problems.

---

to questions in a deliberate, detached manner following what seemed to be careful consideration of his responses. In sum, Carlos portrayed his family as "getting along OK" and minimized his mother's concerns about his violent behavior. Carlos only admitted that his problem was "when I get mad, but that happens only when I have to repeat and repeat things to my mother and either she does not respond or doesn't give me the answer I want." Otherwise, Carlos described himself as a "normal" person who experienced no symptoms of depression, suicidal ideation or plan, or unusual perceptual experiences. He denied the majority of the behavioral concerns reported by his mother.

As part of the evaluation, Carlos was administered tests of cognitive and achievement levels and self-report measures of personality and emotional functioning, including the MMPI-A. Carlos preferred to be interviewed and assessed in English, even though he tended to communicate with his mother in Spanish. Because Carlos had been enrolled in all-English language educa-tion since the fourth grade and had never had bilingual education, both the interview and the testing were conducted in English. Carlos was coopera-tive and compliant with the testing procedures, and the results obtained are considered to represent his level of functioning.

The cognitive evaluation reveals an overall average level of ability, with relative strengths on tasks that involve memory and visual processing over tasks that involve language processing. Carlos's reading and reading comprehension scores are well within the average range for his age group, indicating that he could take the MMPI-A without difficulty.

In one of the self-report inventories he completed, in which he was able to provide relatively open-ended answers, Carlos described himself as getting along well with his family and with school peers. He stated that his school difficulties were due to the teachers because "I don't always understand the assignments they give." It is interesting that Carlos also acknowledged that he tended to befriend others who "get into trouble" and that he "sometimes" disobeyed his mother and felt jealous. He also acknowledged having difficulties with impulsivity, social introversion, bad temper, and suspiciousness.

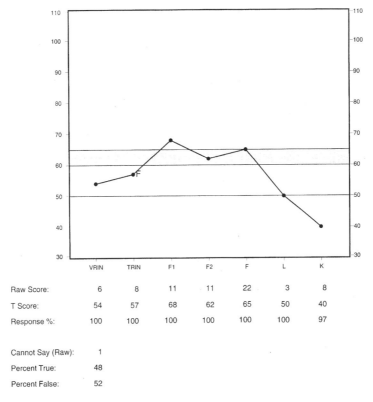

	VRIN	TRIN	F1	F2	F	L	K
Raw Score:	6	8	11	11	22	3	8
T Score:	54	57	68	62	65	50	40
Response %:	100	100	100	100	100	100	97

Cannot Say (Raw):	1
Percent True:	48
Percent False:	52

Figure 8.9. MMPI-A validity scale profile for Carlos F. See Figure 8.1 for scale definitions. F = false.

Carlos completed all 478 items of the English version of the MMPI-A. The validity indexes reveal that Carlos approached the inventory in an open manner (*L* = 50) and that his defenses were rather weak (*K* = 40). No extreme response sets or random responding are evident (*TRIN* raw score = 10; *VRIN* raw score = 6). However, his profile reveals that he acknowledged symptoms of emotional distress, as indicated by his *F* score of 65 (see Figure 8.9).

Carlos's clinical scales profile (see Figure 8.10) reveals two elevations at the clinical level, namely Scales 9 (*Ma*, Hypomania) and 0 (*Si*, Social Introversion). These elevations tend to reflect Carlos's difficulties with impulsivity and possibly other aspects of his functioning, such as ego inflation and amorality. Additionally, the elevation in Scale 0 reflects the long-standing social adjustment problems that Carlos had experienced since childhood. It should be noted that Scale 2 (*D*), although not at the clinically significant level, is at a high-normal level and should be considered in the overall interpretation of the profile and of Carlos's adjustment. It is highly

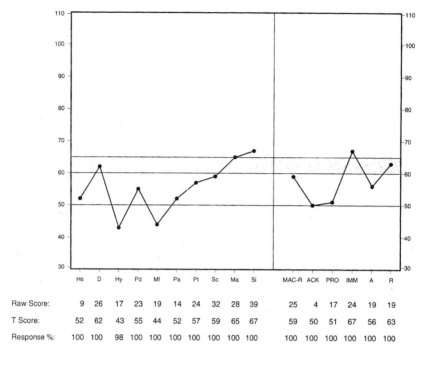

	Hs	D	Hy	Pd	Mf	Pa	Pt	Sc	Ma	Si		MAC-R	ACK	PRO	IMM	A	R
Raw Score:	9	26	17	23	19	14	24	32	28	39		25	4	17	24	19	19
T Score:	52	62	43	55	44	52	57	59	65	67		59	50	51	67	56	63
Response %:	100	100	98	100	100	100	100	100	100	100		100	100	100	100	100	100

Welsh Code: 09+2-87416/53: F+-L/K:

Mean Profile Elevation: 55.6

Figure 8.10. MMPI-A clinical and supplementary scale profiles for Carlos F. See Figure 8.2 for scale definitions.

likely that many of Carlos's difficulties have an affective substrate. Inspection of the subscales reveals that the Scale 2 (*D*) subscales associated with psychomotor retardation and mental dullness appear elevated, with a high-normal elevation in physical symptoms. These elevations appear to be consistent with the mother's observations of Carlos's tendency to isolate and to appear to have limited goals and aspirations. Also of interest is the elevation on the Scale 4 (*Pd*) subscale associated with authority problems, which were pervasive in Carlos's behavioral presentation at home and at school. Other clinical subscales of Scales 8 (*Sc*), 9 (*Ma*), and 0 (*Si*) are seen on the subscales profile. Specifically, the elevation in *Sc3* is associated with the experience of low control over thoughts, which may reflect Carlos's covert preoccupations and anxieties. The elevation in *Ma1* is associated with amorality, which in Carlos's case may be linked to a low level of awareness of the impact of his actions on others and his tendencies to minimize them or explain them away as "other people's fault." Consistent with the pervasive history of poor interpersonal functioning, the elevation in *Si2* is associated

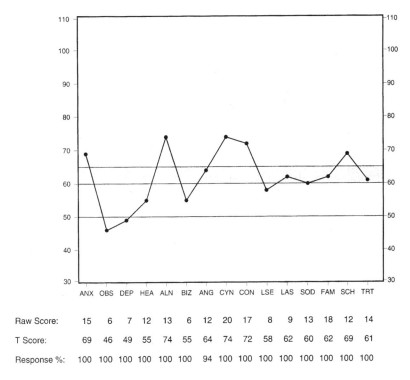

	ANX	OBS	DEP	HEA	ALN	BIZ	ANG	CYN	CON	LSE	LAS	SOD	FAM	SCH	TRT
Raw Score:	15	6	7	12	13	6	12	20	17	8	9	13	18	12	14
T Score:	69	46	49	55	74	55	64	74	72	58	62	60	62	69	61
Response %:	100	100	100	100	100	100	94	100	100	100	100	100	100	100	100

Figure 8.11. MMPI-A content scale profile for Carlos F. See Figure 8.3 for scale definitions.

with active avoidance of social situations, which had been observed in Carlos from an early age.

The content scales profile (see Figure 8.11) reveals elevations in several scales associated with many of Carlos's presenting issues. These include the *A-anx, A-aln, A-cyn, A-con* (Conduct Problems), and *A-sch* scales. These scales appear to capture Carlos's behavioral difficulties in a specific manner, as reflected by the elevations in *A-con* and *A-sch* in particular. It is also interesting that the *A-cyn* scale is elevated, which could be considered consistent with the general attitudes that have been described in Carlos. Nevertheless, his score on the *A-ang* (Anger) scale, although at the high-normal level, does not reach the criterion of T = 65. Content-component analysis of this scale , as well as for other high-normal scales such as *A-las* (Low Aspiration), *A-sod* (Social Discomfort), and *A-fam* (Family Problems), could be useful. Indicators of substance abuse risk appear within the normal range. Nevertheless, an indicator of immaturity is also elevated. This appears to be consistent with several behavioral characteristics of Carlos described by his mother, such as engaging in childlike self-soothing rituals when he was upset, having tantrumlike behaviors, and having difficulty with being separated from home. His mother reported that as part of the initial arraignment process, Carlos had been temporarily referred to a residential facility to address his physical violence and his poor school attendance, but he was not able to tolerate being separated from home and was eventually returned home on condition that he would meet all the expectations set forth by the court.

Comment: Carlos's MMPI-A performance suggests the strong possibility of a conduct disorder. His performance on the *CON* content scale and the elevation on *Ma* suggest a pattern of behavior reflecting antiauthority attitudes, aggressive acting out, impulsive behavior, and disregard for others that are likely to persist unless intervention can bring about more behavior controls. The Minnesota Report (see Exhibit 8.3) indicates that Carlos is not likely to see the need for treatment and may not participate fully in treatment plans. Some suggestions for behavioral treatment are included as a means of bringing about more behavioral controls over his aggressive behaviors.

CASE 5: ADOLESCENT DEPRESSION

This case was originally summarized by E. M. Lucio (2000) in a compendium of cases chosen by MMPI-2 and MMPI-A workshops to illustrate clinical interpretation of the test in international contexts. The Mexican version of the MMPI-A, originally translated by E. Lucio, Reyes-Lagunes, and Scott (1994), was used in the evaluation.

Alejandro Q., an 18-year-old man, had finished high school and was waiting to be admitted to college. Being admitted to public universities in Mexico is difficult, and this situation makes adolescents and their parents anxious. Alejandro had recently failed to obtain admission to a public university and was greatly depressed. He was from a high-middle social class in Mexico City, his reading comprehension was very good, and his family was well educated (see Figures 8.12, 8.13, and 8.14).

Alejandro entered psychological treatment for his depressed mood and was referred for an evaluation by his psychotherapist to obtain a picture of his current mood and behavior. He sought counseling to explore what career options he should follow.

His mother taught art history in college and was from a high social class family; at the time of this evaluation, she was 50 years old. His father was a surgeon, from a middle-class family, and he was 57 years old at the time of the evaluation. Alejandro had two younger sisters, one 15 years old and the other 13. His parents were divorced when he was 10 years old and he lived with his father at the time of the evaluation. However, some months before, he had

EXHIBIT 8.3
Minnesota Report (Carlos F.)

Validity Considerations

This is a valid MMPI-A. This individual was cooperative with the evaluation and appears to be willing to disclose personal information. There may be some tendency on his part to be overly frank and to exaggerate his symptoms in an effort to obtain help. He may be open to the idea of psychological counseling if his MMPI-A profiles reflect psychological symptoms that require attention.

Symptomatic Behavior

This client's MMPI-A clinical scales profile shows relatively few psychological problems at this time. He appears to be energetic, enthusiastic, and busy. He is involved in numerous activities. Although he appears to be very self-confident, he may overestimate his capabilities and overextend himself with projects that he has difficulty completing.

He may outwardly deny difficulties and look on the bright side even in the face of problems. Generally spontaneous and expressive, he may also be impulsive, preferring action to reflection and tending to be somewhat indifferent to details. He seems to enjoy taking risks. Adolescent boys with this MMPI-A clinical profile configuration have one of the most frequent high-point scales, the *Ma* score, among treatment populations. Over 16% of boys in treatment programs have this prime scale score in their profile. It should be noted that this high-point score is also the most frequent peak score in the normative population (21%), although it usually has a lower level of elevation than in treatment samples. In clinical samples, the *Ma* score is elevated above a T score of 65 in 18% of the cases, while almost 11% of the normative sample have this scale elevated above a T score of 65.

His MMPI-A content scales profile reveals important areas to consider in his evaluation. He reports many behavioral problems, including stealing, shoplifting, lying, breaking or destroying property, being disrespectful, swearing, or being oppositional. He may belong to a peer group that is frequently in trouble and encourages deviant behavior. Poor academic performance and behavioral problems in school are also possible, as are behavior problems at home.

This young person reports numerous difficulties in school. He probably has poor academic performance and does not participate in school activities. He may have a history of truancy or suspensions from school. He probably has very negative attitudes about school, possibly reporting that the only positive aspect of school is being with his friends. He may have some anxiety or fears about going to school. He reports many symptoms of anxiety, including excessive worries and sleep disturbances. He may have difficulties with concentration and attending, sometimes becoming confused. Life is probably a strain for him, and he may believe that his problems are so great that he will not be able to solve them.

Interpersonal Relations

At times the client's self-centered behavior is likely to produce interpersonal conflict. He is not very open to considering his contribution to these difficulties. Some problems with his relationships are evident from his extreme endorsement of items on the *A-cyn* scale. He has numerous misanthropic attitudes. The world is a very hostile place to him, and he believes that others are out to get him. He looks for hidden motives whenever someone does anything nice for him. He believes that it is safer to trust no one, because people make friends in order to use them. Because he believes that

(continued)

EXHIBIT 8.3   *(Continued)*

people inwardly dislike helping each other, he reports being on guard when people seem friendlier than he expects. He feels misunderstood by others and thinks they are very jealous of him. In addition to his extreme endorsements on the MMPI-A content scales, he reports other significant interpersonal issues. He feels considerable emotional distance from others. He may believe that other people do not like, understand, or care about him. He reports having no one, including parents or friends, to rely on. He indicates several family problems and may be experiencing increasing discord with his parents and other family members. He reports several problems in social relationships. He finds it difficult to be around others and prefers to be alone. He also reports some irritability and impatience with others. He may have problems controlling his anger.

Behavioral Stability

The relative scale elevation of his highest clinical scale (*Ma*) suggests clear profile definition. His most elevated clinical scales are likely to be present in his profile pattern if he is retested at a later date.

Diagnostic Considerations

No clinical diagnosis is provided for this MMPI-A clinical scales profile. However, possible authority problems and impulsivity should be evaluated. The client's highly elevated *A-con* (Conduct Problems) scale may indicate the presence of an oppositional-defiant disorder or a conduct disorder. Given his elevation on the *A-sch* (School Problems) scale, his diagnostic evaluation could include assessment of possible academic skills deficits and behavior problems. His endorsement of several anxiety-based symptoms should be considered in his diagnostic work-up.

Although the alcohol and other drug problem scales are not elevated, he has some other indicators of possible problems in this area. An evaluation of his alcohol or other drug use is suggested.

Treatment Considerations

Adolescents with this clinical profile who are in outpatient treatment settings usually see no need for therapy. If the other MMPI-A profiles or additional assessments reveal no further problems, they may enter therapy only at the insistence of others. Under these circumstances, behavior change will be difficult to accomplish.

There are some symptom areas suggested by the content scales profile that the therapist may wish to consider in initial treatment sessions. This adolescent's behavior problems may respond best to behavior management strategies such as contracting. His endorsement of several anxiety-based symptoms could be explored further.

He endorsed some items that indicate possible difficulties in establishing a therapeutic relationship. He may be reluctant to self-disclose, may be distrustful of helping professionals and others, and may believe that his problems cannot be solved. He may be unwilling to assume responsibility for behavior change or to plan for his future. His cynical attitudes and beliefs about others and their hidden motivations may create difficulties in therapy. His therapist should be aware of his general mistrust of others.

This adolescent's emotional distance and discomfort in interpersonal situations must be considered in developing a treatment plan. He may have difficulty self-disclosing, especially in groups. He may not appreciate receiving feedback from others about his behavior or problems.

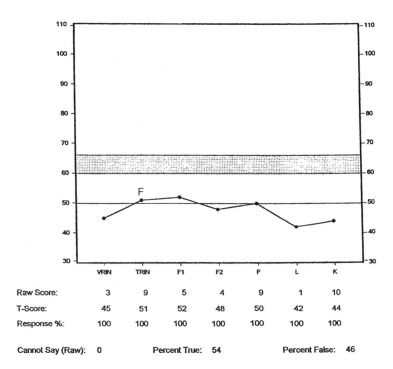

	VRIN	TRIN	F1	F2	F	L	K
Raw Score:	3	9	5	4	9	1	10
T-Score:	45	51	52	48	50	42	44
Response %:	100	100	100	100	100	100	100

Cannot Say (Raw): 0   Percent True: 54   Percent False: 46

Figure 8.12. MMPI-A validity scale profile for Alejandro Q. See Figure 8.1 for scale definitions. F = false.

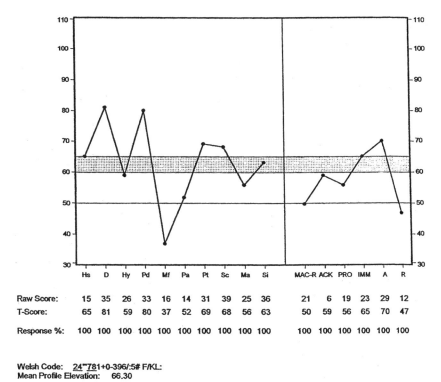

	Hs	D	Hy	Pd	Mf	Pa	Pt	Sc	Ma	Si		MAC-R	ACK	PRO	IMM	A	R
Raw Score:	15	35	26	33	16	14	31	39	25	36		21	6	19	23	29	12
T-Score:	65	81	59	80	37	52	69	68	56	63		50	59	56	65	70	47
Response %:	100	100	100	100	100	100	100	100	100	100		100	100	100	100	100	100

Welsh Code: 24"781+0-396/:5# F/KL:
Mean Profile Elevation: 66.30

Figure 8.13. MMPI-A clinical and supplementary scale profile for Alejandro Q. See Figure 8.2 for scale definitions.

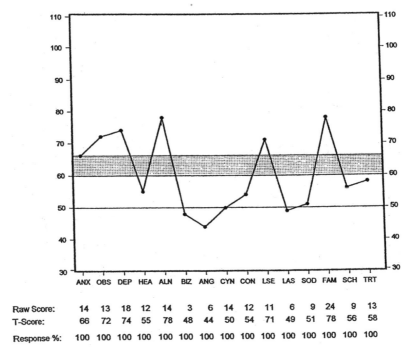

	ANX	OBS	DEP	HEA	ALN	BIZ	ANG	CYN	CON	LSE	LAS	SOD	FAM	SCH	TRT
Raw Score:	14	13	18	12	14	3	6	14	12	11	6	9	24	9	13
T-Score:	66	72	74	55	78	48	44	50	54	71	49	51	78	56	58
Response %:	100	100	100	100	100	100	100	100	100	100	100	100	100	100	100

Figure 8.14. MMPI-A content scale profile for Alejandro Q. See Figure 8.3 for scale definitions.

lived with his mother, his two sisters, and his stepfather. His mother had remarried 6 years before and had no children with her second husband.

At the time of the evaluation, Alejandro was not attending school. He had finished high school (preparatory) at a private school. Before he failed the exams for admission, first to a public university, and then to a private university, he was a very good student; his scores were always high. He was referred for the assessment because he did not know what career to choose and also because he was depressed, so his psychotherapist wanted to know what his aptitudes and interests were. The psychologist who carried out the assessment decided to administer the MMPI-A, because she thought that sometimes personality traits and symptoms can interfere with a person's decision about which career to choose. On the Wechsler Adult Intelligence Scale, he attained an IQ score of 119.

Alejandro was depressed and showed no interest in anything. His symptoms were sleep disturbances such as hypersomnia, feelings of worthlessness, diminished ability to think or concentrate, and indecisiveness. He had also been rejected by the girl with whom he was involved. He felt that his friends were treating him differently because he had failed the admission exam to the university.

He was trying to choose between studying medicine and chemistry. His mother did not want him to study medicine because she felt it required an excessively long educational commitment. To make matters worse, although his father did not tell him what to study, Alejandro felt that his father would like him to study medicine. Alejandro thought he would also like to study literature but was undecided. He liked chemistry but was not enthusiastic about it. He felt perhaps he was not good enough to study anything.

Alejandro reported that he quarreled constantly with his mother because she was too strict and made many comparisons between him and his sisters; she treated his sisters better. He also quarreled with his father because his father wanted him to do something while he was waiting to take the admission exam at the university again—he was neither studying nor working, and his father thought he was depressed because he got up very late in the morning. Alejandro stated that he did not use alcohol or drugs and had never been arrested or confined in prison.

According to the *Diagnostic and Statistical Manual of Mental Disorders* (4th ed.; American Psychiatric Association, 1994), Alejandro's diagnosis would be an adjustment disorder with depressed mood. He was being treated in psychotherapy with a psychodynamic orientation. He was not taking any medication at the time of the assessment but later started taking antidepressant medication. During the course of psychotherapy, Alejandro came to some resolution about his career plans and was determined to pursue chemistry when he entered college.

Comment: Alejandro continued in psychological treatment for a while and showed clear improvement. The results of the MMPI-A were provided to him and he found them useful. He was later admitted to a public university. He decided to apply for the chemistry program and passed the entrance exam. This diminished the negative attitudes he had about himself. He was getting along better with his peers because he did not feel that he was going to fail in everything.

The MMPI-A detected Alejandro's major problems: his low self-esteem, which did not correspond to his abilities; the significant anxiety he was experiencing; and the identity crisis he was going through, which was shown in the elevation of the alienation scale. The Minnesota Report (see Exhibit 8.4) described most of the symptoms and behavior. However, it was not accurate in suggesting that he could present acting-out behavior and problems with alcohol use or drugs. He had not acted impulsively in the past. In fact, he was shy, pessimistic, and rigid. He was worried, and decision making was problematic for him. The high Scale 4 was related to his family

EXHIBIT 8.4
Minnesota Report (Alejandro Q.)

Validity Considerations

This is a valid MMPI-A. The client is neither denying problems nor claiming an excessive number of unusual symptoms. His low *K* score suggests an overly frank self-appraisal, possibly presenting a more negative picture than is warranted. This may reflect a need to get attention for his problems.

Symptomatic Behavior

This adolescent's MMPI-A clinical profile reflects a high degree of psychological distress at this time. He appears rather tense and depressed and may be feeling agitated over problems in his environment. He may be experiencing a great deal of stress following a period of acting-out behavior, possibly including problem use of alcohol or other drugs.

He appears to be developing a pattern of poor impulse control and a lack of acceptance of societal standards. He may also be angry about his present situation and may blame others for his problems. He may be seeking a temporary respite from situational stress. He may attempt to manipulate others through his symptoms to escape responsibility for the problems he has created.

His two highest MMPI-A clinical scales, *D* and *Pd*, which are clearly elevated above other scales, constitute the third most frequent well-defined two-point scale combination among adolescents in mental health and alcohol/drug treatment settings. Over 3% of boys in treatment programs have this clearly defined profile pattern. It should be noted that this well-defined high-point pair is less common in the normative sample, where it occurs in less than 1% of the sample.

Extreme responding is apparent on this client's MMPI-A content scales profile. He endorsed at least 90% of the items on the *A-obs* scale in the deviant direction, indicating that the following is quite important in understanding his problem situation. He reports worrying beyond reason, often over trivial matters. He may be troubled by intrusive thoughts (e.g., "bad words") or unimportant things. His sleep may be disturbed by worries. Decision making is problematic, and he approaches changes with dread.

In addition to the extreme endorsements found in his MMPI-A content scales profile, he also describes other important problem areas. Symptoms of depression are quite prominent in his responses to the MMPI-A. He reports sadness, fatigue, crying spells, and self-deprecatory thoughts. His life may seem uninteresting and not worthwhile. Feelings of loneliness, pessimism, and uselessness are prominent. He reports several symptoms of anxiety, including tension, worries, and difficulties sleeping, and endorses several very negative attitudes about himself and his abilities.

Interpersonal Relations

His relationships may be somewhat superficial. He may use others for his own gratification. He is somewhat hedonistic and may act out impulsively without due concern for the feelings of friends or relatives. He has probably been experiencing strained interpersonal relationships.

He is somewhat shy, with some social anxiety and inhibitions. He is a bit hypersensitive about what others think of him and is occasionally concerned about his relationships with others. He appears to be somewhat inhibited in personal relationships and social situations, and he may have some difficulty expressing his feelings toward others. He may try to avoid crowds, parties, or school activities.

Some interpersonal issues are suggested by his MMPI-A content scales profile. Family problems are quite significant in this person's life. He reports numerous problems with his parents and other family members. He describes his family in terms

(continued)

EXHIBIT 8.4   *(Continued)*

of discord, jealousy, fault finding, anger, serious disagreements, lack of love and understanding, and very limited communication. He looks forward to the day when he can leave home for good, and he does not feel that he can count on his family in times of trouble. His parents and he often disagree about his friends. He indicates that his parents treat him like a child and frequently punish him without cause. His family problems probably have a negative effect on his behavior in school.

He feels considerable emotional distance from others. He may believe that other people do not like, understand, or care about him. He reports having no one, including parents or friends, to rely on.

Behavioral Stability

The relative elevation of the highest scales (*D, Pd*) in his clinical profile shows very high profile definition. His peak scores are likely to remain very prominent in his profile pattern if he is retested at a later date.

This clinical profile reflects some maladaptive characteristics that could develop into personality problems. Although he appears to be experiencing much acute distress, his personality problems may continue even after current stresses subside and he feels more comfortable.

Diagnostic Considerations

An adolescent with this clinical profile may receive a diagnosis of oppositional or conduct disorder with some depressive features. His extreme endorsement of multiple anxiety-based symptoms should be considered in his diagnostic work-up. Recurrent obsessions, including obsessive brooding, may be a part of his diagnostic picture.

Although the alcohol and other drug problem scales are not elevated, he has some other indicators of possible problems in this area. An evaluation of his alcohol or other drug use is suggested.

Treatment Considerations

This young person views himself as having so many problems that he is no longer able to function effectively in day-to-day situations. His low mood and pessimistic outlook on life weigh heavily on him and seemingly keep him from acting to better his situation. His low frustration tolerance and negative attitudes about himself may be very detrimental to progress in treatment and may require attention and support early in therapy to prevent him from becoming discouraged.

Some individuals with this MMPI-A pattern attempt to manipulate others through suicidal gestures when their needs are not being met. Because substance abuse is a strong possibility among individuals with this clinical profile, any use of medications should be cautiously monitored. This client should be evaluated for the presence of suicidal thoughts and any possible suicidal behaviors. If he is at risk, appropriate precautions should be taken. His family situation, which is full of conflict, should be considered in his treatment planning. Family therapy may be helpful if his parents or guardians are willing and able to work on conflict resolution. However, if family therapy is not feasible, it may be advisable during the course of his treatment to explore his considerable anger at and disappointment in his family. Alternative sources of emotional support from adults (e.g., foster parent, teacher, other relative, friend's parent, or neighbor) could be explored and facilitated in the absence of caring parents. This adolescent's emotional distance and discomfort in interpersonal situations must be considered in developing a treatment plan. He may have difficulty self-disclosing, especially in groups. He may not appreciate receiving feedback from others about his behavior or problems. He did endorse content suggesting a desire to succeed in life. There may be some positive aspects about school that could be reinforced. This could be an asset to build on during treatment.

problems, which he was exaggerating because he was sensitive and was depressed when he took the MMPI-2. The elevation of Scale 4 might also be because he judged himself and his father, who was supportive, very strictly. The depressive features were more important than the oppositional conduct. He was disappointed when he failed the admission exam and was feeling different from his peers. There were some small differences between the Mexican and U.S. norms, and perhaps the report would be more accurate if the Mexican norms were used.

CASE 6: AN AGGRESSIVE TEEN

The final case in this chapter, an adolescent from Peru, is included in this book to demonstrate the generalizability of the Hispanic norms in other Latin countries. The case was provided by Pampa and Scott (2000) and developed for the MMPI-2 and MMPI-A workshops case compendium on the international MMPI-A case studies to illustrate cross-cultural test interpretation. The Hispanic translation used in this case was the official University of Minnesota Press Hispanic version of the MMPI-A by Garcia-Peltoniemi, Azan, and Lucio (1998). The MMPI-A Hispania has been widely used and researched in Peru and demonstrates the utility of the instrument in other Spanish language settings.

Adriana L., age 17 at the time of the evaluation, was an only child. Her parents divorced when she was 3 years old. She lived with her mother and stepfather. Her mother had remarried when Adriana was 5.

Adriana was referred to therapy because she became violent toward her mother and broke the mother's arm. Reportedly, she had been demonstrating many aberrant behaviors: aggressiveness, bulimia, and problems with drugs and alcohol. Her mother had also been in therapy for many years and had been admitted to a hospital several times for depression and constant insomnia. Her biological father was a long-term alcoholic who was very abusive toward Adriana's mother; this was the reason for her parents' divorce. Her father married again and has another daughter. He had continued to drink until recently.

When Adriana was 15, she displayed many symptoms of bulimia. More recently, she had had a voluntary or reflective bulimia attack at least twice a week.

At 16, Adriana started smoking and drinking—about three glasses of rum and coke and several bottles of beer over a weekend. She acknowledged that she got drunk easily and became aggressive at times. She also started using marijuana at public parks but stopped 4 months before the evaluation.

She had been in trouble with the police and had been accused of being a small drug dealer and was under police scrutiny. She was smoking four cigarettes per day at the time of the evaluation.

Adriana was having a great deal of difficulty at school. She reported problems with some of her classes, especially math, chemistry, and physics. Her school failures required that she repeat the 7th grade. She was kicked out of school for aggressiveness and smoking and had been in three different middle schools. At the time of the evaluation, she was in the 11th grade and performing poorly.

Her relationship with her father was not particularly problematic, in part because there was not much communication. Most of the time her father was "*borracho*" (drunk) and continued to act aggressively toward Adriana's mother, often calling her names. Adriana only lived with her father sporadically, and he was never very nice to her. He would also call her names and insult her, but he never hurt her physically. Just prior to the time of the evaluation, her father had tried to change his behavior; he had stopped drinking 20 months before, saying he wanted to have a good relationship with his daughter and his ex-wife. Adriana's relationship with her stepfather seemed to be better and she seemed to respect him more. He was very strict with her and always insisted on her being truthful. He reprimanded her when she drank, smoked, or behaved inappropriately.

Her relationship with her mother was troubled. They argued frequently because of Adriana's behavior, especially the drinking and bulimia. Nevertheless, Adriana said that she loved her mother and did not mean to hurt her—sometimes she just lost control. She did not remember breaking her mother's arm; she said she was drunk. She had promised her mother that she would change, a promise she had not fulfilled because she felt her mother was overcontrolling. She claimed the bulimia started as a way to get her mother's attention. She also caused problems because she would not clean up the mess after the vomiting incidents that she would initiate by putting her finger in her throat. When her mother would not let her go out with her friends, Adriana would tell her mother that she was going to kill herself and it would be her mother's fault (see the profiles in Figures 8.15, 8.16, and 8.17).

Comment: As noted in chapter 7, whether one uses the U.S. Hispania norms or the standard U.S. English language norms, the results are virtually identical. Adriana's profile as seen in Figure 8.18 plotted on MMPI-A Hispania norms resulted in profiles highly comparable to those shown in Figure 8.15 (validity scales) and Figure 8.16 (clinical scales). The Minnesota Report (see Exhibit 8.5) summarizing Adriana's MMPI-A performance addresses the personality problems and aggressiveness that she was demonstrating in her relationships with her mother.

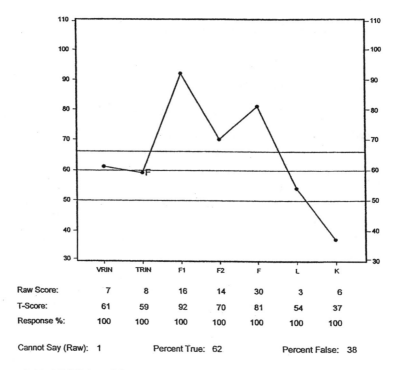

	VRIN	TRIN	F1	F2	F	L	K
Raw Score:	7	8	16	14	30	3	6
T-Score:	61	59	92	70	81	54	37
Response %:	100	100	100	100	100	100	100

Cannot Say (Raw): 1   Percent True: 62   Percent False: 38

Figure 8.15. MMPI-A validity scale profile for Adriana L. See Figure 8.1 for scale definitions.

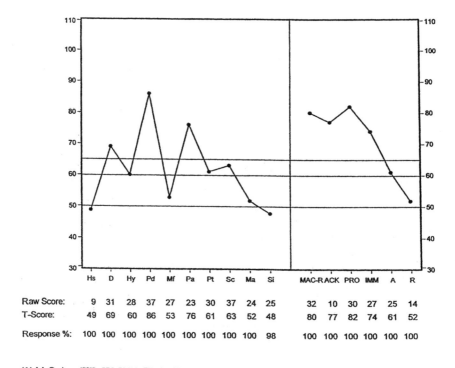

	Hs	D	Hy	Pd	Mf	Pa	Pt	Sc	Ma	Si	MAC-R	ACK	PRO	IMM	A	R
Raw Score:	9	31	28	37	27	23	30	37	24	25	32	10	30	27	25	14
T-Score:	49	69	60	86	53	76	61	63	52	48	80	77	82	74	61	52
Response %:	100	100	100	100	100	100	100	100	100	98	100	100	100	100	100	100

Welsh Code: 4"6'2+873-59/10: F""+-L/:K#
Mean Profile Elevation: 64.50

Figure 8.16. MMPI-A clinical and supplementary scale profile for Adriana L. See Figure 8.2 for scale definitions.

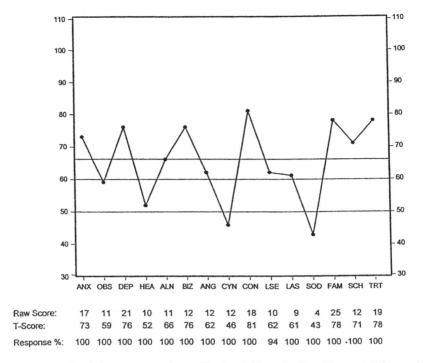

	ANX	OBS	DEP	HEA	ALN	BIZ	ANG	CYN	CON	LSE	LAS	SOD	FAM	SCH	TRT
Raw Score:	17	11	21	10	11	12	12	12	18	10	9	4	25	12	19
T-Score:	73	59	76	52	66	76	62	46	81	62	61	43	78	71	78
Response %:	100	100	100	100	100	100	100	100	100	94	100	100	100	.100	100

Figure 8.17. MMPI-A content scale profile for Adriana L. See Figure 8.3 for scale definitions.

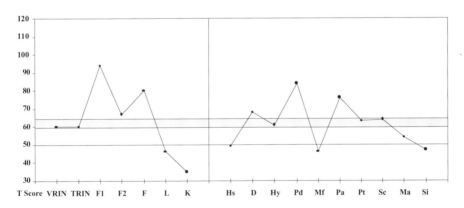

Figure 8.18. MMPI-A validity scale profile for Adriana L. plotted on MMPI-A Hispania norms. The scales include *VRIN* (Variable Responding Inconsistency), *TRIN* (True Responding), *F* (Infrequency), *L* (Lie), *K* (Defensiveness), *Hs* (Hypochondriasis), *D* (Depression), *Hy* (Hysteria), *Pd* (Psychopathic Deviation), *Mf* (Masculinity–Femininity), *Pa* (Paranoia), *Pt* (Psychasthenia), *Sc* (Schizophrenia), *Ma* (Hypomania), and *Si* (Social Introversion).

EXHIBIT 8.5
Minnesota Report (Adriana L.)

Validity Considerations

This is a valid MMPI-A. She is neither denying problems nor claiming an excessive number of unusual symptoms. Her low *K* score suggests an overly frank self-appraisal, possibly presenting a more negative picture than is warranted. This may reflect a need to get attention for her problems.

Symptomatic Behavior

Adolescents with this clinical scales profile show an extreme pattern of psychological maladjustment that combines acting-out problems with more neurotic and dependent behaviors. This individual tends to be quite oppositional, resistant, sneaky, and underhanded. She can be overemotional when things don't go her way. Her behavior is unpredictable and she is very moody. She may tease, bully, or dominate her peers. Anger-control problems may be pronounced. She may have problems with alcohol or other drugs, and she may have difficulties in school. More serious antisocial problems, including acting out sexually, are possible.

She can also be very clinging and dependent on adults (e.g., seeking their help, wanting to be around them). She may be troubled by beliefs that she is evil or deserves severe punishment. These ideas may take on an obsessional quality. Paradoxically, she also tends to externalize blame.

The highest clinical scale in her MMPI-A clinical profile, *Pd*, occurs with very high frequency in adolescent alcohol/drug or psychiatric treatment units. Over 24% of girls in treatment settings have this well-defined peak score (i.e., with the *Pd* scale at least 5 points higher than the next scale). The *Pd* scale is among the least frequently occurring peak elevations in the normative girls' sample (about 3%).

Her MMPI-A content scales profile reveals important areas to consider in her evaluation. She reports several strange thoughts and experiences, which may include hallucinations, persecutory ideas, or feelings of being controlled by others. She may worry that something is wrong with her mind.

She reports many behavioral problems, including stealing, shoplifting, lying, breaking or destroying property, being disrespectful, swearing, or being oppositional. She may belong to a peer group that is frequently in trouble and encourages deviant behavior. Poor academic performance and behavioral problems in school are also possible, as are behavior problems at home. She may be sexually active, flirtatious, provocative, or promiscuous.

Symptoms of depression are quite prominent in her responses to the MMPI-A. She reports sadness, fatigue, crying spells, and self-deprecatory thoughts. Her life may seem uninteresting and not worthwhile. Feelings of loneliness, pessimism, and uselessness are prominent.

She reported numerous problems in school, both academic and behavioral. She reported several symptoms of anxiety, including tension, worries, and difficulties sleeping.

Interpersonal Relations

She has a great deal of difficulty in her social relationships. She feels that others do not understand her and do not give her enough sympathy. She is somewhat aloof, cold, nongiving, and uncompromising, attempting to advance herself at the expense of others. She tends to be hostile, resentful, and irritable.

(continued)

EXHIBIT 8.5   *(Continued)*

Some interpersonal issues are suggested by her MMPI-A content scales profile. Family problems are quite significant in this person's life. She reports numerous problems with her parents and other family members. She describes her family in terms of discord, jealousy, fault finding, anger, serious disagreements, lack of love and understanding, and very limited communication. She looks forward to the day when she can leave home for good, and she does not feel that she can count on her family in times of trouble. Her parents and she often disagree about her friends. She indicates that her parents treat her like a child and frequently punish her without cause. Her family problems probably have a negative effect on her behavior in school. This young person reports feeling distant from others. Other people seem unsympathetic toward her. She feels unliked and believes that no one understands her. She reported some irritability and impatience with others. She may have problems controlling her anger.

Behavioral Stability

The relative scale elevation of the highest scales (*Pd*, *Pa*) in her clinical profile reflects high profile definition. If she is retested at a later date, the peak scores on this test are likely to retain their relative salience in her profile pattern. This adolescent's acting-out behaviors and extreme dependency needs may produce periods of intense interpersonal difficulty.

Diagnostic Considerations

An individual with this MMPI-A clinical scales profile may be viewed as developing characteristics of a personality problem. Externalizing behaviors are likely to be prominent in her clinical pattern.

She admits to having some symptoms of eating disorders (e.g., bingeing, purging, or laxative use for weight loss). She reported several bizarre thoughts and behaviors. If these experiences cannot be explained by alcohol or other drug intoxication, organic problems, a misunderstanding of the items, or an intentional exaggeration of psychopathology, a psychotic process should be considered. Her highly elevated *A-con* (Conduct Problems) scale may indicate the presence of an oppositional–defiant disorder or a conduct disorder.

Given her elevation on the *A-sch* (School Problems) scale, her diagnostic evaluation could include assessment of possible academic skills deficits and behavior problems.

She obtained extremely high scores on all three of the alcohol and drug problem scales, indicative of serious problems in this area. She probably engages in risk-taking behaviors and tends toward exhibitionism. She probably belongs to a peer group who use alcohol or other drugs. Her involvement in an alcohol- or drug-using lifestyle should be further evaluated. She has acknowledged having alcohol or drug abuse problems in her responses to the MMPI-A. Problems at home or school are likely given her problems with alcohol or other drugs.

Treatment Considerations

The MMPI-A clinical scales profile suggests that this individual has serious problems that require intervention. She will probably be a difficult therapy patient because of her distrust, moodiness, and potential for acting out. A supportive, consistent approach may be helpful. A directive strategy focusing on behavioral change may prove more beneficial than insight-oriented techniques. Her dependency needs may be an asset in building a therapeutic relationship. However, the relationship may be stormy at times, with the therapist being inundated with unrealistic demands.

(continued)

EXHIBIT 8.5   *(Continued)*

Her very high potential for developing alcohol or drug problems requires attention in therapy if important life changes are to be made. She has acknowledged some problems in this area, which is a valuable first step for intervention.

She should be evaluated for the presence of suicidal thoughts and any possible suicidal behaviors. If she is at risk, appropriate precautions should be taken.

Her family situation, which is full of conflict, should be considered in her treatment planning. Family therapy may be helpful if her parents or guardians are willing and able to work on conflict resolution. However, if family therapy is not feasible, it may be profitable during the course of her treatment to explore her considerable anger at and disappointment in her family. Alternate sources of emotional support from adults (e.g., foster parent, teacher, other relative, friend's parent, or neighbor) could be explored and facilitated in the absence of caring parents.

There are some symptom areas suggested by the content scales profile that the therapist may wish to consider in initial treatment sessions. Her endorsement of internalizing symptoms of anxiety and depression could be explored further.

During the course of her treatment, it may be important to discuss her sexual behavior. Her knowledge about sexuality and protecting herself against sexually transmitted diseases could be assessed and information provided, if needed. Perhaps in a trusting therapeutic relationship, she will be able to discuss the extent of her sexual activity and its meaning in her life. Alternatives to risky, promiscuous behavior could be discussed and promoted. If she is flirtatious and provocative, a greater awareness of this on her part may prevent unwanted sexual advances or possible victimization. Social skills training may be helpful in changing possibly inappropriate behaviors.

She may have several attitudes and beliefs that could interfere with establishing a therapeutic relationship. These may include very negative opinions about mental health professionals, an unwillingness to self-disclose, and beliefs that her problems are unsolvable. She may be unwilling to accept responsibility for her behaviors or to plan for her future. She may doubt that others care enough to help her or that they are capable of understanding her.

This adolescent's emotional distance and discomfort in interpersonal situations must be considered in developing a treatment plan. She may have difficulty self-disclosing, especially in groups. She may not appreciate receiving feedback from others about her behavior or problems.

9

SUMMARY AND FUTURE DIRECTIONS

The persistent arrival of immigrants into the United States, primarily from Mexico, has resulted in increased cross-cultural assessments in situations in which mental health or forensic practitioners become involved. Psychologists are increasingly being asked to evaluate clients from diverse cultural backgrounds who have varying levels of English language skill and limited awareness of American culture. In this book, we have examined many factors that can affect a Hispanic immigrant's performance on psychological measures such as the MMPI-2 or MMPI-A. We discussed a number of crucial variables that need to be considered for personality evaluation in multicultural assessment settings to be effective:

- *Linguistic factors:* Practitioners need to consider linguistic factors in assessments and to use appropriate Spanish language forms of tests in clinical evaluation of nonindigenous clients who do not speak English.
- *Acculturation level:* Interpreters of tests taken by Hispanic clients need to consider the level of acculturation or the process in which a person becomes adapted to another culture. The extent to which a person has learned the new culture can affect the person's adjustment to new environmental demands and can influence his or her performance on tests. Long-held cultural beliefs or behavior can persist in an immigrant's adaptation efforts, creating adjustment difficulties.

199

- *Stress:* The level of stress a person is experiencing from being an immigrant in a complex society needs to be considered. This variable can add additional ambiguity to the assessment process. When faced with immigration, illegal entry, or other difficult life circumstances, a person's psychological adjustment can be affected substantially. Assessment psychologists need to take stress factors into consideration when conducting an evaluation of Hispanic clients, because high levels of experienced distress can make assessment results appear overly extreme or invalid. Efforts need to be taken when possible to reduce the stress a psychological evaluation can add to the person's already troubled life.

The current need for valid and useful assessment techniques in clinical and forensic settings to provide information needed for decisions about Hispanic clients outweighs any psychometric or cultural factors influencing assessment methodology with minority clients. Personality assessment, usually dictated by the circumstances or context, needs to take place even though the methods may not be perfect and the conclusions provided only provisional. Although there is no perfect or totally accurate assessment device available for Hispanic clients, as the case studies in this volume show, the MMPI-2 and MMPI-A can provide important information in cross-cultural personality assessments and can be valuable tools for providing working hypotheses practitioners can use in their multicultural assessments.

A substantial history of cross-national MMPI adaptation research has produced effective cross-cultural test interpretation strategies that can be applied in ethnic minority assessment evaluations. Consequently, there are a large number of translated and adapted instruments available for use in other languages and cultures. For example, more than 50 years of research and clinical applications of Spanish language MMPI versions have provided a wealth of approved translations (Appendix A) and an extensive database of Spanish language research sources (see Appendix B) that can provide an empirical basis for using the MMPI-2 and MMPI-A with Hispanics who are being assessed in the United States.

IMPORTANCE OF DETERMINING PROTOCOL VALIDITY

Practitioners faced with the task of assessing clients in a multicultural context need to be alert to possible invalidating conditions that may be more pronounced in cross-cultural assessments than in those performed on the general population. For an assessment to provide useful results, the practitioner needs to be confident in the client's response attitudes and determine whether the client has cooperated sufficiently with the evaluation to provide reliable personality information. The MMPI-2 and MMPI-A have validity scales that have been proven to provide insights into a Hispanic client's response strategies (Bagby, Marshall, Bury, Bacchiocci, & Miller, 2006; G. E. Lucio, Duran, Graham, & Ben-Porath, 2002). Research on validity scales has provided the practitioner with the means of detecting invalidating conditions among Hispanic clients. A careful appraisal of the validity indicators for a client can give the practitioner confidence in the results in many cases and provide questions for the clinician to follow up on records of questionable validity.

Effective interpretation strategies for the MMPI-2 and MMPI-A were discussed and illustrated in chapter 4. Some suggested modifications in traditionally used cutoff scores for invalidity were considered because some response variation might be found among Hispanic clients. For example, some elevation on the *F* (Infrequency) scale can result from either stress or cultural factors as well as from linguistic factors. The clinician might be able to obtain clear hypotheses about the source of the client's response pattern by examining his or her performance on other validity scales; for example, if an *F* scale elevation is observed, then one can refine the interpretation by examining whether the person sufficiently understood the items by examining his or her performance on the inconsistency scales *VRIN* (Variable Response Inconsistency) and *TRIN* (True Response Inconsistency). In addition, some elevation on the *L* (Lie) scale has been noted in Hispanics as a result of cultural factors in which there is a need to present an overly favorable self-image. Elevations on the *L* scale can be evaluated further by examining the relative performance of the client on the *S* (Superlative) scale, particularly by comparing the relative performance on the *S* subscales.

IMPROVED MENTAL HEALTH SERVICES

This book has provided a number of case studies in which people of Hispanic background came to be evaluated by a psychologist for mental health, personnel selection, or forensic services. We addressed the topic of how best to fulfill such an assessment with useful and reliable personality-based hypotheses that depict the client's problems from a fair and comprehensive perspective.

Circumstances often require that a Hispanic person be evaluated in a mental health or forensic psychology context. One important goal in this volume has been to provide clearly defined interpretive strategies with clients from Spanish language backgrounds who are living in the United States so that test administrators can better understand their problems and symptoms.

It is encouraging that the test has been validated and shown to be useful when administered in Spanish in Spanish-speaking countries such as Chile, Argentina, Mexico, Peru, and Spain, among others. The traditional clinical scales possess essentially the same meaning and correlates in other countries as in the United States.

A number of examples in this book illustrate the use of computer-based assessment with Hispanic clients. One important value of the use of computer-based test reports is that they are more comprehensive and less influenced by subjective interpretation than are clinical reports (see discussion by Atlis, Hahn, & Butcher, 2006; Butcher, 1986). Although some theorists (e.g., Hays, 2001) have questioned the use of computer-based reports with Hispanic clients, the illustrations provided in this volume support this application. Research in cross-cultural computer-based assessment has supported the utility of this type of assessment in the objective appraisal of clients in cross-cultural settings (Butcher, Berah, et al., 1998; Butcher et al., 2000; Shores & Carstairs, 1998).

RESEARCH DIRECTIONS

Butcher (2005b) recommended that psychologists make more concerted efforts to develop research programs that incorporate multicultural components to develop broader views of psychopathology and psychological disorders:

> The future holds broad possibilities for psychologists to apply objective research methods to acquire more culturally based science of psychopathology. First, psychology is growing as a profession around the world. One has only to look at the expanding research developments in Asia, particularly China, to gain an appreciation of the extent of psychological research in the world today (Butcher et al., 2003). There is a growing assemblage of personality researchers in many countries that have both the motivation and qualifications for collaborative international personality assessment research. Second, the ability to communicate among researchers in today's high speed internet world is an important new development of the past ten years. Only a few years ago, it was extremely difficult to conduct cross-cultural psychological research because of the unavailability of a means for sharing research findings other than through scientific publications that often were years in coming to light. Communications were hampered by the high cost of international telephone communication and the unreliability of mail. In today's world even the most distant sites in the world can have computer internet hook up so that research collaboration can be frequent and thorough. Third, ready access to the extensive body of published research can be a great advantage to collaborating researchers today. For example, the

American Psychological Association's electronic referencing service *PsycLit* includes abstracts for international journals and makes cross cultural studies readily available. One only has to examine the broad array of research coming out of China to recognize that there is indeed a revolution underway in the science of psychology. Fourth, there are a large number of well-developed translations of the MMPI-2 presently available—over 33 (Butcher, 1996) that could serve as a basis for cross-national research studies. Fifth, one can have a high degree of confidence in the equivalence and utility of personality measures, like the MMPI-2. Collaborators in other countries have access to the MMPI-2 because of its availability in many languages. The broad use of more highly standardized and comparable item translations make research done in one country comparable and usable in others. This enables psychological research (even in remote areas of the world) to be cumulative. (p. 563)

Although the psychology literature included in this book gives the test user confidence in conducting multicultural evaluations with existing technology, some facets of Hispanic assessment that have received relatively less attention could benefit from further research evaluation. It would be beneficial to our understanding of the adaptation problems of people undergoing migration stress to pursue empirical research on these individuals. The scarcity of research on this transitory population, however, comes not from the lack of availability of instruments but from the lack of projects using them appropriately. For example, for several reasons, little empirical research has addressed the transitional Hispanic client during early adaptation efforts in the United States that operate to reduce information about refugees who are in the process of adapting to the U.S. culture (see Butcher, 1994; Halcón et al., 2004; Jaranson et al., 2004; Spring et al., 2003): Limited research resources have been available to study the individuals in this group; in addition, there are difficulties in identifying the individuals included in this population for study; finally, when identified, it is often difficult to obtain the cooperation of immigrants in research investigations. For example, during the MMPI-2 normative study in the 1980s, efforts were made to include a representative sample of Hispanics in the norms. We attempted to include newly arrived Hispanics but found that there was great reluctance on the part of identified immigrants to participate because they thought we were involved in federal attempts to deport them.

It is important to study immigrant groups empirically to gain a better understanding of the psychological processes involved in the ever-increasing and often debilitating process of immigration and acculturation. However, problems inherent in this type of research preempt careful extensive study. At this point, given the low level of research support for such a project, it would be valuable for psychologists to implement research that is presently possible with the more limited resources. Given the difficulties of conducting rigorous empirical epidemiological studies with the immigrant population, further information could be obtained by using smaller scale or more targeted clinical studies to document the problems experienced with this population.

With the availability of clearly valid, reliable, and useful objective instruments, there is an excellent opportunity for mental health professionals to engage in cross-cultural comparisons of psychopathology. The availability of carefully developed translations of the MMPI-2 and MMPI-A, such as the Mexican version, provides a means of conducting careful empirical research into the diagnostic and symptomatic problems encountered in mental health settings in the United States and Mexico. Some research on the relative performance of psychiatric patients in Mexico and the United States has been published (G. M. E. Lucio, Palacios, Duran, & Butcher, 1999) suggesting similar patterns of psychopathology among clients; however, no direct comparisons at the scale or interpretation level have been published. More specific information could be obtained by examining similar diagnostic groups across cultures as has been conducted in other countries (e.g., in Greece by Manos, 1985; in Turkey by Savacir & Erol, 1990). A study could be developed to provide information on the cross-cultural generalizability of mental health constructs. As noted above, the field of cross-cultural psychopathology research is in a strong position to provide objective assessments of psychological disorders to undertake a more objective comparison of the manifestation of psychopathology across cultures for a number of reasons: For example, further research on the generalizability of computer-based assessments could be developed by examining psychiatric clients in Mexico and Spanish-speaking people living in the U.S. mainland and Puerto Rico.

Another research direction that is presently needed, as highlighted earlier in the book, is a fuller exploration of the impact of low acculturation on the expression of psychopathology and its impact on the assessment process. Research on personality factors during the process of acculturation could add to understanding of the role of environmental stress on the adjustment process. Some personality patterns that immigrants express on MMPI-2 variables might be influenced by the stress of adaptation. The performance on such scales as F (Infrequency), D (Depression), Pt (Psychasthenia), and Pk (Posttraumatic Stress Disorder) could add to our understanding of the acculturation process if evaluated over time and the course of adaptation.

A third research area that could be explored to advantage with this population involves the role of persistent long-term personality characteristics such as those that make up personality disorders. Are long-term personality characteristics, as manifested in personality disorders, detectable in Hispanic clients who are in the process of adapting to a new culture? Research in cross-cultural settings (for a discussion, see Derksen, 2006) has shown that there are personality profiles suggestive of personality disorders that are addressed by MMPI-2 variables. Do people with pathological personality functioning have more difficulty adapting to the new culture than those without such personality features?

SUMMARY

This chapter has highlighted several life characteristics that can affect the performance of Hispanic clients on psychological measures such as the MMPI-2 and MMPI-A. Inability to communicate in the English language can be a handicap for Hispanic clients seeking help in U.S. mental health clinics. Moreover, being unacculturated or experiencing extreme stress as a result of migration can be a detriment to a reliable psychological appraisal. Both cultural factors and testing circumstances can influence deviant responding. It is crucial that the psychologist pay careful attention to the response attitudes manifested through the validity scales. With valid test performance, test protocols are likely to provide useful hypotheses about a Hispanic client's personality and symptoms.

The traditional clinical scales and content scales in MMPI-2 and MMPI-A have been found to reflect similar psychological symptoms and behaviors in Spanish-speaking clients as in majority clients. Improved clinical decisions with Hispanics in clinical situations can be enhanced by careful use of objective personality test information.

Several examples of the use of computer-based test reports have been included in the book and illustrate that this approach can be used with Hispanic clients to develop personality hypotheses about clients when the protocols are valid. The need for more extensive multicultural research in psychopathology was noted. In particular, there is a scarcity of research on transitory populations such as Hispanic immigrants to the United States.

The field of personality assessment is in a unique position at this time to incorporate multicultural and international research designs into assessment projects with the high number of qualified multicultural and international personality researchers, the rapid communication that is available through the Internet, and the extensive research literature that is now available to psychologists through document sources. Several fruitful avenues were highlighted as possible directions that future research might take to extend the knowledge base of Hispanic-related research.

APPENDIX A

Spanish Language Translations and the Translators and Scale Developers of the MMPI-2 and MMPI-A

MMPI-2

Translations and Distributors

Spanish for Mexico

Manual Moderno
Av Sonora 206 Col. Hipodromo
06100 Mexico, D.F.
Mexico
+ 52-55-5265-1100 (phone)
+ 52-55-5265-1162 (fax)
E-mail: info@manualmoderno.com

Spanish for the United States

Pearson Assessments
5601 Green Valley Drive
Bloomington, MN 55437
800-627-7271 (phone)
612-939-5199 (fax)

Spanish for Spain and Argentina

TEA Ediciones
Fray Bernardino de Sahagun, 24
Madrid 28036
Spain
+ 34-912-705-000 (phone)
+ 34-913-458-608 (fax)
E-mail: madrid@teaediciones.com

Translators and Scale Developers

Spanish/Argentina

Maria Casullo (translator)
University of Buenos Aires
Faculty of Psychology
Tucuman 2162, 8th Floor A
1050 Buenos Aires, Argentina
541-953-1218 (phone)
541-49-4332 (fax)
E-mail: casullo@insinv.psi.uba.ar

Chile

Fernando J. Rissetti (translator)
Departamento de Salud Estudiantil
Pontificia Universidad
Catolicia de Chile
JV Lastarria 65
Santiago, Chile SA5
562-638-0638 (fax)

Mexico

Emilia Lucio and Isabel
  Reyes-Lagunes (translators)
Corregidora 30-1
Col. Miguel Hidalgo Tialpan
CP 14410
Mexico, DF
525-665-6325 (phone)
525-528-5253 (fax)
Manual Moderno (distributor;
  see above for address)

United States

Alex Azan (translator)
Florida International University
Student Counseling Services
University Park-GC 211
Miami, FL 33199
305-348-2880 (phone)
305-348-3448 (fax)

Spain

Alejando Avila-Espade (translator)
Universidad de Salamanca
Department of Psychology

Rosa Garcia-Peltoniemi (translator)
Center for the Victims of Torture
717 East River Road
Minneapolis, MN 55455
612-626-1400 (phone)
612-626-2465 (fax)
Pearson Assessments (distributor; see
  above for address)

MMPI-A

Translators and Distributors

Spanish/Mexico

Emilia Lucio and Isabel
  Reyes-Lagunes (translators;
  see above for address)
Manual Moderno (distributor;
  see above for address)

United States

Alex Azan (translator; see above
  for address)
Rosa Garcia-Peltoniemi (translator;
  see above for address)
Pearson Assessments (distributor;
  see above for address)

APPENDIX B

Compendium of References on Spanish-Language MMPI, MMPI-2, and MMPI-A

Acevedo Corona, M., & Zarabozo, E. D. (1993). Un programa para la calificación automatizada del Inventario Multifásico de la Personalidad de Minnesota (MMPI) [A computerized scoring system for the MMPI]. *Revista Mexicana de Psicología, 10,* 195–202.

Adams, S. V. (2000). MMPI frequency scale using a Hispanic population: An ethnic validity study. *Dissertation Abstracts International, 61,* 2742B.

Adis-Castro, G., & Arayo-Quesada, M. (1971). Mini Mult: Una forma abbreviada del inventario multifasico de la personalidad de Minnesota, MMPI [Mini Mult: A short form of the MMPI]. *Acta Psiquiátrica y Psicológica de América Latina, 17,* 12–18.

Alamo, R. R., Cabiya, J. J., & Pedrosa, O. (1995, March). *Utility of the MMPI-2 in the identification of emotional indicators in a sample of Puerto Ricans who experienced armed assault.* Paper presented at the Annual Symposium on Recent Developments in the Use of the MMPI-2, St. Petersburg, FL.

Alba, C. G. (2004). Reflexiones sobre un grupo de adolescentes no pacientes. Comparación con pacientes anoréxicas y deprimidas [Reflections on a non-patient adolescent group. Comparison with anorexic and depressed female patients]. *Clíníca y Salud, 15*(2), 57–176.

Alfayate, R., Del Palacio, S., Rubio, J. L., Vallejo, M. N., & Fernandez, N. L. (1997, June). Factores de riesgo en la producción de trastorno mental después de un aborto espontáneo [Risk factors for mental disorders following spontaneous abortion]. *Anales de Psiquiatría, 13,* 231–235.

Altus, W. D., & Clark, J. H. (1949). The effect of adjustment patterns upon the intercorrelation of intelligence subtest variables. *Journal of Social Psychology, 30,* 39–48.

Aluja, A. (1991). Evaluación clínica y psicométrica del Trastorno Antisocial de la Personalidad. [Psychometric and clinical evaluation of antisocial personality disorder]. *Revista de Psiquiatría de la Facultad de Medicina de Barcelona, 18,* 59–70.

Aluja, A. (1994). Escalas empíricas derivadas de la escala de Desviación Psicopática del MMPI, para la evaluación del trastorno antisocial de la personalidad del *DSM–III* en delincuentes y no delincuentes [Empirical scales derived from the psychopathic deviate subscale of MMPI to assess the antisocial personality disorder, *DSM–III,* in delinquents and nondelinquents]. *Revista de Psiquiatría de la Facultad de Medicina de Barcelona, 21,* 75–84.

Aluja Fabregat, A., & Pérez Sánchez, J. (1994). Medida del trastorno antisocial de la personalidad del *DSM–III* mediante la escala de desviación psicopática del MMPI [Assessment of *DSM–III* antisocial personality disorder using the psychopathic deviate scale from the MMPI]. *Psiquis: Revista de Psiquiatría, Psicología y Psicosomática, 15*, 41–52.

Aluja, A., & Torrubia, T. (1996). Componentes psicológicos de la personalidad antisocial en delincuentes: Búsqueda de sensaciones y susceptibilidad a las señales de premio y castigo [Psychological elements of antisocial personality in delinquent people: Sensation seeking and susceptibility to reward and punishment]. *Revista de Psiquiatría de la Facultad de Medicina de Barcelona, 23*, 47–56.

Alvarez, M. A., Alvarez, E., & Lastra, R. A. (1982). Desarrollo psicológico en hijos de madres con bocio tóxico difuso [Psychological development in children of mothers with diffuse toxic goiter]. *Revista Cubana de Pediatría, 54*, 206–214.

Amaro, T. (1953). *La personalidad del normalista habanero, segun el MMPI* [The personality of the normal Habanero according to the MMPI]. Unpublished doctoral dissertation, Universidad de la Habana, Havana, Cuba.

Ampudia, R. A., Duran, P. C., & Lucio, G. M. E. (2000). El uso del MMPI-2 en población mexicana de la tercera edad [Use of the MMPI-2 in a Mexican third age population]. *Revista Iberoamericana de Diagnostico y Evaluacion Psicologica, 9*, 115–128.

Ampudia, R. A., Lucio, G. M. E., & Duran, C. P. (1998, March). *Relationship between the MMPI-A and life events in two groups of Mexican adolescents: Normals and psychiatric patients.* Paper presented at the Annual Symposium on Recent Developments in the Use of the MMPI-2, Clearwater, FL.

Ampudia, R. A., Lucio, G. M. E., & Duran, P. C. (1995). Confiabilidad de las escalas suplementarias del MMPI-2 en una poblacion mexicana [Reliability of supplementary scales of the MMPI-2 in a Mexican population]. *Revista Iberoamericana de Diagnostico y Evaluacion Psicologica, 1*(2), 25–49.

Ampudia, S. V. (1977). *Tendencia a la somatizacion en estudiantes de matematicas (estudio comparativo entre estdiantes de matematicas y medicina utilizando la prueba del MMPI)* [Somatization tendency in mathematics students: Comparative study between mathematics and medicine students using the MMPI]. Unpublished doctoral dissertation, National University of Mexico, Mexico City.

Anderson, R. P., Blanco-Picabia, A., Greene, R. L., & Rodríguez-González, J. M. (1988). Utilidad de la Escala de Alcoholismo de MacAndrews en la discriminación de alcohólicos españoles [The utility of the MacAndrews Alcoholism Scale for discrimination of Spanish alcoholics]. *Análisis y Modificación de Conducta, 14*, 431–438.

Anderson, T. R., Thompson, J. P., & Boeringa, J. A. (1993, August). *MMPI-2 and Mississippi scale profiles of Hispanic veterans with posttraumatic stress disorder.* Paper presented at the 101st Annual Convention of the American Psychological Association, New Orleans, LA.

Anderson, U. (1999). Validation of the MMPI-2 Masculinity–Femininity scale with Latino men and women: Preliminary findings. *The SDSU McNair Journal, 6*, 70–77.

Anderson, U., Fernandez, S., Callahan, W. J., & Velasquez, R. J. (2001, May). *Validation of the MMPI-2 Masculinity–Femininity scale with Latino men and women*. Paper presented at the Annual Symposium on Recent Developments in the Use of the MMPI-2, Minneapolis, MN.

Anderson, U., Velasquez, R. J., & Callahan, W. J. (2000, August). *Sex roles, cultural differences and Mf scores of Latinos*. Paper presented at the 108th Annual Convention of the American Psychological Association, Washington, DC.

Anderson, W. P. (1995). Ethnic and cross-cultural differences on the MMPI-2. In J. C. Duckworth & W. P. Anderson (Eds.), *MMPI and MMPI-2: Interpretative manual for counselors and clinicians* (4th ed., pp. 439–460). Bristol, PA: Accelerated Development.

Anthony, A. (2003). The validity of the MMPI-2 with two samples of Mexican American psychiatric outpatients. *Dissertation Abstracts International, 63*, 4359B.

Arayo-Quesada, M. (1967). *Estudio sobre al MMPI en su aplicacion a un grupo de pacientes psiquiatrico costarricenses* [A study of the MMMPI and its applicability with Costa Rican psychiatric patients]. Professional thesis, National University of Mexico, Mexico City.

Arce, R., del Carmen Pampillon, M., & Farina, F. (2002). Desarrollo y evaluación de un procedimiento empírico para detección de la simulación de enajenación mental en el contexto legal [Development and assessment of an empirical procedure for detecting simulated mental insanity in the legal context]. *Anuario de Psicologia, 33*, 385–408.

Arias, G., Mendoza, K., Atlis, M., & Butcher, J. N. (2002, May). *MMPI-2 use in Cuba: An illustration and future directions*. Paper presented at the Annual Symposium on Recent Developments in the Use of the MMPI-2. Minneapolis, MN.

Arqué, J. M., & Beltri, R. T. (1988). Personality, bioelectric profile and platelet monoamine oxidase activity in psychophysiological disorders: Headaches, insomnia and loss of consciousness due to neurocirculatory dystonia. *Psychiatrie & Psychobiologie, 3*, 263–267.

Arqué, J. M., Segura, R., & Torrubia, R. (1987). Correlation of thyroxine and thyroid-stimulating hormone with personality measurements: A study in psychosomatic patients and healthy subjects. *Neuropsychobiology, 18*, 127–133.

Arqué, J. M., Unzeta, M., & Torrubia, R. (1988). Neurotransmitter systems and personality measurements: A study in psychosomatic patients and healthy subjects. *Neuropsychobiology, 19*, 149–157.

Arsuaga, E. N., Higgins, J. C., & Sifre, P. A. (1986). Separation of brain-damaged from psychiatric patients with the combined use of an ability and personality test: A validation study with a Puerto Rican population. *Journal of Clinical Psychology, 42*, 328–331.

Arturo Boizblatt, S., Ruby Baño, A., & Germán Cueto, U. (1983). Depresión postaborto: Estudio de casos y controles [Postabortion depression: Case reports and control]. *Actas Luso-Espanolas de Neurologia, Psiquiatria y Ciencias Afines, 11*, 391–394.

Avila, M. Y., Izaguirre, H. C., & Sanchez, Q. C. (1970). *Normas de calificacion del MMPI en adolescentes en la E.N.E.P. at UNAM* [Norms for the classification of the MMPI in adolescents in the E.N.E.P. at UNAM]. Unpublished degree thesis, National University of Mexico, Mexico City.

Avila Escribano, J. J., & Ledesma Jimeno, A. (1990). Estudio de la personalidad en las esposas de pacientes alcohólicos [Personality study of wives of alcoholic patients]. *Actas Luso-Espanolas de Neurologia, Psiquiatria y Ciencias Afines, 18*, 355–363.

Avila-Espada, A., & Jimenez-Gomez, F. (1996). The Castilian version of the MMPI-2 in Spain: Development, adaptation, and psychometric properties. In J. N. Butcher (Ed.), *International adaptations of the MMPI-2: Research and clinical applications* (pp. 305–328). Minneapolis: University of Minnesota Press.

Avila Espada, A., & Jimenez Gomez, F. (1997). *MMPI-A manual para investigacion (adaptacion Espanola)* [MMPI-A manual for investigation (Spanish adaptation)]. Salamanca, Spain: Laboratorio de Psicologia Clinica y Psicodiagnostico, Universidad de Salamanca.

Azan, A. (1989). The MMPI version Hispanic: Standardization and cross-cultural personality study with a population of Cuban refugees (Doctoral dissertation, University of Minnesota, 1988). *Dissertation Abstracts International, 50*, 2144B.

Bailles, E., Pintor, L., Fernandez-Egea, E., Torres, X., Matrai, S., de Pablo, J., & Arroyo, S. (2004). Psychiatric disorders, trauma, and MMPI profile in a Spanish sample of nonepileptic seizure patients. *General Hospital Psychiatry, 26*, 310–315.

Bamford. K. W. (1991). Bilingual issues in mental health assessment and treatment. *Hispanic Journal of Behavioral Sciences, 13*, 377–390.

Barbenza, C. M., Montoya, O. A., & Borel, M. T. (1978). La tetrada psicotica del MMPI en un grupo de estudiantes universitarios [The psychotic tetrad of the MMPI in a group of college students]. *Revista de Psicologia General y Aplicada, 150*, 79–88.

Barcelata, B., Lucio, E., & Duran, C. (2004) Indicadores de malestar psicológico en un grupo de adolescentes mexicanos [Indicators of psychological distress in a group of Mexican teenagers]. *Revista Colombiana de Psicología, 13*, 64–74.

Barreda, O. (1976). Esquema interpretativo del MMPI en base a los grados de elevacion con factor K. [Interpretive diagram of the MMPI based on degree of elevation of Scale K]. *Revista de Psicologia de II Asociacion de Psicologos de Arequipa, 2*, 71–81.

Barroso, C. C., Alvarez, M. A., & Alvisa, R. (1982). Validación preliminar para Cuba de una nueva versión del MMPI abreviado [Preliminary validation of the new version of the abbreviated MMPI in Cuba]. *Revista del Hospital Psiquiátrico de la Habana, 23*, 581–590.

Becoña, E. (1985). Relación del conservadurismo con personalidad y adaptación en universitarios [The relationship of conservatism with personality and adaptation in university students]. *International Journal of Methodology and Experimental Psychology, 6,* 87–101.

Benavides, G., González, R., Barahona, A., & Paz Tévar, M. (2000). Características del voluntariado para pacientes con cáncer [Characteristics of volunteers for patients with cancer]. *Revista de Psicología Social Aplicada, 10,* 77–96.

Benito, Y., & Moro, J. (1997). *Proyecto de identificación temprana para alumnos superdotados* [Project for early detection of gifted students]. Madrid, Spain: Ministerio de Educación y Cultura de España.

Bernal, A., Colon, A., Fernandez, E., Mena. A., Torres, A., & Torres, E. (1959). *Inventari Multifacetico de la Personalidad* [Translation of the Minnesota Multiphasic Personality Inventory]. New York: Psychological Corporation.

Bernal, A., & Fernandez, E. (1949). *The MMPI in Cuba.* Unpublished manuscript.

Bernstein, I. H., Teng, G., Granneman, B. D., & Garbin, C. P. (1987). Invariance in the MMPI's component structure. *Journal of Personality Assessment, 51,* 522–531.

Bertran, R. P., Gil, C. M., Montoya-Rico, J. L., & Reyes, J. R.(1968). Professional and psychological evaluation of personnel at the psychiatric hospital in Oviedo. *Revista de Psicología General y Aplicada, 23*(91), 77–93.

Blanco, C., Ibáñez, A., Blanco-Jerez, C.-R., Baca-Garcia, E., & Sáiz-Ruiz, J. (2001). Plasma testosterone and pathological gambling. *Psychiatry Research, 105,* 117–121.

Blanco, C., Orensanz-Muñoz, L., Blanco-Jerez, C., & Saiz-Ruiz, J. (1996). Pathological gambling and platelet MAO activity: A psychobiological study. *American Journal of Psychiatry, 153,* 119–121.

Blanco González, A. L., Ledesma, J. A., Llorca, R. G., Delgado, M. M. E., García, C. L., & Matías, P. J. (1988). Aspectos psicopatológicos de las neoplasias hematológicas [Psychopathological aspects of neoplasms]. *Actas Luso-Españolas de Neurología, Psiquiatría y Ciencias Afines, 16,* 375–384.

Bohn, M. J., & Traub, G. S. (1986). Alienation of monolingual Hispanics in a federal correctional institution. *Psychological Reports, 59,* 560–562.

Boscan, D., Penn, N., Gomez, N., Velasquez, R., Reimann, J., & Aguila, J. (1998, March). *MMPI-2 personality of Venezuelan and Colombian university students.* Paper presented at the 16th International Conference on Personality Assessment, Clearwater, FL.

Boscan, D. C., Penn, N. E., Velasquez, R. J., Reimann, J., Gomez, N., Guzman, M., et al. (2000). MMPI-2 profiles of Colombian, Mexican, and Venezuelan university students. *Psychological Reports, 87,* 107–110.

Boscan, D. C., Penn, N. E., Velasquez, R. J., Savino, A., Maness, P., Guzman, M., & Reimann, J. (2002). MMPI-2 performance of Mexican male university students and prison inmates. *Journal of Clinical Psychology, 58,* 465–470.

Boscan, D. C., Savino, A. V., Penn, N. E., Velasquez, R. J., Gomez, F. C., Jr., & Guzman, M. (1999, April). *MMPI-2 performance of Mexican prison inmates: Clinical correlates.* Paper presented at the 34th Annual Symposium on Recent

Developments in the Use of the MMPI-2 and MMPI-A, Huntington, Beach, CA.

Bradford, D. T., & Munoz, A. (1993). Translation in bilingual psychotherapy. *Professional Psychology: Research and Practice, 2*, 52–61.

Brenella, M. E., Dink, L., & Maristany, M. (1992). *Evaluacion objective de la personalidad, aportes del MMPI-2* [Objective personality evaluation with the MMPI]. Buenos Aires, Argentina: Psicoteca Ed.

Butcher, J. N. (1992, October). International developments with the MMPI-2. *MMPI-2 News & Profiles, 4.*

Butcher, J. N. (Ed.). (1996). *International adaptations of the MMPI-2: Research and clinical applications.* Minneapolis: University of Minnesota Press.

Butcher, J. N. (2002, February). *Workshop on the new norms for the Hispanic version of the MMPI-2 for Spanish speaking people in the United States.* Paper presented at the MMPI-2 Workshops and Symposia, Irvine, CA.

Butcher, J. N. (2004). Personality assessment without borders: Adaptation of the MMPI-2 across cultures. *Journal of Personality Assessment, 83*, 90–104.

Butcher, J. N. (2005). Exploring universal personality characteristics: An objective approach. *International Journal of Clinical and Health Psychology, 5*, 553–566.

Butcher, J. N., Azan-Chaviano, A., Cabiya, J. J., & Scott, R. (2002, May). *New norms for the Hispanic version (Garcia–Azan) of the MMPI-2.* Paper presented at the Annual Symposium on Recent Developments in the Use of the MMPI-2, Minneapolis, MN.

Butcher, J. N., Cabiya, J., Lucio, G. M. E., Pena, L., & Scott, R. (1997, June). *New Hispanic version of the MMPI-A for the U.S.* Paper presented at the 32nd Annual Symposium on Recent Developments in the Use of the MMPI-2 and MMPI-A, Minneapolis, MN.

Butcher, J. N., Cabiya, J., Lucio, M. E., Pena, L., Scott, R., & Ruben, D. (1998). *Hispanic version of the MMPI-A manual supplement.* Minneapolis: University of Minnesota Press.

Butcher, J. N., & Clark, L. A. (1979). Recent trends in cross-cultural MMPI research and application. In J. N. Butcher (Ed.), *Recent developments in the use of the MMPI* (pp. 205–257). Minneapolis: University of Minnesota Press.

Butcher, J. N., Coelho, M. S., Tsai, J., & Nezami, E. (2006). Cross-cultural applications of the MMPI-2. In J. N. Butcher (Ed.), *MMPI-2: A practitioner's guide* (pp. 505–537). Washington, DC: American Psychological Association.

Butcher, J. N., Ellertsen, B., Ubostad, B., Bubb, E, Lucio, E., Lim, J., et al. (2000). *International case studies on the MMPI-A: An objective approach.* Minneapolis: University of Minnesota Press.

Butcher, J. N., & Garcia, R. E. (1978). Cross-national application of psychological tests. *Personnel and Guidance Journal, 56*, 472–475.

Butcher, J. N., & Pancheri, P. (1976). *A handbook of cross-national MMPI research.* Minneapolis: University of Minnesota Press.

Cabeza de Vaca, M., & Fuster, A. B. (1993). Relaciones de los miedos y creencias hipocondríacas con ansiedad, depresión y síntomas somáticos [Relationships of hypochondriacal fears and beliefs with anxiety, depression, and somatic symptoms]. *Análisis y Modificación de Conducta, 19,* 461–478.

Cabiya, J. J. (1993, November). *Clinical utility of the MMPI-2 in psychotherapy.* Paper presented at the Second Congress of Psychotherapy in San Juan, Puerto Rico.

Cabiya, J. J. (1994, May). *Application of the Hispanic MMPI-2 in Puerto Rico.* Paper presented at the 29th Annual Symposium on Recent Developments in the Use of the MMPI-2 and MMPI-A, Minneapolis, MN.

Cabiya, J. J. (1996). Use of the MMPI and the MMPI-2 in Puerto Rico. In J. N. Butcher (Ed.), *International adaptations of the MMPI-2: Research and clinical applications* (pp. 284–304). Minneapolis: University of Minnesota Press.

Cabiya, J. (2001, March) *Use of the MMPI-2 in Puerto Rico.* Paper presented at the Annual MMPI-2 and MMPI-A Symposium, Tampa, FL.

Cabiya, J. J., Colberg, E., Perez, S., & Pedrosa, O. (2001, March). *MMPI-2 clinical profiles of female victims of domestic violence and sexual abuse.* Paper presented at the 36th Annual Workshop and Symposium on Recent Developments in the Use of the MMPI-2, Tampa, FL.

Cabiya, J., Costantino, G., & Dana, R. (2004, August). *Cross-cultural validity of current instruments for Latinos.* Paper presented at the 112th Annual Convention of the American Psychological Association, Honolulu, HI.

Cabiya, J., & Cruz, R. (2001, April). *Estudio del MMPI-2 con una muestra de Puertorriqueños normales* [Study of the MMPI-2 with Puerto Rican normals]. Paper presented at the Annual Convention of the Puerto Rican Psychological Association, San Juan, Puerto Rico.

Cabiya, J., Cruz, R., & Bayón, N. (2002, April). *MMPI-2 Hispanic Normative Project—Puerto Rican sample.* Paper presented at the 37th Annual MMPI-2 Workshop and Symposium, Minneapolis, MN.

Cabiya, J., & Dávila, G. (1999). Cultural differences in MMPI-2 scores between North Americans and Puerto Ricans. *Revista Puertorriqueña de Psicología, 12,* 145–158.

Cabiya, J. J., & Dávila, G. (1999, April). *MMPI-2 mean T scores and code-types of Puerto Rican depressed outpatients and inpatients.* Paper presented at the 29th Annual Symposium on Recent Developments in the Use of the MMPI-2 and MMPI-A, Huntington Beach, CA.

Cabiya, J. J., Lucio, E., Chavira, D. A., Castellanos, J., Gomez, F. C., & Velasquez, R. J. (2000). MMPI-2 scores of Puerto Rican, Mexican, and U.S. Latino college students: A research note. *Psychological Reports, 87,* 266–268.

Cabiya, J., Martín, E. A., Despaigne, D. N., & Espinosa, A. L. (1983). Factores de personalidad, depresión y concentración de la atención en el bocio tóxico difuso [Personality factors, depression, and concentration in diffuse toxic goiter]. *Revista Cubana de Investigaciones Biomédicas, 2,* 274–381.

Cabiya, J. J., Reuben, D., García, O., Alvarado, C., Lyons, M., & Butcher, J. (2004) Preliminary validation study of the Spanish version of the MMPI-A with Puerto Rican adolescents. *Ciencias de la Conducta, 19,* 59–71.

Cabiya, J., Reuben, D., García, O., Alvarado, C., Sayers, S., Lyons, M., & Butcher, J. (2001). *Preliminary study of the adequacy of the Spanish translation of the MMPI-A with Puerto Rican adolescents*. Unpublished manuscript.

Cabiya, J., & Velez, R. (1989). Capacidad discriminative del Inventario Multifasico de la Personalidad (MMPI) con tres muestras de poblacion puertorriquena [Discriminative capacity of the Minnesota Multiphasic Personality Inventory (MMPI) with three samples of Puerto Rican population]. *Avances em Psicologia Clinica Latinoamericana, 7*, 105–115.

Calderon, I. (2002). Effects of acculturation on the performance of Mexican-American adolescents on selected scales of the MMPI-A (L, K, SC, and MA). *Dissertation Abstracts International, 63*, 1083B.

Callahan, W. J. (1997). Symptom reports and acculturation of White and Mexican-Americans in psychiatric, college, and community settings. *Dissertation Abstracts International, 58*, 4439B.

Callahan, W. J. (2000, August). *Mexican-American acculturation and MMPI-2 performance*. Paper presented at the 108th Annual Convention of the American Psychological Association, Washington, DC.

Callahan, W. J., Velasquez, R. J., & Saccuzzo, D. P. (1995, August). *MMPI-2 performance of university students by ethnicity and gender*. Paper presented at the 103rd Annual Convention of the American Psychological Association, New York.

Calles, D., Ana, M., & Garriga Trillo, A. J. (1983). Fuerza del Ego = Fuerza del yo? [MMPI Ego Strength Scale = 16PF Feelings Scale?]. *Informes de Psicología, 2*, 209–220.

Campailla, G. (1989). La familia de los enfermos de coronarias [The families of coronary patients]. *Psicopatología, 9*, 39–40.

Campos, L. P. (1989). Adverse impact, unfairness, and bias in the psychological screening of Hispanic peace officers. *Hispanic Journal of Behavioral Sciences, 11*, 122–135.

Cannon, D. S., Bell, W. E., Fowler, D. R., Penk, W. E., & Finkelstein, A. S. (1990). MMPI differences between alcoholics and drug abusers. *Psychological Assessment, 2*, 51–55.

Canul, G. D. (1993). The influence of acculturation and racial identity attitudes on Mexican Americans' MMPI-2 performance. *Dissertation Abstracts International, 54*, 6442B.

Canul, G. D., & Cross, H. J. (1994). The influence of acculturation and racial identity attitudes on Mexican Americans' MMPI-2 performance. *Journal of Clinical Psychology, 50*, 736–745.

Cardenas, Y. (1987). *Estudio de correlacion entre la escala adicional del MMPI AC (Logro Academico) y promedio en una muestra representative de adolescents* [Correlational study between MMPI (Academic Achievement) additional scale and scholar grades on a representative adolescent sample]. Unpublished degree thesis, National University of Mexico, Mexico City.

Carey, R. J., Garske, J. P., & Ginsberg, J. (1986). The prediction of adjustment to prison by means of an MMPI-based classification system. *Criminal Justice and Behavior, 13,* 347–365.

Carrascoso López, F. J. (1999). Terapia de aceptación y compromiso (ACT) en el trastorno de angustia con agorafobia: Un estudio de caso [Acceptance and commitment therapy (ACT) in panic disorder with agoraphobia: A case study]. *Psicothema, 11*(1), 1–12.

Casabal, C., & Wengerman, A. (1974). *Estudio de las características de personalidad utilizando el MMPI en una muestra representative de la generacion 1973 de la Facultad de Psicologia* [Study of personality characteristics using the MMPI in a representative sample of the 1973 class in the Psychology School]. Unpublished degree thesis, National University of Mexico, Mexico City.

Castañeiras, C., Belloch, A., & Martínez, M. P. (2000). Es normal preocuparse por la enfermedad? [Is it normal to worry about illness?]. *Análisis y Modificación de Conducta, 26,* 537–553.

Castellano, M. (2004). A comparative study, of MMPI-2 profiles, between obese Hispanics and non-Hispanics seeking gastric bypass surgery. *Dissertation Abstracts International, 64,* 4097B.

Casullo, M. M. (1964). *Adaptacion del Cuestionario MMPI* [Adaptation of the MMPI questionnaire]. Buenos Aires, Argentina: Departamento de Orientación Vocacional, Universidad de Buenos Aires.

Casullo, M. M. (1996, June). *Assessment of applicants to a military unit using MMPI: Profile comparisons by gender.* Paper presented at the 31st Annual Symposium on Recent Developments in the Use of the MMPI-2 and MMPI-A, Minneapolis, MN.

Casullo, M. M. (1998). *Adolescentes en riesgo* [Adolescents at risk]. Buenos Aires, Argentina: Paidos, Cuadernos de Evaluacion Psicologica.

Casullo, M. M., Samartino, L. G., Brenella, M. E., Marquez, M. A., & Dupertuis, D. G. (1996). Studies of the MMPI-2 in Argentina. In J. N. Butcher (Ed.), *International adaptations of the MMPI-2: Research and clinical applications* (pp. 252–264). Minneapolis: University of Minnesota Press.

Cavior, N., Kurtzberg, R. L., & Lipton, D. S. (1967). The development and validation of a heroin addiction scale with the MMPI. *International Journal of the Addictions, 2,* 129–137.

Cervera, S., Casanova, J., & Lahortiga, F. (1984). Perfil psicopatológico y pruebas neuroendocrinas en el estudio de los trastornos afectivos [Psychopathological features and neuroendocrine tests in the study of affective disorders]. *Revista del Departamento de Psiquiatría de la Facultad de Medicina de Barcelona, 11,* 399–421.

Chacon, M., & Vargas, L. (1976). Exploracion psicologica de las dimensiones de neuroticismo y de introversion–extroversion [Psychological exploration of the dimensions of neuroticism and introversion–extroversion]. *Revista de Psicologia de la Asociacion de Psicologos de Arequipa, 2,* 22–27.

Chavira, D. A., Malcarne, V. L., & Velasquez, R. J. (1997). *The influence of ethnic experience on Mexican-Amercans' MMPI-2 performance.* Unpublished manuscript, San Diego State University, San Diego, CA.

Chavira, D. A., Malcarne, V., Velasquez, R. J., Liu, P. J., & Fabian, G. (1996, August). *Influence of ethnic experience on Spanish MMPI-2 performance.* Paper presented at the 103rd Annual Convention of the American Psychological Association, Toronto, Ontario, Canada.

Chavira, D. A., Montemayor, V., Velasquez, R. J., & Villarino, J. (1995, August). *A comparison of two Spanish translations of the MMPI-2 with Mexican Americans.* Paper presented at the 103rd Annual Convention of the American Psychological Association, New York.

Chavira, D., Velasquez, R. J., Montemayor, V., & Villarino, J. (1995, March). *U.S. Latinos' performance on the Spanish language MMPI-2 & acculturation.* Paper presented at the 30th Annual Symposium on Recent Developments in the Use of the MMPI-2 and MMPI-A, St. Petersburg, FL.

Cirera, E., Belloch, J. V., & Boget, T. (1989). Estudio evolutivo de un estado psicótico tras un intento de suicidio [Psychopathological evolution of a patient suffering from a psychotic state, after a suicide attempt]. *Revista del Departamento de Psiquiatría de la Facultad de Medicina de Barcelona, 16,* 213–219.

Clark, S. A. (1991). A descriptive study of the MMPI and industrially injured immigrant Hispanic workers. *Dissertation Abstracts International, 52,* 2290B.

Clark, S. A., Callahan, W. J., Lichtszajn, J., & Velasquez, R. J. (1996). MMPI performance of Central-American refugees and Mexican immigrants. *Psychological Reports, 79,* 819–824.

Clark, S. A., Velasquez, R. J., & Callahan, W. J. (1991). *MMPI performance of Hispanics by country of origin.* Unpublished manuscript, San Diego State University, San Diego, CA.

Clark, S. A., Velasquez, R. J., & Callahan, W. J. (1992). MMPI-2 two-point codes of industrially injured Hispanic workers by *DSM–III–R* diagnosis. *Psychological Reports, 71,* 107–112.

Clark, S. A., Velasquez, R. J., Callahan, W. J., & Lopez, C. (1993). MMPI-2 differences among Hispanic worker's compensation applicants by psychiatric diagnosis. *Journal of Applied Rehabilitation Counseling, 24*(2), 15–18.

Colon, C. C. (1993). *Relationship between the MMPI-2 content scales and psychiatric symptoms with Puerto Rican college students and psychiatric patients.* Unpublished doctoral dissertation, Caribbean Center for Advanced Studies, San Juan, Puerto Rico.

Conde López, V., Cuesta Zorita, M. J., & Fernández Abeijón, M. D. (1986). Comparación de los perfiles del MMPI en función del resultado en la prueba de supresión con dexametasona en pacientes con depresión mayor [Comparison of MMPI profiles of major depression patients as a function of dexamethasone suppression test results]. *Actas Luso-Espanolas de Neurologia, Psiquiatria y Ciencias Afines, 14,* 351–361.

Contini, N., & Figueroa de Pucci, M. I. (1990a). *Perfil psicologico del adolescente de zona rural de Tucumán* [Psychological profile of the adolescent of rural Tucumán]. Unpublished manuscript.

Contini, N., & Figueroa de Pucci, M. I. (1990b). *Personalidad en adolescentes de Tucumán* [Personality of adolescents in Tucumán]. Unpublished manuscript.

Contini de González, E. N., Figueroa, M. I., Cohen, I. S., & Coronel de Pace, P. (2001). El MMPI-A en la identification de rasgos psicopatológicos. Un estudio con adolescents de Tucumán (Argentina) [The use of the MMPI-A in the identification of psychopathological traits in adolescents of Tucumán (Argentina)]. *Revista Iberoamericana de Diagnóstico y Evaluación Psicológica, 12,* 85–96.

Contini de Gonzalez, N. (1982). *Actualizaciones. Dos tecnias con fines psicodiagnosticos* [Updates. The aims of psychodiagnosis]. Unpublished manuscript, Universidad Nacional de Tucumán: Facultad de Filosofia y Letras, Cuaderno Humanitas, Tucumán, Argentina.

Contini de Gonzalez, N., Figueroa, M. I., & Cohen Imach, S. (2000). Estudio comparativo de psicopatologias prevalentes en adolescentes de dos zonas geograficas de Tucumán (Argentina). [Prevalence study pf psychopathology for adolescents in the geographic zones of Tucumán (Argentina)]. *Revista del Departamento de Investigacion, Facultad de Psicologia, 2,* 7–18.

Cook, W. A. (1996). Item validity of the MMPI-2 for a Hispanic and White clinical sample. *Dissertation Abstracts International, 56,* 5761B.

Corbella, S., Beutler, L. E., Fernández-Álvarez, H., Botella, L., Malik, M. L., Lane, G., & Wagstaff, N. (2003). Measuring coping style and resistance among Spanish and Argentine samples: Development of the systematic treatment selection self-reports in Spanish. *Journal of Clinical Psychology, 59,* 921–932.

Corrales, M. L., Cabiya, J. J., Gomez, F., Ayala, G. X., Mendoza, S., & Velasquez, R. J. (1998). MMPI-2 and MMPI-A research with U.S. Latinos: A bibliography. *Psychological Reports, 83,* 1027–1033.

Crespo, G. S., & Gómez, F. J. (1995). La Escala Superlativa S de Butcher y Han (1995): El fingimiento en la adaptación española del MMPI-2 [The Superlative Scale S of Butcher and Han (1995): The "fake-good" in the Spanish adaptation of the MMPI-2]. *Revista de Psicología, 21,* 5–39.

Cruz-Niemiec, R. (2004). *Factores de tiempo y genero sexual asociados al MMPI-2, versión Hispana, con un muestra de hombres y mujeres puertorriqueños/as* [Factors of time and generated sexual associations to the MMPI-2, Hispanic version, with a sample of Puerto Rican men and women]. Unpublished doctoral dissertation, Albizu University, San Juan, Puerto Rico.

Cuellar, I., Arnold, B., & Maldonado, R. (1995). Acculturation Rating Scale for Mexican Americans II: A revision of the original ARSMA scale. *Hispanic Journal of Behavioral Sciences, 17,* 275–304.

Cuellar, I., & Roberts, R. E. (1997). Relations of depression, acculturation and socio-economic status in a Latino sample. *Hispanic Journal of Behavioral Sciences, 19,* 230–238.

Dahlstrom, L. E. (1986). MMPI findings on other American minority groups. In W. G. Dahlstrom, D. Lachar, & L. E. Dahlstrom (Eds.), *MMPI patterns of American minorities* (pp. 50–86). Minneapolis: University of Minnesota Press.

Dahlstrom, W. G., Lachar, D., & Dahlstrom, L. E. (Eds.) (1986). *MMPI patterns of American minorities*. Minneapolis: University of Minnesota Press.

Dana, R. H. (1988). Culturally diverse groups and MMPI interpretation. *Professional Psychology: Research and Practice, 19*, 490–495.

Dana, R. H. (1995). Culturally competent MMPI assessment of Hispanic populations. *Hispanic Journal of Behavioral Sciences, 17*, 305–319.

Dana, R. H. (1996). Assessment of acculturation in Hispanic population. *Hispanic Journal of Behavioral Sciences, 18*, 317–328.

Dana, R. H. (1997). Multicultural assessment and cultural identity: An assessment-intervention model. *World Psychology, 3*, 121–141.

Dana, R. (2005) *Multicultural assessment: Principles, applications and examples*. Mahwah, NJ: Erlbaum

de Barbenza, C. M., Montoya, O. A., & Borel, M. T. (1978). The psychotic tetrad of the MMPI in a group of university students. *Revista de Psicología General y Aplicada, 33*(150), 79–86.

de Flores, T., Ampudia, M., Tomás, J., Gussinye, M., et al. (1992). Papel de los factores psicológicos en la diabetes mellitus: morbilidad psiquiátrica y perfil psicopatológico [Weight of psychological factors in diabetes mellitus: Psychiatric morbidity and psychopathological profile]. *Revista de Psiquiatría de la Facultad de Medicina de Barcelona, 19*(4), 139–147.

de la Casa, L. G., & Lubow, R. E. (1994). Memory for attended and nominally nonattended stimuli in low and high psychotic-prone normal subjects: The effects of test-anticipation. *Personality and Individual Differences, 17*, 783–789.

de la Casa, L. G., Ruiz, G., & Lubow, R. E. (1993). Latent inhibition and recall/recognition of irrelevant stimuli as a function of pre-exposure duration in high and low psychotic-prone normal subjects. *British Journal of Psychology, 4*, 119–132.

de la Torre, J., Sanchez Nieto, J. A., Dominguez, M. A., & Echevarria, C. (1972). Study of social desirability and differential profiles by course on an attitude questionnaire. *Revista de Psicologia General y Aplicade, 27*, 414–416.

Delgado Martín, M. E., Llorca Ramón, G., Blanco González, A. L., García Carretero, L., et al. (1989). Psicosomática y cáncer [Psychosomatics and cancer]. *Actas Luso-Espanolas de Neurologia, Psiquiatria y Ciencias Afines, 17*, 169–175.

del Palacio, R., Rubio, J. L., de Nicolás, M., & López, N. (1997). Morbilidad psicologica despues de un aborto espontaneo [Psychological morbidity after a spontaneous abortion]. *Psiquis: Revista de Psiquiatría, Psicología y Psicosomática, 18*(10), 15–23

Díaz, A., Jurado, M., Lucio, G. E., & Cuevas, M. (2003). Detección de rechazo al tratamiento en estudiantes universitarios [Detection of treatment dropout in university students]. *Psiquiatría, 19*(1), 1–9.

Díaz González, R. J., Hidalgo Rodrigo, M. I., Santiago Guervós, M. M., Ripoll Lozano, M. A., et al. (1991). Una subescala del M.M.P.I. para la medida de la alexitimia en pacientes con E.U.D. [An MMPI subscale for the assessment of alexithymia in patients with the ulcerative duodenal disorder]. *Actas Luso-Espanolas de Neurologia, Psiquiatria y Ciencias Afines, 19*(1), 52–57.

Dolan, M. P., Roberts, W. R., Robinowitz, R., & Atkins, H. G. (1983). Personality differences among Black, White, and Hispanic-American male heroin addicts on MMPI content scales. *Journal of Clinical Psychology, 39*, 807–813.

Dominguez, M. A. (1970). El cuestionairio MMPI y su aplicacion en el ejercito [Use of the MMPI in the military services]. *Revista de Médico y Cirugía de Guerra, 32*, 351–358.

Donovan, N., Castellanos, J., Velasquez, R. J., & Orozco, V. (2002, May). *The relationship between hypochondriasis, health concerns, cynicism, acculturation, and health locus of control for Chicanos.* Paper presented at the Annual Symposium on Recent Developments in the Use of the MMPI-2, Minneapolis, MN.

DuAlba, L., & Scott, R. L. (1993). Somatization and malingering for workers' compensation applicants: A cross-cultural MMPI study. *Journal of Clinical Psychology, 49*, 913–917.

Dupertuis, D. G., Bolzan, C., Regner, E., & Kunzi, I. (1998, March). *Self-efficacy and personal dominance in severe personality disorders: Control or lack of control? An evaluation with the MMPI-2 and Argentinean alcoholics.* Paper presented at the Annual Symposium on Recent Developments in the Use of the MMPI-2, Clearwater, FL.

Dupertuis, D. G., Bolzan, C., Regner, E., & Kunzi, I. (1998, March). *Eating disorders and MMPI-2: An analysis of serious personality disorders (in Argentina).* Paper presented at the Annual Symposium on Recent Developments in the Use of the MMPI-2, Clearwater, FL.

Duran, P. C. (1996). *Estudios psicométricos del MMPI-2 en estudiantes universitarios* [Psychometric studies of the MMPI-2 on university students]. Unpublished master's thesis, National University of Mexico, Mexico City.

Durán, P. C., Lucio, E., & Reyes-Lagunes, I. (1993, July). *Análisis factorial de las escalas básicas del MMPI-2 español en México* [Factorial analysis of the MMPI-2 Spanish for Mexico]. Paper presented at the 24th Congreso Interamericano de Psicología, Ponencia Sociedad Interamericana de Psicología, Santiago, Chile.

Echevarria, R. C., Torre, R. J., Garcia Santa-Cruz, L., & Dominguez, M. A. (1969). Relacion entre actitudes interpersonales, y neuroticismo y rasgos psicopaticos en universitarios espanoles (MMPI y SIV de Gordon) [Relationship between interpersonal attitudes and neuroticism and psychopathy in Spanish university students (MMPI and SIV de Gordon)]. *Revista de Psicologia General y Applicada, 26*, 894–901.

Erdmann, K., Velasquez, R. J., Flores, L., & Perez, J. (2000, May). *Applying the BSI and MMPI-2 in the assessment of Spanish speaking immigrant DUI offenders.* Paper presented at the 35th Annual Symposium on Recent Developments in the Use of the MMPI-2 and MMPI-A, Minneapolis, MN.

Espina, A. (2003). Eating disorders and MMPI profiles in a Spanish sample. *European Journal of Psychiatry, 17*, 201–211.

Espina, A., Joaristi, L., Ortego, M. A., & de Alda, I. O. (2003). Eating disorders, family interventions and changes in MMPI profiles. An exploratory study. *Estudios de Psicologia, 24*, 359–375.

Estalló Martí, J. A., & Forns, M. (1988). La escala de Esquizofrenia del MMPI en adolescentes normales [The MMPI Schizophrenia subscale in normal adolescents]. *Revista del Departamento de Psiquiatría de la Facultad de Medicina de Barcelona, 15*, 23–32.

Fantoni-Salvador, P., & Rogers, R. (1997). Spanish versions of the MMPI-2 and PAI: An investigation of concurrent validity with Hispanic patients. *Assessment, 4*, 29–39.

Farias, J. M. P., Duran, C., & Gomez-Maqueo, E. L. (2003). MMPI-A temporal stability study through a test–retest design in a Mexican student sample. *Salud Mental, 26*(2), 59–66.

Fierro, R. J. (1986). The psychological effects of early referral to vocational rehabilitation among Mexican-American industrially injured workers (Doctoral dissertation, United States International University, 1986). *Dissertation Abstracts International, 47*, 1657A.

Fierro, R. J., & Leal, A. (1988). The psychological effects of early versus late referral to the vocational rehabilitation process: The case of Mexican origin industrially injured workers. *Journal of Applied Rehabilitation Counseling, 19*, 35–39.

Figueroa, M. I. (2001). *Factores psicosociales y de personalidad asociados con el rendimiento académico en adolescentes del género femenino* [Psychosocial factors related to academic performance in female adolescents]. Unpublished master's thesis, National University of Mexico, Mexico City.

Fisher, G. (1967). The performance of male prisoners on the Marlowe–Crowne Social Desirability Scale: II. Differences as a function of race and crime. *Journal of Clinical Psychology, 23*, 473–475.

Fitch, R. S. (1973). Examination of selected MMPI profiles of four groups of Spanish-American and Anglo-American adolescent females (Doctoral dissertation, Baylor University, 1972). *Dissertation Abstracts International, 38*, 2360B.

Flaskerud, J. H. (1986). Diagnostic and treatment differences among five ethnic groups. *Psychological Reports, 58*, 219–225.

Flores, L., Chavira, D. A., Velasquez, R. J., Perez, J., & Engel, B. (1996, June). *MMPI-2 codetypes of Spanish speaking Hispanic DUI offenders.* Paper presented at the 31st Annual Symposium on Recent Developments in the Use of the MMPI-2 and MMPI-A, Minneapolis, MN.

Fogliatto, H., & Bruno de Cano, M. (1974). Observations on a program of vocational orientation at the secondary level. *Revista de Psicología General y Aplicada, 29*, 781–790.

Fonseca Fábregas, L. E. (1983). Test de supresión de la dexametasona: Valoración a seis meses de experiencia [Dexamethasone suppression test: Evaluation after six months of experience]. *Revista de Psiquiatría y Psicología Médica, 16,* 129–143.

Fournier, M. (2001, March). *Validation of the emotional scale using MMPI-2: A preliminary exploration of aggression predictive factors for the psychiatric population of Puerto Rico.* Paper presented at the Annual Symposium on Recent Developments in the Use of the MMPI-2, Tampa, FL.

Fournier, M., & Cabiya, J. J. (1999, April). *Concurrent validity of MMPI-2 and MCMI-3 Spanish versions.* Paper presented at the 34th Annual Symposium on Recent Developments in the Use of the MMPI-2 and MMPI-A, Huntington Beach, CA.

Fournier, M., & Cabiya J. J. (2000, May). *Comparison between the personality scales of the MCMI–III, Morey's and Ben-Porath's.* Paper presented at the 35th Annual Symposium on Recent Developments in the use of the MMPI-2 and MMPI-A, Minneapolis, MN.

Fowler, R. D., & Blaser, P. (1972, March). *Around the world in 566 items.* Paper given at the Seventh Annual Symposium on Recent Developments in the Use of the MMPI, Mexico City, Mexico.

Fox, D., & Sunlight, C. (1985, March). *The validity of MMPI critical items in different ethnic groups.* Paper presented at the 20th Annual Symposium on Recent Developments in the Use of the MMPI, Honolulu, HI.

Fragoso, J. M., Walker, M. E., Barron, V. L., Lackey, J., & Scott, R. L. (2003, June). *MMPI-2 performance of Mexican villagers and immigrants, Mexican Americans, and White Americans.* Paper presented at the 38th MMPI-2 Conference on Recent Developments in the Use of the MMPI-2 and MMPI-A, Minneapolis, MN.

Francis, B. S. (1964). *Culture and sex role determinants of personality profiles.* Unpublished master's thesis, Trinity University, San Antonio, TX.

Frank, J. G., Velasquez, R. J., Reimann, J., & Salazar, J. (1997, June). *MMPI-2 profiles of Latino, Black, and White rapists and child molesters on parole.* Paper presented at the Annual Symposium on Recent Developments in the Use of the MMPI-2, Minneapolis, MN.

Frye, T. F. (1973). *An evaluative actuarial study of the MMPI utilizing an Anglo and Mexican-American sample.* Unpublished master's thesis, Trinity University, San Antonio, TX.

Fuller, C. G. (1984). Comparisons of unacculturated and acculturated Hispanics with Blacks and Whites on the Minnesota Multiphasic Personality Inventory. *Dissertation Abstracts International, 45,* 1283B.

Fuller, C. G., & Maloney, H. N., Jr. (1984). A comparison of English and Spanish (Nuñez) translations of the MMPI. *Journal of Personality Assessment. 48,* 130–131.

Gaba, R. J. (1988). *Profile constellations of males accused of sexually abusing children.* Unpublished master's thesis, Mount St. Mary's College, Los Angeles, CA.

Gaba, R. J. (1990). *Hispanic sex offenders: Assessment with the MMPI-168.* Paper presented at the Annual Meeting of the California State Psychological Association, San Francisco, CA.

García, C., & Garrido, M. (2000). Minorities in the United States: A sociocultural context for mental health and developmental psychopathology. In A. J. Sameroff, M. Lewis, & S. M. Miller (Eds.), *Handbook of developmental psychopathology* (2nd ed., pp. 177–195). Dordrecht, the Netherlands: Kluwer Academic.

Garcia, O. (1995). *Adecuacidad de la traduccion del MMPI-A* [Adequacy of the translation of the MMPI-A]. Unpublished dissertation, Caribbean Center for Advanced Studies, Miami, FL.

Garcia, O., Cabiya, J. J., & Margarida, M. T. (1996, August). *Adequacy of the Spanish translation of the MMPI-A in Puerto Rico.* Paper presented at the 104th Annual Convention of the American Psychological Association, Toronto, Ontario, Canada.

Garcia, R., Hoffman, N., & Butcher, J. N. (1983). *Spanish translation of the MMPI for Hispanic Americans.* Minneapolis: University of Minnesota Press.

Garcia-Alba, C. (2004). Anorexia and depression: Depressive comorbidity in anorexic adolescents. *Spanish Journal of Psychology, 7,* 40–52.

García Carretero, L., Ledesma Jimeno, A., Llorca Ramón, G., Blanco González, A. L., et al. (1990). Estudio de la personalidad y de la agresividad en pacientes cancerosos [Study of personality and aggressiveness in cancer patients]. *Actas Luso-Espanolas de Neurologia, Psiquiatria y Ciencias Fines, 18,* 34–46.

García-Merita, M., Fuentes, I., Miquel, M., & Rojo, J. (1992). El M.M.P.I. en la evaluación de la esquizofrenia: Un nuevo enfoque [The MMPI in the evolution of schizophrenia: A new approach]. *Anales de Psiquiatría, 8,* 253–257.

García-Merita, M. L., Balaguer, I., & Ibáñez, E. (1984). Problemas de validez en la escala de Depresión del M.M.P.I. [Validity problems in the Depression scale of the MMPI]. *Revista de Psicología General y Aplicada, 39,* 313–340.

Garcia-Peltoniemi, R., & Azan Chaviano, A. (1993). *MMPI-2: Inventario Multifásico de la Personalidad–2 Minnesota* [MMPI-2: Minnesota Multiphasic Personality Inventory–2]. Minneapolis: University of Minnesota Press.

Garrido, M. (1996, June). *Integrating the MMPI-2 and the Thematic Apperception Test for culturally competent evaluations of Latinos: Three cases of Latino parents undergoing child custody evaluations.* Paper presented at the 31st Annual Symposium on Recent Developments in the Use of the MMPI-2 and MMPI-A, Minneapolis, MN.

Garrido, M. (2000, May). *MMPI-A with Latinos: Review of the literature and illustrative case studies.* Paper presented at the 35th Annual Symposium on Recent Developments in the Use of the MMPI-2 and MMPI-A, Minneapolis, MN.

Garrido, M. (2001, March). *The MMPI-2 (Spanish) as indicator of parenting stress among Latinos.* Paper presented at the 36th Annual Symposium on Recent Developments in the Use of the MMPI-2 and MMPI-A, Safety Harbor, FL.

Garrido, M., Diehl, S., Gionta, D., Boscia, M., & Bailey, C. (1999, April). *Prison adjustment: Predictive utility of MMPI-2 scales, Megargee types, and demographic* data. Paper presented at the 34th Annual Symposium on Recent Developments in the Use of the MMPI-2 and MMPI-A, Huntington Beach, CA.

Garrido, M., Gionta, D., Diehl, S., & Boscia, M. (1998, March). *The Megargee MMPI-2 system of inmate classification: A study of its applicability with ethnically diverse prison inmates.* Paper presented at the 33rd Annual Symposium on Recent Developments in the Use of the MMPI-2 and MMPI-A, Clearwater Beach, FL.

Garrido, M., & Velasquez, R. (2005). Interpretation of Latino/Latina MMPI-2 profiles: Review and application of empirical findings and cultural-linguistic considerations. In J. N. Butcher (Ed.), *MMPI-2: The practitioner's handbook* (pp. 477–504). Washington, DC: American Psychological Association.

Garrido, M., Velasquez, R. J., Reimann, J. O., Parsons, J. P., & Salazar, J. (1997, June). *MMPI-2 performance of Hispanic and White abusive and neglectful parents.* Paper presented at the 32nd Annual Symposium on Recent Developments in the Use of the MMPI-2 and MMPI-A, Minneapolis, MN.

Geisinger, K. F. (Ed.). (1992). *Psychologist testing of Hispanics.* Washington, DC: American Psychological Association.

Ghiju, B. G. (1982). *Estudio comparativo del manejo de la agresividad en un grupo de adolescentes mujeres mexicanas de distintos niveles socioeconómicos, utilizando el M.M.P.I.* [Study on aggressiveness of a group of female Mexican adolescents from different socioeconomic levels, using the MMPI]. Unpublished degree thesis, National University of Mexico, Mexico City.

Glatt, K. M. (1969). An evaluation of the French, Spanish, and German translations of the MMPI. *Acta Psychologica, 29,* 65–84.

Goldberg, S. D. (1981). The use of the MMPI psychopathic deviate scale in evaluation of Mexican American patients: A symbolic integrationist's perspective (Doctoral dissertation, United States International University, 1980). *Dissertation Abstracts International, 41,* 4663B.

Gomez, F. C., Johnson, R., Davis, Q., & Velasquez, R. J. (2000). MMPI-A performance of African and Mexican American adolescent first-time offenders. *Psychological Reports, 87,* 309–314.

Gómez de Borda, M. I., González, G. J. A., & Llorca, R. G. (1988). Estudio psicológico del enfermo oncológico [Psychological study of oncological illness]. *Psiquis: Revista de Psiquiatría, Psicología y Psicosomática, 9,* 29–36.

Gondra, J. M. (1975). The relationship of the self/ideal congruence index to change during therapy and to personality adjustment. *Revista de Psicología General y Aplicada, 30,* 585–607.

Gondra Rezola, J. M., & Ortega Martinez, L. (1980). La distribución Q y las dimensiones básicas de la personalidad [Q-sort distribution in basic personality dimensions]. *Revista de Psicología General y Aplicada, 35,* 279–286.

Gonzalez, L. D. (1979). *Estudio de correlacion de las respuestas del Inventario Multifasico de al Personalidad de Minnesota (MMPI) de las escales L, F, K, D y Si de normales, neuroticos, depresivos y esquizofrenicos en poblacion Mexicana.* [Correlation study of the Multiphasic Minnesota Personality Inventory (MMPI) of *L, F, K, D* and *Si* scales in a Mexican sample of normals, neurotics, depressed and schizophrenics]. Unpublished degree thesis, National University of Mexico, Mexico City.

Gonzalez, M. A. A., Martin, E. A., Despaigne, D. N., & Espinosa, A. L. (1983). Factores de personalidad, depression y concentracion de la atencion en el bocio toxico disuso [Personality factors, depression and concentration of toxic goiter]. *Revista Cubana de Investigaciones Biomedicas, 2,* 274–381.

Gonzalez del Pino, D. T., Lopez Navarro, A., & Dominguezo, A. (1969). A differential study of the MMPI neurotic triad and Pd scales for Spanish university students. *Revista de Psicología General y Aplicada, 24,* 728–733.

González Ibañez, A., Mercadé, P. V., Aymamí, N., & Pastor, C. (1990). Variables de personalidad, juego patológico [Personality variables and pathological gambling]. *Revista de Psiquiatría de la Facultad de Medicina de Barcelona, 17,* 203–209.

González-Ibáñez, A., Mora, M., Gutíerrez-Maldonado, J., Ariza, A., & Lourido-Ferreira, M. R. (2005). Pathological gambling and age: Differences in personality, psychopathology, and response to treatment variables. *Addictive Behaviors, 30,* 383–388.

Graham, J. R. (1993). Use of special groups. In J. R. Graham (Ed.), *MMPI-2: Assessing personality and psychopathology* (2nd ed., pp. 193–217). New York: Oxford University Press.

Grassot Esteba, G., & Llinàs Reglà, J. (1997). Psychopatological comparación entre SCL-90-R y otros psychometric instrumento [Psychopathological comparison between SCL-90-R and other psychometric instruments]. *Psiquis: Revista de Psiquiatría, Psicología y Psicosomática, 18*(4), 43–50.

Grau, A. (1991). Estudio neuropsicológico del trastorno obsesivo–compulsivo (primera parte) [Neuropsychological study of obsessive–compulsive disorder: I]. *Revista de Psiquiatría de la Facultad de Medicina de Barcelona, 18*(1), 11–22.

Grau, A. (1992). Estudio neuropsicológico del trastorno obsesivo–compulsivo (segunda parte) [A neuropsychological study of obsessive–compulsive disorder: II]. *Revista de Psiquiatría de la Facultad de Medicina de Barcelona, 18*(2), 49–58.

Greene, R. L. (1987). Ethnicity and MMPI performance: A review. *Journal of Consulting and Clinical Psychology, 55,* 497–512.

Greene, R. L. (1991). Specific groups: Adolescents, the aged, Blacks, and other ethnic minority groups. In R. L. Green (Ed.), *The MMPI-2/MMPI: An interpretive manual* (pp. 331–354). Needham Heights, MA: Allyn & Bacon.

Greenwood, K., Velasquez, R. J., Suarez, R., Rodriguez-Reimann, D., Johnson, A., Flores-Gonzalez, R., & Ledeboer, M. E. (1998, March). *MMPI-2/MMPI-A profiles of Latino mother and daughter dyads in an outpatient community mental health center.* Paper presented at the Annual Symposium on Recent Developments in the Use of the MMPI-2, Clearwater, FL.

Griffith, J. (1983). Relationship between acculturation and psychological impairment in adult Mexican Americans. *Hispanic Journal of Behavioral Sciences, 5,* 431–439.

Grillo, J. (1994, August). *Under-representation of Hispanic Americans in the MMPI-2 normative group*. Paper presented at the 102nd Annual Convention of the American Psychological Association, Los Angeles, CA.

Gumbiner, J. (1998). MMPI-A profiles of Hispanic adolescents. *Psychological Reports*, *82*, 659–672.

Gumbiner, J., Arriaga, T., & Stevens, A. (1999). Comparison of MMPI-A, Marks and Briggs, and MMPI-2 norms for juvenile delinquents. *Psychological Reports*, *84*, 761–766.

Guthrie, G. M., & Lonner, W. J. (1986). Assessment of personality and psychopathology. In W. J. Lonner & J. W. Berry (Eds.), *Field methods in cross-cultural research* (pp. 231–269). Beverly Hills, CA: Sage.

Guzman, D. S. (1979). *Analysis of Mexican-American and Anglo-American differences on the MMPI*. Unpublished master's thesis, San Jose State University, San Jose, CA.

Gynther, M. D. (1983). MMPI interpretation: The effects of demographic variables. In C. Spielberger & J. N. Butcher (Eds.), *Advances in personality assessment* (Vol. 3, pp. 175–193). Hillsdale, NJ: Erlbaum.

Hagemeijer, A. V., Gil, E. G., & Nogues, J. M. P. (2003). Psychopathology and gender identity disorder. *Revista de Psiquiatria de la Facultad de Medicina de Barcelona*, *30*(3), 147–151.

Hall, G. C. N., Bansal, A., & Lopez, I. R. (1999). Ethnicity and psychopathology: A meta-analytic review of 31 years of comparative MMPI/MMPI-2 research. *Psychological Assessment*, *11*, 186–197.

Hargrave, G. E., & Berner, J. G. (1984). *POST psychological screening manual*. Sacramento, CA: California Commission on Peace Officer Standards and Training.

Haskell, A. (1996). Mexican American and Anglo American endorsement of items on the MMPI-2 Scale 2, the Center for Epidemiological Studies Depression Scale, and the Cohen-Hoberman Inventory for Physical Symptoms. *Dissertation Abstracts International*, *57*, 4708B.

Hathaway, S. R. (1970, March). *The MMPI development*. Paper presented at the Conference on Recent Developments in the Use of the MMPI, Mexico City, Mexico.

Hathaway, S. R., Bernal, A., Colon, A., Fernandez, G., Gueits, J., Mena, A., et al. (1959). *Inventario Multifasetico de la Personalidad. Edition limitada y experimental* [Minnesota Multiphasic Personality Inventory. Limited experimental edition]. Minneapolis: University of Minnesota Press.

Herl, D. (1976). Personality characteristics in a sample of heroin addict methadone maintenance applicants. *Journal of Clinical Psychology*, *39*, 807–813.

Hernandez, J. (1994). *The MMPI-2 performance as a function of acculturation*. Unpublished master's thesis, Sam Houston State University, Huntsville, TX.

Hernandez, J. S., & Kordinak, S. T. (1998, March). *The relationship between MMPI-2 performance and acculturation*. Paper presented at the 16th International Conference on Personality Assessment, Clearwater, FL.

Hernandez, Q., & Lucio, G. M. E. (2002, May). *Personality and IQ of high-performance Mexican adolescent students.* Paper presented at the Annual Symposium on Recent Developments in the Use of the MMPI-2, Minneapolis, MN.

Hibbs, B. J., Kobos, J. C., & Gonzales, J. (1979). Effects of ethnicity, sex, and age on MMPI profiles. *Psychological Reports, 45,* 591–597.

Himmel, E., Maltes, S. G., & Rissetti, F. J. (1979). *Valdez de constructo del MMPI en la población universitaria chilena: Un enfoque transcultural* [Construct validity of the MMPI in the Chilean university population: A cross-cultural approach] (Report No. 9). Santiago de Chile: Pontificia Universidad Catolica de Chile, Vicerrectoria Academica, Direccion de Asuntos Estudiantiles, Departamento de Salud Estudiantil.

Hinkle, J. S. (1994). Counselor and cross-cultural assessment: A practical guide to information and training. *Measurement and Evaluation in Counseling and Development, 27,* 103–115.

Hoffmann, T., Dana, R. H., & Bolton, B. (1985). Measured acculturation and MMPI: Performance of Native Americans. *Journal of Cross-Cultural Psychology, 16,* 243–256.

Holland, T. R. (1979). Ethnic group differences in MMPI profile pattern and factorial structure among adult offenders. *Journal of Personality Assessment, 43,* 72–77.

Hudak, K. V. B. (2001). An investigation of variables related to attrition of Hispanic men from a domestic violence treatment program. *Dissertation Abstracts International, 61,* 6137B.

Hutton, H. E., Smith, R., & Langfeldt, V. (1989, May). *Ethnic differences on the MMPI-based over-controlled hostility scale.* Paper presented at the Annual Meeting of the California Forensic Mental Health Association, Asilomar, CA.

Inwald, R. E. (1980, August). *Effect of two-parent background on race differences in psychological testing.* Paper presented at the 88th Annual Convention of the American Psychological Association, Montreal, Quebec, Canada.

Instituto Nacional de Estadistica Geografía e Informática. (1990). *INEGI censo: Nacional de población* [INEGI census: National population]. Mexico City, Mexico: Author.

Izaguirre-Hernandez, C., Sanchez-Quintanar, C., & Avila-Mendez, Y. (1970). *Normas de calificacion del MMPI en adolescentes del E.N.P. de U.N.A.M.* [MMPI norms for classification of adolescents of the National Preparatory School of the UNAM]. Professional thesis, National University of Mexico, Mexico City.

Jacobs, R. (1976). A study of drinking behavior and personality characteristics of three ethnic groups (Doctoral dissertation, California School of Professional Psychology, Los Angeles, 1975). *Dissertation Abstracts International, 36,* 5796B.

Jana, Y. A. (2001). The effectiveness of the MMPI-2 in detecting malingered schizophrenia in adult female inmates in Puerto Rico who receive coaching on diagnostic-specific criteria. *Dissertation Abstracts International, 62,* 1084B.

Jella, S. H., Penn, N., Boscan, D., Maness, P., & Velasquez, R. J. (2001a, May). *MMPI-2 profiles of Mexican DUI offenders and college students.* Paper presented at the Annual Symposium on Recent Developments in the Use of the MMPI-2, Tampa, FL.

Jella, S. H., Penn, N., Boscan, D., Maness, P., & Velasquez, R. J. (2001b, August). *MMPI-2 profiles of Mexican born DUI offenders and non-offenders.* Paper presented at the 109th Annual Convention of the American Psychological Association, San Francisco, CA.

Jenkins, J. H. (1988). Ethno psychiatric interpretations of schizophrenic illness: The problem of nervosa within Mexican American families. *Culture, Medicine, and Psychiatry, 12,* 301–329.

Jiménez Gómez, F., & Sánchez Crespo, G. (2002). Sensibilidad al fingimiento de la Escala Psiquiátrica *Fp* de Arbisi y Ben-Porath (1995, 1998) en la adaptación española del MMPI-2 [Sensitivity to faking in Arbisi and Ben-Porath's Psychiatric *Fp* scale (1995, 1998) in the Spanish adaptation of the MMPI-2]. *Revista Iberoamericana de Diagnostico y Evaluación Psicológica, 14,* 119–134.

Jiménez Gómez, F., Sánchez Crespo, G., & Guadalupe, F. (2001). La contribución de las subescalas Obvio-Sutil del MMPI-2 en la detección del fingimiento [The contribution of Obvious-Subtle subscales of the MMPI-2 to malingering detection]. *Revista Iberoamericana de Diagnostico y Evaluación Psicológica, 11*(1), 111–130.

Jiménez Gómez, F., Sánchez Crespo, G., & Guadalupe, F. (2003). Fingimiento de la imagen e índice de simulación F-K de Gough en la adaptación Española de MMPI-2 [Feigned imagery and Gough's F-K simulation index in the Spanish adaptation of the MMPI-2]. *Revista de Psicología General y Aplicada, 56,* 311–323.

Jiménez-Jiménez, F. J., Santos, J., Zancada, F., Molina, J. A., Irastorza, J., Fernandez-Ballesteros, A., & Roldan, A. (1992). "Premorbid" personality of patients with Parkinson's disease. *Acta Neurologica, 14,* 208–214.

Jones, B. E., Gray, B. A., & Parson, E. B. (1983). Manic–depressive illness among poor urban Hispanics. *American Journal of Psychiatry, 140,* 1208–1210.

Justes, S. M., Cuello, J. D., Manso, J. A., Ortega-Monasterio, L., Fuentes, A. C., Molas, J. V., & Teruel, L. M. P. (2004). Relationship between malingered psychometric profiles and personality styles in prisoners. *Actas Espanolas de Psiquiatria, 32,* 264–268.

Karle, H. R. (1994). *Comparability of the English and Spanish versions of the MMPI-2: A study of Latino bilingual–bicultural students.* Unpublished master's thesis, San Diego State University, San Diego, CA.

Karle, H. R., & Velasquez, R. J. (1995, August). *Comparability of the English and Spanish versions of the MMPI-2: A study of Latinos.* Paper presented at the 103rd Annual Convention of the American Psychological Association, New York.

Knatz, H. F., Inwald, R. E., Brockwell, A. L., & Tran, L. N. (1992). IPI and MMPI predictions of counterproductive job behaviors by racial group. *Journal of Business & Psychology, 7,* 189–201.

Kwant, F., Rice, J. A., & Hays, J. R. (1976). Use of heroin addiction scale to differentiate addicts from rehabilitation clients. *Psychological Reports, 38*, 547–553.

Labastida, V. M. (1988). *Estudio para detenninar las caracteristicas de personalidad que influyen el decision de la carrera de cirujano de la UNAM* [Study of personality characteristics that influence dropouts in the career of surgery at UNAM]. Unpublished degree thesis, National University of Mexico, Mexico City.

Ladd, J. S. (1996). MMPI-2 critical item norms in chemically dependent inpatients. *Journal of Clinical Psychology, 52*, 367–372.

Lapham, S. C., Skipper, B. J., Owen, J. P., Kleyboecker, K., Teaf, D., Thompson, B., & Simpson, G. (1995). Alcohol abuse screening instruments: Normative test data collected for a first DUI offender screening program. *Journal of Studies on Alcohol, 56*, 51–59.

Lapham, S. C., Skipper, B. J., & Simpson, G. L. (1997). A prospective study of the utility of standardized instruments in predicting recidivism among first DWI offenders. *Journal of Studies on Alcohol, 58*, 524–530.

Larraitz de Izaurieta, M. (1980). *Pareja infertiles: Interrelacion de factores de personalidad.* [Infertile parents: Interrelation of personality factors]. Unpublished professional thesis, National University of Mexico, Mexico City.

Lastiri Lopez, M. A. (1971). *Estudio comparative del perfil de la triada neurotica del MMPI en diferentes grupos socio-economicos de adolescents mexicanos* [Comparative study of the MMPI neurotic triad profile in different socioeconomic groups of Mexican adolescents]. Unpublished professional thesis, National University of Mexico, Mexico City.

Lawson, H. H. (1980). Psychopathology and attitude toward mental illness of Mexican-American and European-American patients (Doctoral dissertation, University of Arizona, 1979). *Dissertation Abstracts International, 40*, 3945B–3946B.

Lawson, H. H., Kahn, M. W., & Heiman, E. M. (1982). Psychopathology, treatment outcome and attitudes toward mental illness in Mexican American and European patients. *International Journal of Social Psychiatry, 28*, 20–26.

Ledwin, A. G. (1983a). A comparative study of the MMPI-Español and a culturally sensitive linguistic version (Doctoral dissertation, United States International University, 1982). *Dissertation Abstracts International, 43*, 3884A.

Ledwin, A. G. (1983b, April). *A comparison between the MMPI-Español and a culturally linguistic revision.* Paper presented at the 18th Annual Symposium on Recent Developments in the Use of the MMPI, Minneapolis, MN.

Leon, I., & Lucio, G. M. E. (1998, March). *Consistency and internal structure of the substance abuse scales of the MMPI-2.* Paper presented at the 33rd Annual Symposium of Recent Developments in the Use of the MMPI-2 and MMPI-A, Clearwater, FL.

León, I., & Lucio, E. (1999). Consistencia y estructura interna de las escalas de abuso de sustancias del MMPI-2 [Internal consistency and structure of the MMPI-2 substance abuse scales]. *Salud Mental, 22*(3), 14–19.

León, O. G., & Suero, M. (2000). Regression toward the mean associated with extreme groups and the evaluation of improvement. *Psicothema, 12*, 145–149.

Lessenger, L. H. (1997). Acculturation and MMPI-2 scale scores of Mexican-American substance abuse patients. *Psychological Reports, 80*, 1181–1182.

Leung, R. (1986). MMPI scoring as a function of ethnicity and acculturation: A comparison of Asian, Hispanic, and Caucasian gifted high school students. *Dissertation Abstracts International, 47*, 2622B.

Llorca, G., Martín, T., Derecho, J., & Gómez, M. J. (1991). Personalidad y emesis en el paciente tratado con quimioterapia antineoplásica [Personality and emesis in patients treated with antineoplastic chemotherapy]. *Actas Luso-Espanolas de Neurologia, Psiquiatria y Ciencias Afines, 19*, 327–332.

Llorente, J. M., & Onaindia, E. (1987). Personalidad y dependencia a opiáceos [Personality and opiate dependence]. *Avances en Psicologia Clinica Latinoamericana, 5*, 99–113.

López, F. J. C. (2000). Acceptance and Commitment Therapy (ACT) in panic disorder with agoraphobia: A case study. *Psychology in Spain, 4*, 120–128.

Lopez, S. (1988). The empirical basis of ethnocultural and linguistic bias in mental health evaluations of Hispanics. *American Psychologist, 43*, 1095–1097.

López, S., & Weisman, A. (2004). Integrating a cultural perspective in psychological test development. In R. J. Velásquez, L. M. Arellano, & B. W. McNeill (Eds.), *The handbook of Chicana/o psychology and mental health* (pp. 129–151). Mahwah, NJ: Erlbaum.

Lopez-Ramirez, N. I. (1987). The impact of changing environment on six behavioral and psychological traits in Puerto Rican adults (Doctoral dissertation, Pennsylvania State University, 1986). *Dissertation Abstracts International, 47*, 2960A.

López Ríos, F., & Gil Roales-Nieto, J. (2001). Características del fumador y su relación con el abandono del tabaco en programas de intervención no aversivos [Characteristics of the smoker and their relation with smoking cessation in aversive intervention programs]. *International Journal of Clinical and Health Psychology, 1*, 333–351.

Loy, A., Alvarez, M., Durán, A., & Almagro, D. (1981). Consideraciones psicopatológicas en un grupo de hemofílicos adultos: Informe preliminar [Psychopathological considerations in a group of adult hemophiliacs: Preliminary information]. *Revista Cubana de Medicina, 20*, 38–44.

Loya, F., & Munoz, A. (1981, March). *A comparison of the MMPI scales among Anglo, Black, and Hispanic individuals.* Paper presented at the Seventh International Conference on Personality Assessment, Honolulu, HI.

Lucio, E. (1976). Presencia de algunas caracteristicas hipocondriacas en estudiantes de medicina [Presence of hypochondria characteristics in medical students]. *Revista de Psiquiatria, 6*(3), 44–49.

Lucio, E. (1994). *Manual para la administracion y calificacion del MMPI-2* [Manual for administration and scoring of the MMPI-2]. Mexico City, Mexico: El Manual Moderno.

Lucio, E., Ampudia, A., & Durán, P. C. (1998). *Manual para la administración y calificación del Inventario Multifasico de la Personalidad de Minnesota para adolescentes: MMPI-A* [Manual for the administration and scoring of the Minnesota Multiphasic Personality Inventory for adolescents: MMPI-A]. Mexico City, Mexico: Manual Moderno.

Lucio, E., Ampudia, A., Gallegos, L., & Jurado, F. (1996). Características de personalidad en un grupo de pacientes con dermatitis atópica: Estudio piloto [Personality traits in a group of patients with atopic dermatitis: Pilot study]. *Revista del Centro Dermatológico Pascua, 5,* 166–176.

Lucio, E., Ampudia-Rueda, A., Duran-Patino, C., Gallegos-Mejia, L., & Leon-Guzman, I. (1999). The new version of the Minnesota Multiphasic Personality Inventory for Mexican adolescents. *Revista Mexicana de Psicologia, 16,* 217–226.

Lucio, E., Díaz, A., Jurado, M., & Cuevas, M. (2003). Detección de rechazo al tratamiento en estudiantes universitarios [Detection of treatment rejection in university students]. *Psiquiatría, 19,* 1–9.

Lucio, E., & Labastida, M. (1993). Caracteristicas de personalidad que influyen en la desercion de la carrera de medico cirujano de la U.N.A.M. [Personality traits associated with dropout rates of medical students at UNAM]. *Revista Mexicana de Psicología, 10*(1), 44–49.

Lucio, E., Monzon, G. L., Oyervides, G. S., & Larraguivel, G. (1996, June). *Development of an MMPI-2 infrequency scale for use with Mexican psychopathological populations: The F "psi" scale for Mexico.* Paper presented at the 31st Annual Symposium on Recent Developments in the Use of the MMPI-2 and MMPI-A, Minneapolis, MN.

Lucio, E., & Palacios, H. (1994, May). *MMPI-2 in Mexican psychiatric inpatients: Validity, standard and content scales.* Paper presented at the 29th Annual Symposium on Recent Developments in the Use of the MMPI-2 and MMPI-A, Minneapolis, MN.

Lucio, E., Perez, F. J. M., & Ampudia, R. A. (1996, May). *A reliability test–retest of the MMPI-2 in a group of Mexican university students.* Paper presented at the 31st Annual Symposium on Recent Developments in the Use of the MMPI-2 and MMPI-A, Minneapolis, MN.

Lucio, E., & Reyes-Lagunes, I. (1992, May). *Adaptation of the MMPI-2 Spanish version to Mexican college students.* Paper presented at the 27th Annual Symposium on Recent Developments in the Use of the MMPI-2 and MMPI-A, Minneapolis, MN.

Lucio, E., & Reyes-Lagunes, I. (1994). MMPI-2 for Mexico: Translation and adaptation. *Journal of Personality Assessment, 63,* 105–116.

Lucio, E., Reyes-Lagunes, I., & Scott, R. L. (1994). MMPI-2 for Mexico: Translation and adaptation. *Journal of Personality Assessment, 63,* 105–116.

Lucio, G. E. (2000). Case of Alejandro. In J. N. Butcher, B. Ellertsen, B. Ubostad, E. Bubb, G. E. Lucio, J. Lim, et al. (Eds.), *International case studies on the MMPI-A: An objective approach* (pp. 28–37). Minneapolis, MN: MMPI-2 Workshops.

Lucio, G. E., Ampudia, A., Duran, C., Leon, I., & Butcher, J. N. (2001). Comparison of the Mexican and American norms of the MMPI-2. *Journal of Clinical Psychology, 57,* 1459–1468.

Lucio, G. E., Duran, C., Graham, J. R., & Ben-Porath, Y. S. (2002). Identifying faking bad on the Minnesota Multiphasic Personality Inventory—Adolescent with Mexican adolescents. *Assessment, 9,* 62–69.

Lucio, G. M. E. (1995a, March). *El uso de las escalas clínicas y de contenido del MMPI-2 con personas de habla Hispana* [Use of the MMPI-2 clinical and content scales with Spanish speakers]. Paper presented at the Annual Symposium on Recent Developments in the Use of the MMPI-2, St. Petersburg, FL.

Lucio, G. M. E. (1995b). *MMPI-2: Manual para aplicación y calificacion.* Mexico City: El Manual Moderno.

Lucio, G. M. E., Ampudia, A. R., & Durán, C. P. (1996, May). *Development and normalization of the MMPI-A Spanish version for Mexico.* Paper presented at the Annual Symposium on Recent Developments in the Use of the MMPI-3, Minneapolis, MN.

Lucio, G. M. E., Ampudia, R. A., & Durán, P. C. (1997, June). *A test–retest reliability study of the MMPI-A in a group of Mexican adolescents.* Paper presented at the Clinical Workshops on the MMPI-2 and MMPI-A and the 32nd Annual Symposium on Recent Developments in the Use of the MMPI-2 and MMPI-A, Minneapolis, MN.

Lucio, G. M. E., Córdova, G. V., & Hernández, Q. (2002a, May). *Discriminative sensitivity of the Koss–Butcher and Lachar–Wrobel critical item sets in alcoholic patients.* Paper presented at the Annual Symposium on Recent Developments in the Use of the MMPI-2, Minneapolis, MN.

Lucio, G. M. E., Córdova, I. V., & Hernández, C. Q. (2002b). Sensibilidad discriminativa de los Koss–Butcher and Lachar–Wrobel escalas [Discriminant sensitivity of the Koss–Butcher and Lachar–Wrobel scales]. *Enseñanza e Investigación en Psicología* 6(1), 103–115

Lucio, G. M. E., Gallegos, M. L., Durán, P. C., & Jurado, F. (1999). Factores de personalidad y sucesos de vida que inciden en el tratamiento de pacientes con dermatitis atópica [Personality traits and life-events related to the treatment of patients who suffer from atopic dermatitis]. *Revista del Centro Dermatológico Pascua, 5*(3), 66–75.

Lucio, G. M. E., Loza, G., & Durán, C. (2000). Los sucesos de vida estresantes y la personalidad del adolescente suicida [Stressful life events and the personality of adolescents who attempted suicide]. *Revista Psicología Contemporánea, 7*(2), 58–65.

Lucio, G. M. E., Palacios, H., Duran, C., & Butcher, J. N. (1999). MMPI-2 with Mexican psychiatric inpatients: Basic and content scales. *Journal of Clinical Psychology, 55,* 1541–1552.

Lucio, G. M. E., Perez, F. J. M., & Ampudia, A. (1997). Un estudio de confiabilidad con el MMPI-2 en un grupo de estudiantes universitarios [A reliability study of the MMPI-2 in a group of university students]. *Revista Mexicana de Psicología*, *14*(1), 55–62.

Lucio, G. M. E., & Reyes-Lagunes, I. (1994). La nueva versión del Inventario Multifasico de la Personalidad de Minnesota, MMPI-2 para estudiantes universitarios mexicanos [The new version of the Minnesota Multiphasic Personality Inventory, MMPI-2 for Mexican university students]. *Revista Mexicana de Psicología 11*, 45–54.

Lucio, G. M. E., & Reyes-Lagunes, I. (1996). The Mexican version of the MMPI-2 in Mexico and Nicaragua: Translation, adaptation, and demonstrated equivalency. In J. N. Butcher (Ed.), *International adaptations of the MMPI-2* (pp. 265–283). Minneapolis: University of Minnesota Press.

Madariaga, M., & Guttin, E. (1980). *Estudio comparativo de los rasgos de personalidad de dos grupos diferentes áreas Físico Matemática y el área de Disciplinas Sociales de la escuela preparatoria 5, mediante el uso del MMPI.* [Comparative study of the personality characteristics of two groups from different areas, Physical Mathematics and the Social Disciplines area, of Preparatory School 5, using the MMPI]. Unpublished undergraduate thesis, National University of Mexico, Mexico City.

Maiocco, M. (1996). The relationship between ethnicity and somatization in workers' compensation claimants (African-American, Hispanic). *Dissertation Abstracts International, 57*, 2199B.

Malgady, R. G., & Rogler, L. H. (1993). Mental health status among Puerto Ricans, Mexican-Americans and non-Hispanic Whites: The case of the misbegotten hypothesis. *American Journal of Community Psychology, 21*, 383–388.

Malgady, R. G., Rogler, L. H., & Constantino, G. (1987). Ethno-cultural and linguistic bias in the mental health evaluation of Hispanics. *American Psychologist, 42*, 228–234.

Malinchoc, M., Colligan, R. C., & Offord, K. P. (1996). Assessing explanatory style in teenagers: Adolescent norms for the MMPI Optimism–Pessimism scale. *Journal of Clinical Psychology, 52*, 285–295.

Maness, P. J., Gomez, N., Velasquez, R. J., Silkowski, S., & Savino, A. (2000, May). *Gender differences of the MMPI-2 for Columbian university students.* Paper presented at the 35th Annual Symposium on Recent Developments in the Use of the MMPI-2 and MMPI-A, Minneapolis, MN.

Maness, P. J., Savino, A. V., Lopez, C., Velasquez, R. J., & Spinetta, J. J. (2000, May). *Comparisons of homeless White and African American males on various MMPI-2 scales.* Paper presented at the 35th Annual Symposium on Recent Developments in the Use of the MMPI-2 and MMPI-A, Minneapolis, MN.

Maness, P., Silkowski, S., Velasquez, R. J., Savino, A. V., & Frank, J. (2001, March). *Ethnic comparisons on the MMPI-2 and male sex offenders.* Paper presented at the 36th Annual Symposium on Recent Developments in the Use of the MMPI-2 and MMPI-A, Safety Harbor, FL.

Marcos, T. (1985). Proceso de validación estructural de la escala NF/F para la evaluación de la psicogeneidad del dolor [Structural validation of the NF/

F scale to evaluate the psychological factors involved in pain]. *Revista del Departamento de Psiquiatría de la Facultad de Medicina de Barcelona, 12*, 239–248.

Marcos, T., & Guijarro, A. (1989). Un caso de afasia amnésica postraumática [A case of posttraumatic amnesic aphasia]. *Revista del Departamento de Psiquiatría de la Facultad de Medicina de Barcelona, 16*, 53–55.

Martín, M. J., Riesco, N., Treserra, J., & Valdés, M. (1991). Efectividad en el entrenamiento asertivo y rasgos de personalidad [Effectiveness of assertiveness training and personality traits]. *Análisis y Modificación de Conducta, 17*(51), 7–15.

Martin, R. J., Aksamski, R., & Boenicke, C. (1977). Psychological disorders in patients with epilepsy caused by tumors. *Revista de Psicología General y Aplicada, 32*(145), 193–210.

Martinez, A. D., Baizabal, M. M. J., Maqueo, E. L. G., & Abad, M. C. (2003). Detección de recharzo al tratamiento en estudiantes universitarios [Detection of treatment refusal in undergraduates]. *Psiquiatria, 19*(1), 1–9.

Martinez de Gandell, M. D. (1983). Personality profiles and psychological orientations of employed and unemployed rehabilitated male heroin addicts: A comparison study (Doctoral dissertation, Ohio State University, 1981). *Dissertation Abstracts International, 42*, 4588A.

Mason, K. (1997). Ethnic identity and the MMPI-2 profiles of Hispanic male veterans diagnosed with PTSD. *Dissertation Abstracts International, 58*, 2129B.

Matías, J., Blanco, A. L., Llorca, G., Montejo, A. L., et al. (1995). Psicooncología: Influencia de la Percepción externa sobre los rasgos de personalidad en mujeres con cáncer [Psychooncology: Influence of external perception on the personality characteristics of women with cancer]. *Actas Luso-Espanolas de Neurologia, Psiquiatria y Ciencias Afines, 23*(1), 5–8.

Matías Polo, J., Llorca Ramón, G., Blanco González, A. L., Delgado Martín, E., et al. (1990). Aspectos psicopatológicos del cáncer en ginecología: Cáncer de mama [Psychopathological aspects of cancer in gynecology: Breast cancer]. *Actas Luso-Espanolas de Neurologia, Psiquiatria y Ciencias Afines, 18*(1), 54–61.

McCormick, R. J. (1986). Personality concomitants of the Puerto Rican syndrome as reflected in the Minnesota Multiphasic Personality Inventory (Doctoral dissertation, Rutgers University, 1986). *Dissertation Abstracts International, 47*, 4691B.

McCreary, C., & Padilla, E. (1977). Las diferencias de MMPI como los anglo, africano-americano, y mexicano-americanos delincuentes [MMPI differences among Anglo, African-American, and Mexican-American male offenders]. In R. Núñez (Ed.), *Pruebas psicometricas de la personalidad* (pp. 67–84). Mexico City, Mexico: Trillas.

McGill, J. C. (1980). MMPI score differences among Anglo, Black, and Mexican-American welfare recipients. *Journal of Clinical Psychology, 36*, 147–151.

Meadow, A., Stoker, D. H., & Zurcher, L. A. (1967). Sex role and schizophrenia: A cross-cultural study. *British Journal of Social Psychiatry, 1*, 250–259.

Mena Franco, J. (1965). *Estudio psicologico sobre el Inventario Multifasico de la Personalidad de Minnesota y su aplicacion a dos grupos de pacientes mexicanas* [A psychological study of the MMPI and its application with two groups of Mexican patients]. Unpublished dissertation, National University of Mexico, Mexico City.

Mendizabal, P. (1993). *Grado de correspondencia entre el MMPI y la forma abreviada (Mini-Mult) en una muestra de pacintes del servicio de psiquiatroa del hospital H. Delgado de Arequipa* [Degree of agreement between the MMPI abbreviated form (Mini-Mult) in a sample of patients from the psychiatry department of Delgado Hospital in Arequipa]. Unpublished degree thesis, Universidad Nacional de San Agustín, Arequipa, Peru.

Mendoza-Newman, M. C. (1998, May). *Challenges in the psychological assessment of Latino adolescents: MMPI-A.* Paper presented at the Innovations in Chicano Psychology: Looking Toward the 21st Century Conference, East Lansing, MI.

Mendoza-Newman, M. C. (2000). Level of acculturation, socioeconomic status, and the MMPI-A performance of a non-clinical Hispanic adolescent sample. *Dissertation Abstracts International, 60,* 897B.

Mendoza-Newman, M. C., Greene, R. L., & Velasquez, R. J. (2000, August). *Acculturation, SES, and the MMPI-A of Hispanic adolescents.* Paper presented at the 108th Annual Convention of the American Psychological Association, Washington, DC.

Miranda, A. O., & Umhoefer, D. L. (1998). Depression and social interest differences between Latinos in dissimilar acculturation stages. *Journal of Mental Health Counseling, 20,* 159–171.

Miranda, J., Azocar, F., Organista, K. C., Munoz, R. F., & Lieberman, A. (1996). Recruiting and retraining low-income Latinos in psychotherapy research. *Journal of Consulting and Clinical Psychology, 64,* 868–874.

Modrego, P. J., Pina, M. A., Galindo, M., & Mínguez, J. (2002). Study of psychopathology in patients with chronic non-lesional epilepsy: A Minnesota Multiphasic Personality Inventory Profile controlled study. *European Neurology, 48,* 80–86.

Moncayo, J. (1966). Estudio preliminar a la adaptacion del MMPI en el Ecuador [Preliminary study to the adaptation of the MMPI in Ecuador]. *Archivos de Criminologia, Neuro-Psiquiatria y Disciplinas Conexas, 14,* 543–587.

Monras, M., & Salamero, M. (1998). Criterios de dependencia del alcohol: alidez de sus factores y relación con los perfiles neuropsicológicos [Alcohol dependence criteria: Factor validity and relation with neuropsychological profiles]. *Revista de Psiquiatría de la Facultad de Medicina de Barcelona, 25*(2), 53–61.

Montgomery, G. T., Arnold, B. R., & Orozco, S. (1990). MMPI supplemental scale performance of Mexican Americans. *Journal of Personality Assessment, 54,* 328–342.

Montgomery, G. T., & Orozco, S. (1985). Mexican Americans' performance on the MMPI as a function of level of acculturation. *Journal of Clinical Psychology, 41,* 203–212.

Montoya, O. A., et al. (1977). La triada neurotica del MMPI en un grupo de estudiantes universitarios [The neurotic triad of the MMPI in a group of college students]. *Revista de Psicologia General y Aplicada, 149*, 1077–1083.

Monzon, L. (2001). *Los rasgos de la personalidad del adolescente medidos con el inventario Multifásico de la Personalidad de Minnesota para adolescentes (MMPI-A) y su relación con el desempeño escolar en una muestra de estudiantes de Bachillerato.* [Adolescent personality characteristics measured with the Minnesota Multiphasic Personality Inventory for adolescents (MMPI-A) and their relation to academic achievement in a sample of students from preparatory school]. Unpublished master's thesis, National University of Mexico, Mexico City.

Monzon, L., & Lucio, E. (1996). Scoring and interpretation for the MMPI-2 [Computer software]. Mexico City, Mexico: Author.

Morales Meseguer, J. M., & Ortiz Zabala, M. (1995). Análisis discriminante y validez concurrente de los cuestionarios de personalidad. Las escalas clínicas del MMPI [Discriminant analysis and concurrent validity of personality inventories. The MMPI clinical scales]. *Anales de Psiquiatría, 11*, 274–277.

Moreland, K. L. (1990). Using the MMPI-2 with American minorities. *Critical Items: A Newsletter for the MMPI Community, 6*, 1–2.

Morris, R. B. (1983, May). *A comparison of the Minnesota Multiphasic Personality Inventory and the Inventario Multifasico de la Personalidad with bilingual subjects.* Paper presented at the 18th Annual Symposium on Recent Developments in the Use of the MMPI, Minneapolis, MN.

Murphy, J. R. (1981). Mexican Americans' performance on the MMPI as compared with Anglo Americans (Doctoral dissertation, United States International University, 1978). *Dissertation Abstracts International, 41*, 3582B.

Navarro, R. (1971). El MMPI (Espanol) aplicado a jovenes mexicanos: Influencias de sexo, edad y nivel de inteligencia [The MMPI (Spanish) applied to Mexican youngsters: Sex, age and intelligence influence]. *Revista Latinoamericana de Psicologia, 5*(3–4), 127–137.

Navarro, R. (1973). Orientacion vocacional primer ingreso, cambio de carrera, y sexo en el MMPI [Vocational orientation, college entrance, career change, and sex on the MMPI]. *Revista Inter-Americana de Psicologia, 7*, 1–2.

Negy, C., Leal-Puente, L., Trainor, D. J., & Carlson, R. (1997). Mexican American adolescents' performance on the MMPI-A. *Journal of Personality Assessment, 69*, 205–214.

Negy, C., & Snyder, D. K. (1997). Ethnicity and acculturation: Assessing Mexican-American couples' relationships using the Marital Satisfaction Inventory—Revised. *Psychological Assessment, 9*, 414–421.

Nelson, D. V., Novy, D. M., Averill, M., & Berry, L. A. (1996). Ethnic comparability of the MMPI in pain patients. *Journal of Clinical Psychology, 2*, 485–497.

Netto, D. S., Aguila-Puentes, G., Burns, W. J., Sellars, A. H., & Garcia, B. (1998, August). *Brain injury and the MMPI-2: Neurocorrection for Hispanics.* Paper presented at the 106th Annual Convention of the American Psychological Association, San Francisco.

Nogueras, J. A. (1983). The standardization of the Minnesota Multiphasic Personality Inventory (MMPI) on a selected group of migrant and non-migrant Puerto Rican students (Doctoral dissertation, Pennsylvania State University, 1983). *Dissertation Abstracts International, 44*, 119A.

North, R. C. (1991). *Item analysis of MMPI Scale 8 in a Spanish translation.* Unpublished doctoral dissertation, Cambridge Graduate School of Psychology, Los Angeles.

Novy, D. M., Nelson, D. V., Goodwin, J., & Rowzee, R. D. (1993). Psychometric comparability of the State–Trait Anxiety Inventory for different ethnic subpopulations. *Psychological Assessment, 5*, 343–349.

Novy, D. M., Nelson, D. V., Smith, K. G., & Rogers, P. A. (1995). Psychometric comparability of the English- and Spanish-language versions of the State–Trait Anxiety Inventory. *Hispanic Journal of Behavioral Sciences, 17*, 209–224.

Nuñez, P., Valdés, M., García, L., & Marcos, T. (1986). Alexitimia e inteligencia verbal: Lateralización o déficit hemisférico? [Alexithymia and verbal intelligence: Lateralization or hemispheric deficit?]. *Actas Luso-Espanolas de Neurologia, Psiquiatria y Ciencias Afines, 14*, 392–398.

Núñez, R. (1967). *Inventario Multifasico de la Personalidad MMPI-Espanol* [The Spanish MMPI]. Mexico City, Mexico: Manual Moderno.

Núñez, R. (1979). *Aplicacion del Inventario Multifasico de la Personalidad (MMPI) a la psicopathology* [Application of the Minnesota Multiphasic Personality Inventory (MMPI) for psychopathology]. Mexico City, Mexico: Manual Moderno.

Núñez, R. (1987). *Pruebas psicometricas de la personalidad* [Personality psychometric tests]. Mexico City, Mexico: Trillas.

Ochoa, M. E., López-Ibor Aliño, J. J., Pérez de los Cobos Peris, J. C., & Cebollada Gracia, A. (1992). Tratamiento de deshabituación con naltrexona en la dependencia de opiáceos [Withdrawal treatment with naltrexone in opiate dependence]. *Actas Luso-Espanolas de Neurologia, Psiquiatria y Ciencias Afines, 20*(5), 215–229.

Ojeda, S. (1980). *A cross-cultural comparison of MMPI scores of Chicano and Anglo abusive mothers.* Unpublished master's thesis, San Jose State University, San Jose, CA.

Olea Renovales, M. J. (1993). La red social en el estudio global de los pacientes psiquiátricos [Social network in the global study of psychiatric patients]. *Anales de Psiquiatría, 9*, 355–362.

Olmeda García, M. S., García Cabeza, I., & Morante Fernández, L. (1998). Burnout en profesionales de salud mental [Burnout in mental health workers]. *Anales de Psiquiatría, 14*, 48–55.

Orozco, S. (1994). Acculturation levels of Mexican-American college students and performance on personality assessment inventories (Doctoral dissertation, Texas A&M University, 1994). *Dissertation Abstracts International, 54*, 5950B.

Ordaz, M., & Villegas, C. (2000). *Perfil de personalidad y nivel de asertividad en pacientes con transtorno de personalidad* [Personality profile and assertiveness level of a group of borderline patients]. Unpublished degree dissertation, National University of Mexico, Mexico City.

Padilla, A. M. (1992). Reflections on testing: Emerging trends and new possibilities. In K. F. Geisinger (Ed.), *Psychological testing of Hispanics* (pp. 271–284). Washington, DC: American Psychological Association.

Padilla, A. M., & Ruiz, R. A. (1975). Personality assessment and test interpretation of Mexican Americans: A critique. *Journal of Personality Assessment, 38,* 103–109.

Padilla, E. R., Olmedo, E. L., & Loya, F. (1982). Acculturation and the MMPI performance of Chicano and Anglo college students. *Journal of Behavioral Sciences, 4,* 451–466.

Padrós, F., & Fernández, C. J. (2001). Escala de Gaudibilidad de Padrós: Una propuesta para medir la disposición a experimentar bienestar [Padrós's Scale of the Ability to Enjoy: A proposal for measuring the capacity to experience well-being]. *Boletin de Psicología (Spain), 71,* 7–28.

Page, D. (1987). *Minnesota Multiphasic Personality Inventory differences among Chicano, Anglo, and Black schizophrenics.* Unpublished senior project, California Polytechnic State University, San Luis Obispo.

Page, R. D., & Bozlee, S. (1982). A cross-cultural MMPI comparison of alcoholics. *Psychological Reports, 50,* 639–646.

Palacios, H. (1993). *Analisis de la capacidad discriminative del MMPI-2: Comparacion de perfiles de pacientes psiquiatricos y estudiantes universitarios* [MMPI-2 discrimination: Profile comparison between psychiatric patients and college students]. Unpublished master's thesis, National University of Mexico, Mexico City.

Palacios, H., & Lucio, E. (1993, March). *Resultados preliminares de las escalas de validez del MMPI-2 en pacientes psiquiatricos.* [Preliminary results of MMPI-2 validity scales in psychiatric patients]. Paper presented at the Third Institutional Clinical Psychology Convention, Fray Bernandino Alvarez Hospital, Mexico City, Mexico.

Pampa, W. M., & Scott, R. L. (1998, March). *The MMPI-2 in Peru: A pilot normative sample.* Paper presented at the Annual Symposium on Recent Developments in the Use of the MMPI-2, Clearwater, FL.

Pampa, W., & Scott, R. (2000). Case of Adriana. In J. N. Butcher, B. Ellertsen, B. Ubostad, E. Bubb, E. Lucio, J. Lim, et al. (Eds.), *International case studies on the MMPI-A: An objective approach* (pp. 62–70). Minneapolis, MN: MMPI-2 Workshops.

Pando, J. R. (1974). Appraisal of various clinical scales of the Spanish version of the Mini-Mult with Spanish Americans (Doctoral dissertation, Adelphi University, 1974). *Dissertation Abstracts International, 34,* 5688B.

Paz, J. M. (1952). *La personalidad de los estudiantes de medicina, segun el MMPI* [The personality of medical students, according to the MMPI]. Unpublished doctoral thesis, University of Havana, Havana, Cuba.

Pena, C., Cabiya, J. J., & Echevarria, N. (1995, March). *Ambios en los promedios de puntauaiones T en al MMPI-2 de confinados convictos por crimenes violentos participantes en un programa de tratamiento basado en un modelo de apreniazaje social* [Changes in mean MMPI-2 T scores of violent offenders in a social learning treatment program]. Paper presented at the Annual Symposium on Recent Developments in the Use of the MMPI-2, St. Petersburg, FL.

Pena, C., Cabiya, J. J., & Echevarria, N. (1996, November). *MMPI-2 scores of a representative sample of state prison inmates in Puerto Rico.* Paper presented at the 43rd Convention of the Puerto Rican Psychological Association, Mayaguez, Puerto Rico.

Pena, C., Cabiya, J., & Echevarría, N. (2000). MMPI-2 scores of a representative sample of state inmates in Puerto Rico. *Revista Ciencias de la Conducta, 15,* 39–52.

Pena, L. M. (1996, June). *Spanish MMPI-A and Cuban Americans MMPI-A profiles of Cuban American adolescents using the Spanish version of the MMPI-A.* Paper presented at the 31st Annual Symposium on Recent Developments in the Use of the MMPI-2 and MMPI-A, Minneapolis, MN.

Pena, L., & Megargee, E. (1994, May). *MMPI-A patterns among juvenile delinquents.* Paper presented at the 29th Annual Symposium on Recent Developments in the Use of the MMPI-2 and MMPI-A, Minneapolis, MN.

Pena, L. M., & Megargee, E. I. (1998, March). *Predictions of institutional adjustment using the MMPI-A.* Paper presented at the Annual Symposium on Recent Developments in the Use of the MMPI-2, Clearwater, FL.

Penk, W. (1981). MMPI differences of male Hispanic-American, Black, and White heroin addicts. *Journal of Consulting and Clinical Psychology, 49,* 488–490.

Penk, W. E., Robinowitz, R., Bell, W., Shattner, H. H., Black, J., & Flores, E. (1983). *A comparison of Hispanic-American, Black, and White combat veterans seeking treatment for substance abuse (heroin).* Paper presented at the 18th annual symposium on Recent Developments in the Use of the MMPI, Minneapolis, MN.

Penk, W. E., Robinowitz, R., Black, J., Dolan, M. P., Bell, W., Dorsett, D., et al. (1989). Ethnicity: Post-traumatic stress disorder (PTSD) differences among Black, White, and Hispanic veterans who differ in degrees of exposure to combat in Vietnam. *Journal of Clinical Psychology, 45,* 729–735.

Penk, W. E., Robinowitz, R., Roberts, W. R., Dolan, M. P., & Atkins, H. G. (1981). MMPI differences of male Hispanic-American, Black, and White heroin addicts. *Journal of Consulting and Clinical Psychology, 49,* 488–490.

Penn, M. P. (1963). *A cross-cultural comparison using MMPI profiles from college students.* Unpublished master's thesis, University of Tucson, Tucson, AZ.

Penn, N., Savino, A. V., Velasquez, R. J., Boscan, D., & Gomez, F. C., Jr. (1999, April). *MMPI-2 performance of Mexican prison inmates: Clinical correlates.* Paper presented at the 34th Annual Symposium on Recent Developments in the Use of the MMPI-2 and MMPI-A, Huntington Beach, CA.

Pérez, D., & Sandín, B. (1982). Actividad hipófiso–tiroidea y personalidad [Pituitary–thyroid activity and personality]. *Psiquis: Revista de Psiquiatría, Psicología y Psicosomática, 3*(3), 46–62.

Pérez Solera, A. (1992). Tratamiento de trastornos hipocondríacos mediante un cambio de atribución: Estudio del tratamiento y sequimiento a 1 año, de un grupo de 4 pacientes [Treatment in hypochondriacal disorders through a change in attributions: Treatment study in a group of 4 patients and follow-up for 1 year]. *Análisis y Modificación de Conducta, 18*(58), 279–290.

Plemons, G. (1977). A comparison of MMPI scores of Anglo- and Mexican-American psychiatric patients. *Journal of Consulting and Clinical Psychology, 45,* 149–150.

Plemons, G. (1980). *The relationship of acculturation to MMPI scores of Mexican American psychiatric outpatients.* Unpublished doctoral dissertation, Palo Alto School of Professional Psychology, Palo Alto, CA.

Polishuk, P. (1980). Personality characteristics and role preferences among Hispanic Protestant ministers (Doctoral dissertation, Fuller Theological Seminary, 1980). *Dissertation Abstracts International, 41,* 2342B.

Pons, R., Benedito, S., & Salamero, M. (1993). El MMPI en pacientes que han cometido intento de suicidio [The MMPI in patients with suicide attempts]. *Revista de Psiquiatría de la Facultad de Medicina de Barcelona, 19*(5), 193–200.

Prewitt-Diaz, J. O., Norcross, J. A., & Draguns, J. (1985). MMPI (Spanish translation) in Puerto Rican adolescents: Preliminary data on reliability and validity. *Hispanic Journal of Behavioral Sciences, 2,* 179–190.

Pucheu, C., & Rivera, O. (1971). *The use of the MMPI in a program to prevent mental disorders.* Unpublished manuscript, National University of Mexico, Mexico City.

Quevedo, K. M., & Butcher, J. N. (2005). The use of MMPI and MMPI-2 in Cuba: A historical overview from 1950 to the present. *International Journal of Clinical and Health Psychology, 5*(2), 335–347.

Quintana, J. P. (1997). Acculturation of Hispanic-American college students and its relationship to MMPI-2 scores. *Dissertation Abstracts International, 57,* 7265B.

Quiroga, I. R. (1972). The use of a linear discriminant function on Minnesota Multiphasic Personality Inventory scores in the classification of psychotic and nonpsychotic Mexican-American psychiatric patients (Doctoral dissertation, University of Oklahoma, 1972). *Dissertation Abstracts International, 33,* 448B–449B.

Ramos Platón, M. J., & Sierra, J. E. (1992). Changes in psychopathological symptoms in sleep apnea patients after treatment with nasal continuous positive airway pressure. *International Journal of Neuroscience, 62,* 173–195.

Rangel, S., Velasquez, R. J., & Castellanos, J. (2000, May). *Utilization and opinions of the MMPI-2 by Latino psychologists: Preliminary results of a national survey.* Paper presented at the 35th Annual Symposium on Recent Developments in the Use of the MMPI-2 and MMPI-A, Minneapolis, MN.

Rangel, S. J., Yanez, E. M., Jaghab, K., & Velasquez, R. J. (2001, March). *MMPI-2 correlates for neglectful/abusive Latino and non-Latino parents: Preliminary results.* Paper presented at the 36th Annual Symposium on Recent Developments in the Use of the MMPI-2 and MMPI-A, Safety Harbor, FL.

Ray, J. B., Solomon, G. S., Doncaster, M. G., & Mellina, R. (1983). First offender adult shoplifters: A preliminary profile. *Journal of Clinical Psychology, 39*, 769–770.

Rechea Alberola, C., & Belloch Fuster, A. (1982). Factorización dinámica: Imposición de hipótesis [Dynamic factorization: Hypothesis imposition]. *Revista de Psicología General y Aplicada, 37*, 719–731.

Rees, W. L. (1974). A controlled epidemiological study of the role of psychological factors in migraine. *Archivos de Neurobiología, 37*, 243–251.

Reilley, R. R., & Knight, G. E. (1970). MMPI scores of Mexican-American college students. *Journal of College Student Personnel, 11*, 419–422.

Reuben, D. L., Lyons, M. J., Cabiya, J. J., & Harrison, R. (1996, August). *Male juvenile delinquents in Puerto Rico: MMPI-A (Spanish version)*. Paper presented at the Annual Convention of the American Psychological Association, Toronto, Ontario, Canada.

Reyes-Lagunes, E. L., Reyes-Lagunes, I., & Scott, R. L. (1994). MMPI-2 for Mexico: Translation and adaptation. *Journal of Personality Assessment, 63*, 105–116.

Reyes-Lagunes, I., Ahumada, R., & Diaz Guerrero, R. (1967). *Consideraciones acerca de la estandarizacion de pruebas en Lationamerica. Aportaciones de la psiologia a la investigacion transcultural* [Considerations about test standardization in Latin America: Contributions from psychology to cross-cultural research]. Mexico City, Mexico: Trillas.

Reynoso, H. (1989). *Inventario Multifasico de la Personalidad (MMPI): Version abreviada (Mini-Mult)* [Minnesota Multiphasic Personality Inventory (MMPI): Abbreviated version (Mini-Mult)]. Unpublished manuscript, Universidad Nacional de San Agustín, Arequipa, Peru.

Riesco, Y., Pérez Urdániz, A., Rubio, V., Izquierdo, J. A., Sánchez Iglesias, S., Santos, J. M., & Carrasco, J. L. (1998). Evaluación de trastornos de la personalidad en una población penal con el IPDE y el MMPI [Evaluation of personality disorders in a penal population using the IPDE and the MMPI]. *Actas Luso-Espanolas de Neurologia, Psiquiatria y Ciencias Afines, 26*(3), 151–154.

Rincón, V. D. R., & Lastra, R. A. (1987). Contribución a la caracterización psicológica de los enfermos de lepra [Contribution to the psychological characterization of leprosy patients]. *Revista Cubana de Medicina Tropical, 39*, 45–65.

Rissetti, F. J., Butcher, J. N., Agostini, J., Elguetta, M., Gaete, S., Margulies, T., et al. (1979a, July). *Estudios transnacionales y transculturales con el MMPI* [Transnational and transcultural studies with the MMPI]. Paper presented at the 17th Congreso Interamericano de Psicologia, Lima, Peru.

Rissetti, F. J., Butcher, J. N., Agostini, J., Elguetta, M., Gaete, S., Margulies, T., et al. (1979b, July). *La experiencia chilena con el MMPI* [The Chilean experience with the MMPI]. Paper presented at the 17th Congreso Interamericano de Psicologia, Lima, Peru.

Rissetti, F. J., Butcher, J. N., Agostini, J., Elguetta, M., Gaete, S., Margulies, T., et al. (1979c, March). *Translation and adaptation of the MMPI in Chile: Use in*

a university student health service. Paper presented at the 14th Annual Symposium on Recent Developments in the Use of the MMPI, St. Petersburg, FL.

Rissetti, F., Himmel, E., & Gonzalez, H. A. (1996). Use of the MMPI-2 in Chile.
In J. N. Butcher (Ed.), *International adaptations of the MMPI-2: Research and
clinical applications* (pp 221–251). Minneapolis: University of Minnesota Press.

Rissetti, F., Himmel, E., Maltes, S., Gonzalez, H. A., et al. (1989). Estandarizacion
del Inventario Multifasico de la Personalidad de Minnesota (MMPI), en poblacion adulta Chilena [Standardization of the Minnesota Multiphasic Personality
Inventory (MMPI) in the adult Chilean population]. *Revista Chilena de Psicologia, 10*(1), 41–62.

Rissetti, F. J., & Maltes, S. G. (1985a). Use of the MMPI in Chile. In J. N. Butcher
& C. D. Spielberger (Eds.), *Advances in personality assessment* (Vol. 4, pp.
209–257). Hillsdale, NJ: Erlbaum.

Rissetti, F. J., & Maltes, S. G. (1985b). Validez predictive del MMPI en la poblacion
universitaria de la P. Universidad Catolica de Chile [Predictive validity of
the MMPI in the university population of P. Catholic University of Chile].
Cuadernos Consejo de Rectores, Universidades Chilenas, 24, 192–203.

Rissetti, F. J., Montiel, F., Maltes, S., Hermosilla, M., & Fleischili, A. M. (1978a).
Chilean version of the MMPI. Santiago, Chile: Catholic University of Chile.

Rissetti, F. J., Montiel, F., Maltes, S., Hermosilla, M., & Fleischili, A. M. (1978b).
Traduccion al castellano del Minnesota Multiphasic Personality Inventory (MMPI)
[Translation to the Castilian of the Minnesota Multiphasic Personality Inven-
tory (MMPI)]. Santiago, Chile: Pontificia Universidad Catolica de Chile,
Direccion de Asuntos Estudiantiles, Servicio de Salud Estudiantil.

Rivera, O. (1991). *Interpretacion del MMPI en psicologia clinica, laoral y educative*
[MMPI interpretation in clinical, industrial and education psychology]. Mexico
City, Mexico: Manual Moderno.

Rivera, O., & Ampudia, I. (1976). El MMPI en la deteccion precoz delas alteraciones
mentales en pablaciones universitarias [The MMPI in the early detection of
mental disorders in college populations]. *Revista de Psiquiatria, 6*(2), 162–169.

Roche Psychiatric Service Institute. (1978). *Survey of summary statistics on basic
MMPI scales of various ethnic groups of mental health clients.* Unpublished
manuscript.

Rodriguez, L. (1952). *La personalidad del novato universitario segun el MMPI* [The
personality of the beginning university student according to the MMPI].
Unpublished doctoral dissertation, Universidad de la Habana, Havana, Cuba.

Rodriguez, L. (1980). *La normalizacion del MMPI con una muestra de estudiantes
universitarios* [Normalization of the MMPI with a college sample]. Unpublished
doctoral dissertation, Universidad de Puerto Rico, Rio Piedras.

Rogado, A. Z., Harrison, R. H., & Graham, J. R. (1974). Personality profiles in
cluster headache, migraine and normal controls. *Archivos de Neurobiología,
37*, 227–241.

Rogler, L. H., Cortes, D. E., & Malgedy, R. G. (1991). Acculturation and mental health status among Hispanics. Convergence and new directions for research. *American Psychologist, 46*, 585–597.

Rosario-Hernandez, E., Rovira-Millan, L., Rodriguez-Irrizary, A., & Alvarez, C. (2005, October). *Effectivity of the MMPI-2 Validity and Clinical Scales in differentiating response patterns for honesty, simulation (faking good) and malingering.* Paper presented at the 50th Convention of the Puerto Rican Psychological Association, San Juan, Puerto Rico.

Rossi, L. E. (2003). Comparability of the English and Spanish translations of the MMPI-2 and MCMI-III. *Dissertation Abstracts International, 63*, 4961B.

Rowell, R. K. (1992). Differences between Black, Mexican American, and White probationers on the revised MacAndrew Alcoholism Scale of the MMPI-2. *Dissertation Abstracts International, 54*, 821A.

Ruiz, P. (1997). Assessing, diagnosing, and treating culturally diverse individuals: A Hispanic perspective. *Psychiatric Quarterly, 66*, 329–341.

Ruiz Ruiz, M., Bedia Gómez, M. A., Rodríguez-Rosado, A., León Macía, M., Carpintero Avellaneda, J. L., & de la Torre Prados, M. V. (1998). Factores psicológicos y trastornos de personalidad en pacientes ingresados en cuidados intensivos: I [Psychological factors and personality disturbances in hospitalized patients in intensive care: I]. *Anales de Psiquiatría, 14*, 147–153.

Ruiz Ruiz, M., Rodríguez Rosado, A., Torres Ojeda, J., Bedia Gómez, M. A., Ruiz Ruiz de León, F., & Cano Domínguez, P. (1999). Factores psicológicos en pacientes ingresados en cuidados intensivos: II. Actitudes y trastornos psicosomáticos [Psychological factors in patients suffering in intensive care units: II. Psychosomatic factors and disorders]. *Anales de Psiquiatría, 15*, 336–346.

Saavedra, L. T. (2000). The translation and validation of the SCT-75 for assessing malingering among Hispanics involved in personal injury litigation. *Dissertation Abstracts International, 61*, 2814B.

Saba, L. (1996). Predictors of an elevated Scale 8 (Sc) on the MMPI, Version Hispana, in Hispanic workers (Doctoral dissertation, Fielding Institute, 1996). *Dissertation Abstracts International, 57*, 4776B.

Saiz-Ruiz, J., Aguilera, J. C. (1985). Personality traits and acetylator status. *Biological Psychiatry, 20*, 1138–1140.

Salamero, M., & Corominas, J. (1983). Utilidad de las escalas "Obvias" y "Sutiles" del MMPI en pacientes psiquiátricos [Usefulness of "Obvious" and "Subtle" scales for the MMPI in psychiatric patients]. *Revista del Departamento de Psiquiatría de la Facultad de Medicina de Barcelona, 10*, 385–389.

Salamero, M., Marcos, T., Rodríguez, X. A., & Corominas, J. (1983). Una forma abreviada del M.M.P.I., el Mini-Mult, para la evaluación de rasgos psicopatológicos [A shortened form of the M.M.P.I., the Mini-Mult form evaluation of psychopathological features]. *Revista del Departamento de Psiquiatría de la Facultad de Medicina de Barcelona, 10*, 311–321.

Salamero, M., & Mestre, L. (1986). El MMPI en una muestra de pacientes psiquiátricos: Perfiles medios y estructura factorial [The MMPI in a psychiatric sample:

Average profiles and factor analysis]. *Revista del Departamento de Psiquiatría de la Facultad de Medicina de Barcelona, 13*, 20–27.

Sanchez, N., Africa, D., & Santa-Cruz, L. N. (1969). Correlations between vocational preferences and the neurotic and psychopathic scales of the MMPI for Spanish university students. *Revista de Psicología General y Aplicada, 24*, 734–740.

Sánchez Martín, M. (1991). Psicopatología y delincuencia: Estudio de una muestra de reclusos salmantinos [Psychopathology and delinquency: A sample of a prison population at the Penitentiary Center of Salamanca]. *Psiquis: Revista de Psiquiatría, Psicología y Psicosomática, 12*(4), 46–55.

Sanchez Nieto, J. A., Dominguez, M. A., & Lopez Navarro, A. (1969). Correlaciones entre preferencias vocacionales y rasgos Neuroticos y Psicopaticos en universitarios espanoles [Correlations between vocational preferences and the Neurotic and Psychopathic scales of the MMPI for Spanish university students]. *Revista de Psicologia General y Aplicada, 24*, 734–740.

Sanchez Nieto, J. A., Santa Cruz, L. G., Dominguez, M. A., & Lopez Navarro, J. A. (1969). Inter-correlaciones entre preferencias vocacionales y tetrada psicotica del MMPI en universitarios espanoles ([ntercorrelations between vocational preferences and psychotic tetrad of the MMPI for Spanish university students]. *Revista de Psicologia General y Aplicada, 25*, 979–986.

Sanchez Nieto, J. A., et al. (1971). Relaciones entre el desajuste de la personalidad, inteligencia general, intereses vocacionales y estudios universitarios [Relationships between personality maladjustment, general intelligence, and vocational interests in university students]. *Revista de Médicos y Cirugía de Guerra, 33*, 39–50.

Sánchez Turet, M., & Abella Pons, F. (1999). Perfil psicopatológico en una muestra de jóvenes consumidores de drogas de diseño [Psychopathological profile in a group of youngsters using designer drugs]. *Revista de Psiquiatría Infanto-Juvenil, 2*, 85–91.

Sandín, B., & Chorot, P. (1985). Escala de anhedonia física revisada (EAF-r) de Chapman y Chapman: Primeros datos empíricos con sujetos españoles [The revised Physical Anhedonia Scale of Chapman and Chapman: First empirical evidence with a Spanish population]. *Psiquis: Revista de Psiquiatría, Psicología y Psicosomática, 6*(2), 9–18.

Sanso, T. P. (1984). Personalidad y evolución ponderal durante el tratamiento de sujetos con sobrepeso [Personality and weight evolution during the treatment of overweight people]. *Análisis y Modificación de Conducta, 10*, 463–481.

Sanz-Carrillo, C., García-Campayo, J. J., & Sánchez Blanque, A. (1993). Estudio de personalidad en pacientes con trastorno de pánico [Personality assessment in patients with panic disorder]. *Actas Luso-Espanolas de Neurologia, Psiquiatria y Ciencias Afines, 21*, 243–249.

Schluter-Sartorius, H. L. (1969). *Estudio sobre la validez diagnostica del MMPI a trvez del Rorschach y el diagnostico psiquiatrico* [A study of the diagnostic validity of the MMPI and Rorschach in psychiatric diagnosis]. Unpublished thesis, Universidad Iberoamericana, Mexico City, Mexico.

Scott, R. L., Butcher, J. N., Young, T. L., & Gomez, N. (2002). The Hispanic MMPI-A across five countries. *Journal of Clinical Psychology, 58*, 407–417.

Scott, R. L., Knoth, R. L., Beltran-Quiones, M., & Gomez, N. (2003). Assessment of psychological functioning in adolescent earthquake victims in Colombia using the MMPI-A. *Journal of Traumatic Stress, 16*(1), 49–57.

Scott, R. L., & Pampa, W. M. (2000). The MMPI-2 in Peru: A normative study. *Journal of Personality Assessment, 74*, 95–105.

Seco, F. L., Molinero, J. L., González, L., & Esteller, B. T. (2003). Personalidad y trastornos de la conducta alimentaria: Uso del Mini-Mult en la valoración de pacientes externas con trastorno alimentario [Personality and eating disorders: Use of the Mini-Mult in the outpatient assessment of patients with eating disorders]. *Revista Psiquis, 24*(5), 32–40.

Seisdedos, N., & Roig Fuste, J. M. (1986). *MMPI. Suplemento tecnico e interpretacion clinica* [Technical supplement and clinical interpretation]. Madrid, Spain: TEA Edicones.

Seisdedos Cubero, N. (1977). Personality characteristics of students receiving school counseling. *Revista de Psicología General y Aplicada, 32*(145), 287–295.

Selters, R. R. (1974). An investigation of the relationship between ethnic origin and reactions to the MMPI (Doctoral dissertation, Baylor University, 1973). *Dissertation Abstracts International, 34*, 5210B.

Serrano Prieto, F., & Diéguez Sánchez, J. (1995). Estudio del riesgo de suicidio en enfermos drogodependientes seropositivos al V.I.H. [A study of suicide risk in HIV-seropositive drug addicts]. *Folia Neuropsiquiatrica, 30*(1), 47–54.

Sesteaga, N. B. (1980). *Relación entre características de personalidad y preferencias vocacionales en mujeres adolescentes estudiantes de preparatoria* [The relation between personality traits and career election in female adolescents from preparatory school]. Unpublished undergraduate dissertation, National University of Mexico, Mexico City.

Shaffer, J. N., Nurco, D. N., Hanlon, T. E., Kinlock, T. W., Duzynski, K. R., & Stephenson, P. (1988). MMPI-168 profiles of male narcotic addicts by ethnic group and city. *Journal of Clinical Psychology, 44*, 292–298.

Sopena Alcorlo, A. (1972). La motivacion y tiempo perspectivo y los relaciones con personalidad: Una estudia empirica psychiatric [Motivation and time perspective in their relationships with personality: An empirical psychiatric study]. *Revista de Psicología General y Aplicada, 27*, 955–981.

Starke, J. (1979). *Trastonzos emocionales en pacientes gestantes, un estudio en base al MMPI* [Emotional disturbance in pregnant patients, a study based on the MMPI]. Unpublished degree thesis, Universidad Nacional de San Agustin, Arequipa, Peru.

Steinman, D. (1993). MMPI-2 profiles of inpatient polysubstance abusers. *Dissertation Abstracts International, 54*, 3354B.

Straeter, S. V. (2003). Body image and acculturation status, eating disorder symptomatology, psychopathology and self-esteem in Latina college students. *Dissertation Abstracts International, 63*, 4388B.

Sundberg, N. D., & Gonzales, L. R. (1981). Cross-cultural and cross-ethnic assessment: Overview and issues. In P. McReynolds (Ed.), *Advances in psychology assessment* (Vol. 5, pp. 460–536). New York: Plenum Press.

Swickard, D. L., & Spilka, B. (1961). Hostility expression among delinquents of minority and majority groups. *Journal of Consulting Psychology, 25*, 216–220.

Taboada, A. L. (1994). *Normalizacion del MMPI-2 en poblacion universitaria de Nicaragua* [MMPI-2 normalization for Nicaraguan college students]. Unpublished master's thesis, National University of Mexico, Mexico City.

Telander, C. M. (1999). Asian and Hispanic-American performance on the supplementary scales of the MMPI-2. *Dissertation Abstracts International, 59*, 6108B.

Toro, J., Nicolau, R., & Castro, J. (1989). Tratamiento de una fobia simple y depresión [Treatment of a simple phobia and depression]. *Revista de Psiquiatría de la Facultad de Medicina de Barcelona, 16*, 163–165.

Torre, C. (1977). *Psicología Latinoamericana. Entre la dependencia y la identidad* [Latin American psychology: Between dependency and identity]. Havana, Cuba: Félix Varela.

Torre Rodriguez, J., et al. (1970). Estudio diferencial de la "tetrada psicotica" del MMPI en univrsitarios espanoles [Differential study of the "psychotic tetrad" of the MMPI in Spanish university students]. *Revista de Psicologia General y Aplicada, 25*, 987–995.

Torres, A. A. (1956). *La normalizacion del MMPI para Cuba* [The normalization of the MMPI for Cuba]. Unpublished doctoral dissertation, Universidad de la Habana, Cuba.

Traub, G. S., & Bohn, M. J., Jr. (1985). Note on the reliability of the MMPI with Spanish-speaking inmates in the federal prison system. *Psychological Reports, 56*, 373–374.

Triana, R. M., Delgado, N. F., Sarraff, T. F., & Felipe, L. M. S. (1999). Aspectos psicológicos en pacientes con policitemia relativa hipovolémicos y normovolémicos [Psychological aspects of patients with relative hypovolemic and normovolemic polycythemia]. *Revista Cubana de Hematología, Inmunología y Hemoterapia, 15*, 127–131.

Triana, R. M., Espinosa, A. L., Triana, Y. G., Espinosa, M. A. D., & Abascal, D. P. (1987). Particularidades psíquicas de un grupo de pacientes con policitemia relativa [Psychiatric peculiarities of a group of patients with relative polycythemia]. *Revista Cubana de Hematología, Inmunolgía y Hemoterapia, 3*, 135–144.

Triana, R. M., Espinosa, A. L., Valdés, H. R., & González, L. G. (1988). Estilo de enfrentamiento al estrés en pacientes con hemopatías [Style of stress in patients with hemophilia]. *Revista del Hospital Psiquiátrico de la Habana, 29*, 555–560.

Triana, R. M., Valdés, M. E. A., & Felipe, L. M. S. (2000). Personalidad y estabilidad psíquica en un grupo de pacientes adultos con inmunodeficiencia celular

[Stability of personality in a group of adult patients with immunocellular deficiency]. *Revista Cubana de Hematología, Inmunología y Hemoterapia, 16,* 56–61.

Tsai, J. L., Butcher, J. N., Munoz, R. F., & Vitousek, K. (2001). Culture, ethnicity, and psychopathology. In H. E. Adams & P. B. Sutker (Eds.), *Comprehensive handbook of psychopathology* (3rd ed., pp. 105–127). New York: Plenum Press.

Valcárcel, E. C., & Ríos, J. M. (1974). La dimensionalidad de la escala L del MMPI [The dimensionality of the MMPI scale]. *Ciencias, Serie 6: Psicología, 1,* 1–12.

Valdés, T. L. G. (1979). Estudio valorativo de algunas características del MMPI en pacientes con trastornos psíquicos [Study of the value of MMPI characteristics in patients with severe psychological problems]. *Revista del Hospital Psiquiátrico de la Habana, 20,* 249–258.

Valdivia, J. (1996). *La normalidad estadistica segt/n el MMPI y el riesgo de sus implicancia diagnosticas: Un estudio con alullmos de la Universidad Nacional de San Agustin de Arequipa* [The statistical norm according to the MMPI and the risk of its diagnostic implications: A study of students in the Universidad Nacional de San Agustin de Arequipa]. Unpublished degree thesis, Universidad Nacional de San Agustin, Arequipa, Peru.

Varela, M. J. (1955). *La histeria en al estudiantado cubano, segun el MMPI* [Hysteria in the Cuban student, according to the MMPI]. Unpublished doctoral dissertation, Universidad de la Habana, Cuba.

Vazquez, A. (1994). MMPI: Results of a study of 500 students of professional development. *Revista de Psicologia General y Aplicada, 47,* 349–350.

Vega, A. (1971). Cross-validation of four MMPI scales for alcoholism. *Quarterly Journal of Studies on Alcohol, 32,* 791–797.

Vega, S. (1984). The cultural effects upon MMPI responses of industrially-injured Mexican and Anglo-American males (Doctoral dissertation, University of Southern California, 1983). *Dissertation Abstracts International, 44,* 2278B.

Vega, W. A., Gil, W. G., Warheit, G, J., Zimmerman, R. S., & Apospori, E. (1993). Acculturation and delinquent behavior among Cuban American adolescents: Toward an empirical model. *American Journal of Community Psychiatry, 21,* 113–115.

Vega, W. A., Kaloda, B., Aguilar-Gaxiola, S., Aldrete, E., Catalano, R., & Carereo-Anduaga, J. (1998). Lifetime prevalence of *DSM–III–R* psychiatric disorders among urban and rural Mexican Americans in California. *Archives of General Psychiatry, 55,* 771–778.

Vega, W. A., Kaloda, B., Aguilar-Gaxiola, S., & Catalano, R. (1999). Gaps in service utilization by Mexican-Americans with mental health problems. *American Journal of Psychiatry, 156,* 928–934.

Velasquez, R. J. (1984). *An atlas of MMPI group profiles on Mexican Americans* (Occasional Paper No. 19). Los Angeles: Spanish Speaking Mental Health Research Center.

Velasquez, R. J. (1987). Minnesota Multiphasic Personality Inventory differences among Chicano state hospital patients (Doctoral dissertation, Arizona State University, 1986). *Dissertation Abstracts International, 47,* 4668B.

Velasquez, R. J. (1991). *Hispanic–White differences on the MMPI as a function of profile validity.* Unpublished manuscript, San Diego State University, San Diego, CA.

Velasquez, R. J. (1992). Hispanic-American MMPI research (1949–1992): A comprehensive bibliography. *Psychological Reports, 70,* 743–754.

Velasquez, R. J. (1995). Personality assessment of Hispanic clients. In J. N. Butcher (Ed.), *Clinical personality assessment: Practical approaches* (pp. 120–139). New York: Oxford University Press.

Velasquez, R. J., Ayala, G. X., & Mendoza, S. A. (1998). *Psychodiagnostic assessment of U.S. Latinos with the MMPI, MMPI-2, and MMPI-A: A comprehensive resource manual.* East Lansing: Julian Samora Research Institute, Michigan State University.

Velasquez, R. J., Ayala, G. X., Mendoza, S., Nezami, E., Castillo-Canez, I., Pace, T., et al. (2000). Culturally competent use of the Minnesota Multiphasic Personality Inventory–2 with minorities. In I. Cuellar & F. A. Paniagua (Eds.), *Handbook of multicultural mental health* (pp. 389–417). San Diego, CA: Academic Press.

Velasquez, R. J., & Callahan, W. J. (1990). MMPI comparisons of Hispanic- and White-American veterans seeking treatment for alcoholism. *Psychological Reports, 67,* 95–98.

Velasquez, R. J., & Callahan, W. J. (1990). MMPIs of Hispanic, Black, and White DSM–III schizophrenics. *Psychological Reports, 66,* 819–822.

Velasquez, R. J., & Callahan, W. J. (1992). Psychological testing of Hispanic Americans in clinical settings: Overview and issues. In K. F. Geisinger (Ed.), *Psychological testing of Hispanics* (pp. 253–265). Washington, DC: American Psychological Association.

Velasquez, R. J., Callahan, W. J., & Carrillo, R. (1989). MMPI profiles of Hispanic-American inpatient and outpatient sex offenders. *Psychological Reports, 65,* 1055–1058.

Velasquez, R. J., Callahan, W. J., & Carrillo, R. (1991). MMPI differences among Mexican-American male and female psychiatric inpatients. *Psychological Reports, 68,* 123–127.

Velasquez, R. J., Callahan, W. J., & Young, R. (1993). Hispanic–White MMPI comparisons: Does psychiatric diagnosis make a difference? *Journal of Clinical Psychology, 49,* 528–534.

Velasquez, R. J., Callahan, W. J., Reimann, J., & Carbonell, S. (1998, August). *Performance of bilingual Latinos on an English–Spanish MMPI-2.* Paper presented at the 106th Annual Convention of the American Psychological Association, San Francisco.

Velasquez, R. J., Castellanos, J., Garrido, M., Maness, P., & Anderson, U. (2006). Interpreting forensic interview and test data of Latino children: Recommendations for culturally competent evaluations. In S. N. Sparta & G. P. Koocher

(Eds.), *Forensic mental health assessment of children and adolescents* (pp. 97–114). New York: Oxford University Press.

Velasquez, R. J., Chavira, D. A., Karle, H., Callahan, W. J., Garcia, J. A., & Castellanos, J. (2000). Assessing Spanish-speaking Latinos with translations of the MMPI-2: Initial data. *Cultural Diversity and Ethnic Minority Psychology, 6,* 65–72.

Velasquez, R. J., Garrido, M., Castellanos, J., & Burton, M. P. (2004). Culturally competent assessment of Chicana/os with the MMPI-2. In R. J. Velasquez, L. M. Arrellano, & B. W. McNeill (Eds.), *The handbook of Chicana/o psychology and mental health* (pp. 153–175). Mahwah, NJ: Erlbaum.

Velasquez, R. J., & Giminez, L. (1987). MMPI differences among three diagnostic groups of Mexican-American state hospital patients. *Psychological Reports, 60,* 1071–1074.

Velasquez, R. J., Gonzales, M., Butcher, J. N., Castillo-Canez, I., Apaca, J. X., & Chavira, D. (1997). Use of the MMPI-2 with Chicanos: Strategies for counselors. *Journal of Multicultural Counseling & Development, 25,* 107–120.

Velasquez, R. J., Gutierrez, N. M., & Jimenez, R. (1999, April). *Development of a bilingual MMPI-2 for Mexican Americans: Initial psychometric data.* Paper presented at the 34th Annual Symposium on Recent Developments in the Use of the MMPI-2 and MMPI-A, Huntington Beach, CA.

Velasquez, R. J., Jimenez, R., McClendon, V., Arellano, L. M., Callahan, W. J., & Reimann, J. (1998, August). *Performance of bilingual Latinos on an English–Spanish MMPI-2.* Paper presented at the 106th Annual Convention of the American Psychological Association, San Francisco, CA.

Velasquez, R. J., Karle, H., & Callahan, W. (1994, May). *Comparability of the English and Spanish versions of the MMPI-2: A study of Latino university students.* Paper presented at the 29th Annual Symposium on Recent Developments in the Use of the MMPI-2 and MMPI-A, Minneapolis, MN.

Velasquez, R. J., Maness, P. J., & Anderson, U. (2002). Culturally competent assessment of Latino clients: The MMPI-2. In J. N. Butcher (Ed.), *Clinical personality assessment: Practical approaches* (2nd ed., pp. 154–170). New York: Oxford University Press.

Velasquez, R. J., Page, D., & Gimenez, L. (1987, August–September). *A comparison of Chicano, Anglo, and Black schizophrenics on the MMPI.* Paper presented at the 95th Annual Convention of the American Psychological Association, New York.

Velasquez, R. J., & Quijada, P. (1992). *Use of the MMPI to assess Hispanics in substance abuse treatment programs: A review.* Unpublished manuscript, San Diego State University, San Diego, CA.

Velasquez, R. J., Ryszka, C., Gomez, F. C., Jr., Smith, M., King, D., Biskar, J., & Stokes, C. (1999, April). *Correlations between the MMPI-2 and Personality Assessment Screener (PAS) for persons seeking services in a homeless shelter.* Paper presented at the 34th Annual Symposium on Recent Developments in the Use of the MMPI-2 and MMPI-A, Huntington Beach, CA.

Velazquez, J. J. (1970). *A comparative study of two culturally different groups of Catholic priests on the basis of the MMPI.* Master's thesis, University of the Americas, Mexico City, Mexico.

Velez de Pava, M. (1967). Inventario multifasico de la personalidad (MMPI): Construccion de una escale T en 500 estudiantes de universidad [Multiphasic personality inventory (MMPI): Construction of a T scale for 500 university students]. *Revista de Psicologia, 12,* 41–54.

Vélez, R., & Cabiya, J. J. (1987) Limited utility of the MMPI-168 and of the Mini-Mult in the prediction of diagnostic profile. *Ciencias de la Conducta, 2,* 1–5.

Venn, J. (1988). MMPI profiles of Native-, Mexican-, and Caucasian-American male alcoholics. *Psychological Reports, 62,* 427–432.

Vidal Gómez, J., & Tous Ral, J. M. (1990). Psicoinmunología: Dimensiones de personalidad y respuesta inmune [Psychoneuroimmunology: Personality dimensions and immune response]. *Revista de Psicología General y Aplicada, 43,* 339–342.

Vilalta, J. (1989). Heredabilidad de la drogadicción [Inheritance of drug addiction]. *Revista del Departamento de Psiquiatría de la Facultad de Medicina de Barcelona, 16*(4), 187–192.

Vilalta, J., Garcia Esteve, L. I., Treserra, J., & Garcia Giral, M. (1986). Respuesta al tratamiento del síndrome de abstinencia a opiáceos: Influencias de variables psicológicas [Therapeutic outcome of opioid withdrawal syndrome: Influences of psychological variables]. *Revista del Departamento de Psiquiatria de la Facultad de Medicina de Barcelona, 13*(2), 63–72.

Villa Canal, A., Saiz Martínez, P. A., González García-Portilla, M. P., & Fernández Miranda, J. J. (1996). Hacia una definición del perfil psicosocial y psicopatológico de los consumidores de éxtasis [Toward a a psychosocial and psychopathological profile of ecstasy users]. *Anales de Psiquiatría, 12*(5), 183–189.

Villatoro, J. A., Medina-Mora, M. E., Hernandez, M., Fleiz, C., Amador, N., & Bermudez, P. (2005). La encuesta de estudiantes de nivel medio y medio superior de la Ciudad de México: Noviembre 2003. Prevalencias y evolución del consumo de drogas [Survey of students of superior and average mean level of the City of Mexico: November 2003. Prevalency and evolution of drug consumption]. *Salud Mental, 28*(1), 38–51.

Villatoro, C., & Ramírez, G. F. (1998) *Estudio comparativo de perfiles de personalidad de delincuentes, basado en el Inventario Multifásico de la Personalidad Minnesota-2 (MMPI-2)* [Comparative study of personality traits assessed with the MMPI-2 of a group of felons]. Unpublished degree dissertation, National University of Mexico, Mexico City.

Vinet, E. V., & Alarcon, B. P. (2003). Evaluacion psicometrica del Inventario Multifasico de Personalidad de Minnesota para Adolescentes (MMPI-A) en muestras Chilenas. [Psychometric assessment of the Minnesota Multiphasic Personality Inventory (MMPI-A) in Chilean samples]. *Terapia Psicologica, 21*(2), 87–103.

Vinet, E., Brio, C., Correa, P., Diaz, P., Diez, M., Echeverría, M., et al. (1999). MMPI-A. *Traducción y adaptación chilena para uso exclusivo en investigación* [MMPI-A. Chilean translation and adaptation for exclusive use in research]. Unpublished manuscript, Universidad de La Frontera, Santiago, Chile.

Vinet, E., & Lucio, M. E. (2006). *Aplicabilidad de las normas mexicanas y estadounidenses del MMPI-A en la evaluación de adolescentes chilenos* [Applicability of Mexican and United States norms for the MMPI-A in the assessment of Chilean adolescents]. Manuscript under review.

Wallace, J. E., MacCrimmon, D. J., & Goldberg, W. M. (1980). Acute hyperthyroidism: Cognitive and emotional correlates. *Journal of Abnormal Psychology, 89,* 519–527.

Watson, L., Chavira, D., Velasquez, R. J., & Castellanos, J. (2000, May). *MMPI-2 performance of Filipino- and Mexican-Americans: Initial findings.* Paper presented at the Annual Symposium on Recent Developments in the Use of the MMPI-2, Minneapolis, MN.

Weisman, C. P., Angline, M. D., & Fisher, D. G (1989). MMPI profiles of narcotics addicts: II. Ethnic and criminal history effects. *International Journal of the Addictions, 24,* 881–896.

Wexler, A. K. (1996). Gender and ethnicity as predictors of psychological qualifications for police officer candidates. *Dissertation Abstracts International, 57,* 2924B.

Whatley, P. R., & Dana, R. H. (1990. April). *Racial identity and the MMPI.* Paper presented at the meeting of the Southeastern Psychological Association, Atlanta, GA.

Whitworth, R. H. (1988). Anglo- and Mexican-American performance on the MMPI administered in Spanish or English. *Journal of Clinical Psychology, 44,* 891–899.

Whitworth, R. H., & McBlaine, D. D. (1993). Comparison of the MMPI and MMPI-2 administered to Anglo and Hispanic American university students. *Journal of Personality Assessment, 61,* 19–27.

Whitworth, R. H., & Unterbrink, C. (1994). Comparison of MMPI-2 clinical and content scales administered to Hispanic and Anglo-Americans. *Hispanic Journal of Behavioral Sciences, 16,* 255–264.

Woychowski, B. C. (1987). MMPI differences and interaction effects caused by race, sex, and stress experience levels of narcotic dependent patients receiving methadone maintenance treatment (Doctoral dissertation, Florida Institute of Technology, 1987). *Dissertation Abstracts International, 48,* 1825B.

Wright, T., & Velasquez, R. J. (2001, March). *Focus of control and MMPI-2 for Latinos.* Paper presented at the 36th Annual Symposium on Recent Developments in the Use of the MMPI-2 and MMPI-A, Safety Harbor, FL.

Zalewski, C., & Greene, R. L. (1996). Multicultural usage of the MMPI-2. In L. A. Suzuki, P. J. Miller, & J. G. Ponterotto (Eds.), *Handbook of multicultural assessment* (pp. 77–225). San Francisco: Jossey-Bass.

Zanolo, B. (1993). Pruebas derivadas del MMPI: Alternativas para la exploracion de diversas variables de la personalidad [MMPI derived tests: Alternatives for the exploration of diverse variables of personality]. *Revista del Departamento de Grados y Titulos de la Facilitad de Psicologia de la Universidad Inca Garcilazo de la Vega, 1*, 18–28.

Zevallos, M. (1991). *Estudio psicopatologico de internos por homicidio calificado del E.P. de Socabaya* [Psychopathological study of jailed inmates for homicide at the Socobaya jail]. Unpublished degree thesis, Universidad Nacional de San Agustín, Arequipa, Peru.

Zuckerman, M. (2003). Are there racial and ethnic differences in psychopathic personality? A critique of Lynn's (2002) racial and ethnic differences in psychopathic personality. *Personality and Individual Differences, 35*, 1463–1469.

Zuniga, O. V. (1958). *Inventario multifasico de la personalidad de Minnesota: Estudios preliminares en Mexico del MMPI* [MMPI: Preliminary studies in Mexico with the MMPI]. Unpublished degree thesis, National University of Mexico, Mexico City.

APPENDIX C

T-Score Tables for the Mexican Version
of the MMPI-2

EXHIBIT C.1
TRIN

Raw score	Male	Female
23	120	120
22	120	120
21	120	120
20	120	120
19	112	111
18	106	105
17	100	99
16	93	93
15	87	87
14	81	80
13	75	74
12	68	68
11	62	62
10	56	56
9	49	50
8	57	56
7	63	63
6	69	69
5	76	75
4	82	81
3	88	87
2	95	93
1	101	99
0	107	105

255

EXHIBIT C.2
VRIN

Raw score	Male	Female
27	120	120
26	120	119
25	118	115
24	114	112
23	110	108
22	107	104
21	103	100
20	99	97
19	96	93
18	92	89
17	88	85
16	84	82
15	81	78
14	77	74
13	73	70
12	70	67
11	66	63
10	62	59
9	58	55
8	55	52
7	51	48
6	47	44
5	44	40
4	40	37
3	36	33
2	32	29
1	29	25
0	25	22

EXHIBIT C.3
T Uniformes Para las Escalas Básicas Hombres con K

Raw score	L	F	K	Hs	D	Hi	Dp	Mf	Pa	Pt	Es	Ma	Is
79													
78													
77													
76													
75											120		
74											118		
73											117		
72											115		
71											114		
70											112		
69											111		108
68											109		106
67											108		105
66											107		104
65											105		102
64											104		101
63											102		100
62										120	101		98
61										118	99		97
60										116	98		96
59										114	96		95
58										112	95		93
57										110	93		92
56										108	92		91
55						120				106	91		89
54					119	120				104	89		88
53					117	119				102	88		87

(continued)

EXHIBIT C.3 (Continued)

Raw score	L	F	K	Hs	D	Hi	Dp	Mf	Pa	Pt	Es	Ma	Is
52					115	116		119		100	86		85
51					113	114		116		98	85		84
50					111	112	115	114		96	83		83
49					109	110	113	111		94	82		81
48				120	107	108	110	109		92	80		80
47				118	105	106	108	106		90	79		79
46				115	103	103	105	104		88	77	120	77
45				113	101	101	103	102		86	76	118	76
44				111	99	99	100	99		84	75	115	75
43				109	97	97	98	97		82	73	112	73
42				107	95	95	95	94		80	72	109	72
41				105	93	93	93	92		78	70	106	71
40				103	91	91	90	89		76	69	103	69
39				101	89	88	88	87		74	67	100	68
38				99	87	86	86	85		72	66	97	67
37				97	85	84	83	82		70	64	94	66
36				95	83	82	81	80		68	63	91	64
35				93	81	80	78	77		66	62	88	63
34				91	79	78	76	75		64	60	85	62
33				89	77	76	73	72		62	58	82	60
32				87	75	73	71	70		60	57	79	59
31				85	73	71	68	68	120	58	55	76	58
30		119	77	83	71	69	66	65	116	56	53	73	56
29		117	75	81	69	67	63	63	113	54	51	70	55
28		114	73	79	67	65	61	60	110	52	49	67	54
27		111	71	77	65	63	58	58	107	49	48	64	52
26		108	69	74	63	60	56	55	104	47	46	61	51
25		105	67	72	61	58	53	53	101	45	44	58	50

	1	2	3	4	5	6	7	8	9	10	11	12	13
24	48	55	42	42	97	51	51	56	59	70	65	102	
23	47	53	40	40	94	48	49	54	57	68	63	100	
22	46	50	38	38	91	46	46	52	54	66	61	97	
21	44	48	37	36	88	43	44	49	52	64	59	94	
20	43	46	35	35	85	41	42	47	50	62	56	91	
19	42	43	34	33	82	38	40	45	47	60	54	88	
18	40	41	32	32	78	36	38	43	45	58	52	85	
17	39	39	31	31	75	34	36	41	43	55	50	83	
16	38	37	30	30	72	31	34	39	41	53	48	80	
15	37	35			69		33	38	39	50	46	77	100
14	35	34			66		32	36	37	48	44	74	96
13	34	32			63		31	35	35	45	42	71	91
12	33	30			59		30	34	33	43	40	68	87
11	31				56			33	32	40	38	66	83
10	30				53			33	31	38	36	63	78
9					49			33	31	36	34	60	74
8					46			32	30	34	32	57	70
7					43			31		33	30	54	65
6					39			30		31		52	61
5					37					31		49	56
4					34					30		46	52
3					32							43	48
2					31							40	43
1					30							37	39
0												35	35

EXHIBIT C.4
T Uniformes de las Escalas Básicas Mujeres con K

Raw score	L	F	K	Hs	D	Hi	Pd	Mf	Pa	Pt	Es	Ma	Is
78													
77													
76													
75													
74													
73													
72													
71													
70													
69											120		101
68											119		99
67											117		98
66											115		97
65											113		96
64										120	112		95
63										118	110		93
62										116	108		92
61										115	106		91
60										113	104		90
59										111	102		88
58										109	101		87
57						117				107	99		86
56						115	120			105	97		85
55						113	118			103	95		84
54						111	116			101	93		82
53						109	114			99	92		81
52						107	112			97	90		80

	L	K	J	I	H	G	F	E	D	C	B	A
51				105	110	117			95	88		79
50				103	107	114			93	86		78
49				101	105	112			91	84		76
48			120	100	103	109			89	83		75
47			118	98	101	107			87	81		74
46			116	96	99	104			85	79	117	73
45			114	94	97	102			83	77	114	71
44			112	92	95	99			81	75	111	70
43			109	90	93	97			79	73	109	69
42			107	88	90	94			77	72	106	68
41			105	86	88	91			75	70	103	67
40			103	84	86	89			73	68	101	65
39			101	83	84	86			71	66	98	64
38			98	81	82	84			69	64	95	63
37			96	79	80	81	32		67	63	93	62
36			94	77	78	79	34		65	61	90	61
35			92	75	76	76	37		63	59	87	59
34			90	73	73	74	40		61	57	85	58
33			87	71	71	71	42		59	56	82	57
32			85	69	69	69	45		57	54	79	56
31			83	67	67	66	48	120	55	52	77	54
30	119	79	81	66	65	63	51	117	53	51	74	53
29	116	77	79	64	63	61	53	114	51	49	71	52
28	113	75	76	62	61	58	56	111	49	48	69	51
27	111	73	74	60	59	56	59	107	47	46	66	50
26	108	71	72	58	57	53	61	104	45	44	63	48
25	105	69	70	56	54	51	64	101	43	43	61	47
24	102	67	67	54	52		67	97	41	41	58	46

(continued)

APPENDIX C   *261*

EXHIBIT C.4 (Continued)

Raw score	L	F	K	Hs	D	Hi	Pd	Mf	Pa	Pt	Es	Ma	Is
23		99	64	65	52	50	49	69	94	39	40	55	45
22		96	62	63	49	48	46	72	90	37	38	52	44
21		94	60	61	47	46	44	75	87	35	36	50	42
20		91	58	59	45	45	42	78	84	34	35	47	41
19		88	56	56	43	43	40	80	80	33	33	44	40
18		85	54	54	41	41	38	83	77	31	31	42	39
17		82	52	52	39	39	37	86	74	30	30	39	37
16		80	50	50	37	38	35	88	70			37	36
15	105	77	47	47	35	36	34	91	67			35	35
14	100	74	45	45	33	35	32	94	64			34	34
13	95	71	43	43	31	33	31	96	60			33	33
12	90	68	41	41	30	32	30	99	57			33	31
11	86	65	39	39		31		102	53			32	30
10	81	63	37	37		30		104	50			31	
9	76	60	35	35				107	47			30	
8	71	57	33	33				110	44				
7	66	54	30	31				113	41				
6	62	51		30				115	38				
5	57	48						118	36				
4	52	46							34				
3	47	43							32				
2	43	40							31				
1	38	37							31				
0	33	34							31				

EXHIBIT C.5
T Uniformes Escalas de Contenido Hombres

Raw score	ANS	MIE	OBS	DEP	SAU	DEL	ENJ	CIN	PAS	PTA	BAE	ISO	FAM	DTR	RTR
36					105										
35					103										
34					101										
33				106	99									105	
32				104	98									103	
31				102	96									101	
30				101	94									99	
29				99	92									97	
28				97	90									95	
27				95	89									93	
26				93	87									91	106
25				91	85								101	89	103
24				89	83						99	88	98	87	101
23	91	96		87	82	118		81			97	86	96	85	98
22	88	93		85	80	114		77	95		94	84	93	83	95
21	86	91		83	78	111		73	91		92	82	91	81	93
20	83	88		81	76	108		69	87		90	80	88	79	90
19	81	86		79	74	104		65	83	86	87	77	85	77	88
18	78	83		77	73	101		61	79	82	85	75	83	75	85
17	76	81		75	71	98		58	75	78	83	73	80	73	83
16	73	78	88	73	69	94	86	55	70	75	80	71	78	71	80
15	71	75	84	72	67	91	83	52	66	71	78	69	75	69	78
14	68	73	81	70	66	88	79	50	62	67	76	67	73	67	75
13	66	70	78	68	64	84	76	48	59	63	73	65	70	65	73
12	63	68	74	66	62	81	72	47	55	59	71	63	68	63	70
11	61	65	71	64	60	78	69	46	52	56	69	61	65	61	68
10	58	63	67	62	58	74	66	45	50	53	66	58	62	59	65

(continued)

EXHIBIT C.5 (Continued)

Raw score	ANS	MIE	OBS	DEP	SAU	DEL	ENJ	CIN	PAS	PTA	BAE	ISO	FAM	DTR	RTR
9	56	60	64	60	57	71	62	44	48	50	64	56	60	57	63
8	54	58	61	58	55	68	59	43	46	48	62	54	58	55	60
7	53	55	58	56	52	65	56	42	44	46	59	51	55	54	58
6	51	53	55	53	50	61	53	41	42	44	57	48	53	52	55
5	49	50	52	51	48	58	51	40	40	42	54	46	51	50	53
4	46	47	49	48	45	55	48	38	38	39	51	43	48	48	50
3	44	44	46	44	42	52	45	37	37	37	47	40	45	45	47
2	41	41	43	41	38	48	42	35	34	35	44	37	42	42	44
1	37	38	39	37	34	43	38	32	32	32	40	34	39	39	40
0	33	34	34	32	30	37	34	30	30	30	36	31	35	35	35

EXHIBIT C.6
T Uniformes Escalas de Contenido Mujeres

Raw score	ANS	MIE	OBS	DEP	SAU	DEL	ENJ	CIN	PAS	PTA	BAE	ISO	FAM	DTR	RTR
36					103										
35					101										
34					99										
33				107	97									104	
32				105	96									102	
31				103	94									100	
30				101	92									98	
29				99	90									96	
28				97	88									94	
27				95	86									91	
26				93	84									89	109
25				91	83								97	87	106
24				88	81						99	93	95	85	103
23	90	90		86	79	120		83			96	90	92	83	100
22	88	87		84	77	118		79	102		94	88	90	81	97
21	85	83		82	75	114		75	98		91	85	87	78	95
20	82	80		80	73	111		72	94	92	89	83	84	76	92
19	79	77		78	72	107		68	90	88	87	80	82	74	89
18	76	74		76	70	104		64	85	83	84	77	79	72	86
17	74	71		74	68	100		61	81	79	82	75	77	70	83
16	71	67	89	72	66	97	91	57	77	74	79	72	74	68	80
15	68	64	85	70	64	93	87	55	73	70	77	69	72	66	78
14	65	61	81	68	62	90	83	52	69	66	75	67	69	63	75
13	62	58	78	65	61	86	78	50	64	61	72	64	67	61	72
12	60	56	74	63	59	83	74	49	60	57	70	61	64	59	69
11	57	53	70	61	57	79	70	47	56	57	67	59	62	57	66
10	55	52	67	59	55	76	66	46	53	54	65	57	59	55	63

(continued)

EXHIBIT C.6 (Continued)

Raw score	ANS	MIE	OBS	DEP	SAU	DEL	ENJ	CIN	PAS	PTA	BAE	ISO	FAM	DTR	RTR
9	53	50	63	57	53	72	62	45	50	51	62	54	57	54	60
8	52	48	59	55	51	69	58	44	48	48	60	52	55	52	58
7	50	47	56	53	49	65	55	43	46	46	58	50	52	51	56
6	48	45	53	50	47	62	52	41	44	44	55	48	50	49	54
5	46	43	50	48	45	58	49	40	42	42	53	46	47	47	51
4	44	42	47	45	42	55	47	39	39	39	50	44	45	45	49
3	42	39	44	42	39	52	44	37	37	37	47	41	43	43	46
2	40	37	41	39	36	49	41	35	35	35	43	38	40	40	43
1	37	34	37	36	33	44	37	33	32	32	39	34	37	37	39
0	33	31	33	32	30	37	33	30	30	30	35	30	34	34	34

EXHIBIT C.7
Suplementarias Hombres

CAL	A	R	Es	MAC	O-H	Do	Re	Mt	GM	GF	PK	PS	Fp
78													
77													
76													
75													
74													
73													
72													
71													
70													
69													
68													
67													
66													
65													
64													
63													
62													
61													
60												110	
59												108	
58												107	
57												106	
56												105	
55												104	
54												102	
53												101	
52			83									100	
51			81									99	
50			79									98	
49			76	118								96	
48		120	74	116								95	
47		118	72	113					73			94	
46		115	70	111					71	98	113	93	
45		113	68	108					69	95	111	92	
44		111	66	106					67	93	109	90	
43		108	63	103					65	90	108	89	
42		106	61	101					63	87	106	88	
41		104	59	98				99	61	85	105	87	
40		102	57	96				98	59	82	103	85	
39	92	99	55	93				96	57	79	101	84	
38	91	97	53	91				94	55	77	100	83	
37	89	95	50	88				93	53	74	98	82	
36	88	93	48	86				91	51	72	96	81	
35	86	90	46	83				89	49	69	95	79	
34	85	88	44	81				88	47	66	93	78	
33	84	86	42	78				86	45	64	91	77	
32	82	83	40	76				84	43	61	90	76	
31	81	81	38	73				83	41	58	88	75	

(continued)

EXHIBIT C.7   *(Continued)*

CAL	A	R	Es	MAC	O-H	Do	Re	Mt	GM	GF	PK	PS	Fp
30	79	79	35	71			74	81	39	56	86	73	
29	78	77	33	68			71	79	37	53	85	72	
28	77	74	31	65	92		69	77	35	50	83	71	
27	75	72		63	89		66	76	32	48	82	70	
26	74	70		60	86		63	74	30	45	80	69	
25	72	68		58	82	82	61	72		43	78	67	
24	71	65		55	79	79	58	71		40	77	66	
23	69	63		53	76	75	56	69		37	75	65	
22	68	61		50	72	72	53	67		35	73	64	118
21	67	59		48	69	68	50	66		32	72	63	115
20	65	56		45	66	65	48	64			70	61	111
19	64	54		43	63	61	45	62			68	60	108
18	62	52		40	59	58	42	61			67	59	104
17	61	49		38	56	55	40	59			65	58	100
16	60	47		35	53	51	37	57			64	57	97
15	58	45		33	49	48	35	56			62	55	93
14	57	43		30	46	44	32	54			60	54	90
13	55	40			43	41		52			59	53	86
12	54	38			39	37		50			57	52	83
11	53	36			36	34		49			55	51	79
10	51	34			33	30		47			54	49	76
9	50	31			30			45			52	48	72
8	48	29						44			50	47	68
7	47	27						42			49	46	65
6	46	25						40			47	45	61
5	44	22						39			46	43	58
4	43	20						37			44	42	54
3	41	18						35			42	41	51
2	40	15						34			41	40	47
1	38	13						32			39	39	44
0	37	11						30			37	37	40

EXHIBIT C.8
Suplementarias Mujeres

CAL	A	R	Es	MAC	O-H	Do	Re	Mt	GM	GF	PK	PS	Fp
78													
77													
76													
75													
74													
73													
72													
71													
70													
69													
68													
67													
66													
65													
64													
63													
62													
61													
60												105	
59												104	
58												103	
57												102	
56												100	
55												99	
54												98	
53												97	
52			84									96	
51			82									95	
50			80									93	
49			78									92	
48			77									91	
47			75						80			90	
46		119	73						78	82	109	89	
45		116	71	120					77	79	108	88	
44		114	69	117					75	76	106	86	
43		111	67	114					73	73	104	85	
42		109	65	112					72	70	103	84	
41		106	63	109				95	70	67	101	83	
40	89	104	61	106				93	68	64	100	82	
39	88	101	59	103				91	66	61	98	81	
38	86	98	57	100				90	65	58	96	79	
37	85	96	55	98				88	63	55	95	78	
36	84	93	54	95				86	61	52	93	77	
35	82	91	52	92				85	60	49	92	76	
34	81	88	50	89				83	58	46	90	75	
33	80	86	48	86				82	56	43	89	74	
32	78	83	46	83				80	54	40	87	72	
31	77	81	44	81				78	53	37	85	71	

(continued)

EXHIBIT C.8 *(Continued)*

CAL	A	R	Es	MAC	O-H	Do	Re	Mt	GM	GF	PK	PS	Fp
30	75	78	42	78			74	77	51	34	84	70	
29	74	76	40	75			71	75	49	31	82	69	
28	73	73	38	72	94		68	73	47		81	68	
27	71	71	36	69	91		65	72	46		79	67	
26	70	68	34	67	87		62	70	44		77	65	
25	69	66	32	64	84		59	68	42		76	64	
24	67	63	30	61	80		56	67	41		74	63	
23	66	61		58	77		53	65	39		73	62	118
22	64	58		55	73		50	64	37		71	61	114
21	63	56		53	70	102	47	62	35		69	60	111
20	62	53		50	66	99	44	60	34		68	58	107
19	60	51		47	63	96	41	59	32		66	57	104
18	59	48		44	59	92	38	57	30		65	56	101
17	58	46		41	56	89	35	55			63	55	97
16	56	43		38	52	85	32	54			61	54	94
15	55	41		36	49	82		52			60	53	90
14	53	38		33	45	78		50			58	51	87
13	52	35		30	42	75		49			57	50	83
12	51	33			38	72		47			55	49	80
11	49	30			35	68		45			53	48	76
10	48	28			31	65		44			52	47	73
9	47	25				61		42			50	46	70
8	45	23				58		41			49	44	66
7	44	20				55		39			47	43	63
6	42	18				51		37			45	42	59
5	41	15				48		36			44	41	56
4	40	13				44		34			42	40	52
3	38	10				41		32			41	39	49
2	37	8				38		31			39	37	45
1	36	5				34					37	36	42
0	34	3				31					36	35	39

APPENDIX D
T-Score Tables for the Mexican Version of the MMPI-A

EXHIBIT D.1
Uniform and Linear T-Score Conversions for Boys—Basic Scales (*N* = 1,904)

Raw score	VRIN	TRIN	F1	F2	F	L	K	Hs	D	Hy	Pd	Mf	Pa	Pt	Sc	Ma	Si
78																	117
77															105		116
76															104		115
75															103		113
74															102		112
73															101		111
72															100		110
71															99		108
70															98		107
69															97		106
68															96		104
67															95		103
66															94		102
65															93		101
64															92		99
63															91		98
62															90		97
61															89		95
60															88		94
59															87		93
58															86		92
57					119					120					85		90
56					118				120	118					84		89
55					116				119	116					83		88
54					115				117	114					82		87
53					113				115	112					81		85
52					112				113	110					80		84
51					110				111	109					79		83
50					109				109	107					78		81

Raw																	
49	80		77				113	105	107				108				
48	79		76	91			111	103	105				106				
47	78		75	90			109	101	103				105				
46	76	118	74	89			107	99	101				103				
45	75	115	73	87			105	97	99		119		102				
44	74	112	72	86			103	95	97		117		100				
43	72	109	71	85		118	101	94	95		114		99				
42	71	106	70	83		115	99	92	94		112		97				
41	70	104	69	82		112	97	90	92		110		96				
40	69	101	68	81	118	109	95	88	90		108		94				
39	67	98	68	79	116	107	93	86	88		106		93				
38	66	95	67	78	114	104	91	84	86		103		91	120			
37	65	93	66	77	111	101	89	82	84		101		90	118			
36	63	90	65	75	109	98	86	80	82		99		88	115			
35	62	87	64	74	107	95	84	79	80		97		87	113			
34	61	84	63	73	104	92	82	77	78		95		85	111			
33	60	82	62	71	102	89	80	75	76		92		84	109			
32	58	79	61	70	99	86	78	73	74	107	90		82	107			
31	57	76	60	69	97	83	76	71	72	105	88		81	104			
30	56	73	59	67	95	80	74	69	70	103	86		80	102			
29	54	70	58	66	92	77	72	67	68	100	84		78	100			
28	53	68	57	65	90	74	70	65	67	98	81		77	98			
27	52	65	56	63	88	71	68	64	65	96	79		75	96			
26	51	62	55	62	85	68	66	62	63	93	77		74	93			
25	49	59	54	61	83	65	64	60	61	91	75		72	91	120		
24	48	57	53	59	81	62	62	58	59	89	73		71	89	117		
23	47	54	52	58	78	59	60	56	57	86	70		69	87	114		
22	45	52	51	57	76	56	58	54	55	84	68		68	85	110		
21	44	50	51	55	74	53	56	52	53	82	66	119	66	82	107	120T	
20	43	48	50	54	71	50	54	50	50	79	64	115	65	80	104	114T	120
19	42	46	49	53	69	47	52	48	48	77	62	111	63	78	100	108T	119
18	40	44	48	52	67	44	50	46	46	75	59	107	62	76	97	102T	114
17	39	42	47	51	64	41	48	44	44	73	57	103	60	74	94	96T	110

Raw score	VRIN	TRIN	F1	F2	F	L	K	Hs	D	Hy	Pd	Mf	Pa	Pt	Sc	Ma	Si
16	105	90T	90	71	59	98	55	70	42	42	46	38	62	49	46	40	38
15	100	84T	87	69	57	94	53	68	40	40	44	35	59	48	45	39	36
14	96	78T	84	67	56	90	51	66	38	38	42	32	57	47	44	37	35
13	91	72T	81	65	54	86	48	63	36	36	40		55	46	43	35	34
12	86	66T	77	63	53	82	46	61	34	35	38		52	45	42	34	33
11	82	60T	74	61	52	78	44	59	33	33	36		50	43	41	32	33
10	77	54T	71	58	50	74	42	56	32	32	35		47	42	40	30	31
9	72	48T	67	56	49	70	40	54	31	31	33		45	41	39		30
8	68	58F	64	54	47	66	37	52	30	30	31		42	39	38		
7	63	64F	61	52	46	61	35	49			30		40	38	36		
6	58	70F	57	50	44	57	33	47					37	37	35		
5	54	76F	54	47	43	53	31	44					35	35	34		
4	49	81F	51	45	41	49		41					32	34	32		
3	45	87F	48	43	40	45		39					30	32	31		
2	40	93F	44	41	38	41		36						30	30		
1	35	99F	41	39	37	37		33									
0	31	105F	38	36	35	33		30									

Uniform T-Score Conversions for Boys—Content Scales ($N = 1,904$)

Raw score	ANS	OBS	DEP	SAU	ENA	DEL	ENJ	CIN	PCO	BAE	ASL	ISO	FAM	ESC	RTR	Raw score
37				109												37
36				107												36
35				105									97			35
34				103									95			34
33				101									93			33
32				99									91			32
31				97									90			31
30				95									88			30
29				93									86			29
28				91									84			28
27				89									82			27
26			85	87									81		94	26
25			83	85									79		92	25
24			82	83								88	77		89	24
23			80	81					93			85	75		86	23
22			78	79				80	90			83	73		84	22
21	87		76	77				76	87			80	72		81	21
20	84		74	75	93			72	83			78	70	98	78	20
19	81		73	73	90	95		68	80			75	68	94	76	19
18	79		71	71	87	92		64	77	87		73	66	91	73	18
17	76		69	70	84	89	83	60	73	85		70	64	88	70	17
16	73		67	68	81	86	79	56	70	82	96	67	63	84	68	16
15	70	80	66	66	78	83	75	53	67	79	92	65	61	81	65	15
14	67	77	64	64	75	79	71	50	63	76	88	62	59	77	62	14
13	64	73	62	62	72	76	67	48	60	73	83	60	57	74	60	13
12	62	69	60	60	69	73	63	45	57	71	79	57	56	71	57	12
11	59	65	58	58	66	70	59	44	54	68	75	55	54	67	55	11

(continued)

EXHIBIT D.2 (Continued)

Raw score	ANS	OBS	DEP	SAU	ENA	DEL	ENJ	CIN	PCO	BAE	ASL	ISO	FAM	ESC	RTR	Raw score
10	56	61	57	56	62	67	56	42	51	65	70	52	52	64	52	10
9	54	57	55	54	59	64	52	40	49	62	66	50	50	60	50	9
8	51	53	52	52	56	61	49	39	46	59	61	48	49	57	48	8
7	49	50	50	50	54	58	47	37	44	56	57	45	47	54	46	7
6	47	47	48	48	51	55	44	36	42	54	53	43	45	51	44	6
5	45	45	45	45	48	52	42	34	39	51	50	40	43	48	42	5
4	43	42	42	43	45	49	40	32	37	48	46	38	41	45	40	4
3	40	39	39	40	43	46	37	30	34	45	43	35	39	42	38	3
2	38	36	36	36	39	42	34	30	31	41	40	33	36	39	35	2
1	35	33	33	32	36	38	31	30	30	37	36	30	33	35	33	1
0	31	30	30	30	32	33	30	30	30	33	32	30	30	31	30	0

EXHIBIT D.3
Uniform and Linear T-Score Conversions for Boys—
Supplementary Scales (*N* = 1,904)

Raw score	MAC-R	ACK	PRO	IMM	A	R
78						
77						
76						
75						
74						
73						
72						
71						
70						
69						
68						
67						
66						
65						
64					120	
63					119	
62					118	
61					116	
60					115	
59					113	
58					112	
57					111	
56					109	
55					108	
54					106	
53				119	105	
52				117	104	
51	120			116	102	
50	118			114	101	
49	115			112	99	
48	113			110	98	
47	110			109	97	
46	108			107	95	
45	106			105	94	
44	103		119	103	92	
43	101		116	102	91	120
42	98		114	100	90	117
41	96		111	98	88	115
40	94		109	97	87	112
39	91		107	95	85	110
38	89		104	93	84	108
37	86		102	91	83	105
36	84		99	90	81	103
35	82		97	88	80	100
34	79		94	86	78	98
33	77		92	85	77	95
32	74		90	83	76	93

(continued)

EXHIBIT D.3   *(Continued)*

Raw score	MAC-R	ACK	PRO	IMM	A	R
31	72		87	81	74	90
30	69		85	79	73	88
29	67		82	78	71	85
28	65		80	76	70	83
27	62		77	74	69	80
26	60		75	72	67	78
25	57		73	71	66	75
24	55		70	69	64	73
23	53		68	67	63	70
22	50		65	66	62	68
21	48		63	64	60	66
20	45		60	62	59	63
19	43		58	60	57	61
18	41	119	55	59	56	58
17	38	114	53	57	55	56
16	36	110	51	55	53	53
15	33	105	48	54	52	51
14	31	100	46	52	50	48
13		96	43	50	49	46
12		91	41	48	48	43
11		87	38	47	46	41
10		82	36	45	45	38
9		77	34	43	43	36
8		73	31	42	42	33
7		68		40	41	31
6		63		38	39	
5		59		36	38	
4		54		35	36	
3		50		33	35	
2		45		31	34	
1		40			32	
0		36			31	

EXHIBIT D.4
Uniform and Linear T-Score Conversions for Girls—Basic Scales (N = 2,146)

Raw score	VRIN	TRIN	F1	F2	F	L	K	Hs	D	Hy	Pd	Mf	Pa	Pt	Sc	Ma	Si
78																	113
77															107		112
76															106		111
75															105		110
74															104		108
73															103		107
72															102		106
71															101		105
70															100		103
69															99		102
68															98		101
67															97		100
66															96		99
65															95		97
64															94		96
63															93		95
62															92		94
61															91		93
60															90		91
59										120					89		90
58										118					88		89
57									112	117					87		88
56									110	115					86		86
55									108	113					85		85
54									107	111					84		84
53									105	109					83		83
52					120				103	107					82		82
51					119				101	105					80		80

(continued)

EXHIBIT D.4 (Continued)

Raw score	VRIN	TRIN	F1	F2	F	L	K	Hs	D	Hy	Pd	Mf	Pa	Pt	Sc	Ma	Si
50					117				100	103	109				79		79
49					115				98	101	107				78		78
48					114				96	100	105			90	77		77
47					112				94	98	103			89	76		76
46					111				93	96	101			88	75	117	74
45					109				91	94	100			86	74	114	73
44					107				89	92	98			85	73	111	72
43					106				87	90	96			83	72	109	71
42					104				86	88	94			82	71	106	69
41					102				84	86	92			80	70	103	68
40					101				82	84	90		120	79	69	100	67
39					99				80	83	88		119	78	68	98	66
38					98				79	81	86		116	76	67	95	65
37					96				77	79	84		114	75	66	92	63
36					94				75	77	82		111	73	65	90	62
35					93				73	75	80		109	72	64	87	61
34				120	91				72	73	78		106	71	63	84	60
33				117	89			93	70	71	76		104	69	62	82	59
32				115	88			91	68	69	75	30	101	68	61	79	57
31				113	86			89	67	67	73	32	99	66	60	76	56
30				110	85		86	88	65	65	71	35	96	65	59	73	55
29				108	83		84	86	63	64	69	38	93	63	58	71	54
28				105	81		81	84	61	62	67	41	91	62	57	68	52
27				103	80		79	82	60	60	65	44	88	61	56	65	51
26				100	78		77	81	58	58	63	47	86	59	55	63	50
25				98	76		75	79	56	56	61	50	83	58	54	60	49
24				95	75		73	77	54	54	59	53	81	56	53	57	48
23				93	73		71	75	52	52	57	56	78	55	52	55	46
22		120T	119	91	72		69	73	50	50	55	59	76	54	52	52	45
21			115	88	70		66		48	48		62	73	53	51	50	44

Row	A	B	C	D	E	F	G	H	I	J	K	L	M	N	O	P	Q
20		118T	112	86	68	117		72									
19		111T	108	83	67	113		70				65			50		
18		105T	104	81	65	108		68				68		52	49		
17	116	99T	100	78	63	104		66				71	71	51	48		
16	111	93T	97	76	62	100	64	65				74	68	50	48		
15	106	87T	93	73	60	96	62	63				77	66	49	47		
14	101	80T	89	71	59	91	60	61				80	63	48	46		
13	96	74T	86	69	57	87	58	59				83	61	47	45		
12	91	68T	82	66	55	83	56	58			54	86	58	46	44		
11	85	62T	78	64	54	79	54	56		46	52	89	56	45	43		
10	80	55T	75	61	52	74	51	54		44	50	92	53	44	42	48	43
9	75	49F	71	59	50	70	49	52	46	43	48	95	50	43	41	46	42
8	70	57F	67	56	49	66	47	50	44	41	46	98	48	41	40	44	40
7	65	63F	63	54	47	62	45	47	42	39	45	101	45	40	39	42	39
6	60	69F	60	52	46	58	43	45	40	37	43	104	43	39	38	40	38
5	55	76F	56	49	44	53	41	43	38	36	41	107	40	38	36	39	37
4	50	82F	52	47	42	49	39	40	36	35	39	110	38	36	36	37	35
3	45	88F	49	44	41	45	36	37	35	33	37	113	35	35	35	35	34
2	40	94F	45	42	39	41	34	35	33	32	34	116	33	33	33	34	33
1	35	100F	41	39	37	36	32	32	31	31	32	116	31	31	32	32	32
0	30	107F	38	37	36	32	30	30	30	30	30	120	30	30	30	30	31

EXHIBIT D.5
Uniform T-Score Conversions for Girls—Content Scales (N = 2,146)

Raw score	ANS	OBS	DEP	SAU	ENA	DEL	ENJ	CIN	PCO	BAE	ASL	ISO	FAM	ESC	RTR	Raw score
37				100												37
36				98												36
35				97									94			35
34				95									92			34
33				93									90			33
32				92									88			32
31				90									87			31
30				88									85			30
29				87									83			29
28				85									82			28
27				83									80			27
26			86	82									78		94	26
25			84	80									76		92	25
24			82	78								87	75		89	24
23			80	77					97			85	73		87	23
22			78	75				83	94			82	71		84	22
21	85		76	73				79	91			80	70		81	21
20	82		74	71	91			75	88			77	68	98	79	20
19	79		71	70	88	96		71	85			75	66	95	76	19
18	76		69	68	85	93		67	82	84		72	64	92	74	18
17	73		67	66	82	90	82	63	79	82		70	63	89	71	17
16	70		65	65	79	87	78	59	76	79	94	67	61	85	69	16
15	67	81	63	63	76	84	74	55	73	76	90	65	59	82	66	15
14	64	76	61	61	73	81	70	52	70	74	86	63	57	79	64	14
13	61	72	59	60	71	77	66	49	67	71	82	60	56	76	61	13
12	58	68	57	58	68	74	61	47	64	68	78	58	54	73	59	12
11	55	63	55	56	65	71	57	45	61	66	74	55	53	70	56	11
10	53	59	53	55	62	68	54	44	58	63	70	53	51	67	54	10

EXHIBIT D.6
Uniform and Linear T-Score Conversions for Girls—
Supplementary Scales (*N* = 2,146)

Raw score	MAC-R	ACK	PRO	IMM	A	R
78						
77						
76						
75						
74						
73						
72						
71						
70						
69					120	
68					118	
67					117	
66					116	
65					114	
64					113	
63					112	
62					111	
61					109	
60					108	
59					107	
58					105	
57					104	
56					103	
55					101	
54					100	
53					99	
52					98	
51				119	96	
50				117	95	
49				115	94	
48	120			114	92	
47	117			112	91	
46	115			110	90	
45	112			108	89	
44	110			107	87	
43	107		120	105	86	
42	105		118	103	85	
41	102		115	102	83	120
40	100		113	100	82	117
39	97		110	98	81	114
38	95		108	96	79	111
37	92		105	95	78	109
36	90		103	93	77	106
35	87		100	91	76	103
34	85		98	90	74	100
33	82		95	88	73	98
32	80		93	86	72	95

(continued)

EXHIBIT D.3 *(Continued)*

Raw score	MAC-R	ACK	PRO	IMM	A	R
31	77		90	84	70	92
30	75		88	83	69	90
29	72		85	81	68	87
28	69		83	79	67	84
27	67		80	77	65	81
26	64		78	76	64	79
25	62		75	74	63	76
24	59		73	72	61	73
23	57		70	71	60	71
22	54		68	69	59	68
21	52		65	67	57	65
20	49		63	65	56	62
19	47		60	64	55	60
18	44		58	62	54	57
17	42		55	60	52	54
16	39	120	53	59	51	51
15	37	115	50	57	50	49
14	34	110	48	55	48	46
13	32	104	45	53	47	43
12	29	99	43	52	46	41
11	27	94	40	50	44	38
10	24	89	38	48	43	35
9	22	84	35	47	42	32
8	19	79	33	45	41	30
7	17	74	30	43	39	27
6	14	68	27	41	38	24
5	12	63	25	40	37	21
4	9	58	22	38	35	19
3	7	53	20	36	34	16
2	4	48	17	34	33	13
1	2	43	15	33	32	11
0	−1	37	12	31	30	8

REFERENCES

Abad, V., & Boyce, E. (1979). Issues in psychiatric evaluations of Puerto Ricans: A sociocultural perspective. *Journal of Operational Psychiatry, 10,* 28–30.

Adis-Castro, G., & Arayo-Quesada, M. (1971). Mini Mult: Una forma abbreviada del inventario multifasico de la personalidad de Minnesota, MMPI [Mini Mult: A short form of the MMPI]. *Acta Psiquiatrica y Psicologica de America Latina, 17,* 12–18.

Alamo, R. R., Cabiya, J. J., & Pedrosa, O. (1995, March). *Utility of the MMPI-2 in the identification of emotional indicators in a sample of Puerto Ricans who experienced armed assault.* Paper presented at the Annual MMPI Symposium on Recent Developments in the Use of the MMPI-2/MMPI-A, St. Petersburg, FL.

Alvarez, M. A., Alvarez, E., & Lastra, R. A. (1982). Desarrollo psicológico en hijos de madres con bocio tóxico difuso [Psychological study of children with mothers with diffuse toxic goiter]. *Revista Cubana de Pediatría, 54,* 206–214.

American Psychiatric Association. (1994). *Diagnostic and statistical manual of mental disorders* (4th ed.). Washington, DC: Author.

American Psychological Association. (2002). Ethical principles of psychologists and code of conduct. *American Psychologist, 57,* 1060–1073.

Anderson, S. J. (2001). On the importance of collecting local neuropsychological normative data. *South African Journal of Psychology, 31,* 29–34.

Arayo-Quesada, M. (1967). *Estudio sobre al MMPI en su aplicacion a un grupo de pacientes psiquiatrico costarricenses* [A study of the MMPI and its applicability with Costa Rican psychiatric patients]. Unpublished thesis, National Autonomous University of Mexico, Mexico City, Mexico.

Arbisi, P. A., Ben-Porath, Y. S., & McNulty, J. L. (2003). Empirical correlates of common MMPI-2 two-point codes in male psychiatric inpatients. *Assessment, 10,* 237–247.

Archer, R. P. (1992). *MMPI-A: Assessing adolescent psychopathology.* Hillsdale, NJ: Erlbaum.

Archer, R. P. (2005). *MMPI-A: Assessing adolescent psychopathology* (3rd ed.). Mahwah, NJ: Erlbaum.

Archer, R. P., Bollnskey, P. K., Morton, T. L., & Farris, K. L. (2003). MMPI-A characteristics of male adolescents in juvenile justice and clinical treatment settings. *Assessment, 10,* 400–410.

Archer, R. P., & Gordon, R. A. (1988). MMPI and Rorschach indices of schizophrenic and depressive diagnoses among adolescent inpatients. *Journal of Personality Assessment, 52,* 276–287.

Archer, R. P., Griffin, R., & Aiduk, R. (1995). Clinical correlates for ten common code types. *Journal of Personality Assessment, 65,* 391–408.

Arias, G., Mendoza, K., Atlis, M., & Butcher, J. N. (2002, May). *MMPI-2 use in Cuba: An illustration and future directions*. Paper presented at the Annual MMPI Symposium on Recent Developments in the Use of the MMPI-2/MMPI-A, Minneapolis, MN.

Arita, A. A., & Baer, R. A. (1998). Validity of selected MMPI-A content scales. *Psychological Assessment, 10,* 59–63.

Arqué, J. M., Segura, R., & Torrubia, R. (1987). Correlation of thyroxine and thyroid-stimulating hormone with personality measurements: A study in psychosomatic patients and healthy subjects. *Neuropsychobiology, 18,* 127–133.

Atkinson, D. R., Morten, G., & Sue, D. W. (1998). *Counseling American minorities* (5th ed.). Boston: McGraw-Hill.

Atlis, M. M., Hahn, J., & Butcher, J. N. (2006). Computer-based assessment with the MMPI-2. In J. N. Butcher (Ed.), *MMPI-2: The practitioner's handbook* (pp. 445–476). Washington, DC: American Psychological Association.

Avila-Espada, A., & Jimenez-Gomez, F. (1996). The Castilian version of the MMPI-2 in Spain: Development, adaptation, and psychometric properties. In J. N. Butcher (Ed.), *International adaptations of the MMPI-2: Research and clinical applications* (pp. 305–328). Minneapolis: University of Minnesota Press.

Azan, A. (1989). The MMPI Version Hispanic: Standardization and cross-cultural personality study with a population of Cuban refugees (Doctoral dissertation, University of Minnesota, 1988). *Dissertation Abstracts International, 50,* 2144B.

Bagby, R. M., Marshall, M. B., Bury, A., Bacchiocci, J. R., & Miller, L. (2006). Assessing underreporting and overreporting styles on the MMPI-2. In J. N. Butcher (Ed.), *MMPI-2: The practitioner's handbook* (pp. 39–69). Washington, DC: American Psychological Association.

Barbenza, C. M., Montoya, O. A., & Borel, M. T. (1978). La tetrada psicotica del MMPI en un grupo de estudiantes universitarios [The psychotic tetrad of the MMPI in a group of college students]. *Revista de Psicologia General y Aplicada, 150,* 79–88.

Barroso, C. C., Alvarez, M. A., & Alvisa, R. (1982). Validación preliminar para Cuba de una nueva versión del MMPI abreviado [Preliminary validation of a new version of the abbreviated MMPI for Cuba]. *Revista del Hospital Psiquiátrico de la Habana, 23,* 581–590.

Bartram, D. (2001). The development of international guidelines on test use: The International Test Commission Project. *International Journal of Testing, 1,* 33–45.

Ben-Porath, Y. S. (1990). Cross-cultural assessment of personality: The case for replicatory factor analysis. In J. N. Butcher & C. D. Spielberger (Eds.), *Recent advances in personality assessment* (pp. 27–48). Mahwah, NJ: Erlbaum.

Ben-Porath, Y. S., & Davis, D. L. (1996). *Case studies for interpreting the MMPI-A.* Minneapolis: University of Minnesota Press.

Benito, Y., & Moro, J. (1997). *Proyecto de identificación temprana para alumnos superdotados* [Project for early detection of gifted students]. Madrid, Spain: Ministerio de Educación y Cultura de España.

Berger, K. (1995, March). *Personality factors in incarcerated women who commit murder: An MMPI-2 study of infanticides, filicides, and homicides*. Paper presented at the 30th Annual MMPI Symposium on Recent Developments in the Use of the MMPI-2/MMPI-A, St. Petersburg, FL.

Bernal, A., & Fernandez, E. (1949). *The MMPI in Cuba*. Unpublished manuscript.

Berry, D. T. (1996, June). *Assessment of profile validity: Malingering and related response*. Paper presented at the 31st Annual MMPI Symposium on Recent Developments in the Use of the MMPI-2/MMPI-A, Minneapolis, MN.

Berry, J. W. (1997). Immigration, acculturation, and adaptation. *Applied Psychology, 46*, 5–68.

Betancourt, H., & López, S. R. (1993). The study of culture, ethnicity, and race in American psychology. *American Psychologist, 48*, 629–637.

Brenella, M. E., Dink, L., & Maristany, M. (1992). *Evaluacion objective de la personalidad, aportes del MMPI-2* [Objective evaluation of personality with the MMPI-2]. Buenos Aires, Argentina: Psicoteca Ed.

Brook, R., Kaplun, J., & Whitehead, P. C. (1974). Personality characteristics of adolescent amphetamine users as measured by the MMPI. *British Journal of Addiction to Alcohol and Other Drugs, 69*, 61–66.

Bryant, F. B., & Yarnold, P. R. (1995). Principal components analysis and exploratory and confirmatory factor analysis. In L. G. Grimm & P. R. Yarnold (Eds.), *Reading and understanding multivariate statistics* (pp. 99–136). Washington, DC: American Psychological Association.

Burke, E. L., & Eichberg, R. H. (1972). Personality characteristics of adolescent users of dangerous drugs as indicated by the Minnesota Multiphasic Personality Inventory. *Journal of Nervous and Mental Disease, 154*, 291–298.

Butcher, J. N. (1986). *Cross-cultural psychological assessment: Issues and procedures for the psychological appraisal of refugee patients* (Tech. Rep. prepared for the Technical Assistance Center, National Institute of Mental Health Project). Minneapolis: University of Minnesota.

Butcher, J. N. (1994). Psychological assessment by computer: Potential gains and problems to avoid. *Psychiatric Annals, 20*, 20–24.

Butcher, J. N. (1996a). *International adaptations of the MMPI-2: Research and clinical applications*. Minneapolis: University of Minnesota Press.

Butcher, J. N. (1996b). Understanding abnormal behavior. In J. N. Butcher (Ed.), *International adaptations of the MMPI-2* (pp. 3–25). Minneapolis: University of Minnesota Press.

Butcher, J. N. (1997). [Pearson Assessments, National Computer Systems archival base rate data]. Unpublished data, University of Minneapolis.

Butcher, J. N. (2004). Personality assessment without borders: Adaptation of the MMPI-2 across cultures. *Journal of Personality Assessment, 83*, 90–104.

Butcher, J. N. (2005a). *A beginner's guide to the MMPI-2* (2nd ed.). Washington, DC: American Psychological Association.

Butcher, J. N. (2005b). Exploring universal personality characteristics: An objective approach. *International Journal of Clinical and Health Psychology, 5,* 553–566.

Butcher, J. N. (Ed.). (2006). *MMPI-2: A practitioner's guide.* Washington, DC: American Psychological Association.

Butcher, J. N., Berah, E., Ellertsen, B., Miach, P., Lim, J., Nezami, E., et al. (1998). Objective personality assessment: Computer-based MMPI-2 interpretation in international clinical settings. In C. Belar (Ed.), *Comprehensive clinical psychology: Sociocultural and individual differences* (pp. 277–312). New York: Elsevier.

Butcher, J. N., Cabiya, J., Lucio, M. E., Pena, L., Scott, R., & Ruben, D. (1998). *Hispanic version of the MMPI-A manual supplement.* Minneapolis: University of Minnesota Press.

Butcher, J. N., Cheung, F. M., & Lim, J. (2003). Use of the MMPI-2 with Asian populations. *Psychological Assessment, 15,* 248–256.

Butcher, J. N., Coelho Mosch, S., Tsai, J., & Nezami, E. (2006). Cross-cultural applications of the MMPI-2. In J. N. Butcher (Ed.), *MMPI-2: A practitioner's guide* (pp. 505–537). Washington, DC: American Psychological Association.

Butcher, J. N., Dahlstrom, W. G., Graham, J. R., Tellegen, A. M., & Kaemmer, B. (1989). *Minnesota Multiphasic Personality Inventory–2 (MMPI-2): Manual for administration and scoring.* Minneapolis: University of Minnesota Press.

Butcher, J. N., Derksen, J., Sloore, H., & Sirigatti, S. (2003). Objective personality assessment of people in diverse cultures: European adaptations of the MMPI-2. *Behavior Research and Therapy, 41,* 819–840.

Butcher, J. N., Ellertsen, B., Ubostad, B., Bubb, E., Lucio, E., Lim, J., et al. (2000). *International case studies on the MMPI-A: An objective approach.* Minneapolis: University of Minnesota Press.

Butcher, J. N., & Garcia, R. E. (1978). Cross-national application of psychological tests. *Personnel and Guidance Journal, 56,* 472–475.

Butcher, J. N., Graham, J. R., Ben-Porath, Y. S., Tellegen, Y. S., Dahlstrom, W. G., & Kaemmer, B. (2001). *Minnesota Multiphasic Personality Inventory–2: Manual for administration and scoring* (Rev. ed.). Minneapolis: University of Minnesota Press.

Butcher, J. N., Graham, J. R., Dahlstrom, W. G., & Bowman, E. (1990). The MMPI-2 with college students. *Journal of Personality Assessment, 54,* 1–15.

Butcher, J. N., Graham, J. R., Kamphuis, J., & Rouse, S. (2006). Evaluating MMPI-2 research: Considerations for practitioners. In J. N. Butcher (Ed.), *MMPI-2: The practitioner's handbook* (pp. 15–38). Washington, DC: American Psychological Association.

Butcher, J. N., Hamilton, C. K., Rouse, S. V., & Cumella, E. J. (2006). The deconstruction of the *Hy* scale of MMPI-2: Failure of RC3 in measuring somatic symptom expression. *Journal of Personality Assessment, 87,* 199–205.

Butcher, J. N., & Han, K. (1996). Methods of establishing cross-cultural equivalence. In J. N. Butcher (Ed.), *International adaptations of the MMPI-2* (pp. 44–66). Minneapolis: University of Minnesota Press.

Butcher, J. N., & Hostetler, K. (1990). Abbreviating MMPI item administration: Past problems and prospects for the MMPI-2. *Psychological Assessment, 2,* 12–22.

Butcher, J. N., Jeffrey, T., Cayton, T. G., Colligan, S., DeVore, J., & Minnegawa, R. (1990). A study of active duty military personnel with the MMPI-2. *Military Psychology, 2,* 47–61.

Butcher, J. N., Nezami, E., & Exner, J. (1998). Psychological assessment of people in diverse cultures. In S. Kazarian & D. R. Evans (Eds.), *Cross-cultural clinical psychology* (pp. 61–105). New York: Oxford University Press.

Butcher, J. N., Ones, D. S., & Cullen, M. (2006). Personnel screening with the MMPI-2. In J. N. Butcher (Ed.), *MMPI-2: The practitioner's handbook* (pp. 381–406). Washington, DC: American Psychological Association.

Butcher, J. N., & Pancheri, P. (1976). *A handbook of cross-national MMPI research.* Minneapolis: University of Minnesota Press.

Butcher, J. N., Tsai, J., Coelho, S., & Nezami, E. (2006). Cross-cultural applications of the MMPI-2. In J. N. Butcher (Ed.), *MMPI-2: The practitioner's handbook* (pp. 505–537). Washington, DC: American Psychological Association.

Butcher, J. N., & Williams, C. L. (1992). *MMPI-2 and MMPI-A: Essentials of clinical interpretation.* Minneapolis: University of Minnesota Press.

Butcher, J. N., & Williams, C. L. (2000). *Essentials of MMPI-2 and MMPI-A interpretation* (2nd ed.). Minneapolis: University of Minnesota Press.

Butcher, J. N., Williams, C. L., Graham, J. R., Archer, R., Tellegen, A., Ben-Porath, Y. S., & Kaemmer, B. (1992). *MMPI-A manual for administration, scoring, and interpretation.* Minneapolis: University of Minnesota Press.

Cabiya, J. J. (1994, May). *Application of the Hispanic MMPI-2 in Puerto Rico.* Paper presented at the 29th Annual MMPI Symposium on Recent Developments in the Use of the MMPI-2/MMPI-A, Minneapolis, MN.

Cabiya, J. (1996). Use of the MMPI and MMPI-2 in Puerto Rico. In J. N. Butcher (Ed.), *Handbook of cross-national MMPI-2 research and clinical applications* (pp. 284–304). Minneapolis: University of Minnesota Press.

Cabiya, J. (1997). *MMPI-2 study of Puerto Rican prison inmates.* Manuscript in preparation, Center for Caribbean Studies, San Juan, Puerto Rico.

Cabiya, J., Colberg, E., Pérez, S., & Pedrosa, O. (2001, April). *MMPI-2 clinical scales profiles of female victims of domestic violence and sexual abuse.* Paper presented at the 36th Annual MMPI Symposium on Recent Developments in the Use of the MMPI-2/MMPI-A, Tampa, FL.

Cabiya, J., Cruz, R., & Bayón, N. (2002, May). *MMPI-2 Hispanic Normative Project: Puerto Rican sample.* Paper presented at the 37th Annual MMPI Symposium on Recent Developments in the Use of the MMPI-2/MMPI-A, Minneapolis, MN.

Cabiya, J., & Davila, G. (1999a). Cultural differences in MMPI-2 scores between North Americans and Puerto Ricans. *Revista Puertorriqueña de Psicología, 12,* 145–158.

Cabiya, J. J., & Davila, G. (1999b, April). *MMPI-2 mean T scores and code-types of Puerto Rican depressed outpatients and inpatients.* Paper presented at the 34th Annual MMPI Symposium on Recent Developments in the Use of the MMPI-2/MMPI-A, Huntington Beach, CA.

Cabiya, J., Reuben, D., García, O., Alvarado, C., Sayers, S., Lyons, M., & Butcher, J. (2001). *Preliminary study of the adequacy of the Spanish translation of the MMPI-A with Puerto Rican adolescents.* Unpublished manuscript.

Calderon, I. (2002). Effects of acculturation on the performance of Mexican-American adolescents on selected scales of the MMPI-A (L, K, SC, and MA). *Dissertation Abstracts International: Section B: Sciences and Engineering, 63*(2-B), 1083.

Callahan, W. J. (1997). Symptom reports and acculturation of White and Mexican-Americans in psychiatric, college, and community settings. *Dissertation Abstracts International, 58*(8-B), 4439.

Capwell, D. F. (1945). Personality patterns of adolescent girls: I. Girls who show improvement in IQ. *Journal of Applied Psychology, 29,* 212–228.

Carey, R. J., Garske, J. P., & Ginsberg, J. (1986). The prediction of adjustment to prison by means of an MMPI-based classification system. *Criminal Justice and Behavior, 13,* 347–365.

Cashel, M. L., Ovaert, L., & Holliman, N. G. (2000). Evaluating PTSD in incarcerated male juveniles with the MMPI-A: An exploratory analysis. *Journal of Clinical Psychology, 56,* 1535–1550.

Casullo, M. M. (1964). *Adaptacion del Cuestionario MMPI* [Adaptation of the MMPI Questionnaire]. Buenos Aires, Argentina: Universidad de Buenos Aires, Departamento de Orientación Vocacional.

Casullo, M. M., Samartino Garcia, L. G., Brenella, M. E., Marquez, M. A., & Dupertuis, D. G. (1996). Studies of the MMPI-2 in Argentina. In J. N. Butcher (Ed.), *International adaptations of the MMPI-2: Research and clinical applications* (pp. 252–264). Minneapolis: University of Minnesota Press.

Cheung, F. M., & Ho, R. M. (1997). Standardization of the Chinese MMPI-A in Hong Kong: A preliminary study. *Psychological Assessment, 9,* 499–502.

Cheung, F. M., Song, W. Z., & Butcher, J. N. (1991). An infrequency scale for the Chinese MMPI. *Psychological Assessment, 3,* 648–653.

Cigrang, J. A., & Staal, M. A. (2001). Readministration of the MMPI-2 following defensive invalidation in a military job applicant sample. *Journal of Personality Assessment, 76,* 472–481.

Colligan, R. C., & Offord, K. P. (1992). Age, stage, and the MMPI: Changes in response patterns over an 85-year age span. *Journal of Clinical Psychology, 48,* 476–493.

Colligan, R. C., & Osborne, D. (1977). MMPI profiles from adolescent medical patients. *Journal of Clinical Psychology, 33,* 186–189.

Colon, C. C. (1993). *Relationship between the MMPI-2 content scales and psychiatric symptoms with Puerto Rican college students and psychiatric patients.* Unpublished doctoral dissertation, Caribbean Center for Advanced Studies, San Juan, Puerto Rico.

Comas-Diaz, L. (1992). The future of psychotherapy with ethnic minorities. *Psychotherapy, 29*, 88–94.

Comas-Diaz, L. (2001). Hispanics, Latinos, or Americanos: The evolution of identity. *Cultural Diversity and Ethnic Minority Psychology, 7*, 115–120.

Comas-Diaz, L., & Grenier, J. R. (1998). Migration and acculturation. In J. Sandoval, C. L. Frisby, K. F. Geisinger, J. D. Scheuneman, & J. R. Grenier (Eds.), *Test interpretation and diversity: Achieving equity in assessment* (pp. 213–240). Washington, DC: American Psychological Association.

Comas-Diaz, L., & Jacobsen, F. M. (1987). Ethnocultural identification in psychotherapy. *Psychiatry, 50*, 232–241.

Contini de Gonzalez, E. N., Figueroa, M. I., Cohen Imach, S., & Coronel de Pace, P. (2001). The use of the MMPI-A in the identification of psychopathological traits in adolescents of Tucuman (Argentina). *Revista Iberoamericana de Diagnostico y Evaluacion Psicologica, 12*, 85–96.

Coohey, C. (2001). The relationship between familism and child maltreatment in Latino and Anglo families. *Journal of the American Professional Society on the Abuse of Children, 6*, 130–142.

Cook, W. W., & Medley, D. M. (1954). Proposed hostility and pharisaic-virtue scales for the MMPI. *Journal of Applied Psychology, 38*, 414–418.

Crespo, G. S., & Gomez, F. J. (2003). La Escala Superlativa S de Butcher y Han (1995): El fingimiento en la adaptación española del MMPI-2 [The Superlative Scale S of Butcher and Han (1995): The "fake-good" in the Spanish adaptation of the MMPI-2]. *Revista de Psicologia, 21*(1), 5–39.

Cruz-Niemiec, R. (2004). *Factores de tiempo y genero sexual asociados al MMPI-2, Versión Hispana, con un muestra de hombres y mujeres puertorriqueños/as* [Factors of time and generated sexual association to the MMPI-2, Hispanic version, with a sample of Puerto Rican men and women]. Unpublished doctoral dissertation, Albizu University, San Juan, Puerto Rico.

Cuellar, I. (2000). Acculturation as a moderator of personality and psychological assessment. In R. H. Dana (Ed.), *Handbook of cross-cultural and multicultural personality assessment* (pp. 113–129). Mahwah, NJ: Erlbaum.

Cumella, E. J., Wall, A. D., & Kerr-Almeida, N. (1999). MMPI-A in the inpatient assessment of adolescents with eating disorders. *Journal of Personality Assessment, 73*, 31–44.

Cummins, J. (1984). *Bilingualism and special education: Issues in assessment and pedagogy.* Austin, TX: Pro-Ed.

Cusick, G. M., & Fafrak, L. L. (1992, Spring). Development of local norms and their vocational evaluation. *Vocational Evaluation and Work Adjustment Bulletin, 15–18.*

Dahlstrom, W. G., Welsh, G. S., & Dahlstrom, L. E. (1975). *An MMPI handbook: Research applications* (Vol. 2). Minneapolis: University of Minnesota Press.

Dana, R. H. (1988). Culturally diverse groups and MMPI interpretation. *Professional Psychology: Research and Practice, 19,* 490–495.

Dana, R. H. (1997). Multicultural assessment and cultural identity: An assessment–intervention model. *World Psychology, 3,* 121–141.

Dana, R. (2005). *Multicultural assessment: Principles, applications and examples.* Mahwah, NJ: Erlbaum.

Deinard, A. S., Butcher, J. N., Thao, U. D., Moua Vang, S. H., & Hang, K. (1996). Development of Hmong translation of the MMPI-2. In J. N. Butcher (Ed.), *International adaptation of the MMPI-2* (pp. 194–205). Minneapolis: University of Minnesota Press.

Derksen, J. (2006). The contributions of the MMPI-2 to the diagnosis of personality disorders. In J. N. Butcher (Ed.), *MMPI-2: The practitioner's handbook* (pp. 99–120). Washington, DC: American Psychological Association.

Derksen, J., de Mey, H., Sloore, H., & Hellenbosch, G. (1993). *MMPI-2: Handleiding bij afname, scoring en interpretatie* [MMPI-2: Handbook for scoring and interpretation]. Nijmegen, the Netherlands: PEN Tests.

Derksen, J., Ven Dijk, J., & Cornelissen, A. (2003). The Dutch version of the MMPI-A [In Dutch]. *Psycholoog, 38,* 304–311.

Díaz, A., Jurado, M., Lucio, G. E., & Cuevas, M. (2003). Detección de rechazo al tratamiento en estudiantes universitarios [Detection of treatment dropout in university students]. *Psiquiatría, 19,* 1–9.

Durán, P. C., Lucio, E., & Reyes-Lagunes, I. (1993, July). *Análisis factorial de las escalas básicas del MMPI-2 español en México* [Factorial analysis of the MMPI-2 Spanish for Mexico]. Paper presented at the 24th Congreso Interamericano de Psicología. Ponencia "Sociedad Interamericana de Psicología," Santiago, Chile.

Egan, J. P. (1975). *Signal detection theory and ROC analysis.* New York: Academic Press.

Farias, J. M. P., Duran, C., & Gomez-Maqueo, E. L. (2003). MMPI-A temporal stability study through a test–retest design in a Mexican student sample. *Salud Mental, 26,* 59–66.

Figueroa, M. I. (2001). *Factores psicosociales y de personalidad asociados con el rendimiento académico en adolescentes del género femenino* [Psychosocial factors related to academic performance in female adolescents]. Unpublished master's dissertation, National Autonomous University of Mexico, Mexico City.

Fink, A., & Butcher, J. N. (1972). Reducing objections to personality inventories with special instructions. *Educational and Psychological Measurements, 27,* 631–639.

Fitzgibbons, D. J., Berry, D. F., & Shearn, C. R. (1973). MMPI and diagnosis among hospitalized drug abusers. *Journal of Community Psychology, 1,* 79–81.

Flores, L., Chavira, D. A., Velasquez, R. J., Perez, J., & Engel, B. (1996, June). *MMPI-2 codetypes of Spanish speaking Hispanic DUI offenders.* Paper presented at the 31st Annual MMPI Symposium on Recent Developments in the Use of the MMPI-2/MMPI-A, Minneapolis, MN.

Forbey, J. D., & Ben-Porath, Y. S. (2003). Incremental validity of the MMPI-A content scales in a residential treatment facility. *Assessment, 10*, 191–202.

Frank, J. G., Velasquez, R. J., Reimann, J., & Salazar, J. (1997, June). *MMPI-2 profiles of Latino, Black, and White rapists and child molesters on parole.* Paper presented at the 32nd Annual MMPI Symposium on Recent Developments in the Use of the MMPI-2/MMPI-A, Minneapolis, MN.

Gallucci, N. T. (1997). On the identification of patterns of substance abuse with the MMPI-A. *Psychological Assessment, 9*, 224–232.

Garcia, R., Hoffman, N., & Butcher, J. N. (1983). *Spanish translation of the MMPI for Hispanic Americans.* Minneapolis: University of Minnesota Press.

Garcia-Peltoniemi, R., Azan, A. A., & Lucio, E. (1998). *Inventario Multifasico de la Personalidad para Adolescentes (MMPI-A)* [Multiphasic Personality Inventory for Adolescents (MMPI-A)]. Minneapolis: University of Minnesota Press.

Garcia-Peltoniemi, R., & Azan Chaviano, A. (1993). *MMPI-2: Inventario Multifásico de la Personalidad-2 Minnesota* [MMPI-2: Minnesota Multiphasic Personality Inventory]. Minneapolis: University of Minnesota Press.

Garrido, M., Diehl, S., Gionta, D., Boscia, M., & Bailey, C. (1999, April). *Prison adjustment: Predictive utility of MMPI-2 scales, Megargee types, and demographic data.* Paper presented at the 34th Annual MMPI Symposium on Recent Developments in the Use of the MMPI-2/MMPI-A, Huntington Beach, CA.

Garrido, M., Gionta, D., Diehl, S., & Boscia, M. (1998, March). *The Megargee MMPI-2 system of inmate classification: A study of its applicability with ethnically diverse prison inmates.* Paper presented at the 33rd Annual MMPI Symposium on Recent Developments in the Use of the MMPI-2/MMPI-A, Clearwater Beach, FL.

Garrido, M., Parsons, J. P., Velasquez, R., Reimann, J. O., & Salazar, J. (1997, June). *MMPI-2 performance of Hispanic and White abusive and neglectful parents.* Paper presented at the 32nd Annual MMPI Symposium on Recent Developments in the Use of the MMPI-2/MMPI-A, Minneapolis, MN.

Garrido, M., & Velasquez, R. J. (2006). Interpretation of Latino/a MMPI-2 profiles: Review and application of empirical findings and cultural–linguistic considerations. In J. N. Butcher (Ed.), *MMPI-2: A practitioner's guide* (pp. 477–504). Washington, DC: American Psychological Association.

Geisinger, K. F. (1998). Psychometric issues in test interpretation. In J. Sandoval, C. L. Frisby, K. F. Geisinger, J. D. Scheuneman, & J. R. Grenier (Eds.), *Test interpretation and diversity: Achieving equity in assessment* (pp. 17–30). Washington, DC: American Psychological Association.

Genshaft, J. L. (1980). Personality characteristics of delinquent subtypes. *Journal of Abnormal Child Psychology, 8*, 279–283.

Ghiju, B. G. (1982). *Estudio comparativo del manejo de la agresividad en un grupo de adolescentes mujeres mexicanas de distintos niveles socioeconómicos, utilizando el MMPI* [Comparative study of the management of aggressiveness in a group of Mexican female adolescents from different socioeconomic levels, using the

MMPI]. Unpublished thesis, National Autonomous University of Mexico, Mexico City, Mexico.

Gilberstadt, H., & Duker, J. (1965). *A handbook for clinical and actuarial MMPI interpretation*. Philadelphia: Saunders.

Glaser, B. A., Calhoun, G. B., & Petrocelli, J. V. (2002). Personality characteristics of male juvenile offenders by adjudicated offenses as indicated by the MMPI-A. *Criminal Justice and Behavior, 29*, 183–201.

Gómez, F. C. J., Johnson, R., Davis, Q., & Velasquez, R. J. (2000). MMPI-A performance of African and Mexican American adolescent first-time offenders. *Psychological Reports, 87*, 309–314.

Gomez de Borda, M. I., Gonzalez, G. J. A., & Llorca, R. G. (1988). Estudio psicológico del enfermo oncológico [Psychological study of oncology patients]. *Psiquis: Revista de Psiquiatría, Psicología y Psicosomática, 9*, 29–36.

Gonzalez, M. A. A., Martin, E. A., Despaigne, D. N., & Espinosa, A. L. (1983). Factores de personalidad, depresión y concentración de la atención en el bocio tóxico difuso [Factors of personality, depression, and concentration of attention in diffuse toxic goiter]. *Revista Cubana de Investigaciones Biomédicas, 2*, 274–381.

Good, B., & Kleinman, A. (1985). Epilogue: Culture and depression. In A. Kleinman & B. Good (Eds.), *Culture and depression* (pp. 491–506). Berkeley: University of California Press.

Graham, J. R. (2006). *MMPI-2: Assessing personality and psychopathology* (4th ed.). New York: Oxford University Press.

Graham, J. R., Ben-Porath, Y. S., & McNulty, J. (1999). *MMPI-2 correlates for outpatients*. Minneapolis: University of Minnesota Press.

Graham, J. R., & Butcher, J. N. (1988, March). *Differentiating schizophrenic and major affective disorders with the revised form of the MMPI*. Paper presented at the 23rd Annual MMPI Symposium on Recent Developments in the Use of the MMPI-2/MMPI-A, St. Petersburg, FL.

Green, S. B., & Kelley, C. K. (1988). Racial bias in prediction with the MMPI for a juvenile delinquent population. *Journal of Personality Assessment, 52*, 263–275.

Greene, R. L. (1987). Ethnicity and MMPI performance: A review. *Journal of Consulting and Clinical Psychology, 35*, 497–512.

Greene, R. L. (1991). *The MMPI-2/MMPI: An interpretive manual*. Boston: Allyn & Bacon.

Greene, R. L. (2000). *The MMPI-2: An interpretive manual* (2nd ed.). Needham Heights, MA: Allyn & Bacon.

Greene, R. L., Robin, R. W., Albaugh, B., Caldwell, A., & Goldman, D. (2003). Use of the MMPI-2 in American Indians: II. Empirical correlates. *Psychological Assessment, 15*, 360–369.

Gregory, R. J. (1974). Replicated actuarial correlates for three MMPI code types in juvenile delinquency. *Journal of Clinical Psychology, 30*, 390–394.

Guarnaccia, P. J., Lewis-Fernández, R., & Marano, M. R. (2003). Toward a Puerto Rican popular nosology: Nervios and ataque de nervios. *Culture, Medicine and Psychiatry, 27,* 339–366.

Gucker, D., & McNulty, J. (2004, May). *The MMPI-2, defensiveness, and an analytic strategy.* Paper presented at the 39th Annual MMPI Symposium on Recent Developments in the Use of the MMPI-2/MMPI-A, Minneapolis, MN.

Gynther, M. D., Altman, H., & Sletten, I. W. (1973). Development of an empirical interpretive system for the MMPI: Some after-the-fact observations. *Journal of Clinical Psychology, 29,* 232–234.

Hahn, J. (2003). Faking and defensive responding in Korean MMPI-2. *Dissertation Abstracts International: Section B: Sciences and Engineering, 64*(6-B), 2971.

Halcón, L., Robertson, C. L., Savik, K., Johnson, D. R., Spring, M. A., Butcher, J. N., et al. (2004). Trauma and coping in Somali and Oromo refugee youth. *Journal of Adolescent Health, 35,* 17–25.

Hall, G. C. N., Bansal, A., & Lopez, I. R. (1999). Ethnicity and psychopathology: A meta analytic review of 31 years of comparative MMPI/MMPI-2 research. *Psychological Assessment, 11,* 186–197.

Han, K., Weed, N., Calhoun, R., & Butcher, J. N. (1995). Psychometric characteristics of the MMPI-2 Cook–Medley Hostility Scale. *Journal of Personality Assessment, 65,* 567–586.

Handler, L., & Meyer, G. J. (1998). The importance of teaching and learning personality assessment. In L. Handler & M. J. Hilsenroth (Eds.), *Teaching and learning personality assessment* (pp. 3–30). Mahwah, NJ: Erlbaum.

Harkness, A., McNulty, J., Ben-Porath, Y., & Graham, J. R. (1999). *MMPI-2 Personality Psychopathology 5 (PSY-5) scales: MMPI-2 test reports.* Minneapolis: University of Minnesota Press.

Haskell, A. (1996). Mexican American and Anglo American endorsement of items on the MMPI-2 Scale 2, the Center for Epidemiological Studies Depression Scale, and the Cohen–Hoberman Inventory for Physical Symptoms. *Dissertation Abstracts International, 57,* 4708B.

Hathaway, S. R. (1970, March). *The MMPI development.* Paper presented at the Annual MMPI Symposium on Recent Developments in the Use of the MMPI-2/MMPI-A, Mexico City, Mexico.

Hathaway, S. R., & McKinley, J. C. (1940). A multiphasic personality schedule (Minnesota): I. Construction of the schedule. *Journal of Psychology, 10,* 249–254.

Hathaway, S. R., & Monachesi, E. D. (1951). The prediction of juvenile delinquency using the Minnesota Multiphasic Personality Inventory. *American Journal of Psychiatry, 108,* 469–473.

Hathaway, S. R., & Monachesi, E. D. (1952). The Minnesota Multiphasic Personality Inventory in the study of juvenile delinquents. *American Sociological Review, 17,* 704–710.

Hathaway, S. R., & Monachesi, E. D. (1957).The personalities of predelinquent boys. *Journal of Criminal Law and Criminology, 48*, 149–163.

Hathaway, S. R., & Monachesi, E. D. (1961). *An atlas of juvenile MMPI profiles.* Minneapolis: University of Minnesota Press.

Hathaway, S. R., & Monachesi, E. D. (1963). *Adolescent personality and behavior: MMPI patterns of normal, delinquent, drop-out, and other outcomes.* Minneapolis: University of Minnesota Press.

Hays, P. (2001). *Addressing cultural complexities in practice: A framework for clinicians and counselors.* Washington, DC: American Psychological Association.

Helms, J. E., & Cook, D. A. (1999). *Using race and culture in counseling and psychotherapy: Theory and process.* Needham Heights, MA: Allyn & Bacon.

Henard, D. H. (2000). Item response theory. In L. G. Grimm & P. R. Yarnold (Eds.), *Reading and understanding more multivariate statistics* (pp. 67–98). Washington, DC: American Psychological Association.

Hernandez, Q., Lucio, E., & Manzo, C. (2002, May). *Personality and IQ of high performance Mexican adolescent student patients.* Paper presented at the 37th Annual MMPI Symposium on Recent Developments in the Use of the MMPI-2/MMPI-A, Minneapolis, MN.

Hilliard, A. (1996). Either a paradigm shift or no mental measurement: The non-science of the bell curve. *Cultural Diversity and Mental Health, 2*, 1–20.

Himmel, E., Maltes, S. G., & Rissetti, F. J. (1979). *Valdez de constructo del MMPI en la población universitaria chilena: Un enfoque transcultural* [Construct validity of the MMPI in the Chilean university population: A transcultural approach]. Santiago, Chile: Pontificia Universidad Carolica de Chile, Vicerrectoria Academica, Direccion de Asuntos Estudiantiles, Departamento de Salud Estudiantil.

Hjemboe, S., Almagor, M., & Butcher, J. N. (1992). Empirical assessment of marital distress: The Marital Distress Scale (MDS) for the MMPI-2. In J. N. Butcher & C. D. Spielberger (Eds.), *Advances in personality assessment* (Vol. 9, 141–152). Hillsdale, NJ: Erlbaum.

Instituto Nacional de Estadistica Geografía e Informática. (1990). *INEGI censo: Nacional de población* [INEGI census: National population]. Mexico City, Mexico: Author.

Instituto Nacional de Estadistica Geografía e Informática. (2000). *INEGI censo: Nacional de población* [INEGI census: National population]. Mexico City, Mexico: Author.

Izaguirre-Hernandez, C., Sanchez-Quintanar, C., & Avila-Mendez, Y. (1970). *Normas de calificacion del MMPI en adolescentes del E.N.P. de U.N.A.M.* [MMPI norms for classification of adolescents of the National Preparatory School of the UNAM]. Unpublished thesis, College of Psychology, National Autonomous University of Mexico, Mexico City, Mexico.

Jaranson, J., Butcher, J. N., Halcón, L., Johnson, D. R., Robertson, C., Savik, K., et al. (2004). Somali and Oromo refugees: Correlates of torture and trauma history. *American Journal of Public Health, 94*, 591–597.

Keane, T. M., Malloy, P. F., & Fairbank, J. A. (1984). Empirical development of an MMPI subscale for the assessment of posttraumatic stress disorder. *Journal of Consulting and Clinical Psychology, 52,* 888–891.

Kopper, B. A., Osman, A., Soman, J. R., & Hoffman, J. (1998). Clinical utility of the MMPI-A content scales and Harris–Lingoes subscales in the assessment of suicidal risk factors in psychiatric adolescents. *Journal of Clinical Psychology, 54,* 191–200.

Lapham, S. C., Skipper, B. J., & Simpson, G. L. (1997). A prospective study of the utility of standardized instruments in predicting recidivism among first DWI offenders. *Journal of Studies on Alcohol, 58,* 524–530.

León, I., & Lucio, E. (1999). Consistencia y estructura interna de las escalas de abuso de sustancias del MMPI-2 [Internal consistency and structure of the MMPI-2 substance abuse scales]. *Salud Mental, 22*(3), 14–19.

Lilienfeld, L. R. (1994). *The use of the MMPI-A in the identification of risk factors for the future development of eating disorders.* Doctoral dissertation, University of Minnesota, Minneapolis.

Lindgren, S. D., Harper, D. C., Richman, L. C., & Stehbens, J. A. (1986). "Mental imbalance" and the prediction of recurrent delinquent behavior. *Journal of Clinical Psychology, 42,* 821–825.

Lindsey, M. L. (1998). Culturally competent assessment of African-American clients. *Journal of Personality Assessment, 70,* 43–53.

Lonner, W. I., & Ibrahim, F. A. (1996). Appraisal and assessment in cross-cultural counseling. In P. B. Pedersen, J. G. Draguns, W. J. Lonner, & J. E. Trimble (Eds.), *Counseling across cultures* (pp. 293–322). New York: Guilford Press.

López, S., & Weisman, A. (2004). Integrating a cultural perspective in psychological test development. In R. J. Velásquez, L. M. Arellano, & B. W. McNeill (Eds.), *The handbook of Chicana/o psychology and mental health* (pp. 129–151). Mahwah, NJ: Erlbaum.

Loy, A., Alvarez, M., Duran, A., & Almagro, D. (1981). Consideraciones psicopatológicas en un grupo de hemofílicos adultos: Informe preliminar [Psychopathological considerations in a group of adult hemophiliacs: Preliminary study]. *Revista Cubana de Medicina, 20,* 38–44.

Lucio, E. (1976). Presencia de algunas características hipocondriacas en estudiantes de medicina [Hypochondriasis personality traits in students]. *Revista Psiquiatría, 6*(3), 46–49.

Lucio, E., Ampudia, A., & Durán, P. C. (1998). *Manual para la administración y calificación del Inventario Multifasico de la Personalidad de Minnesota para adolescentes: MMPI-A* [Manual for the administration and scoring of the Minnesota Multiphasic Personality Inventory for Adolescents: MMPI-A]. Mexico City, Mexico: Manual Moderno.

Lucio, E., Reyes-Lagunes, I., & Scott, R. L. (1994). MMPI-2 for Mexico: Translation and adaptation. *Journal of Personality Assessment, 63,* 105–116.

Lucio, G. E. (2000). Case of Alejandro. In J. N. Butcher, B. Ellertsen, B. Ubostad, E. Bubb, G. E. Lucio, J. Lim, et al. (Eds.), *International case studies on the*

MMPI-A: An objective approach (pp. 28–37). Minneapolis, MN: University of Minnesota Press.

Lucio, G. E., Ampudia, A., Duran, C., Leon, I., & Butcher, J. N. (2001). Comparisons of Mexican and American norms of the MMPI-2. *Journal of Clinical Psychology, 57,* 1459–1468.

Lucio, G. E., Duran, C., Graham, J. R., & Ben-Porath, Y. S. (2002). Identifying faking bad on the Minnesota Multiphasic Personality Inventory–Adolescent with Mexican adolescents. *Assessment, 9,* 62–69.

Lucio, G. M. E., Ampudia, R. A., & Durán, P. C. (1997, June). *A test–retest reliability study of the MMPI-A in a group of Mexican adolescents.* Paper presented at the 32nd Annual MMPI Symposium on Recent Developments in the Use of the MMPI-2/MMPI-A, Minneapolis, MN.

Lucio, G. M. E., Córdova, G. V., & Hernandez, Q. (2002a, May). *Discriminative sensitivity of the Koss–Butcher and Lachar–Wrobel critical item sets in alcoholic patients.* Paper presented at the 36th Annual MMPI Symposium on Recent Developments in the Use of the MMPI-2/MMPI-A, Minneapolis, MN.

Lucio, G. M. E., Córdova, I. V., & Hernandez, C. Q. (2002b). Sensibilidad discriminativa de los reactivos significativos [Discriminative sensitivity of significant Koss–Butcher and Lachar–Wrobel items in alcoholic patients]. *Enseñanza e Investigación en Psicología, 6*(1), 103–115.

Lucio, G. M. E., Loza, G., & Durán, C. (2000). Los sucesos de vida estresantes y la personalidad del adolescente suicida [Stressful life events and the personality of adolescents who attempted suicide]. *Revista Psicología Contemporánea, 7*(2), 58–65.

Lucio, G. M. E., Palacios, H., Duran, C., & Butcher, J. N. (1999). MMPI-2 with Mexican psychiatric inpatients. *Journal of Clinical Psychology, 55,* 1541–1552.

Lucio, G. M. E., & Reyes-Lagunes, I. (1996). The Mexican version of the MMPI-2 in Mexico and Nicaragua: Translation, adaptation, and demonstrated equivalency. In J. N. Butcher (Ed.), *International adaptations of the MMPI-2* (pp. 265–283). Minneapolis: University of Minnesota Press.

Lueger, R. J., & Hoover, L. (1984). Use of the MMPI to identify subtypes of delinquent adolescents. *Journal of Clinical Psychology, 40,* 1493–1495.

Macmillan, N. A., & Creelman, C. D. (1991). *Detection theory: A user's guide.* New York: Cambridge University Press

Madariaga, M., & Guttin, E. (1980). *Estudio comparativo de los rasgos de personalidad de dos grupos diferentes áreas Físico Matemática y el área de Disciplinas Sociales de la escuela preparatoria 5, mediante el uso del MMPI* [Study of personality traits with the MMPI, of two groups from Social Sciences and Physical–Chemical areas from the Preparatory School 5]. Unpublished dissertation, National Autonomous University of Mexico, Mexico City, Mexico.

Malgady, R. G., Rogler, L. H., & Constantino, G. (1987). Ethnocultural and linguistic bias in the mental health evaluation of Hispanics. *American Psychologist, 42,* 228–234.

Manos, N. (1985). Adaptation of the MMPI in Greece: Translation, standardization, and cross-cultural comparisons. In J. N. Butcher & C. D. Spielberger (Eds.), *Advances in personality assessment* (Vol. 4, pp. 159–208). Hillsdale, NJ: Erlbaum.

Manson, S., & Kleinman, A. (1998). *DSM–IV*, culture and mood disorders: A critical reflection on recent practice. *Transcultural Psychiatry, 35,* 377–386.

Marin, G., & Triandis, H. C. (1985). Allocentrism as an important characteristic of the behavior of Latin American and Hispanics. In R. Diaz-Guerrero (Ed.), *Cross-cultural and national studies in social psychology* (pp. 85–104). Amsterdam: Elsevier Science.

Marks, P. A., Seeman, W., & Haller, D. L. (1974). *The actuarial use of the MMPI with adolescents and adults.* Baltimore: William & Wilkins.

Mason, K. (1997). Ethnic identity and the MMPI-2 profiles of Hispanic male veterans diagnosed with PTSD. *Dissertation Abstracts International, 58*(4-B), 2129.

McGrath, R. E., Pogge, D. L., & Stokes, J. M. (2002). Incremental validity of selected MMPI-A content scales in an inpatient setting. *Psychological Assessment, 14,* 401–409.

Megargee, E. I. (1993, March). *Using the Megargee offender classification system with the MMPI-2: An update.* Paper presented at the 28th Annual MMPI Symposium on Recent Developments in the Use of the MMPI-2/MMPI-A, St. Petersburg Beach, FL.

Mendizabal, P. (1993). *Grado de correspondencia entre el MMPI y la forma abreviada (Mini-Mult) en una muestra de pacintes del servicio de psiquiatroa del hospital H. Delgado de Arequipa* [Degree of agreement between the MMPI abbreviated form (Mini-Mult) in a sample of patients from the psychiatry department of Delgado Hospital in Arequipa]. Unpublished thesis, Universidad Nacional de San Agustin, Arequipa, Peru.

Micucci, J. A. (2002). Accuracy of MMPI-A scales *ACK, MAC-R,* and *PRO* in detecting comorbid substance abuse among psychiatric inpatients. *Assessment, 9,* 111–122.

Montoya, O. A. (1977). La triada neurotica del MMPI en un grupo de estudiantes universitarios [The neurotic triad of the MMPI with a group of college students]. *Revista de Psicologia General y Aplicada, 149,* 1077–1083.

Monzon, L. (2001). *Los rasgos de la personalidad del adolescente medidos con el inventario Multifásico de la Personalidad de Minnesota para adolescentes (MMPI-A) y su relación con el desempeño escolar en una muestra de estudiantes de bachillerato* [The relation between personality traits assessed with the MMPI-A and academic achievement in a sample of students from preparatory school]. Unpublished master's thesis, National Autonomous University of Mexico, Mexico City, Mexico.

Monzon, L., & Lucio, E. (1996). Scoring and interpretation for the MMPI-2 [Computer software]. Mexico City, Mexico: Author.

Moore, J. M., Jr., Thompson-Pope, S. K., & Whited, R. M. (1996). MMPI-A profiles of adolescent boys with a history of firesetting. *Journal of Personality Assessment, 67,* 116–126.

Morton, T. L., Farris, K. L., & Brenowitz, L. H. (2002). MMPI-A scores and high points of male juvenile delinquents: Scales 4, 5, and 6 as markers of juvenile delinquency. *Psychological Assessment, 14,* 311–319.

Navarro, R. (1971). El MMPI (Español) aplicado a jóvenes mexicanos: Influencias de sexo, edad y nivel de inteligencia [The MMPI (Spanish) applied to Mexican youngsters: Sex, age and intelligence influence]. *Revista Latinoamericana de Psicología, 5,* 127–137.

Negy, C., Leal-Puente, L., Trainor, D. J., & Carlson, R. (1997). Mexican American adolescents' performance on the MMPI-A. *Journal of Personality Assessment, 69,* 205–214.

Nichols, D. S. (2006). The trials of separating bath water from baby: A review and critique of the MMPI-2 restructured clinical scales. *Journal of Personality Assessment, 87,* 121–138.

Nichols, D. S., & Crowhurst, B. (2006). The use of the MMPI-2 in inpatient mental health settings. In J. N. Butcher (Ed.), *MMPI-2: The practitioner's handbook* (pp. 195–252). Washington, DC: American Psychological Association.

Nieves-Grafals, S. (1995). Psychological testing as a diagnostic and therapeutic tool in the treatment of traumatized Latin-American and African refugees. *Cultural Diversity and Mental Health, 1,* 19–27.

Nordström, P., Schalling, D., & Asberg, M. (1995). Temperamental vulnerability in attempted suicide. *Acta Psychiatrica Scandinavica, 92,* 155–160.

Núñez, R. (1967). *Inventario multifasico de la personalidad MMPI—Español* [The Spanish MMPI]. Mexico City, Mexico: Manual Moderno.

Núñez, R. (1979). *Aplicacion del Inventario Multifasico de la Personalidad (MMPI) a la psicopathology* [Application of the Minnesota Multiphasic Personality Inventory (MMPI) for psychopathology]. Mexico City, Mexico: Manual Moderno.

Núñez, R. (1987). *Pruebas psicometricas de la personalidad* [Personality psychometric tests]. Mexico City, Mexico: Trillas.

Ordaz, M., & Villegas, C, (2000). *Perfil de personalidad y nivel de asertividad en pacientes con transtorno de personalidad* [Personality profile and assertiveness level of a group of borderline patients). Unpublished dissertation, National Autonomous University of Mexico, Mexico City, Mexico.

Ortega, D. M. (2001). Parenting efficacy, aggressive parenting and cultural connections. *Family Social Work, 6*(1), 47–57.

Padilla, A. M. (1992). Reflections on testing: Emerging trends and new possibilities. In K. F. Geisinger (Ed.), *Psychological testing of Hispanics* (pp. 271–284). Washington, DC: American Psychological Association.

Pampa, W., & Scott, R. (2000). Case of Adriana. In J. N. Butcher, B. Ellertsen, B. Ubostad, E. Bubb, E. Lucio, J. Lim, et al. (Eds.), *International case studies on the MMPI-A: An objective approach* (pp. 62–70). Minneapolis: University of Minnesota Press.

Pearson Assessments–National Computer Systems. (1994). [Archival base rate data]. Minneapolis, MN: Author.

Pena, C., Cabiya, J. J., & Echevarria, N. (1995, March). *Cambios en los promedios de puntuaciones T en al MMPI-2 de confinados convictos por crímenes violentos participantes en un programa de tratamiento basado en un modelo de aprendizaje social* [Changes in mean MMPI-2 T scores of violent offenders in a social learning treatment program]. Paper presented at the 29th Annual MMPI Symposium on Recent Developments in the Use of the MMPI-2/MMPI-A, St. Petersburg, FL.

Pena, C., Cabiya, J., & Echevarria, N. (2000). MMPI-2 scores of a representative sample of state inmates in Puerto Rico. *Revista Ciencias de la Conducta, 15,* 39–52.

Pena, L. M., Megargee, E. I., & Brody, E. (1996). MMPI-A patterns of male juvenile delinquents. *Psychological Assessment, 8,* 388–397.

Phinney, J. S. (1996). When we talk about American ethnic groups, what do we mean? *American Psychologist, 51,* 918–927.

Pinderhughes, E. (1989). *Understanding race, ethnicity, and power: The key to efficacy in clinical practice.* New York: Free Press.

Pope, K. S., Butcher, J. N., & Seelen, J. (2006). *The MMPI/MMPI-2/MMPI-A in court* (3rd ed.). Washington DC: American Psychological Association.

Quevedo, K. M., & Butcher, J. N. (2005). The use of MMPI and MMPI-2 in Cuba: A historical overview from 1950 to the present. *International Journal of Clinical and Health Psychology, 5,* 335–347.

Ricks, J. H. (1971). Local norms: When and why. *Test Service Bulletin, 58,* 1–6.

Rinaldo, J. C. B., & Baer, R. A. (2003). Incremental validity of the MMPI-A content scales in the prediction of self-reported symptoms. *Journal of Personality Assessment, 80,* 309–318.

Rincon, V. D. R., & Lastra, R. A. (1987). Contribución a la caracterización psicológica de los enfermos de Lepra [Psychological characteristics of patients with leprosy]. *Revista Cubana de Medicina Tropical, 39,* 45–65.

Rissetti, F. J., Butcher, J. N., Agostini, J., Elguetta, M., Gaete, S., Margulies, T., et al. (1979a, March). *Estudios transnacionales y transculturales con el MMPI* [Cross-national and cross-cultural studies with the MMPI]. Paper presented at the 17th Congreso Interamericano de Psicologia, Lima, Peru.

Rissetti, F. J., Butcher, J. N., Agostini, J., Elguetta, M., Gaete, S., Margulies, T., et al. (1979b). *La experiencia chilena con el MMPI* [The Chilean experience with the MMPI]. Santiago, Chile: Pontificia Universidad Catolica de Chile, Direccion de Asuntos Estudiantiles, Departamento de Salud Estudiantil.

Rissetti, F. J., Butcher, J. N., Agostini, J., Elguetta, M., Gaete, S., Margulies, T., et al. (1979c, July). *Translation and adaptation of the MMPI in Chile: Use in a university student health service.* Paper presented at the 13th Annual MMPI

Symposium on Recent Developments in the Use of the MMPI-2/MMPI-A, St. Petersburg, FL.

Rissetti, F. J., Himmel, E., & Gonzalez-Moreno, J. A. (1996). Use of the MMPI-2 in Chile. In J. N. Butcher (Ed.), *International adaptations of the MMPI-2: Research and clinical applications* (pp. 221–251). Minneapolis: University of Minnesota Press.

Rissetti, F. J., Himmel, E., Maltes, S. G., Gonzalez, J. A., & Olmos, S. (1989a). Estandarizacion del inventario Multifasico de Personalidad de Minnesota (MMPI) en poblacion adulta chilena [Standardization of the MMPI in an adult Chilean population]. *Revista Chilena de Psicologia, 1*, 41–62.

Rissetti, F. J., Himmel, E., Maltes, S. G., Gonzalez, J. A., & Olmos, S. (1989b, March). *Standardization of the Minnesota Multiphasic Personality Inventory (MMPI) in Chilean adult population.* Paper presented at the 24th Annual MMPI Symposium on Recent Developments in the Use of the MMPI-2/MMPI-A, Honolulu, HI.

Rissetti, F. J., & Maltes, S. G. (1985a). Use of the MMPI in Chile. In J. N. Butcher & C. D. Spielberger (Eds.), *Advances in personality assessment* (Vol. 4, pp. 209–257). Hillsdale, NJ: Erlbaum.

Rissetti, F. J., & Maltes, S. G. (1985b). Validez predictive del MMPI en la poblacion universitaria de la P. Universidad Catolica de Chile [Predictive validity of the MMPI in the university population at the Catholic University of Chile]. *Cuadernos Consejo de Rectores, Universidades Chilenas, 24*, 192–203.

Rissetti, F. J., Montiel, F., Maltes, S., Hermosilla, M., & Fleischili, A. M. (1978). *Traduccion al castellano del Minnesota Multiphasic Personality Inventory (MMPI)* [Castilian translation of the Minnesota Multiphasic Personality Inventory (MMPI)]. Santiago, Chile: Pontificia Universidad Catolica de Chile, Direccion de Asuntos Estudiantiles, Servicio de Salud Estudiantil.

Rogers, R., Sewell, K. W., Harrison, K. S., & Jordan, M. J. (2006). The MMPI-2 restructured clinical scales: A paradigmatic shift in scale development. *Journal of Personality Assessment, 87*, 139–147.

Rogler, L. H. (1999). Methodological sources of cultural insensitivity in mental health research. *American Psychologist, 54*, 424–433.

Rowell, R. K. (1992). Differences between Black, Mexican American, and White probationers on the revised MacAndrew Alcoholism Scale of the MMPI-2. *Dissertation Abstracts International, 54*, 821A.

Sandoval, J., & Duran, R. P. (1998). Language. In J. Sandoval, C. L. Frisby, K. F. Geisinger, J. D. Scheuneman, & J. R. Grenier (Eds.), *Test interpretation and diversity: Achieving equity in assessment* (pp. 181–212). Washington, DC: American Psychological Association.

Santiago-Rivera, A., Arredondo, P., & Gallardo-Cooper, M. (2002). *Counseling Latinos and la familia: A practical guide*. Thousand Oaks, CA: Sage.

Savacir, I., & Erol, N. (1990). The Turkish MMPI: Translation, standardization, and validation. In J. N. Butcher & C. D. Spielberger (Eds.), *Advances in personality assessment* (Vol. 8, pp. 49–62). Hillsdale, NJ: Erlbaum.

Schinka, J. A., Elkins, D. E., & Archer, R. P. (1998). Effects of psychopathology and demographic characteristics on MMPI-A scale scores. *Journal of Personality Assessment, 71*, 295–305.

Scott, R. L., Butcher, J. N., Young, T. L., & Gomez, N. (2002). The Hispanic MMPI-A across five countries. *Journal of Clinical Psychology, 58*, 407–417.

Scott, R. L., Knoth, R. L., Beltran-Quiones, M., & Gomez, N. (2003). Assessment of psychological functioning in adolescent earthquake victims in Colombia using the MMPI-A. *Journal of Traumatic Stress, 16*, 49–57.

Scott, R. L., & Pampa, W. M. (2000). The MMPI-2 in Peru: A normative study. *Journal of Personality Assessment, 74*, 95–105.

Sechrest, L., Fay, T., & Zaida, S. (1972). Problems of translation in cross-cultural research. *Journal of Cross-Cultural Psychology, 1*, 41–56.

Seisdedos, N. (1977). Personality characteristics of students receiving school counseling. *Revista de Psicología General y Aplicada, 32*, 287–295.

Seisdedos, N., & Roig Fuste, J. M. (1986). *MMPI: Suplemento tecnico e interpretacion clinica* [MMPI: Technical supplement and clinical interpretation]. Madrid, Spain: TEA Edicones.

Sesteaga, N. B. (1980). *Relación entre características de personalidad y preferencias vocacionales en mujeres adolescentes estudiantes de preparatoria* [The relation between personality traits and vocational preferences in female adolescents from preparatory school]. Unpublished thesis, National Autonomous University of Mexico, Mexico City, Mexico.

Shores, A., & Carstairs, J. R. (1998). Accuracy of the MMPI-2 computerized Minnesota Report in identifying fake-good and fake-bad response sets. *Clinical Neuropsychologist, 12*, 101–106.

Sirigatti, S. (2000). Toward an Italian version of the MMPI–Adolescent. *Bollettino di Psicologia Applicata, 230*, 67–72.

Sirigatti, S., & Giannini, M. (2000). Detection of faking good on the MMPI-2: Psychometric characteristics of the S scale. *Bollettino di Psicologia Applicata, 232*, 61–69.

Smith, W. R., Monastersky, C., & Deisher, R. M. (1987). MMPI-based personality types among juvenile sexual offenders. *Journal of Clinical Psychology, 43*, 422–430.

Spanier, G. B. (1976). Measuring dyadic adjustment: New scales for assessing the quality of marriage and similar dyads. *Journal of Marriage and the Family, 38*, 15–28.

Spiro, R., Butcher, J. N., Levenson, M., Aldwin, C., & Bosse, R. (1993, August). *Personality change over five years: The MMPI-2 in older men.* Paper presented at the 101st Annual Convention of the American Psychological Association, Toronto, Ontario, Canada.

Spring, M., Westermeyer, J., Halcón, L., Savik, K. , Jaranson, J., Robertson, C., et al. (2003). Sampling in difficult-to-access refugee and immigrant communities. *Journal of Nervous and Mental Disease, 191*, 813–819.

Stein, L. A., McClinton, B. K., & Graham, J. R. (1998). Long-term stability of MMPI-A scales. *Journal of Personality Assessment, 70*, 103–108.

Steinman, D. (1993). MMPI-2 profiles of inpatient polysubstance abusers. *Dissertation Abstracts International, 54*, 3354B.

Sue, D. W., & Sue, D. (1999). *Counseling the culturally different.* New York: Wiley.

Suzuki, L. A., & Valencia, R. R. (1997). Race–ethnicity and measured intelligence: Educational implications. *American Psychologist, 52*, 1103–1114.

Swets, J. A. (1988, June 3). Measuring the accuracy of diagnostic systems. *Science, 240*, 1285–1293.

Tellegen, A., Ben-Porath, Y. S., McNulty, J., Arbisi, P., Graham, J. R., & Kaemmer, B. (2003). *MMPI-2: Restructured clinical (RC) scales.* Minneapolis: University of Minnesota Press.

Toyer, E. A., & Weed, N. C. (1998). Concurrent validity of the MMPI-A in counseling program for juvenile offenders. *Journal of Clinical Psychology, 54*, 395–400.

Triana, R. M., Delgado, N. F., Sarraff, T. F., & Felipe, L. M. S. (1999). Aspectos psicológicos en pacientes con policitemia relativa hipovolémicos y normovolémicos [Psychological aspects of patients with relative hypovolemic and normovolemic polycythemia]. *Revista Cubana de Hematología, Inmunología y Hemoterapia, 15*, 127–131.

Triana, R. M., Espinosa, A. L., Triana, Y. G., Espinosa, M. A. D., & Abascal, D. P. (1987). Particularidades psíquicas de un grupo de pacientes con policitemia relativa [Psychological aspects in a group of patients with relative polycythemia]. *Revista Cubana de Hematología, Inmunolgía y Hemoterapia, 3*, 135–144.

Triana, R. M., Espinosa, A. L, & Valdes, H. R. (1995). Aspectos psicológicos en leucémicos adultos [Psychological aspects of adults with leukemia]. *Revista Cubana de Hematología, Inmunología y Hemoterapia, 37*, 112–119.

Triana, R. M., Espinosa, A. L., Valdes, H. R., & Gonzales, L. G. (1988). Estilo de Enfrentamiento al estrés en pacientes con hemopatías [Strategies of facing stress in hemopathological patients]. *Revista del Hospital Psiquiátrico de la Habana, 29*, 555–560.

Triana, R. M., Valdes, M. E. A., & Felipe, L. M. S. (2000). Personalidad y estabilidad psíquica en un grupo de pacientes adultos con inmunodeficiencia celular [Stability of personality in a group of adult patients with cellular immunodeficiency]. *Revista Cubana de Hematología, Inmunología y Hemoterapia, 16*, 56–61.

Triandis, H. C. (1994). *Culture and social behavior.* New York: McGraw-Hill.

U.S. Census Bureau. (2004). *Annual demographic supplement to the March 2002 Current Population Survey.* Washington, DC: Author.

Valcarcel, E. C., & Rios, J. M. (1974). La dimensionalidad de la escala *L* del MMPI [Dimensions of the MMPI *L* scale]. *Ciencias: Psicología, 6*(1).

Valdes, T. L. G. (1979). Estudio valorativo de algunas características del MMPI en pacientes con trastornos psíquicos [Validity study of some MMPI characteristics in psychiatric patients]. *Revista del Hospital Psiquiátrico de la Habana, 20,* 249–258.

Velasquez, R. J., Ayala, G. X., & Mendoza, S. A. (1998). *Psychodiagnostic assessment of U.S. Latinos with the MMPI, MMPI-2, and MMPI-A: A comprehensive resource manual.* East Lansing: Michigan State University, Julian Samora Research Institute.

Velasquez, R. J., Callahan, W. J., Reimann, J., & Carbonell, S. (1998, August). *Performance of bilingual Latinos on an English–Spanish MMPI-2.* Paper presented at the 106th Annual Convention of the American Psychological Association, San Francisco.

Velasquez, R. J., Chavira, D. A., Karle, H. R., Callahan, W. J., Garcia, J. A., & Castellanos, J. (2000). Assessing bilingual and monolingual Latino students with translations of the MMPI-2: Initial data. *Cultural Diversity and Ethnic Minority Psychology, 6,* 65–72.

Velasquez, R. J., Gonzales, M., Butcher, J. N., Castillo-Canez, I., Apodaca, J. X., & Chavira, D. (1997). Use of the MMPI-2 with Chicanos: Strategies for counselors. *Journal of Multicultural Counseling and Development, 25,* 107–120.

Velasquez, R. J., Maness, P. J., & Anderson, U. (2002). Culturally competent assessment of Latino clients: The MMPI-2. In J. N. Butcher (Ed.), *Clinical personality assessment: Practical approaches* (2nd ed., pp. 154–170). New York: Oxford University Press.

Villatoro, C., & Ramírez, G. F. (1998) *Estudio comparativo de perfiles de personalidad de delincuentes, basado en el Inventario Multifásico de la Personalidad Minnesota-2 (MMPI-2)* [Comparative study of personality traits assessed with the MMPI-2 of a group of felons]. Unpublished dissertation, National Autonomous University of Mexico, Mexico City, Mexico.

Vinet, E. V., & Alarcon, P. B. (2003). Evaluacion psicometrica del Inventario Multifasico de Personalidad de Minnesota para Adolescentes (MMPI-A) en muestras chilenas [Psychometrical assessment of the MMPI-A in Chilean samples]. *Terapia Psicologica, 21*(2), 87–103.

Wallace, A., & Liljequist, L. (2005). A comparison of the correlational structures and elevation patterns of the MMPI-2 restructured clinical (RC) scales and clinical scales. *Assessment,* 290–294.

Weed, N. C., Butcher, J. N., McKenna, T., & Ben-Porath, Y. S. (1992). New measures for assessing alcohol and drug abuse with the MMPI-2: The APS and AAS. *Journal of Personality Assessment, 58,* 389–404.

Weed, N. C., Butcher, J. N., & Williams, C. L. (1994). Development of MMPI-A alcohol and drug problem scales. *Journal of Studies on Alcohol, 55,* 296–302.

Whitworth, R. H. (1988). Anglo and Mexican American performance on the MMPI administered in Spanish or English. *Journal of Clinical Psychology, 44,* 891–897.

Whitworth, R. H., & McBlaine, D. C. (1993). Comparison of the MMPI and MMPI-2 administered to Anglo and Hispanic American university students. *Journal of Personality Assessment, 61,* 19–27.

Whitworth, R. H., & Unterbrink, C. (1994). Comparison of MMPI-2 clinical and content scales administered to Hispanic and Anglo Americans. *Hispanic Journal of Behavioral Sciences, 16,* 255–260.

Williams, C. L., & Butcher, J. N. (1989a). An MMPI study of adolescents: I. Empirical validity of the standard scales. *Psychological Assessment, 1,* 251–259.

Williams, C. L., & Butcher, J. N. (1989b). An MMPI study of adolescents: II. Verification and limitations of code types classifications. *Psychological Assessment, 1,* 260–265.

Williams, C., Butcher, J. N., Ben-Porath, Y. S., & Graham, J. R. (1992). *MMPI-A: Assessing psychopathology in adolescents.* Minneapolis: University of Minnesota Press.

Woodcock, R. W., Munoz, A. F., Ruef, M. L., & Alvarado, C. G. (2005). *Woodcock–Munoz Language Survey—Revised.* Itasca, IL: Riverside.

Zane, N., & Mak, W. (2003). Major approaches to the measurement of acculturation among ethnic minority populations: A content analysis and an alternative empirical strategy. In K. M. Chun, P. B. Organista, & G. Marin (Eds.), *Acculturation: Advances in theory, measurement, and applied research* (pp. 39–60). Washington, DC: American Psychological Association.

Zanolo, B. (1993). Pruebas derivadas del MMPI: Alternativas para la exploracion de diversas variables de la personalidad [MMPI derived tests: Alternatives for the exploration of diverse variables of personality]. *Revista del Departamento de Grados y Titulos de la Facilitad de Psicología de la Universidad Inca Garcilazo de la Vega, 1,* 18–28.

INDEX

307

MMPI-A content scale profile for, 166
MMPI-A validity scale profile for, 164

K. See Defensiveness scale
Keane Post-Traumatic scale (PK), 100
Kopper, B. A., 157
Korea, 74

L. See Lie scale
Language
    dominance/preference, 65
    of Hispanic people in United States, 17
    of test, 65–67
Language proficiency, 19
Language switching, 66
LAS (Adolescent–Low Aspirations) scale, 136
Lie scale (L), 75, 201
    in Mexican MMPI-A study, 153–154
    on MMPI-2, 83
    on MMPI-A, 132
Linguistic equivalence, 7
Linguistic factors, 199
Literal translation, 30
Local norm, 139
Low Aspirations scale, Adolescent (LAS), 136
Low Self-Esteem scale (LSE)
    on MMPI-2, 98–99
    on MMPI-A, 136
Loza, G., 156
LSE. See Low Self-Esteem scale
Lucio, Emilia, 59, 138, 147–148, 149, 156, 158, 192, 184

Ma. See Hypomania scale
MacAndrew Alcoholism—Revised (MAC-R), 35, 36, 100, 166
Machismo, 89–90
MAC-R. See MacAndrew Alcoholism— Revised
Malgady, R. G., 66
Manzo, C., 158
Marianismo, 89, 90

Marital Distress scale (MDS), 100–101
Masculinity–Femininity scale (Mf) (Scale 5)
    in Mexican MMPI-A study, 154
    on MMPI-2, 89–91
    on MMPI-A, 133
MDS. See Marital Distress scale
Medical patients study, 38–39
Megargee Felon Classification System, 59, 63
Mendoza, S. A., 61
Mental health services, improved, 201–202
Mexican people in United States
    demographics, 17
    studies of, 43–44
Mexican version of MMPI-2, 66–67
Mexico, MMPI-2 use in, 29–42, 74
    comparative research, 34
    criminal offenders study, 41–42
    development steps for, 30–34
    medical patients study, 38–39
    personality disorders study, 39–40
    psychiatric patients study, 37–38
    substance-abusers study, 35–37
    treatment settings studies, 40–41
Mf. See Masculinity–Femininity scale
Migration stress, 203
Minnesota Multiphasic Personality Inventory (MMPI), xii
    adolescent evaluation with, 130
    in Argentina, 47
    in Chile, 44–45
    in Cuba, 28–29
    in Mexico, 29
    in Peru, 49
    references on Spanish language version of, 209–253
    in Spain, 51
    translations of, 25
Minority status, 62
MMPI. See Minnesota Multiphasic Personality Inventory
MMPI–Adolescent (MMPI-A), 68, 129–161
    content scales, 131, 135–137
    development of, 130–137
    distributors of, 208
    Mexican norms for, 152–160
    Mexican version, 144, 147–152
    normative study for Hispanics, 138–146

ABOUT THE AUTHORS

James N. Butcher, PhD, was born in West Virginia. He enlisted in the U.S. Army when he was 17 years old and served in the airborne infantry for 3 years, including a 1-year tour in Korea during the Korean War. After military service, he attended Guilford College, graduating in 1960 with a bachelor of arts in psychology. He received a master of arts in experimental psychology in 1962 and a PhD in clinical psychology from the University of North Carolina at Chapel Hill. He was awarded Doctor Honoris Causa from the Free University of Brussels, Belgium, in 1990. In 2005, he was also awarded an honorary doctorate (Laurea Honoris Causa in Psicologia) from the University of Florence, Florence, Italy.

He was associate director and director of the clinical psychology program at the University of Minnesota for 19 years and is currently professor emeritus of psychology in the Department of Psychology. He was a member of the University of Minnesota Press's Minnesota Multiphasic Personality Inventory (MMPI) Consultative Committee, which undertook the revision of the MMPI in 1989. He was formerly the editor of *Psychological Assessment*, a journal of the American Psychological Association, and serves as consulting editor or reviewer for numerous other journals in psychology and psychiatry. Throughout most of his career he maintained a private clinical practice specializing in psychological assessment and psychotherapy.

Dr. Butcher has worked in the cross-cultural psychology field since 1970, conducting research and training psychologists in the use of the MMPI. He has written extensively on cross-cultural personality assessment and has worked with psychologists in many countries on MMPI and MMPI-2 assessment projects. He is a fellow of the American Psychological Association and the Society for Personality Assessment. He has published more than 50 books and more than 175 articles in the fields of abnormal psychology, cross-cultural psychology, and personality assessment.

Jose Cabiya, PhD, earned his doctorate in clinical psychology in 1983 from the State University of New York at Albany. He has been a professor at the Carlos Albizu University (CAU), San Juan, Puerto Rico, since 1983, and has been the director of the Scientific Research Institute at CAU since 1998. He has trained many of the Latino clinical psychologists now practicing or performing research in Puerto Rico and in the U.S. mainland. He has published extensively in national and international scientific journals on clinical interventions and psychological assessment, especially on the MMPI. He has been performing research with the MMPI since the middle of the 1980s and was one of the coauthors of the Manual Supplement for the Hispanic Version of the MMPI-A. He has been project director of the Center for Research and Outreach in Hispanic Mental Health and Other Health Disparities funded by the National Center on Minority Health and Health Disparities of the National Institutes of Health since 2002. He also has had extensive clinical experience as director of the Psychology Department of the Puerto Rico State Psychiatric Hospital from 1984 to 1998 and in independent clinical practice from 1983 to the present.

Emilia Lucio, PhD, was born in Mexico City, Mexico. She is a full-time professor at the National Autonomous University of Mexico (UNAM), Mexico City, the most prestigious university in Latin America. She earned her bachelor's degree, master's degree, and PhD at UNAM. She was also a special student at Queens University, Kingston, Ontario, Canada. She has two specializations, one in humanist psychoanalysis and the other in narrative therapy. She is now the coordinator of a master's program in child psychotherapy and was the head of the Department in Clinical Psychology at UNAM for 8 years.

She has written more than 40 articles in national and international journals on the subjects of assessment, psychotherapy, and adolescence. She has also written 6 books. She has been assessor of more than 50 students in their master's and PhD theses. In 2006, she received an award for psychologist of the year from Psychologist College, Mazatlan Sinaloa, Mexico. Dr. Lucio has been in clinical practice for more than 30 years.

Maria Garrido, PsyD, was born in San Juan, Puerto Rico and obtained her PsyD in clinical psychology from the Graduate School of Applied and Professional Psychology at Rutgers University, New Jersey, in 1988. She has worked as a private practitioner in Providence, Rhode Island, since 1991 and has been affiliated with the Psychology Department at the University of Rhode Island as adjunct professor since 1995. She has taught courses in personality assessment and provided clinical supervision to graduate students with a focus on the application of culturally competent strategies in all aspects of clinical work. Much of her clinical work has focused on assessment of Spanish-speaking clients in forensic and educational settings. Most recently, she has taught objective personality assessment with the MMPI-2 and MMPI-A as visiting faculty at the Ponce School of Medicine, Ponce, Puerto Rico. She has made numerous presentations on the use of the MMPI-2 in the culturally appropriate assessment of Latino and Latina clients and has collaborated in recently published chapters that deal with the interpretation of the MMPI-2 and MMPI-A profiles of Latino and Latina clients.